CA Proficiency
Taxation 2 (NI)
2014–2015

Chartered Accountants Ireland

Published in 2014 by
Chartered Accountants Ireland
Chartered Accountants House
47–49 Pearse Street
Dublin 2
www.charteredaccountants.ie

This publication is designed to provide accurate and authoritative information in regard to the subject matter covered. It is provided on the understanding that the Institute of Chartered Accountants in Ireland is not engaged in rendering professional services. The Institute of Chartered Accountants in Ireland disclaims all liability for any reliance placed on the information contained within this publication and recommends that, if professional advice or other expert assistance is required, the services of a competent professional should be sought.

ISBN: 978-1-908199-91-1

Typeset by Deanta Global Publishing Services
Printed and bound by eprint, Dublin

Contents

PART ONE   CORPORATION TAX

PART TWO   CAPITAL GAINS TAX

PART THREE   INHERITANCE TAX

PART FOUR   STAMP DUTY

Chartered Accountants Ireland Code of Ethics

The Chartered Accountants Ireland *Code of Ethics* applies to all aspects of a Chartered Accountant's professional life, including dealing with corporation tax issues, capital gains tax issues, inheritance tax issues and stamp duty issues. The *Code of Ethics* outlines the principles that should guide a Chartered Accountant, namely:

- Integrity
- Objectivity
- Professional Competence and Due Care
- Confidentiality
- Professional Behaviour

As a Chartered Accountant, you will have to ensure that your dealings with the tax aspects of your professional life are in compliance with these fundamental principles. Set out in **Appendix 2** is further information regarding these principles and their importance in guiding you on how to deal with issues which may arise throughout your professional life, including giving tax advice and preparing tax computations.

Part One

Corporation Tax

Introduction and General Principles of Corporation Tax

Learning Objectives

After studying this chapter you will have developed competency in the following:

- Companies are liable to corporation tax on the profits that they earn.
- The computation of taxable profits is based on the profits per the financial statements, with certain tax adjustments.
- Income tax principles generally apply to the computation of taxable total profits.
- Each source of income and each chargeable gain is computed separately, in accordance with income tax law and practice, but excluding provisions relating solely to individuals and subject to corporation tax provisions. The various sources of income are:
  - trading income – profits from a trade carried out in the UK or overseas;
  - loan relationships – interest and other income from loans, including bank deposits (generally this is the net position);
  - miscellaneous income – any taxable income not taxed under any other specific provisions; and
  - property income – profits from rents and other income from property in the UK and overseas.
- Chargeable gains/(losses) are the profits or losses from the disposal of capital assets and are broadly computed in accordance with normal capital gains tax (CGT) principles, with the exception that, unlike for individuals, there is annual exemption. However, indexation relief is not frozen as it was at April 1998 for individuals.
- The principles for determining when an accounting period for corporation tax purposes begins and ends, including scenarios greater than and less than 12 months.
- The applicable rates of corporation tax to differing taxable profit levels.
- Residence principles for corporation tax – generally a company is UK tax resident if it is incorporated in the UK. If a company is not incorporated in the UK, it will still be UK resident if it is **centrally managed and controlled** in the UK. A company resident in the UK is chargeable to corporation tax on all its profits wherever the income arises and whether or not they are received or transmitted to the UK. A non-resident company is chargeable to corporation tax if it carries on a business in the UK through a permanent establishment.

> ■ Administrative aspects of paying corporation tax and filing corporation tax returns including the charging of interest and penalties for late payment of corporation tax and late submission of corporation tax returns.
> ■ An awareness of the new failure to notify penalties for corporation tax and Senior Accounting Officer duties.
> ■ Corporation tax enquiry procedures including the new penalty regime from 1 April 2009.
> ■ Record-keeping requirements for companies.
> ■ Details of the HMRC initiative, Managing Deliberate Defaulters (MDD).
> ■ Details of the rules for publishing deliberate tax defaulters.

> The Chartered Accountants Ireland *Code of Ethics* applies to all aspects of a Chartered Accountant's professional life, including dealing with corporation tax issues. As outlined at the beginning of this book, further information regarding the principles in the *Code of Ethics* is set out in **Appendix 2**.

1.1 The UK Corporation Tax Regime

Corporation tax chargeable is calculated by applying the relevant corporation tax rate to the company's taxable total profits (TTP). The financial year (FY) for corporation tax commences on 1 April (so the FY 2014 commences on 1 April 2014). The main rate of corporation tax for FY 2014 is 21%. The small profits rate of corporation tax is 20% for 2014. From 1 April 2015, the main rate of corporation tax is set to fall by 1% to 20%, whereby it will align with the existing small profits rate.

"Profits" lower than £300,000 are chargeable at the small profits rate, while those exceeding £1,500,000 are chargeable at the main rate. "Profits" which lie between £300,000 and £1,500,000 are initially chargeable at the main rate but can avail of a marginal relief claim. In essence, the tax rate moves from the small profits rate of 20% to the main rate of 21% on a gradual basis as the profits increase from £300,000 to £1,500,000. For 2014, the effective rate of tax for profits which fall in the above tranche is 21.25%.

■ "Profits" for the above purposes are deemed to be TTP plus non-group franked investment income (FII), where FII is the net dividend received together with the associated tax credit. However, whilst one measures "profits" against the above limits to establish the relevant band, the actual applicable rate is only ever applied to TTP. It should be noted that the above limits are proportionately reduced where the company has one or more "associated companies" and for accounting periods of less than 12 months.

■ A small or medium-sized company's corporation tax is due and payable nine months and one day after the end of the accounting period. However "large" companies are required to pay their corporation tax liabilities in up to four quarterly instalments. A company is deemed to be "large" if its "profits" exceed the upper amount, £1,500,000 currently. The upper amount should be divided by the total number of associates at the end of the previous accounting period (including the company itself) to determine if quarterly instalments are required for an accounting period. However, the company will not be required to pay by instalments in an accounting period where the "profits" for that period do not exceed £10 million **and** it was not large in the previous period. Again this £10 million is required to be divided by the total number of associates at the end of the previous accounting period (including the company itself).

- The maximum four quarterly instalments are payable as follows: the first is due six months and 13 days after the start of the accounting period, the second after a further three months, the third after a further three months, with the fourth and final instalment due three months and 14 days after the end of the accounting period.
- Where the accounting period is less than 12 months, the final instalment remains due on the normal date, three months and 14 days after the end of the accounting period. In this scenario, earlier instalments only fall due if their due date is prior to the date of the final instalment.
- The liability due at each instalment is calculated using the formula: $3 \times$ (company's total liability divided by the number of months in the accounting period). Interest is charged on instalments paid late at the late instalment rate.

1.2 Overview – Application and Accounting Periods

A company is defined as "any body corporate or unincorporated association". Therefore, unincorporated societies, trade and voluntary associations and members' clubs will find themselves within the corporation tax regime. Partnerships are specifically excluded from the definition of a "body corporate".

Corporation tax is levied on the profits of companies, as defined, and is payable by the company. The profits that are chargeable to corporation tax consist of income and chargeable gains. A dividend payment is not an expense of the company and therefore does not attract tax relief per se. A company's income and gains are generally calculated using income tax and CGT principles and the rules for the various types of income apply, in the main, to the UK corporation tax regime.

The FY for corporation tax purposes commences on 1 April and ends on the following 31 March with corporation tax rates fixed for financial years.

Directors of UK companies are required to prepare and file statutory accounts with the Companies Registry (or Companies House) for every 12-month accounting period. At the end of an accounting period, HM Revenue & Customs (HMRC) will issue a notice which will specify a 12-month period for which HMRC consider that a corporation tax return (Form CT600 (2008) Version 2) is due. Whilst the corporation tax accounting period would normally follow the statutory accounting period, there are specific rules which determine the date of the commencement and cessation of a corporation tax accounting period.

A corporation tax accounting period first begins when a company comes within the scope of corporation tax – be that when it acquires a source of income or when it becomes UK resident.

A corporation tax accounting period ends on the earliest occurrence of the following:

1. 12 months from the beginning of the accounting period;
2. the date to which the company draws up its accounts;
3. the date the company begins or ceases to be UK resident;
4. the date the company begins or ceases to be in administration;
5. the date the company goes into liquidation or winds up; or
6. the date the company begins or ceases to trade or ceases to be within the charge to corporation tax.

Thus, a corporation tax accounting period will generally be for a period of 12 months and will usually coincide with the period for which the company draws up its accounts. Where a company's statutory accounts are drawn up for a period in excess of 12 months then, for corporation tax purposes, it is split into accounting periods of 12 months, followed by a residual period of less than 12 months. **Each** of the split periods will require the preparation of a separate company tax return and have separate due dates for the payment of corporation tax.

Where a company prepares statutory accounts for a period longer than 12 months, the profits will generally be apportioned on a time basis between the two corporation tax accounting periods. However, HMRC reserve the right to amend this general rule where there is "a more accurate and fairer estimate of the profits or loss" that could be applied to the chargeable periods. It should be noted that chargeable gains are always **allocated to the period in which they occur**.

For companies, all transactions should be included in the financial statements. Therefore, the computation of corporation tax requires the analysis of those profits between the various sources of income and chargeable gains.

As each company has its own accounting year end, the law relates payment of tax and filing of returns to that year end, split if necessary as discussed above. Companies report their liability to corporation tax to HMRC via the self-assessment procedures and each company must calculate its own liability. Thus companies are required to prepare a corporation tax computation, setting out the liability due, and submit this to HMRC in conjunction with the corporation tax return (Form CT600, to include any relevant supplementary pages) and a copy of their statutory accounts, which are the accounts the company must file at Companies House or the organisation must prepare under its constitution. They include directors' and auditors' reports. However, if the company files abbreviated accounts at Companies House, it **must** file full accounts as part of its company tax return. Accounts can be prepared under IFRS or UK GAAP.

To summarise, a complete company tax return should include the following:

1. a completed Form CT600;
2. any relevant supplementary pages;
3. a copy of the statutory accounts (as previously defined);
4. a corporation tax computation setting out how the various figures recorded on Form CT600 have been arrived at and how they have been derived from entries within their statutory accounts and associated schedules.

1.3 The Charge to Corporation Tax

Corporation tax is assessed on the profits of companies for accounting periods. Accordingly the concept of basis periods in the income tax code is not carried into the corporation tax system.

The question whether, and how, a company is to be charged to corporation tax depends on whether or not it is resident in the UK. A company is resident in the UK if it is incorporated in the UK. If it is not incorporated in the UK, it will still be deemed resident in the UK (for corporation tax purposes) if it is centrally managed and controlled in the UK.

In the case of a **company resident in the UK,** the charge to corporation tax is imposed on **all its income** wherever arising and **its chargeable gains** wherever the assets were situated irrespective of whether or not they are remitted to the UK.

In the case of a **non-resident company,** the charge is imposed only if the company is carrying on a trade in the UK through **a permanent establishment (PE)**. Such a company is chargeable to corporation tax on any **trading income** arising directly or indirectly through, or from, the **PE; any income** from property or rights used by the **PE**; and on **any chargeable gains** on the disposal of assets situated in the UK used for the purposes of the trade of the PE.

There are three special rules in the corporation tax code which should be noted at this stage:

1. Until 1 July 2009, corporation tax was not charged on dividends or other distributions of a UK resident company received by another UK resident company. **Franked investment income (FII) is the net dividend plus the relevant tax credit**. Finance Act 2009 introduced new rules

on the taxation of dividends received by UK companies, which came into effect on 1 July 2009. These rules are covered in **Chapter 5**.

2. A paying company is not required to withhold income tax from annual interest, royalties or annuities if the recipient is also a company resident in the UK. However, such payments made to individuals, partnerships, etc. are made under deduction of income tax (generally at the basic rate of 20%). Companies may receive income which has suffered income tax at source. Corporation tax is charged on the gross amount of any payments received by a company under deduction of income tax. Therefore, if any tax has been deducted at source it will be necessary to gross the income up for the purposes of the corporation tax computation. However, the income tax already suffered by deduction may be set-off against the final corporation tax chargeable.

3. No deduction is allowed for dividends paid by a company (or any item treated as a distribution of profits under tax rules) when computing taxable profits. Nor indeed is any deduction allowed for the corporation tax payment itself.

1.4 Rates of Corporation Tax

Rate	Name	As From	Profits = TTP + FII
24%	Main rate	1 April 2012	Greater than £1,500,000
23%	Main rate	1 April 2013	Greater than £1,500,000
21%	Main rate	1 April 2014	Greater than £1,500,000
20%	Small profits rate	1 April 2011	Less than £300,000
25%	Marginal rate	1 April 2012	£300,001 to £1,500,000
23.75%	Marginal rate	1 April 2013	£300,001 to £1,500,000
21.25%	Marginal rate	1 April 2014	£300,001 to £1,500,000

The above rates are applicable for single companies with a full 12-month accounting period.

1.4.1 Main Rate of Corporation Tax

The main rate of corporation tax for FY 2014, i.e. the year commencing on 1 April 2014, is 21%. The main rate for FY 2015 is 20%, subject to Finance Act 2015. The main rate until 31 March 2008 was 30% and 28% for FY 2008, 2009 and 2010. It then fell by 2% to 26% for FY 2011 (the table above shows the changes since then).

1.4.2 Associated Companies

For corporation tax purposes, a company is associated with another company if it either controls the other or if both are under the control of the same person or persons. For this purpose, person is deemed to include individuals, partnerships or companies. Control is deemed to be either a holding of over 50% of the issued share capital or voting power or being entitled to over 50% of the distributable income or net assets on a winding up.

If a company has one or more associated companies, then the "profits" limits for small profits rate purposes are reduced and are effectively divided by the number of associated companies PLUS 1. That is, if a company has "profits" for the year ended 31 March 2014 of

£600,000 and it has three associated companies, then the limits of £300,000 and £1,500,000 for small profits rate purposes will be reduced to £75,000 and £375,000 respectively (i.e. divided by 4).

The residence of any associated company is irrelevant for this calculation. Hence, even though such companies cannot themselves avail of the UK small profits rate, they have a detrimental impact as regards the potential effective rate that the UK company may be charged.

For example, assume a UK company, Joe Bloggs Ltd, had taxable profits of £280,000 for the year ended 31 March 2014 and it had a non-resident associate, Foreign Ltd, with taxable profits for the same period of £25,000. In this scenario, Joe Bloggs Ltd would have its limits reduced to £150,000 and £750,000 respectively, notwithstanding the fact that Foreign Ltd could not itself avail of the small profits rate.

It is also important to note that companies which have only been associated for part of any accounting period are deemed to have been associated for the whole of the accounting period for the purposes of determining the profit limits. However, an associated company is ignored for these purposes if it has not carried on any trade or business at any time in the accounting period (or for the part of the period during which it was associated); generally this applies to dormant companies. There may also be other limited scenarios where a company may have a source of income and is not deemed to be carrying on a business for the purposes of the associated company rules.

Finally, a holding company will count as not carrying on a trade or business (and thus not be included in the calculation to reduce the profits limit by the number of associates) provided that:

1. its only assets are shares in subsidiaries;
2. it is not entitled to deduct any outgoings as charges or management expenses; and
3. its only profits are dividends from subsidiaries and these are distributed in full to its shareholders.

All of the above conditions must be satisfied.

The associated company rules also play an important part in determining if a company is required to pay corporation tax in instalments. This is discussed at **Section 1.5.1**.

1.4.3 Short Accounting Periods

If a company produces accounts for a period of less than 12 months, then the "profit limits" are proportionately reduced.

Example 1.1
Mary Ltd, which had no associated companies, had taxable total profits (TTP) from selling clothes of £200,000 in the year ended 31 March 2015. Corporation tax payable by Mary Ltd is £40,000 (£200,000 @ 20%).

Example 1.2
For the year ended 31 March 2015, Sunset Ltd, a company with two subsidiaries, had TTP of £110,000.

Since there are two associated companies, the lower and upper limits (of £300,000 and £1,500,000) have to be divided by three, giving £100,000 and £500,000 respectively. The corporation tax payable by the company would thus be £100,000 @ 20% + £10,000 @ 21.25%, a total of £22,125.

> **Example 1.3**
> Oslot Ltd has three associated companies and its results for the nine-month period to 31 December 2014 showed TTP of £120,250.
>
> In order to calculate the company's corporation tax liability, one must first adjust both the lower and upper profits limit to take account of the short accounting period **and** the number of associated companies, as follows:
>
> (£300,000 $\times$ 9/12) $\div$ 4   =   £56,250
>
> (£1,500,000 $\times$ 9/12) $\div$ 4   =   £281,250
>
> Thus the corporation tax liability is calculated as £56,250 @ 20% + £64,000 @ 21.25%, a total of £24,850.

Substantial commercial interdependence

In establishing who controls a company and whether two companies are under common control and thus associated, the law (sections 450 and 451 Corporation Tax Act 2010) currently automatically attributes to an individual all the rights and powers held by his or her associates. Associates is generally defined as a person with a familial relationship to the participator and includes husband or wife, parent or remote forebear, children, brothers or sisters and partner.

Previously, HMRC Extra Statutory Concession (ESC) C9 limited such attribution between relatives (apart from spouses and minor children) solely to circumstances where substantial commercial interdependence exists between the companies.

Legislation was introduced in Finance Act 2011 to ensure that companies are not held to be associated by mere accident of circumstance but only where the level of commercial interdependence between companies makes it appropriate to do so.

Finance Act 2011 brought into primary legislation what was previously available only by concession (ESC C9). It is now necessary to solely use a direct control test, unless one company has a relationship of "substantial commercial interdependence" with another company. Where there is substantial commercial interdependence between the companies, the control test is extended to consider indirect control. These new rules are set to apply to accounting periods ending on or after 1 April 2011.

Substantial commercial interdependence is determined by taking into account the degree to which the companies are:

- Financially interdependent – where one company gives financial support (directly or indirectly) to the other; or each has a financial interest in the affairs of the same business. Companies are financially interdependent where one makes a loan or provides a guarantee on behalf of another. Intercompany loans will generally provide first-hand evidence of financial interdependence.

- Economically interdependent – where the companies seek to realise the same economic objective, the activities of one benefit the other; or the companies have common customers.

- Organisationally interdependent – where the companies share common management, employees, premises or equipment.

1.4.4   Marginal Relief

Marginal relief applies where the "profits" of an accounting period of a UK resident company are over £300,000 but under £1,500,000. In this situation, 'profits' means taxable total profits (TTP) *added to* the grossed-up amount of dividends received from non-group companies.

In this scenario, the corporation tax liability is calculated by first multiplying the TTP by the main rate and then deducting a figure arrived at by the following formula,

$$(M - P) \times I/P \times \text{marginal relief fraction}$$

where M is the upper limit (currently £1,500,000), P is "profits" (as defined above) and I is TTP.

The marginal relief fractions for each of the financial years are as follows:

Financial Year	Fraction
2014	1/400
2013	3/400
2012	1/100
2011	3/200
2010	7/400
2009	7/400
2008	7/400

It should be noted that the latter formula is circumvented by the methodology applied in Examples 1.2 and 1.3 previously, where the company was not in receipt of FII during the relevant period.

Thus another method of calculating the corporation liability for **Example 1.2** could have been as follows, where M = £500,000, I = P = £110,000 and the fraction is 1/400.

	£
£110,000 @ 21%	23,100
Less (marginal relief)	
$(500,000 - 110,000) \times 110,000/110,000 \times 1/400$	(975)
Liability	22,125

Thus, one might choose to only apply the marginal relief formula where the company has been in receipt of non-group dividends during the relevant period. In all other cases, one might adopt the more succinct method used in Examples 1.2 and 1.3.

Example 1.4

Marmalade Ltd had taxable total profits of £295,000 for the year ended 31 March 2015. The company had also received dividends from other UK companies of £9,000 in the same period. Marmalade Ltd had no associated companies.

In the absence of the latter formula, one might suspect that all £295,000 would fall to be taxed at 20% (the small profits rate) as this falls below the £300,000 limit. However, while the dividends themselves are not taxable, they do have an impact on the effective tax charge that is eventually applied to the TTP. This is because the sum of the TTP of £295,000 and the grossed-up dividend of £10,000 (being £9,000 dividend multiplied by 10/9 to gross up for the notional tax credit), gives a figure of £305,000 to be compared with the lower and upper "profits limit". Thus, in this situation, M is £1,500,000, I is £295,000 and P is £305,000. The corporation tax liability is calculated as follows:

continued overleaf

TTP multiplied by the main rate LESS relevant marginal relief, being:	
	£
£295,000 @ 21%	61,950.00
Less:	
(1,500,000 − 305,000) × 295,000/305,000 × 1/400	(2,889.55)
Total liability	59,060.45

1.4.5 Split Financial Years

It is possible that a company's accounting period could straddle two financial years. For example, if a company prepares accounts to 31 December 2010 then the resultant profits would be split (based on actual days) to 90 days for the 2009 financial year (commencing 1 April 2009) and 275 days for 2010. After making this apportionment, the rates applicable to each financial year are applied to each portion of profits using the above methodology. As the corporation tax rates are the same for 2009 and 2010, there will be no need to split the accounting period in this way. However, as there has been a change in rate between FY 2013 and FY 2014, it will be necessary to split the profits of any companies with accounting periods straddling the date of the change.

Example 1.5

Camelot Ltd had taxable total profits of £2,500,000 for the year ended 30 September 2014. The company has no associated companies.

The corporation tax liability is calculated as follows:

	£
FY 2013	
£2,500,000 × 182/365 = £1,246,575.34 × 23%	286,712.33
FY 2014	
£2,500,000 × 183/365 = £1,253,424.66 × 21%	263,219.18
Total liability	549,931.51

TTP must be apportioned between FY 2013 and FY 2014.

Generally you make the apportionment on a time basis. However you can work out the profits of an accounting period by reference to the transactions which took place in that accounting period where this gives a more accurate result than time apportionment. HMRC may seek to use this basis also but generally this will only apply where there are a few easily identifiable transactions.

1.5 Dates of Payment of Corporation Tax

1.5.1 Overview

A small or medium-sized company's corporation tax is due and payable nine months and one day after the end of the accounting period. However, "large" companies are required to pay their corporation tax liabilities in up to four quarterly instalments. The number of quarterly instalment payments a company needs to make depends on the length of the accounting period. A company is deemed to be "large" if its "profits" exceed the upper amount, currently £1,500,000 as adjusted for associates. However, the company will not be required to pay by instalments in an accounting period where the "profits" for that period do not exceed £10 million **and** it was not large in the previous period. Also a company is not treated as large for an accounting period if its corporation tax liability does not exceed £10,000. Once again "profits" means TTP plus non-group FII.

The above limits (of £10 million and £10,000) are reduced (as with the marginal relief calculation) where the company has associated companies and where the accounting period is less than 12 months. The number of associated companies to be taken into account for this purpose are those in existence **on the last day of the previous accounting period**. In other words, if a company has three associates at that point in time then the £1,500,000 and £10,000,000 limits previously described must be divided by 4, i.e. the number of associated companies plus 1.

The first of the maximum four quarterly instalments falls due six months and 13 days after the start of the accounting period, the second after a further three months, the third after a further three months with the fourth and final instalment due three months and 14 days after the end of the accounting period. In essence, for a company with a 12-month accounting period, the instalments are due on the 14th day of the seventh and tenth months during the accounting period and the first and fourth months after the end of the accounting period.

Where the accounting period is less than 12 months, the final instalment remains due on the normal date, three months and 14 days after the end of the accounting period. In this scenario, earlier instalments only fall due if their due date is prior to the date of the final instalment.

The liability due at each instalment is calculated using the following formula, namely $3 \times$ (company's total liability divided by the number of months in the accounting period). Interest is charged on instalments paid late at the late instalment rate as set by HMRC.

Example 1.6

Trust Limited is a large company with an accounting year end of 31 December. Its instalments of corporation tax will fall due for payment on:

(a) 14 July and 14 October in the accounting period; and

(b) 14 January and 14 April after the accounting period.

Example 1.7

Syracuse Limited had a corporation liability for the year ended 31 March 2015 of £1,000,000. The amount of each instalment is $3 \times (1,000,000/12) = £250,000$ and these payments will fall due on:

14 October 2014, 14 January 2015, 14 April 2015 and 14 July 2015.

Example 1.8

Andes Limited has a corporation tax liability of £990,000 for the nine-month period ended 31 October 2014. The instalment amount is calculated initially by applying the above formula, giving a figure of £330,000 (namely $3 \times (£990,000/9)$). The instalments and due dates are thus:

£330,000 on 14 August 2014, £330,000 on 14 November 2014 and £330,000 on 14 February 2015

The first instalment is always due six months and 13 days after the first day of the accounting period, i.e. 14 August 2014 which is six months and 13 days after 1 February 2014.

It should be noted that the instalments are based on the estimated corporation tax liability for the current period (and not the previous period as with self-assessment for individuals). Thus it is very important that companies accurately forecast their potential corporation tax liabilities to avoid incurring significant interest charges. This will invariably entail the company reviewing its estimates each quarter and adjusting payments already made and still to be made accordingly.

1.5.2 Interest

If a company pays its corporation tax liability after the due date, then it will be charged late payment interest, calculated from the day after the normal due date until the effective date of payment. The position is considered after the due date for each instalment (where applicable) on a cumulative basis and the interest position is calculated by HMRC after the company submits its corporation tax return.

If a company has overpaid corporation tax, it may make a repayment claim and it will also be entitled to interest on the repayment. The repayment interest runs from the "material date" to the date when the repayment was issued. Interest paid/received on late payments or overpayments of corporation tax are treated as interest paid/received on a non-trading loan relationship and included in the calculation of the net loan relationship debit or credit. The effect of this is that interest paid is deductible for tax and any interest received is taxable.

Example 1.9

Wright Limited, a large company, has always prepared accounts to 31 March. It had paid the following instalments in respect of the accounting period ending 31 March 2015:

£2.5 million on 14 October 2014, £6.5 million on 14 January 2015, £3 million on 14 April 2015 and £3 million on 14 July 2015, a total of £15 million.

On submission of its corporation tax return, the company's tax liability was actually £16 million, and the balance of £1 million was paid on 1 January 2016.

Thus the £16 million should have been paid in instalments of £4 million each ($3 \times$ (£16 million/12)) and the schedule below sets out the under/over payments:

Date	Paid	Actually Due	Under/(over)	Cumulative
	£	£	£	£
14 October 2014	2.5m	4m	1.5m	1.5m
14 January 2015	6.5m	4m	(2.5m)	(1m)
14 April 2015	3m	4m	1m	Nil
14 July 2015	3m	4m	1m	1m

Interest would thus be charged/(received) as follows:

- Charged on £1.5 million from 14 October 2014 until 13 January 2015.
- Received on £1 million from 14 January 2015 until 13 April 2015.
- Charged on £1 million from 14 July 2015 until 31 December 2015.

1.5.3 Penalties

In order to dissuade companies from deliberately understating their instalments, HMRC reserve the right to impose penalties (on top of the above interest charges) where they find no justifiable reasons for inadequate instalment payments. This would normally involve consideration of the contemporaneous records of the company and a request for the company's explanation of why their estimates were incorrect.

A penalty can arise where:

- a company, or person acting on its behalf, deliberately or recklessly fails to pay the right amount on a particular instalment date; or
- a company, or person acting on its behalf, fraudulently or negligently makes a claim for repayment under the Instalment Regulations.

The penalty is an amount not exceeding twice the amount of interest charged on any unpaid amount in respect of the total liability of the company for its accounting period.

1.5.4 Group Payment Arrangements

Given the potential uncertainties over the tax liabilities of individual group members and, until such time as all relevant group relief and other claims have been determined after the end of the accounting period, HMRC permits arrangements whereby instalments can be paid by one company in the group and subsequently allocated amongst the group in line with their eventual individual final liabilities. This is particularily efficient from an interest perspective as often the final liabilities in groups are dependent on group relief allocations.

1.6 Computation of Income

The basic rule for the calculation of income is that, apart from certain special provisions relevant only to companies, it is to be computed in accordance with income tax principles.

The income tax scheme of capital allowances and balancing charges is brought into the corporation tax system. However, **capital allowances** due to trading companies are **treated as trading expenses** for corporation tax purposes and not as a deduction from the assessable income as in the case of income tax. Similarly, balancing charges are treated for corporation purposes as trading receipts.

Furthermore, for the purposes of claiming capital allowances, capital expenditure is incurred on the date on which the obligation to pay becomes unconditional even if there is a later payment date. For capital allowances purpose, if the contractual payment date is longer than four months, the expenditure is treated as incurred on the payment due date.

For the purposes of computing the tax-adjusted profits of a company from its profit and loss account for an accounting period, the following particular points should be noted:

- Bona fide directors' salaries, fees, benefits payable for directors, etc. are deductible, unlike the drawings/salary of a self-employed person. Such income is, of course, assessable in the hands of the individual director as employment income.
- Where a director has a company car available for private use, there is no deduction for "personal element" for corporation tax purposes, unlike the personal element of a self-employed person. Again, a director with the use of a company car for private purposes will, of course, suffer a benefit in kind assessment.

Example 1.10

Joe and Ann jointly own Deduction Ltd and are both directors on the board of the company. Deduction Ltd pays all the motor expenses incurred in running Joe's car. Only 75% of the expenses are incurred in respect of the business. The balance of 25% is personal. Deduction Limited will be entitled to a full deduction for all the motor expenses, even though some of the expense is personal; however Joe will be liable to income tax on the personal motor expenses paid by the company.

▓ Dividend payments by a company are not deductible as they are treated as appropriations of profit.

▓ Interest on borrowings, which are used for trading purposes (e.g. financing of stock, debtors and fixed assets used for the purpose of the trade), are fully allowable on the **accruals** basis. If, on the other hand, a company has borrowed money and applies the funds for non-trading purposes, e.g. say for the purchase of speculative oil shares or to purchase shares in a subsidiary, then such interest charges are not deductible against trading income. However, these would generally qualify as non-trade deficits under the loan relationship rules.

A pro forma corporation tax computation, together with notes on important adjustments, is set out in **Chapter 2**.

1.7   Computation of Investment Income

A company's investment income would, in the main, include property income and income from non-trading loan relationships. Companies that qualify as an investment business can claim a deduction for management expenses.

1.7.1   Property Income (Income from Land and Buildings)

Companies are charged corporation tax on income arising from the letting of land and property, wherever situated. Income generated from land and property in the UK is aggregated into one "UK property business". Income from all land and property outside the UK will be combined into the company's "overseas property business".

Property business profits/(losses) are computed in accordance with generally accepted accounting principles and the types of income assessable under this schedule would include payments for a licence to occupy, exercise or use of a right over land, income from furnished lettings (to include furnished holiday lettings), ground rents and other annual payments in respect of land and so forth.

While capital allowances are available for plant used in a letting business, they are not available for plant let for use in a dwelling house. Instead, relief can be obtained by a wear and tear deduction.

This latter relief is given for furnished lettings and calculated as 10% of the gross property income net of the water rates and council tax (if applicable).

It should be noted that, unlike for individuals, **interest is excluded** from a property income computation; it is dealt with as a non-trading "debit" under the loan relationship rules (see **Section 2.6.2**).

Basis of Assessment
Tax is charged on the income arising during the accounting period. The rent taken into account is the amount receivable whether or not it is actually received, i.e. on an accruals rather than a cash basis.

1.7.2   Premiums on Short Leases

Calculation of Taxable Portion of Premium
Where a company receives a premium on the creation of a "short lease" (i.e. the duration of the lease does not exceed 50 years), the premium will be treated partly as a disposal for CGT purposes and partly as income. The latter is treated as property income in the year in which the lease is

granted (in addition to any actual rent for that period) and is computed as the amount of the premium less 2% for each complete year of the lease except the first (or by the formula P × (50 − Y)/50, where P is the premium and Y is the number of complete years in the term of the lease excluding the first.

Example 1.11

A Ltd lets premises to B Ltd on 1 April 2014 for 21 years at a rent of £18,000 per annum subject to a premium of £20,000.

Property Income	£
Premium receivable	20,000
Less (proportion chargeable as capital gain − 2% of £20,000 × 20 years)	(8,000)
Chargeable as additional rent	12,000
Annual rent	18,000
Property income	30,000

Alternatively: $\dfrac{P \times (50 - Y)}{50}$ = £20,000 × (50−20)/50 = £12,000

This is treated as additional rent for the purposes of calculating A Ltd's taxable property income for the year ended 31 March 2015.

The lessee, B Ltd, leases the property for business purposes and claims the following deduction against Trading Income in its accounting period ending 31 March 2015:

	£
Rental costs	18,000
Amount of premium treated as additional rent, namely £12,000, divided by lease term (£12,000/21)	571
Total Trading Income deduction	18,571

Allowable Deductions Incurred in Calculating Property Income

The following amounts may be deducted from the gross rents:

1. Rent payable.
2. Rates (if any), property insurance, etc.
3. Cost of goods or services which the landlord is obliged to provide and for which he receives no separate consideration, e.g. gas, electricity, waste disposal.
4. Cost of repairs (excluding improvements (where the asset is taken beyond its condition prior to the repair) and items treated as capital expenditure). However, repair expenditure of the subsidiary parts of an asset is classed as revenue expenditure.

   Examples of common repairs that are normally deductible in computing rental business profits include:

   - exterior and interior painting and decorating;
   - stone cleaning;
   - damp and rot treatment;
   - mending broken windows, doors, furniture and machines such as cookers or lifts;
   - re-pointing; and
   - replacing roof slates, flashing and gutters.

5. Accountancy fees incurred in drawing up rental accounts and keeping rental records. Strictly speaking, such expenses are not allowable as they relate more to the management of the landlord's affairs rather than to the receipt of rent or the management of the premises. In practice, however, HMRC allow a deduction for such expenses as they recognise that the efficient running of a business of letting premises requires that financial accounts should be prepared.

6. A claim for wear and tear allowances calculated as 10% of gross rents (less water and council rates, if applicable).

7. Legal fees of a revenue nature wholly and exclusively incurred in connection with the rental business. Legal costs involved with the first letting of a property for more than one year are deemed to be of a capital nature and are not allowable. However, legal and professional costs incurred in respect of the renewal of short-term leases (a lease of less than 50 years) are allowable, though not the payment of a premium. Finally, legal costs incurred in acquiring or adding to a property and those involved with the change of use of a property in vacant periods between lets are disallowable.

Allowable expenses are normally deducted on an accruals basis rather than on a paid basis. In order to be deductible, the expense must be incurred wholly and exclusively for the purpose of earning the rent and must be revenue rather than capital in nature. Expenses incurred in respect of a property before a lease commences in respect of that property are, in the main, not deductible. In the case of interest and rent, no deduction is allowed for either interest or rent payable in respect of a period before the property is first **occupied** by a lessee. However, relief may be available for items such as these under the legislative provisions for pre-trading expenditure.

Expenses incurred after the termination of a lease are not deductible. However, expenses incurred after the termination of one lease and before the commencement of another lease in respect of the property are deductible, provided the following three conditions are satisfied:

1. the expenses would otherwise be deductible;
2. the person who was the lessor of the property does not occupy the premises during the period when the property is not let; and
3. the property is let by the same lessor at the end of the period.

Example 1.12

A company purchased a rental property on 1 April 2014. Between the date of purchase and 31 May 2014 the company spent £25,000 refurbishing the property. On 1 June 2014 the property was leased for £800 per month payable in advance.

The following expenses were incurred up to 31 May 2014:

	£
Auctioneers/advertising fees for first tenants	800
Repairs and maintenance	600
Light and heat	300
Security and insurance	500
Interest on loan	1,200

continued overleaf

The following expenses were incurred in the period 1 June 2014 to 31 March 2015:

	£
Water charges	600
Light and heat	350
Security	400
Interest	2,250
Repairs/maintenance of a revenue nature	870

Calculate the taxable rental profits for the year ended 31 March 2015.

Solution

	£	£
Gross rents receivable (£800 × 10)		8,000
Less qualifying expenses		
Auctioneers/advertising for first tenants	800	
Water charges	600	
Light and heat	350	
Security	400	
Repairs/maintenance	870	(3,020)
Property income		4,980

1.7.3   Property Income Losses

It is possible that a company could incur losses from their rental business. Such losses incurred in an accounting period from a property business carried on commercially can be set against the company's total profits for the same accounting period. If the losses still exceed the profits, then they can be carried forward to the next accounting period and set against total profits of that period. Excess losses are carried forward in this way until the property business ceases. At this point, any remaining loss will be treated as management expenses and available to be carried forward to set-off under the relevant rules. This is dealt with in more detail in **Chapter 4.**

1.7.4   Letting of Surplus Accommodation

By virtue of section 44 CTA 2009, the letting of surplus business accommodation (not land held as trading stock and part of a building another part of which is used to carry on the trade) on a short-term basis is taxed under the trading income, rather than the property income, provisions. Thus, receipts which are relatively small may be treated as trading income.

Accommodation is deemed to be surplus to requirements only if it has been used in the last three years to carry on the trade (or was acquired in the last three years), the trader intends to use it for the trade at a later date and the letting is for a term of not more than three years.

1.8   Computation of Chargeable Gains

Where a chargeable gain accrues to a company in an accounting period, the chargeable gain is included in the company's total profits subject to corporation tax. The gain calculated is after deducting both allowable capital losses in the current accounting period and those brought forward from previous years.

Since company chargeable gains are included within the company's total profits, they will fall to be taxed at the same rate as trading profits and other income. Note that companies are not liable to CGT but rather pay corporation tax on their chargeable gains.

1.8.1   Disposals

It is important to note that the disposal of intangible assets comes within the intangible assets regime, whilst the disposal of loan stock is dealt with under the loan relationship rules. Thus the main category of disposals that will be relevant to companies will be the disposal of land and property and share holdings.

These chargeable gains are liable to corporation tax and not CGT. However, this does not change the basic calculation which is broadly computed in accordance with normal CGT principles, with a few important exceptions. Unlike the situation for individuals, a company does not have any annual exemption nor is it entitled to entrepreneur's relief (or its predecessor, taper relief). However, whilst indexation was frozen for individuals as of 31 March 1998, companies can still avail of indexation up to the date of disposal.

1.8.2   Basic Computation

The basic capital gains computation considers the difference between the net selling price of the asset being disposed of compared with its original cost (or March 1982 value if relevant) coupled with any further allowable items of expenditure.

Since one is comparing money values at different times, HMRC recognises this and companies can thus apply indexation to the historical costs of the item being disposed of.

The gross sales proceeds are reduced by the incidental costs of sale, which could include such things as legal fees, estate agent fees, valuation fees, etc. The costs associated with the purchase are added to the actual purchase cost (or March 1982 valuation) and these items will attract indexation from the relevant date up to the date of disposal.

Indexation allowance is calculated by multiplying the relevant allowable expenditure by the retail price percentage increase over the relevant time (where this percentage is expressed as a decimal to three decimal places). The relevant time is from the date of acquisition (or 31 March 1982 valuation if applicable) up to the date of sale. However, indexation allowance can neither create nor increase a capital loss.

1.8.3   Capital Losses

The above basic calculation could result in a capital loss, although note that the indexation allowance cannot create or increase a loss. If the company had other chargeable gains in the same period, this loss is first set against such chargeable gains. If unutilised, the capital loss is carried forward to set against future capital gains of subsequent accounting periods.

Unlike in the case of death for individuals, there are no provisions for the carry back of capital losses. Nor are there any provisions for the surrender of capital loss between group members or, in the main, for setting capital losses against total profit. However, it is possible to transfer gains within a CGT group under section 171A TCGA 1992 (see **Chapter 10**).

Note: in a situation where a company has an accounting period exceeding 12 months, whilst the trading and other income are time-apportioned, the chargeable gains are allocated to the period in which the disposal took place (and are not time-apportioned).

Example 1.13

X Ltd prepares accounts to 31 March. In the year ended 31 March 2015, the tax-adjusted trading profit was £20,000. During that year the company sold a chargeable asset for £16,000, incurring incidental costs of sale of £1,000. It had purchased the asset for £10,000 some three years previously and the indexation factor was 0.105.

X Ltd – Year ended 31 March 2015

	£
Trading income	20,000
Chargeable gain (Note)	3,950
	23,950
Corporation tax due £23,950 @ 20%	4,790
Note – Chargeable gain	
Gross sales proceeds	16,000
Less: incidental costs of sale	(1,000)
	15,000
Purchase cost	(10,000)
	5,000
Indexation £10,000 × 0.105	(1,050)
Indexed chargeable gain	3,950

Example 1.14

Lauren Ltd prepares accounts to 31 March each year.

In February 2003 the company bought an asset for £12.6m. The costs of acquisition were £0.7m. In April 2004, enhancement capital expenditure of £1.8m was incurred on this asset. Lauren Ltd disposed of this asset in July 2014 for £37.9m, having incurred £1.1m on incidental costs of sale. Set out the chargeable gain to be included within the corporation tax computation of the above company for the year ended 31 March 2015.

Assume the following Retail Price Index (RPI) figures:

July 2014	256.0
February 2003	179.3
April 2004	185.7

continued overleaf

Solution

	£ 000	£ 000
Gross sales proceeds		37,900
Less: incidental costs of sale		(1,100)
Net sales proceeds		36,800
Acquisition costs	12,600	
Incidental costs of acquisition	700	
Enhancement expenditure	1,800	
		(15,100)
Unindexed gain		21,700
Indexation allowance:		
Acquisition cost (£12.6m × 0.428)	5,393	
Incidental costs of acquisition (£0.7m × 0.428)	300	
Enhancement (£1.8m × 0.379)	682	
		(6,375)
Chargeable gain		15,325

Indexation Factor

Cost	(256.0 − 179.3)/179.3 = 0.428
Enhancement	(256.0 − 185.7)/185.7 = 0.379

Notes

In the corporation tax computation, the chargeable gain amount is included immediately after the total income has been ascertained as follows:

	£
Trading income	X
Net credit from loan relationships	X
Miscellaneous income	X
Property income	X
Total income	X
Chargeable gains	X
Taxable total profits (TTP)	X

1.9 Accounting Periods

Corporation tax is assessed on the profits arising in the company's accounting period. The term "accounting period" is given a special meaning for corporation tax purposes. Ordinarily, it is the period for which the company makes up its accounts ("period of account") **but an accounting period cannot exceed 12 months**.

The first accounting period of a company for corporation tax purposes begins whenever the company comes within the charge to corporation tax. A company may come within the charge to corporation tax in one of several ways:

1. A company not resident in the UK which is carrying on a trade outside the UK may become resident in the UK. Its first accounting period will start on the day it becomes resident.

2. A company may acquire for the first time a source of income chargeable to corporation tax, for example, a non-resident company may start to trade in the UK through a permanent establishment, such as a branch or agency here; at that point an accounting period will start.
3. A new company may be created and acquire a source of profits.
4. An unincorporated partnership or sole trade may become incorporated.

An accounting period runs for a maximum of 12 months from its start. It will end earlier if the company's own accounting date falls within the 12 months. A new accounting period starts immediately at the end of an accounting period unless the accounting period ended because the company ceased altogether to be within the charge to corporation tax.

An accounting period ends when any one of the following happens:

- the expiry of 12 months from the beginning of the accounting period;
- the accounting date of the company, that is the date to which it makes up its accounts;
- the end of a period for which a company does not make up accounts;
- the company begins to trade;
- the company comes within the charge to corporation tax in respect of its trade or, if it carries on more than one trade, of all its trades;
- the company ceases to trade;
- the company ceases to be within the charge to corporation tax in respect of its trade or, if it carries on more than one trade, of all its trades;
- the company begins to be resident in the UK;
- the company ceases to be resident in the UK;
- the company ceases to be within the charge to corporation tax; or
- the commencement of the winding-up of the company.

Example 1.15
Start Ltd was incorporated on 1 June 2014. The money subscribed for share capital was put on deposit. The company commenced to trade on 1 September 2014. It prepared its first set of financial statements for the period ended 31 December 2014 and intends to prepare annual financial statements to 31 December each year thereafter.

As Start Ltd acquired a source of income on 1 June, an accounting period commenced. As it commenced to trade on 1 September, an accounting period is deemed to end, even though no actual set of financial statements are prepared. Therefore, Start Ltd has an accounting period of three months, ending on 31 August 2014. Its next accounting period is from 1 September to 31 December 2014. Thereafter it will have accounting periods ending on 31 December each year.

Companies that Prepare Accounts for a Period of less than 12 Months
The main implications here are as follows:

- If the short accounting period has resulted from a change in the normal annual accounting date of the company then, unlike the income tax position for a sole trader who changes his accounting date, HMRC has no special powers. For example, if a company has prepared a 12-month set of accounts to 31 December 2012, then an eight-month set of accounts to 31 August 2013, followed by a 12-month set of accounts to 31 August 2014, then corporation tax is simply payable for each of these three accounting periods.
- Where the company's accounting period is less than 12 months long, then the normal capital allowances available must be scaled down appropriately. For example, if an accounting period is eight months long, then the normal writing down allowances must be scaled down to 8/12ths.

Companies that Prepare Accounts for a Period Exceeding 12 Months

As the maximum length of an accounting period is 12 months, where a company prepares a set of accounts for a period exceeding 12 months, this "period of account" must be broken down into tranches, each a maximum of 12 months long.

Example 1.16

X Ltd prepared a set of accounts for 30 months ending on 30 June 2014. In these circumstances corporation tax is payable for the following "accounting periods":

1. 12-month accounting period to 31 December 2012.

2. 12-month accounting period to 31 December 2013.

3. Six-month accounting period to 30 June 2014 (remember an accounting period is terminated automatically by reference to the date to which a set of accounts is prepared).

As you can see from this example, **if the period of account is longer than 12 months, the first accounting period will always be at least 12 months long.**

In the above example, the profit and loss account was 30 months long, meaning a tax-adjusted profits computation would have to be prepared. This would involve adjusting for the various normal add-backs and deductions to produce a tax-adjusted profits computation (ignoring capital allowances for the moment) corresponding to a 30-month period. One would then **time-apportion** the tax-adjusted trading profits for this 30-month period to arrive at the relevant trading income for each of the accounting periods mentioned above.

It should be particularly noted that, as a general rule, the profits should be apportioned on a time basis, according to the number of days in the accounting period. However, HMRC reserves the right to divide and apportion profits in a different fashion if they believe and can demonstrate that it was a "more accurate and fairer estimate". Notwithstanding this, chargeable gains are **always** allocated to the period in which they occurred. For example, if there was only one capital disposal in the 30-month period, say on 1 May 2014, then the adjusted chargeable gain would be assessed and brought into the computation for the six-month accounting period ending on 30 June 2014.

In the above example, the capital allowances would have to be computed separately for each of the three accounting periods by reference to additions and disposals of assets which occurred during year ended 31 December 2012, 31 December 2013, and six months to 30 June 2014. In the case of the last six-month period, clearly the writing down allowances would have to be restricted appropriately as discussed above. Therefore, in this situation, capital allowances are not allowed as a trading expense until after the trading income has been time-apportioned.

(**Note:** Past exam questions have required students to deal with companies that have long periods of account and therefore require this type of time-apportionment to be done by the student.)

1.10 Residence of Companies

The most important factor in determining a company's liability to corporation tax is the company's **residence**. In broad terms, a UK resident company is liable on all profits, whereas a non-resident company is liable only on profits attributable to a PE established in the UK.

The rules for determining the residence of a company have evolved from case law. The earliest case that dealt with company tax residence is *Calcutta Jute Mills Co Ltd v. Nicholson*. This case established that residence is located where a company's centre of control is located. The most important subsequent case is *de Beers Consolidated Mines v. Howe* (1906). In this case, it was held that a company's residence is where its real business is carried on and that place was where the central management and control actually abides.

The "central management and control" test was further endorsed in *Bullock v. Unit Construction Co Ltd* (1959). This case emphasised the point that central management and control is a question of fact and is not necessarily located where it appears to be located, e.g. where the board of directors held its meetings. These principles were reaffirmed by the Court of Appeal in 2006 in the case of *Wood v. Holden*.

These and other UK court decisions determined that the key factor in determining where a company is resident is where it is **managed and controlled**. The following are the factors which have been taken into account by the UK courts in determining the centre of the company's management and control and, therefore, its place of residence:

- Where are the questions of important policy determined?
- Where are the directors' meetings held?
- Where do the majority of the directors reside?
- Where are the shareholders' meetings held?
- Where is the negotiation of major contracts undertaken?
- Where is the head office of the company?
- Where are the books of account and the company books (minute book, share register, etc.) kept?
- Where are the company's bank accounts?

As you can see, control is generally determined by reference to where the directors hold their meetings and **whether real decisions affecting the company are taken at those meetings**. In each case, one needs to look at the facts to determine where the company is actually managed and controlled.

In summary, a company is resident in the UK if it is incorporated in the UK. If it is not incorporated in the UK, it will be resident in the UK if it is centrally managed and controlled in the UK. A company resident in the UK is chargeable to corporation tax on all its profits wherever the income arises. Corporation tax is also payable on the disposal of chargeable assets irrespective of where the asset was situated and whether or not the proceeds were received or transmitted to the UK.

As stated above, a non-resident company is chargeable to corporation tax if it carries on a trade in the UK through a permanent establishment (PE). If it has a PE, then it will be chargeable on its trading income, income from property and on any chargeable gains arising on the disposal of assets situated in the UK and which are used for the purposes of the PE trade. A company is deemed to have a PE in a particular country if it has a fixed place of business (or a dependent agent) there through which the company carries out, either wholly or partly, its business.

It should be noted that a non-resident company which does not carry on a trade in the UK through a PE remains chargeable to income tax at the basic rate on any other UK income that it may have.

Where a UK company becomes non-UK resident, it must inform HMRC and its departure will be deemed to be the cessation of an accounting period with all of the resultant taxation implications as regards capital allowances and on the deemed disposal of all of its chargeable assets at their then market value. The exit charge arising may be postponed in certain circumstances.

1.10.1 Dual Resident Companies

It is sometimes the case that a former non-resident company, having become UK resident, may be deemed, under the domestic law of the foreign jurisdiction, to continue to be resident in that jurisdiction. In this scenario, the company has dual residence and the terms of the relevant double taxation treaty have to be examined. Double taxation treaties will generally contain a "tie-breaker" clause which will be applied to determine if the company is "treaty resident" in the UK or the foreign jurisdiction for tax purposes.

1.11 Substantial Shareholdings Exemption (SSE)

This relief, subject to all of the relevant conditions being fulfilled, will result in there being no chargeable gain on the disposal of shares or an interest in shares held by a company in another company.

For the gain not to be chargeable, the investing company most hold at least 10% of the investee company's shares and be entitled to at least 10% of the profits and assets available for distribution, and the company must have held the shares for a continuous period of at least 12 months ending not more than one year before the disposal in question.

Both the investing company and the investee company must have been a trading company or a member of a trading group throughout the 12-month period before the disposal, and immediately after the disposal.

In this context, a trading company is defined as a company which is either "a company existing wholly for the purpose of carrying on one or more trades" or a company that would fall within that definition "apart from purposes capable of having no substantial effect on the extent of the company's activities". In this context, any non-trading activities should be insubstantial – normally taken to mean not more than 20% of all activities.

1.12 Self-assessment and Administration

1.12.1 Filing of Company Tax Return

Companies are obliged to notify and report their liability to corporation tax to HMRC through the Corporation Tax Self-Assessment (CTSA) procedures.

The resultant company tax return must include a declaration by the person making the return that, to the best of their knowledge and belief, the return is correct and complete.

A complete company tax return should include:

1. completed form CT600;
2. any appropriate supplementary pages;
3. a copy of the relevant statutory accounts, to normally include detailed trading and profit and loss accounts;
4. a tax computation showing how the figures on the CT600 have been derived from the above statutory accounts.

This company tax return is due for filing with HMRC by the due date (in response to a notice to deliver sent by HMRC on form CT603). The due date is the last day of whichever of the following periods is the last to end:

1. within 12 months of the end of the accounting period.
2. if the company's statutory accounting period lies between 12 and 18 months, then 12 months from the end of the accounting period.
3. if the company's statutory accounts are for a period longer than 18 months, then 30 months from the beginning of that period.
4. within three months of receiving a notice to deliver (where the notice has been forwarded late to the company).

Corporation tax returns can be filed online with HMRC via its website at www.hmrc.gov.uk/businesses.

Since 1 April 2011, all companies and organisations are required to file their company tax return online in iXBRL format. This means that data within the accounts and computations must be XBRL tagged.

From the same date, companies and organisations are required to pay any corporation tax and related payments due electronically (for example by direct debit).

It is always the responsibility of the company to inform HMRC in writing within three months when it comes within the charge to corporation tax and this is normally satisfied by completing and submitting form CT41G. However, in many cases, Companies Registry will have informed HMRC of the formation of the new company. HMRC would then write to the company (sending them form CT41G) requesting all the relevant information and details relating to the new company.

Whilst HMRC will generally write to the new company (provided they have been supplied with the relevant details), the responsibility for notification always rests with the company. If a company fails to notify HMRC, then it will assume that the first accounting period will run for 12 months from the date of incorporation, which may or may not be the actual position. It is thus imperative that the company keep HMRC appraised of any relevant changes in the company's details (address, accounting period, directors, etc.).

From 1 April 2010 new penalties for failure to notify were introduced, which are applicable to most taxes. However, in respect of corporation tax, these generally mean that a company which has not received a company tax return or notice to file must tell HMRC if it becomes chargeable to tax within 12 months from the end of the relevant accounting period.

Different companies can have different accounting dates, so the time limit for notifying HMRC will differ accordingly. If a company's accounting date is 30 June 2014 and it is liable to corporation tax for that period, notification of chargeability must be given to HMRC by 29 June 2015.

Penalties for failure to notify are calculated based on the potential lost revenue to HMRC that could have arisen due to failure to notify (so this could be calculated on the basis of the corporation tax liability in the first accounting period).

The level of penalty will depend on how the failure to notify arose, and how HMRC became aware of it (see table below).

Type of failure to notify	Unprompted disclosure	Prompted disclosure
Non-deliberate – notified within 12 months	0%–30%	10%–30%
Non-deliberate – notified after 12 months	10%–30%	20%–30%
Deliberate but not concealed	20%–70%	35%–70%
Deliberate and concealed	30%–100%	50%–100%

> **Example 1.17**
> An example of "deliberate and concealed" failure to notify would be as follows:
>
> Ferdinand Ltd has never submitted tax returns. The company bought a property in 2011 from which it has been receiving rental income. When questioned by HMRC about the source of funds to purchase the property, Ferdinand, the sole shareholder and director, says the money was lent to the company by overseas family members. HMRC later find that Ferdinand Ltd owned a number of rental properties prior to 2011 and that the money actually came from the sale of one of those properties. For the earlier years when asked to explain the source of the company's funds, Ferdinand took active steps to conceal the company's liability. For those years the failure is deliberate and concealed. There may also be a failure-to-notify penalty on the company for the chargeable gain on the sale of the property.

The act of concealment can include:

- creating false stock records;
- creating false evidence of a non-taxable source to explain undisclosed taxable income;
- creating false invoices to support inaccurate figures of turnover;
- back-dating or post-dating invoices or contracts;
- deliberately destroying records so that they are no longer available;
- creating sales records that deliberately understate the value of the goods sold.

1.12.2 Company Records

A company must keep all business records and accounts, including contracts and receipts, until the latest of:

1. six years from the end of the relevant accounting period;
2. the date that any enquiries are completed; and
3. the date after which enquiries may not be commenced.

If a return is demanded more than six years after the end of the accounting period, any records which the company still has must be retained until the later of the end of the enquiry and the expiry of the right to start an enquiry.

The maximum penalty for failing to preserve records is £3,000. However, there is no penalty for failing to keep or preserve records which might have been needed only for the purposes of claims, elections or notices not included in the return.

1.12.3 Company Tax Return

Directors of UK companies are required to file statutory accounts with Companies Registry for every 12-month accounting period. In general, the corporation tax accounting period follows the statutory accounting period but, for corporation tax purposes, there are specific dates at which an accounting period will begin or end and, as discussed earlier, these can differ from those for the statutory accounts.

If the statutory period of account is greater than 12 months, it is divided for corporation tax purposes into 12-month tranches and a residue period. For example, if A Ltd prepared accounts for the 19-month period ending 31 December 2014, it would be required to submit company tax returns for the 12 months ended 31 May 2014 and for the seven-month period ended 31 December 2014. The filing date for both returns is 31 December 2015, being 12 months after the end of the period of accounts. However, there will be two deadlines for payment of corporation tax, providing the instalment payment rules do not apply.

Penalties

If the company's tax return is not filed within three months of the due date, it will incur a flat rate penalty of £100. The penalty rises to £200 after this and is increased to £500 and £1,000 where the failure occurs for a third successive time.

Whilst the above penalties are not tax-related, if a company fails to deliver a return within 18 months of the end of an accounting period (or a later filing date, if applicable), then the penalty becomes 10% of the unpaid tax at that date if it remains undelivered within two years of the due date, rising to 20% thereafter. The latter tax-related penalties are in addition to the flat rate penalties above.

1.12.4 Enquiry

For accounting periods ending after 31 March 2008, the time span for which HMRC may give notice that it is enquiring into a company tax return (where the company is small or part of a small group) is 12 months from the date that the return was filed. Previously, HMRC could raise an enquiry at any time within 12 months of the filing date or, if the return was delivered late, 12 months from after the next quarter dates (31 January, 30 April, 31 July and 31 October) following the date on which the return was actually delivered.

Normally HMRC would conduct its enquiries under procedures set out in their Code of Practice. With many UK companies being family owned and run, it would not be unusual to find that HMRC would open an enquiry into the tax affairs of the directors/working shareholders at the same time. During the course of the enquiry, the company and/or its professional advisors will be asked to supply various documents and details relating to the queries raised by HMRC. In some circumstances a meeting may take place. Minutes of all such meetings would be taken and HMRC would normally request that the company would sign a copy of these minutes as a verification of their content.

The enquiry would be complete when HMRC issues a closure notice. If HMRC believes that the original company tax return requires amendment, it notifies the company in writing. Any additional corporation tax which is deemed to be now due will attract interest and will most likely include a tax-geared penalty. HMRC will make an offer to the company to encompass all outstanding liabilities. If the company is dissatisfied, it has the right to appeal and it must lodge its appeal with the Tax Tribunal within 30 days from the date that an assessment was issued.

If either the company or HMRC disagrees with the decision of the First-tier Tax Tribunal, they can ask for a review by the Upper-tier Tax Tribunal. Ultimately, if the company remains dissatisfied, it can appeal the decision of the Tax Tribunal. Appeals from the Tax Tribunal can only be made by HMRC or a taxpayer on points of law, and not in respect of findings of fact by the Tax Tribunal.

Tax cases appealed from the Tax Tribunal now skip the High Court and go straight to the Court of Appeal. From a commercial point of view, companies must be mindful of the potentially huge costs involved in such a course of action and these must be weighed against the tax at stake.

Penalties

The existing penalty regime came into force on 1 April 2009. It applies to income tax, CGT, corporation tax and VAT and has effect for return periods commencing after 31 March 2008, where the return is filed after 31 March 2009. Therefore, it applies to companies for accounting periods commencing on or after 1 April 2009.

The penalty regime was extended to other taxes and duties, including stamp duty and inheritance tax, from 1 April 2010.

1.12.5 Taxpayer's Behaviour

The new penalty regime focuses on the behaviour of the taxpayer, i.e. the company acting through its directors and officers. Where a company has made a mistake in a return submitted to HMRC, but has taken reasonable care in the preparation of that return, no penalty will be applied by HMRC.

In its *Compliance Handbook*, HMRC states that appointing a tax adviser does not automatically mean that the company has taken reasonable care in the preparation of a return. The tax adviser should be competent and qualified. The company still bears responsibility for the return and the director is expected, within his ability and competence, to make sure that the return which he is signing is correct.

The categories of behaviour where penalties will be imposed are:

1. Careless (failure to take reasonable care)
2. Deliberate but not concealed (the inaccuracy is deliberate but there are no arrangements to conceal it)
3. Deliberate and concealed (the inaccuracy is deliberate and there are arrangements to conceal it).

Once HMRC has categorised the "behaviour" of the taxpayer, the potential lost revenue (PLR) will be computed. The penalty imposed is based on a percentage of PLR, which is the additional amount of tax due or payable as a result of correcting the inaccuracy.

However, HMRC may apply reductions to the proposed penalty where the company has disclosed the inaccuracy. Disclosure is split into two types (unprompted and prompted), with greater reductions being given where the company makes a disclosure which has not been prompted by HMRC.

HMRC states in its *Compliance Handbook* that a disclosure is unprompted if it is made at a time when the person making it has no reason to believe that HMRC has discovered or is about to discover the inaccuracy.

The ranges of percentage penalties which will be applied by HMRC to the PLR, based on the behaviour of the taxpayer and the extent of the disclosure, are summarised in the table below.

Behaviour	Careless	Deliberate but not concealed	Deliberate and concealed
Minimum penalty with unprompted disclosure	0%	20%	30%
Minimum penalty with prompted disclosure	15%	35%	50%
Maximum penalty	30%	70%	100%

Example 1.18

HMRC discovers an arithmetical error in Peony Ltd's tax return for the year ended 31 March 2014. The PLR is calculated to be £5,000. The return had been prepared by the company's financial controller and signed by its sole director, Dee. She had not checked the tax return before signing it and so was not aware of the error.

The company has been careless in the preparation of its tax return and was not able to disclose the error to HMRC before it was discovered. Because the error was arithmetical, it was within Dee's competence and ability to find it. HMRC may impose a penalty of 30% of £5,000, i.e. £1,500, in addition to charging interest for late payment.

The types of documents on which a penalty is potentially payable are:

1. CT600 (company tax return);
2. any document in connection with a claim for an allowance, deduction or relief;
3. the accounts for the relevant period;
4. any other document which HMRC could reasonably be expected to rely upon in ascertaining the company's corporation tax liability/repayment claims, etc. – this could include the computation submitted to support the return.

HMRC will assess the penalty and notify the company accordingly in respect of the tax period for which the penalty is being assessed. The penalty assessment must be made within 12 months of the period beginning with the end of the appeal period for the decision correcting the inaccuracy, or the date the inaccuracy is corrected (if there is no penalty assessment).

As previously mentioned, the company will have a right to appeal to the Tax Tribunal against the imposition of the penalty, its amount and/or the conditions of the penalty (it will also be able to appeal the non-suspension of a penalty).

In the case of deliberate inaccuracy which is found to be attributable to an officer (to include a director, secretary or shadow director) of the company, both the company and the officer are liable for the penalty.

1.12.6 Duties of Senior Accounting Officers of Qualifying Companies

All companies have an obligation to deliver correct and complete tax returns, but compliance with this obligation can be compromised if the company's tax accounting arrangements are not fit for purpose. Previously there was no requirement on anyone within a qualifying company to ensure that the underlying tax accounting arrangements were fit for purpose. This measure addresses that potential "accountability gap" by making the senior accounting officer (SAO) of a qualifying company responsible for ensuring that appropriate tax accounting arrangements are in place. In many cases the SAO will be the chief financial officer (CFO) of the company or group.

These measures apply to qualifying companies, which are generally defined as a UK incorporated company that, in the preceding financial year, either alone or when its results are aggregated with other UK companies in the same group, has turnover of more than £200 million or has a relevant balance sheet total of more than £2 billion.

The SAO is the director or officer with overall responsibility, as appropriately delegated, for the company's financial accounting arrangements. The company will judge who best fits this definition, and in most cases this will be evident from the established governance arrangements.

This requires the SAO of a qualifying company to take reasonable steps to ensure that the company establishes and maintains appropriate tax accounting arrangements.

The SAO of a qualifying company must also provide HMRC with a certificate stating whether the company has appropriate tax accounting arrangements or, where it does not, provide an explanation. The certificate must be submitted no later than the end of the period for filing the accounts for the financial year.

Penalties may arise for failure to comply with this legislation as follows:

- there could be a penalty of £5,000 assessable on the SAO if they fail to comply with the main duty to take reasonable steps to ensure that the company establishes and maintains appropriate tax accounting arrangements;
- there could be a penalty of £5,000, again assessable on the SAO, if they fail to provide a certificate or if they provide an incorrect certificate; or

▨ there could be a penalty where a company fails to notify HMRC of the name/s of the person who was the SAO throughout the financial year.

1.13 Publishing Details of Deliberate Tax Defaulters

HMRC states that more than 90% of citizens pay their taxes and, to tackle the small minority who deliberately do not, HMRC deals seriously with such cases, using civil or criminal powers to penalise or prosecute evaders. From April 2010, in addition to recovering the tax due, interest and a penalty up to 100% of the tax lost, new legislation came into force allowing HMRC to publish the details of people or companies caught deliberately evading more than £25,000.

Previously, HMRC could not publish details of the evaders in civil cases, only in criminal cases. Parliament decided to set the threshold at £25,000 to ensure that only the most serious cases of tax evasion will result in publication.

Section 94 FA 2009 enables HMRC to publish the names and details of individuals and companies who are penalised for deliberate tax defaults. Deliberate tax defaults are: incorrect returns, failures to notify and certain VAT and excise duty wrongdoings. Section 94 does not, however, apply to late filing or late payment penalties.

The legislation was brought into effect by Treasury Order on 3 March 2010 and applies to return periods starting on or after 1 April 2010 and failures or wrongdoings occurring on or after 1 April 2010. No details of deliberate defaults committed prior to the legislation becoming effective will be published.

1.13.1 Details of the Scheme

For HMRC to consider publication of a person's (including company's) name and details, the following conditions must apply:

▨ a relevant penalty within Schedule 24 FA 2007 or Schedule 41 FA 2008 must be incurred;
▨ the taxpayers must be penalised for one or more deliberate or deliberate and concealed defaults; and
▨ the amount of tax evaded must be greater than £25,000. In working out whether this threshold is reached, all tax (of any sort, and for any year after 1 April 2010) which has been subject to a penalty for deliberate errors will be added together.

However, even where the above criteria are met, HMRC will not publish details where individuals make a full disclosure to HMRC, either unprompted or immediately when challenged, and co-operate fully throughout the course of HMRC's enquiries, thereby receiving the maximum penalty reduction available.

1.13.2 Publication Rules

Publication will follow a strict set of rules:

▨ All the penalty decisions which underpin the scheme can be appealed to an independent tribunal.
▨ No publication is possible until all appeals are concluded or opportunities to appeal have expired.
▨ The publication process will not form part of the enquiry process. At the conclusion of a compliance check the compliance officer will refer any case that meets the criteria for publication to a specialist team, which will ensure that:

- The taxpayer is notified in advance of HMRC's intention to publish, and the details to be published.
- The taxpayer will be given an opportunity to make representations, explaining why their details should not be published.
- The strict time limits are adhered to. HMRC must publish within 12 months of the penalty becoming final and cease publishing that information 12 months thereafter.

HMRC will publish the details necessary to uniquely identify the person and the extent of their evasion. This may include the person's name, address, nature of business, period covered by the evasion, amount of evaded tax and the penalty for that evasion. HMRC plans to publish a list quarterly on the HMRC website with an accompanying press notice.

HMRC will publish if the criteria are met, unless there are exceptional circumstances. Any representations made by the taxpayer will be taken into account in reaching this decision. Examples might include prejudice to an ongoing criminal investigation or risk to a person's security. HMRC are unlikely to decide not to publish because of a possible impact on the person's reputation, business interests or creditworthiness. The decision to publish will be made by a senior HMRC officer.

1.14 Managing Deliberate Defaulters Programme

In February 2011 HMRC launched a programme aimed at closely monitoring the tax affairs of individuals and businesses, including companies, classed as "deliberate defaulters" (DD). HMRC have openly stated that a key objective of the new programme will be to ensure taxpayers in the programme are compliant with their tax obligations and "have demonstrated a permanent change in their behaviour".

This new programme is in addition to existing legislation allowing HMRC to publish the names of those with errors resulting in a tax loss in excess of £25,000, as discussed previously.

The programme is not voluntary in nature and thus any taxpayer/company classed as a DD may become part of this enhanced monitoring and activity programme known as Managing Deliberate Defaulters (MDD).

In future, if a person/company is classed as having deliberately evaded tax, HMRC will normally write to warn them that they may be included in MDD. When HMRC considers that enhanced monitoring should apply, it will advise the taxpayer in writing of their inclusion in the programme at the end of the relevant compliance check.

HMRC's accompanying Q&A guidance on MDD defines deliberate default for the purposes of the programme as follows:

"Generally speaking, deliberate default will be most easily identified where a penalty under Schedule 24 Finance Act 2007 or Schedule 41 Finance Act 2008 for Deliberate or Deliberate with Concealment applies."

Furthermore, the programme will be applied retrospectively to any taxpayer having already been charged with a penalty under this behavioural penalty regime.

However, where a full unprompted disclosure is made, the defaulter will not be placed into the MDD programme, subject to having been given the maximum 50% penalty reduction for deliberate without concealment behaviour, having reduced the maximum possible penalty from 70% to 20% (maximum 70% penalty reduction for deliberate with concealment behaviour reducing the maximum possible penalty from 100% to 30%).

It should be noted that there is no *de minimis* penalty limit which would apply to allow taxpayers to avoid inclusion in the programme. Therefore, the MDD programme applies to businesses and individual taxpayers who have been found to have made a deliberate understatement of any size (whether or not concealed) resulting in a "tax loss" (overclaims and overstatements are similarily targeted).

HMRC has also made it clear that a DD may also be identified without a compliance check having been carried out, for example where a person has been convicted of a criminal offence involving tax evasion. Other instances of deliberate evasion may be identified through Civil Investigation of Fraud or specific disclosure campaigns.

It is also important to note that the MDD programme extends across all the defaulter's tax affairs rather than just the area(s) from which the initiating behaviour originated.

In addition to the penalty for the original offence, for a five-year period afterwards, the taxpayer may be subject to additional monitoring, with the level and term of monitoring depending on the seriousness of the offence. However, HMRC does not envisage that anyone will be released from the programme within a two-year period.

HMRC will continue to check that returns are filed on time and that any tax due is paid on time, but there will also be regular reviews of DDs' tax affairs to check that any errors or failings have been rectified. There are a variety of measures HMRC may use to monitor a DD's tax affairs. These include:

- Making announced or unannounced inspection visits to carry out pre-return checks of books and records.
- Asking for certain records so that they can be checked.
- Requiring that additional information or documents are sent in with the relevant tax returns.
- Conducting in-depth compliance checks into all or any part of the DD's tax affairs.
- Observing and recording the DD's business activities and cross-checking details in their accounts. For example, HMRC may make test purchases or inspect the records of one or more of their suppliers or customers.
- For VAT customers, HMRC may:
  - require submission of quarterly or monthly VAT returns;
  - require the same accounting periods for VAT and income tax or corporation tax; and
  - withdraw the use of certain schemes (for example, cash accounting, annual accounting, flat-rate scheme, retail schemes) if HMRC deem this necessary for the protection of tax revenue.

Those who fail to keep their tax affairs in order will face increasingly intrusive interventions from HMRC and, if "deliberate evasion" continues, HMRC may also start criminal proceedings.

Monitoring will continue until HMRC has been satisfied that the defaulter has demonstrated a sustained and permanent change in behaviour, at which time HMRC will write to advise them of this change in status.

When included in the programme, HMRC will explain the minimum requirements that the DD will need to meet and what, if any, additional documents or information will be required with future tax returns. At a minimum level, the scheme will require that DDs submit all relevant returns and make all relevant payments on time, including tax under a Time to Pay arrangement (an arrangement whereby tax is paid on an instalment basis as agreed with HMRC where the business is experiencing cash flow difficulties).

Furthermore, a DD will not be entitled to use the "Short" pages option when filing returns. In cases where the DD's tax "loss" is £5,000 or more, HMRC may also require the following additional information to be submitted with the relevant tax returns for a period of up to five years:

- a copy of the detailed trading and profit and loss accounts (and property income accounts if relevant);

- a detailed balance sheet;
- detailed computations and explanations that identify and explain the nature and amount of any figures contained in the accounts that cannot be vouched by physical or electronic records made at the time that the underlying transactions took place. If there were no such figures, HMRC will require written confirmation of this; and
- defaulting businesses registered for VAT may be required to submit VAT accounts for any and all periods included within the period of the trading accounts required.

The above information will be required regardless of the additional cost involved. Given the potentially serious consequences for taxpayers coming under the auspices of this new programme, practitioners should be fully aware of the implications of MDD status when discussing with clients disclosure opportunities of any nature or for those clients currently in the process of reaching any settlement of tax with HMRC likely to result in a penalty categorised in the "deliberate" category.

Computation of Corporation Tax

Learning Objectives

After studying this chapter you will have developed competency in the following:
- The format of a corporation tax computation – as you deal with the other chapters, make sure that you understand how they fit into the pro forma corporation tax computation.
- The understanding that there are many items in the financial statements that are required to be adjusted in moving from profit per the accounts to Trading Income, and the competence to make these adjustments resulting in the ability to calculate the liability to corporation tax.
- An awareness that there is additional tax relief for expenditure on R&D which may be claimed by companies of all sizes.

2.1   Pro Forma Corporation Tax Computation

Complex Company Limited Corporation Tax Computation for the 12-month accounting period to 31 March 2015

	Notes	£	£
Trading income:			
Tax-adjusted trading profits	2	X	
Losses forward under section 45 CTA 2010		(X)	
			X
Loan relationships:			
Net income from non-trading loan relationships	3		X
Chargeable gains	4		X
"Total profits"			X
Deduct: Qualifying charitable donations	5		(X)
Taxable total profits (TTP)			X

Note 1

The computation should always have the name of the company at the top and an appropriate heading, i.e. "corporation tax computation for the 12-month accounting period to...".

Remember: it is possible for a corporation tax accounting period to be less than 12 months but it can never exceed 12 months. This is discussed in detail in **Chapter 1**.

Note 2

The tax-adjusted trading profits are arrived at after making a number of adjustments.

It should be particularly noted that the tax-adjusted trading profits represent the final trading income figure **after** capital allowances have been deducted, but **before** relief for unutilised trading losses carried forward from the **same trade**.

A small or medium-sized enterprise (SME) may qualify for an enhanced deduction from trading profits of 225% of its qualifying research and development (R&D) expenditure. This deduction should be included within the Trading Income computation under the heading "deductible expenditure not included in the accounts". For a large company, the relevant deduction is 130%. Finance Act 2013 saw the introduction of a 10% 'above the line' tax credit for large company R&D expenditure. Companies can elect to apply this scheme, in preference to the enhanced deduction of 130%, for their qualifying expenditure incurred on or after 1 April 2013.

Note 3

The income to be included here is income receivable during the accounting period, *without* deduction of UK income tax. For example, deposit interest earned by a **company** on deposits with a UK bank or building society will normally be **paid gross**.

Interest relating to non-trading loan relationships is taxed as investment income on an accruals basis. A company will have a non-trading loan relationship if it is not a party to that loan relationship for the purposes of its trade. Any debits and credits that are not brought into account as trading income and expenses are termed non-trading profits and deficits.

Non-trading credits and debits are added together to arrive at the net amount to be brought into account.

Note 4

A corporation tax computation also includes chargeable gains by companies. The computation method for arriving at the appropriate chargeable gains to include in the corporation tax computation was dealt with in detail in **Chapter 1**. See also **Section 13.7** for more information on computation of a chargeable gain.

Note 5

Qualifying charitable donations or non-trade charges

Following Corporation Tax Act 2010 (CTA 2010), for corporation tax purposes charges on income are now reduced to charitable donations only; therefore these are now referred to as "qualifying charitable donations" as this gives a more accurate description. Qualifying charitable donations (QCDs) made by a company are allowed as deductions from the company's total profits in calculating the corporation tax chargeable for an accounting period. They are deducted from the company's total profits for the period after any other relief from corporation tax other than group relief.

The amount of the deduction is limited to the amount that reduces the company's taxable total profits for the period to nil. As there is no facility to carry forward surplus donations, any excess is effectively lost. For accounting periods ending prior to 1 April 2010, these were known as excess non-trade charges.

Extra-Statutory Concession B7, which allowed small local gifts to charities, is no longer applicable and hence all gifts or donations to charity fall to be treated as QCDs.

2.2 Badges of Trade

The full amount of the profits or gains of a trade are taxable as trading income. "Trade" is defined as including "every trade, manufacture, adventure or concern in the nature of trade". This definition does not give any detailed guidance as to whether a particular activity constitutes a trading activity. Each case where the meaning of "trade" is an issue must be decided on its own facts.

The approach of the Commissioners and the courts over the years has been to examine the facts and look for the presence or absence of common features or characteristics of trade. These are known as the "badges of trade" which have been identified as case law has developed before the courts.

The report of the Royal Commission on the Taxation of Profits and Income in 1955 reviewed the case law and identified six "badges". Since then the concept has been refined and enlarged.

A useful modern summary of the badges of trade is contained in *Marson v. Morton and Others* (1986) 59 TC 381 at page 391, although the court disclaimed any intention of the review being exhaustive.

The six "badges" to be taken into account in determining if a trade exists are as follows:

2.2.1 The Nature of the Asset

The nature of the asset can be of great, even decisive, importance. Some assets are generally realised by way of trade (e.g. chemicals) and, for transactions in such assets, the existence of a trade is rarely in doubt. The area of difficulty concerns assets that are generally bought:

- as an investment that usually, but not necessarily, yields income, e.g. shares; or
- for personal use or enjoyment, e.g. paintings and classic cars; or
- as a fixed asset of an admitted trade, e.g. plant and machinery.

Their very nature provides an initial presumption that these types of assets are acquired other than as a subject of trade. That presumption can be overturned but there is, in practice, a greater onus on those who assert that there is a trade than is the case with assets that are commonly dealt with by way of trade.

Generally, property which does not generate any income or enjoyment is more likely to have been purchased with a view to selling it than property which produces income or enjoyment. For example, the disposal of a valuable painting may generate a gain of a capital nature rather than trading income. In contrast, the disposal of one million rolls of toilet paper is more likely to be presumed to be a trading transaction.

2.2.2 Length of Period of Ownership

In general, property purchased and sold within a short time period is presumed to be of a trading nature.

Assets that are the subject of trade will normally, but not always, be sold quickly. Therefore, an intention to resell an asset shortly after purchase will generally support trading. However, an asset, which is to be held indefinitely, is much less likely to be a subject of trade. Each situation will depend on the specific facts of the case.

2.2.3   Existence of Similar Trading Transactions or Interests

Transactions that are similar to those of an existing trade may themselves be trading. Transactions which would be treated as being of a capital nature if carried out in isolation will be treated as trading transactions if there is in fact a succession of such transactions over a period of years or there are several such transactions in or around the same time.

2.2.4   Changes to the Asset

Was the asset repaired, modified or improved to make it more easily saleable or saleable at a greater profit? What happens to the asset pending resale may be a relevant factor. There may be modifications to the asset by way of processing or manufacture, or some kind of adaptation to make it more readily marketable. All these actions are typical of trading activities. Where there is an organised effort to generate profit, then there is likely to be a source of trading income. However, if there is no such effort the result would tend to go the other way. However, remember that if an asset does not need any modification or other work, then absence of any modification, etc. is neutral.

2.2.5   The Way in which the Sale is Carried out

Was the asset sold in a way that was typical of trading organisations? Alternatively, did it have to be sold to raise cash for an emergency? This is a pointer towards trade that the transactions are carried out in the same manner as those of an undisputed trader.

2.2.6   Profit Motive

An intention to make a profit supports trading, but by itself is not conclusive. However, motive is extremely important in all cases. There are cases in which the purpose of the transaction is clearly discernible. Circumstances surrounding the particular transaction may indicate the motive of the seller and this may in fact overrule the seller's own evidence.

2.3   Adjustments in Arriving at Trading Income

In arriving at "trading income" the following steps should **always** be considered:

1.   Deduct non-trading income and gains.
2.   Add back any expenses not properly associated with the trading activities.
3.   Watch out for receipts that are not taxable.

2.3.1   Deduction of Non-trading Income and Gains

Deduct	**Then tax instead as follows:**
Interest	Generally taxed under the loan relationship rules.
	If miscellaneous income, then tax gross amount with credit for tax deducted (if applicable).
Rents	Property income, deduct related expenses and wear and tear allowances.
Dividends from other UK companies	Not taxable if received prior to 1 July 2009. After 1 July 2009, should also be tax-free provided one of the exemptions is met.
Foreign dividends	Prior to 1 July 2009 are taxable with credit given for foreign tax up to limit of UK tax on dividend. After 1 July 2009, should be tax-free provided one of the exemptions is met.

▨ Profits on disposal   If a chargeable asset, then compute chargeable gain as described in
of assets   **Chapter 1**.

2.3.2   Add Back of Expenses not Properly Associated with the Trading Activities

Summary of Expenses Commonly Disallowed

1. Expenses or losses of a capital nature:

▨ Depreciation.
▨ Loss on sale of fixed assets (if a chargeable asset remember to compute the chargeable gain/
loss position as discussed in **Chapter 1**).
▨ Improvements to premises.
▨ Purchase of fixed assets.

2. Expenses not wholly and exclusively laid out for the purposes of the trade or business:

▨ Rental expenses (may be allowable against property income).
▨ Political donations. Qualifying charitable donations should be added back and then allowed as
a deduction from total profits.
▨ Fines and penalties and interest on late payment of tax (however, interest on late corporation tax
will be allowed as a non-trade debit to be deducted from non-trade loan relationships).

Treatment of Certain Specific Items

(a) Bad debts
Under UK generally accepted accounting principles (or UK GAAP), a company may have general
and specific bad debts provisions. Under general tax principles, general provisions are not deductible.
Therefore, if there are any movements on the general bad debts provision account, an adjustment
must be made, i.e.:

▨ Increase in a general provision for bad debts – not allowable; therefore, add this back.
▨ Decrease in a general provision for bad debts – not taxable; therefore, deduct this amount.

As there is no difference between the tax and accounting rules in relation to any other movements
on bad debts, there is no adjustment required for the following items:

▨ Bad debts written off – deducted in profit and loss account and also allowed for tax purposes.
▨ Bad debts recovered – credited to profit and loss account and therefore taxable.
▨ Increase in a specific provision for bad debts – deducted in P&L account and therefore allowed
for tax purposes.
▨ Decrease in a specific provision for bad debts – credited to P&L account and therefore taxable.

For the avoidance of doubt, UK GAAP includes accounts of companies prepared under International
Accounting Standards, International Financial Standards and accounts prepared under Financial
Reporting Standards including FRS 102 *The FRS applicable in the UK and the Republic of Ireland.*
     Students should note that the adoption of FRS 102 may result in the need for transitional
adjustments for tax purposes. These transitional adjustments are beyond the scope of this book.

IFRS   Under IFRS, the manner of calculating a provision for doubtful debts is more specific than
under UK GAAP. As a result, increases in bad debt provisions are treated as deductible for tax
purposes, provided that they are properly calculated in accordance with the new standards.

(b) Entertainment Expenses

General entertainment expenses incurred are completely disallowed. Entertainment includes the provision of accommodation, food, drink or any other form of hospitality including the provision of gifts.

Expenditure on bona fide staff entertainment is not subject to the foregoing restrictions provided its provision is not incidental to the provision of entertainment to third parties. Entertaining for and gifts to employees are normally deductible for the company but one should watch out for excessive amounts. Gifts to customers not costing more than £50 per donee per year are allowable if they carry a conspicuous advertisement for the business and are not food, drink or tobacco. In looking at whether the £50 limit has been breached it is necessary to take into account the cost of all such gifts carrying a conspicuous advertisement (excluding any gifts already disallowed) given to the same person in the same accounting period.

Extra-Statutory Concession B7 was a concessionary arrangement which allowed traders to deduct the cost of gifts (not to be confused with monetary donations otherwise known as qualifying charitable donations (QCDs) or non-trade charges on income) to local bodies or associations established for educational, cultural, religious, recreational or benevolent purposes, as long as the expenditure was incurred for the purposes of the trade and was reasonably small in relation to the scale of the donor's business. This was withdrawn from 9 December 2010 as effectively companies can now avail of relief for gifts to charities as a result of section 1300(5) CTA 2009.

(c) Legal Expenses

- Debt recovery – allowable.
- Acquisition of assets – not allowable.
- Renewal of short lease (defined as being < 50 years) – allowable.
- Product liability claims and employee actions – allowable.
- Maintaining existing trading rights and assets – allowable.

(d) Repairs

Replacement/redecoration, repairs not involving material improvements – expenditure is allowable.

(e) Motor Vehicle Hire

New rules were introduced on 1 April 2009. Where a car is held on operating lease, the deduction available for the lease hire charges depends on the CO_2 emissions of the car.

For leases entered into from 1 April 2013 onwards, where the CO_2 emissions exceed 130g/km (160g/km for leases entered into prior to 1 April 2013), 15% of the lease hire charge will be disallowed.

Example 2.1

A company, which prepares annual accounts to 31 December, leased a new car on 1 June 2014. The car's CO_2 emissions are 143g/km.

In the annual accounts to 31 December 2014 lease hire charges of £10,000 were incurred.
Disallowable: £10,000 × 15% = £1,500

Prior to 1 April 2009, an amount was disallowed if the list price of the car exceeded £12,000. The list price of the car is no longer relevant to this calculation.

(f) Interest on Late Payment of Tax

Interest on late payment of any tax (including VAT, PAYE, etc.) is not allowed in computing tax-adjusted profits; neither are any penalties arising from VAT, PAYE or any other tax. However, interest on late payment of corporation tax should be added back and then treated as a non-trade debit.

(g) Accountancy/Taxation Fees

▨ Normal routine accounting, auditing and taxation compliance costs are allowable.
▨ Special costs associated with Appeal Hearings are likely to be disallowed following the decision of *Allen v. Farquharson Brothers,* where the costs of employing solicitors and counsel in connection with an appeal against income tax assessments were held to be disallowed.
▨ Fee protection insurance charges to cover the risk of incurring additional costs are only allowable if the additional costs are of a revenue nature.

(h) Pre-trading Expenses

Pre-trading expenses, as their name indicates, are incurred before the trade has commenced. As a general rule, relief is given for allowable business expenditure incurred in the seven years prior to the commencement of a trade. The relief is given in the accounting period in which the trade commences in respect of those revenue items which satisfy the relevant test.

The qualifying expenses are those:

▨ incurred in the seven years prior to the commencement, and
▨ which would be allowed as a deduction in calculating trading profits, if they had been incurred after trading commenced.

Examples of qualifying pre-trading expenses include: accountancy fees, market research, feasibility studies, salaries, advertising, preparing business plans and rent.

These pre-trading expenses are deductible against income of the trade if they were incurred in the seven-year period prior to commencement. If these expenses exceed the company's trading income, resulting in a loss, this loss **can** be offset against other profits of the company, and it can be group relieved. It can also be carried forward against future income of the same trade.

QCDs (previous non-trading charges on income) incurred before a trade commences are treated as paid when the trade commences, i.e. are deductible as non-trade charges in the first year of trading.

Any interest that a company incurs before trading commences is classified as a non-trade debit under the loan relationship rules. As non-trade debits carried forward can only be set-off against future non-trade income, the company has a choice to elect that the pre-trading non-trade debits be treated as a trading expense of the year when it commences trading.

Example 2.2

Ray Ltd commenced to trade on 1 July 2014. It incurred the following pre-trading expenditure:

		£
December 2006	Market research	8,000
December 2013	Director's salary	30,000
January 2014	Business entertainment	5,000
May 2014	Marketing expenditure	17,000

Notes: The market research expenditure is not deductible as it was not incurred within seven years before the trade commenced. The business entertainment expenditure is never allowable. The expenditure on the director's salary and marketing are allowable. Therefore, Ray Ltd incurs deductible expenses of £47,000 on 1 July 2014. These are fully deductible in calculating Trading Income of the first accounting period. Should this expenditure exceed this income, the excess is available for offset against other profits, for group relief if applicable or against future income of this trade.

(i) Expenditure on Research and Development (R&D)

A small or medium-sized company (SME) qualifies for an enhanced deduction from its trading profits of 225% of its qualifying R&D expenditure with effect from 1 April 2012. The tax relief is obtained by adjusting the trading income computation. Where the deduction creates a deemed trading loss, the company may (instead of any loss relief that it may be entitled to) surrender the loss for a cash payment of 14.5% of the loss for the chargeable period in respect of qualifying expenditure incurred on or after 1 April 2014. Prior to this the rate was 11%.

A large company's tax deduction is 130% of qualifying expenditure, being expenditure that would be allowable as a deduction in computing the taxable profits of a trade carried on by the company. Alternatively, as a large company, it could elect into the newly introduced 'above the line' R&D tax credit regime for expenditure incurred from 1 April 2013.

See **Section 2.5** below for more on this specific relief for companies.

(j) Payments for "Intangible Assets"

The intangible asset regime was introduced in the UK with effect from 1 April 2002 and it provides companies with tax relief on their intangible assets, to include their intellectual property – see **Section 2.6** below. The definition of intangible asset in CTA 2009 is that "it has the same meaning it has for accounting purposes". It also includes intellectual property which is defined as:

(i) any patent, trademark, registered design, copyright or design right;

(ii) any right under the law of a country or territory outside the UK corresponding or similar to a right under (a);

(iii) any information or technique not protected by a right within paragraph (a) or (b) but having industrial, commercial or other economic value; or

(iv) any licence or other right in respect of anything within paragraph (a), (b) or (c).

Intangible asset is defined for accounting purposes in FRS 10 as "non-financial fixed assets that do not have a physical substance but are identifiable and are controlled by the entity through custody or legal rights". Included within "intangible assets" therefore are items such as patents, trademarks, brand names, copyrights, goodwill, know-how agreements and publishing copyrights. For taxation purposes, intellectual property includes both UK and overseas rights.

Accounting gains and accounting losses relating to intangible assets used in a company's business are translated, respectively, into credits and debits for tax purposes. Although all the credits and debits are brought into account as revenue items, different rules govern how they enter the calculation depending on the nature of the business activity for which the intangible fixed asset in respect of which they arise is held, e.g. whether the assets are held for trading purposes, a property business or a non-trading company. Expenditure is a "debit", whereas income is a "credit".

(k) Redundancy Payments

The following rules apply if a company as employer makes a redundancy payment (statutory) or an approved contractual payment to an employee and the payment is in respect of the employee's employment in the employer's trade. An approved "contractual payment" means a payment which, under an agreement, an employer is liable to make to an employee on the termination of the employee's contract of employment.

Statutory redundancy payments are specifically allowable as are approved contractual payments up to the statutory limit. If such payments are made after the employer has permanently ceased to carry on the trade, they are treated as made on the last day on which the employer carried on the trade.

The deduction under this section is allowed for the accounting period in which the payment is made unless the trade has permanently ceased in which case it is treated as made on the last day of the trade.

For any voluntary payments in excess of the statutory (or approved) payments, these additional voluntary payments are allowable only if the sole reason for their disallowance is the cessation of the trade or part of the trade.

(l) Subscriptions
Political subscriptions and donations are generally not allowable. Subscriptions to a relevant professional body are generally allowable.

(m) Lease Payments for Assets Capitalised in the Balance Sheet
In accordance with FRS 21, where a finance leased asset is capitalised in the balance sheet, the amounts expensed in the P&L are the interest expense and depreciation. The lease payment is not expensed to the P&L. Where the burden of the wear and tear of the asset is borne by the lessor – the typical situation – the lessee is not entitled to capital allowances. Rather, the accounts depreciation charge will be deductible for tax purposes, provided it is based on normal commercial accounting principles. This means, in effect, that no tax adjustment needs to be made in respect of finance leased assets. However, note that, if the finance lease depreciation relates to a motor vehicle, new rules were introduced on 1 April 2009. Where a car is held on finance lease, the deduction available for the depreciation on the finance lease depends on the CO_2 emissions of the car.

For the financial year 2014/15, where the CO_2 emissions exceed 130g/km, 15% of the depreciation will be disallowed.

Example 2.3

A company, which prepares annual accounts to 31 March, purchased a new car under finance lease for £26,775 on 1 October 2014. The car's CO_2 emissions are 193g/km.

In the annual accounts to 31 March 2015 depreciation of £2,678 has been charged. Disallowable: £2,768 @ 15% = £415.

Prior to 1 April 2009, an amount was disallowed if the list price of the car exceeded £12,000. The list price of the car is no longer relevant to this calculation.

(n) Pension Contributions
Where the payments to a pension scheme meet the "wholly and exclusively for the purposes of the trade" test and they are of a revenue nature, they will be an allowable deduction from profits on a **paid** basis. Thus, the amount included within the P&L account may well require adjustment in the Trading Income computation. Given the large number of owner managed companies, HMRC would be anxious to establish that contributions in respect of controlling directors (or the wider family circle) meet the above criteria. HMRC is also likely to enquire into the deductibility of the pension contributions paid in connection with the sale or transfer of shares.

Thus, ordinary annual contributions by an employer to a registered pension scheme for the benefit of his employees are generally allowable for tax purposes in the year in which they are paid if the company is carrying on a trade, or as management expenses if the company has an investment business.

HMRC also consider contributions made to preserve the reputation and morale of staff as allowable deductions.

However, whilst allowable, pension contributions may have to be spread forward where they exceed certain limits. An initial comparison is done with the **contributions** made in the previous chargeable period and spreading may have to take place where the current year contributions are greater than 210% of the previous period. In this situation, HMRC considers the excess of the current year's payment over 110% of the previous year. Where this excess is less than £500,000, then there is no forward spreading of the contributions. Where the excess is between £500,000 and less than £1 million, half of the excess is spread into the following year. If the excess lies between £1 million and less than £2 million, then one-third of the excess is spread into each of the next two accounting periods. Where the excess is £2 million or more, then one-quarter of the excess is spread over the next three accounting periods.

If spreading of the payments is required, a deferred tax implication arises, as the timing of relief for the payment differs to the actual timing of the payment itself in the accounts.

Example 2.4

An employer makes the following pension contributions for the two years ended 31 December 2014:

	£
31 December 2013	200,000
31 December 2014	1,420,000

As the 2014 contribution is greater than 210% of that of 2013, HMRC will then calculate the potential amount, if any, to be spread forward.

The excess is found by comparing the current year (2014) contribution with 110% of that of the previous period, namely £220,000. The resultant excess is thus £1,200,000. Since this figure lies between £1 million and £2 million, one-third of the excess is spread as follows into each of the following two accounting periods.

	£
31 December 2014	620,000
31 December 2015	400,000
31 December 2016	400,000

(o) Keyman Insurance

Generally premiums paid under loss of profits insurance policies are tax deductible and any sums received from the insurance company are taxable as trading receipts.

Policies which provide indemnity for loss or damage to fixed or intangible assets, trading stock and trade debts are allowable if they are deemed to be wholly and exclusively for the purpose of the trade.

Keyman insurance is insurance taken out by a company in its own favour against the death or critical illness of key employees (the keyman) whose services are vital to the success of the employer's business. Such premiums are generally allowable and the proceeds of any such policies are taxable as trading receipts. However, one should be mindful that there is a potential argument that, if the key person is also the sole shareholder, HMRC may seek to argue that there is a dual purpose to the premiums, i.e. that they seek to protect the value of the shares of the company and that there is also a private benefit as well. This could result in the premiums not being allowable for tax but, potentially, if the policy did pay out, they may still seek to argue for taxing the payout.

Note: in cases where there is a personal benefit to the policy and the premiums are paid on behalf of a participator or an associate of a participator (see **Chapters 6** and **7**), the amounts are disallowed for corporation tax and will also result in either a benefit-in-kind if the participator is an employee or director or as a distribution (see **Chapter 7**).

2.3.3 Non-taxable Receipts

If the company is applying generally accepted accounting principles, the number of receipts that are not taxable should be considered – there should not be too many of such items.

2.3.4 Provisions made under IAS 37/FRS 102

Provisions made under IAS 37 *Provisions, Contingent Liabilities and Contingent Assets* and FRS 102 *The FRS applicable in the UK and the Republic of Ireland* are generally allowable for tax purposes, provided that the provision would be allowable under general rules if it were an expense, e.g. a provision in relation to a capital item would not be deductible.

2.3.5 Interest

Interest is deductible on an accruals basis if it is **trade-related**, i.e. it is treated the same as in the financial statements and, therefore, no adjustment is required. This is the case even if the money is borrowed to buy capital assets. However, these assets must be used in the trade and must not be used for investment purposes.

Other interest, which is not trade-related, must be disallowed in calculating trading income and may then be relievable as a non-trade debit as follows:

- If the interest is on monies borrowed for a property generating property income, the interest will be dealt with as a non-trading "debit" under the loan relationship rules.
- If the interest is on monies borrowed to lend to or invest in another company, it will either qualify for relief as a non-trade debit if certain conditions are satisfied or it will be deemed to be a debit arising from an "unallowable" purpose. An unallowable purpose is any non-business, non-commercial purpose or any purpose that consists of securing a tax advantage.

2.3.6 Payments to Directors and Other Employees

Bona fide directors' salaries, fees, and benefits payable for directors, etc. are deductible, unlike the drawings/salary of a self-employed person. Such income is, of course, assessable in the hands of the individual director as employment income. Where a director has a company car available for private use, there is no disallowance for the inevitable "personal element" for corporation tax purposes unlike the personal element of a self-employed person. Again, a director with the use of a company car for private purposes will, of course, suffer tax under the benefit in kind regime.

2.4 Capital Allowances

The computation of capital allowances is beyond the scope of this textbook. However, remember to deduct capital allowances from trading income to arrive at tax-adjusted trading profits.

2.5 Research and Development

2.5.1 Overview

Relief is available for capital Research and Development (R&D) via the capital allowances regime and for revenue R&D through the various tax reliefs available for expenditure on R&D.

Capital Expenditure
The definition of R&D for tax purposes follows its definition under UK GAAP SSAP 13 or IAS 38, as appropriate. For capital expenditure, relief may be claimed on providing facilities to carry out the research but land does not qualify and neither does any dwelling whose cost exceeds more than 25%

of the overall cost of the building. A 100% capital allowances deduction may be claimed on qualifying R&D capital expenditure during the accounting period. Whilst a reduced claim can be made, there is no facility to claim any disclaimed allowances in future periods. On disposal or destruction, a balancing charge may arise, being the difference between the disposal value and the balance of unclaimed expenditure and the R&D allowance claimed. As noted above, the computation of capital allowances is beyond the scope of this textbook. Relevant figures for capital allowances are provided in the examples and questions contained in this textbook.

Revenue Expenditure

The enhanced tax relief for revenue R&D can only be claimed on "relevant" R&D, i.e. R&D is related to the trade carried on by the company or from which it is intended that a trade be carried on. This also includes R&D activities which may lead to or facilitate an extension of the trade, and R&D of a medical nature which has a special relation to the welfare of workers employed in the trade.

2.5.2 Qualifying Company

The tax relief for qualifying expenditure on R&D may be claimed by all companies, and the enhanced deduction is included within the adjusted trading profits computation. It was previously the case that tax relief was only available if a company spent at least £10,000 a year on qualifying R&D costs in an accounting period. This R&D threshold was removed in Finance Act 2012 for expenditure incurred on or after 1 April 2012.

2.5.3 Qualifying R&D Expenditure

Whilst the definition of R&D follows that of SSAP 13 and IAS 38, HMRC recommends that the Department of Trade and Industry (DTI) guidance tests must be applied. In essence, a project will qualify as an R&D project if it is carried on in the field of science or technology and is undertaken to extend knowledge and to address scientific or technological uncertainties.

Qualifying revenue expenditure is similar (but not identical) under the SME and large companies regimes. However, under both regimes, the expenditure must meet the following conditions and, *inter alia*:

1. must not be capital in nature;
2. must be attributable to relevant R&D that is either directly undertaken by the company or on its behalf; and
3. must be incurred on staffing costs (to include salaries and wages (but not redundancy payments), employer's NIC, employer's pension fund contributions (but not non-cash benefits in kind), consumable or transformable materials, software, externally provided workers, utilities (such as power, water and fuel), subcontracted R&D expenditure and on payments to participants in clinical trials.

One difference between the SME and large company relief is the ability to claim the enhanced deduction on 65% of the qualifying subcontracted R&D but only where the company and the subcontractor are not connected (or where an election has not been made under section 1135 CTA 2009 to treat the company and the subcontractor as connected). For a large company the expenditure on R&D contracted to other persons is generally not allowable. However, it can be qualifying expenditure if it is revenue expenditure on relevant R&D and the company contracts for work to be directly undertaken by a qualifying body or an individual or a partnership (each member of which is an individual).

2.5.4   Tax Relief: Small and Medium-sized Companies

A small or medium-sized company (SME as defined in accordance with the EU guidelines) qualifies for an enhanced deduction from its trading profits of 225% of its qualifying R&D expenditure from 1 April 2012. The qualifying expenditure must be such that it would have been allowable as a deduction in computing the taxable profits of a trade carried on by the company. Unlike the normal situation, pre-trading expenditure in this scenario is treated as incurred when it is actually incurred **and not** deemed to be treated on the first day of trading.

The tax relief is claimed as an adjustment to the trading income computation. Where the deduction creates a deemed trading loss, the company can choose to surrender the loss for a cash payment of 14.5% of the loss for the chargeable period from 1 April 2014. The rate was previously 11% for qualifying expenditure incurred on or after 1 April 2012 until it was increased to 14.5% in Finance Act 2014. The restriction that the cash payment cannot exceed the total of the company's PAYE and NIC liabilities for the period has been removed for accounting periods ending on or after 1 April 2012.

2.5.5   Tax Relief: Large Companies

Finance Act 2013 introduced a further R&D tax relief for large companies called 'Above the Line' (ATL) credit. Its aim is to incentivise R&D activity amongst large companies and to increase the attractiveness of the UK to multinationals seeking a competitive jurisdiction from which to base their R&D activity. It is designed to give greater visibility of large company R&D activity and to provide greater cash flow support where a company is carrying losses.

The taxable credit is 10% of qualifying expenditure incurred on or after 1 April 2013. Any company with no corporation tax liability (i.e. loss-making) may be entitled to a payable credit.

The ATL credit scheme is initially optional and will become mandatory after 1 April 2016. Any large companies looking to avail of the new scheme will be required until 2016 to elect for its use. Otherwise the existing enhanced 30% deduction of qualifying expenditure will continue to apply by reducing chargeable profits (or increasing losses) but which does not permit a payable credit.

Example 2.5

Conan Limited is a large company with the following results for the year to 31 March 2015.

	£
Turnover	7,500,000
R&D expenditure	(750,000)
Other expenditure	(5,750,000)
Net profit	1,000,000

Demonstrate how the corporation tax charge is calculated under both options available to a large company assuming the R&D expenditure qualifies for tax relief

Solution
Using the enhanced deduction of 130%

	£
Profit before tax	1,000,000
R&D (£750,000 x 30%)	(225,000)
Taxable profits	775,000
Corporation tax @ 21%	162,750

continued overleaf

Using the "Above the Line" Credit

	£	£
Turnover		7,500,000
R&D activity	(750,000)	
ATL tax credit	<u>75,000</u>	(675,000)
Other expenditure		<u>(5,750,000)</u>
Net profit		1,075,000
Corporation tax @ 21%		<u>(225,750)</u>
Profit after tax		<u>849,250</u>
Corporation tax calculation		
Taxable profits		<u>1,075,000</u>
Corporation tax @ 21%		225,750
ATL tax credit		<u>(75,000)</u>
Net tax payable		<u>150,750</u>
In this instance, it would be preferable for the company to elect for the ATL scheme.		

A large company will qualify for an enhanced deduction from trading profits of 130% (from 1 April 2008) on its qualifying R&D expenditure. An SME may make a claim under the large companies rules if it fails to meet the specific criteria for that regime, but in so doing will be restricted to the limits for such companies.

2.6 Intangible Fixed Assets Regime

As noted at **Section 2.3.2(j)**, a special corporation tax regime has been in place since 1 April 2002 which applies to a company's expenditure in respect of intangible fixed assets (IFAs), which are the company's "intellectual property" and include such things as patents, copyrights, trademarks and goodwill.

Companies will generally obtain tax relief on expenditure on IFAs created or acquired after 1 April 2002 through their amortisation policy. The company can, if it chooses, instead apply a fixed rate allowance of 4% per annum, effectively writing the IFA off over 25 years.

In the new regime, the loss or gain on the disposal of an IFA asset created or acquired on or after 1 April 2002 will be eligible to be relieved/taxed accordingly. There is also a form of "rollover" relief available in the situation where an IFA is disposed of for more than the original cost and the disposal proceeds are re-invested in newly acquired IFAs. The amount by which the disposal proceeds exceed the original cost may be rolled over against the cost of the new IFA assets. In this situation, the company will be taxed as if the disposal proceeds of the old assets and the cost of the newly acquired IFAs were both reduced by this excess.

Patent royalties are also within the scope of the new regime and fall to be taxed on the "accruals" basis.

Under the regime, gains and losses relating to intangible assets used in a company's business are generally taxed as revenue items. Expenditure is a "debit", whereas income is a "credit". The actual tax treatment of these "debits and credits" depends on whether the assets are held for trading purposes, a property business or a non-trading company.

2.6.1 Trading Debits and Credits

Debits and credits in respect of assets held for the purposes of a trade are dealt with in the normal trading income computation as expenses and receipts of that particular trade. If they relate to a property business, then they are dealt with as property income.

2.6.2 Non-trading Debits and Credits

However, non-trading debits and credits are initially grouped together and netted off against each other. If there is a resultant net gain, then it is assessable under the catch-all Miscellaneous Income provisions.

If there is a net "loss", then the company has a choice about how they wish to relieve this loss, i.e. either to group relief the loss or to set it against the company's total profits of that accounting period. Any unutilised loss is carried forward to the next accounting period and treated as if it were a non-trading debit of that period.

Finally, gains or losses on the disposal of assets such as goodwill acquired **before** 1 April 2002 will continue to be dealt with under the CGT regime and be either chargeable gains or allowable capital losses. However, gains on such "old" assets may only be rolled over into the new IFA regime and follow the treatment outlined above.

Questions

Review Questions
(See Suggested Solutions to Review Questions at the end of this textbook.)

Question 2.1

Telestar Ltd, a company which commenced to trade many years ago, makes up its accounts each year to 31 March. It is a "small" company and has no subsidiaries.

The profit and loss account to 31 March 2015 is as follows:

	£
Gross profit	239,800
Grant for extension of premises	10,000
Employment grant	1,000
Patent royalty received from individual (net of 20%) (Note 1)	1,600
Discount received	3,300
Dividends from Bank of Ireland received on 10 May 2014 (UK company)	1,300
Profit on sale of van (Note 2)	1,000
Profit on sale of shares (Note 3)	3,000
Bank deposit interest (paid gross)	600
	261,600

		£	
Less:	Discount given	3,000	
	Goods stolen	3,000	
	Business overdraft interest	5,800	
	Depreciation	15,389	
	Van expense	3,400	
	Motor expenses	2,400	
	Bad debts	2,300	
	Obsolete stock – written off	2,600	
	Salaries and wages	100,000	
	Telephone	311	
	Entertainment (Note 4)	2,700	
	Depreciation on finance leases (Note 5)	1,300	
	Legal fees (Note 6)	2,400	144,600
	Profit before tax		117,000

Notes

1. The patent royalty was received in December 2014 and relates to the company's non-trading activities.
2. Profit on sale of van – the van was acquired second-hand on 03/02/2002 for £12,000. It was sold on 05/05/2014 for £4,000. The net book value of the van at 31/03/2014 was £3,000.
3. Profit on sale of shares – these shares in Video Plc were acquired on 31/03/2002 for £3,000 and sold on 30/04/2014 for £6,000. Indexation factor is 0.456. The shares represented 0.25% of Video Plc's share capital and the company owns no other shares in Video Plc.
4. The charge for entertainment is made up as follows:

	£
Prizes for top salespersons of the year	900
Christmas party for staff	750
Christmas gifts for suppliers (hampers)	150
Reimbursement of managing director for costs incurred entertaining customers at home	350
General customer entertainment	550
	2,700

5. Finance lease depreciation – this relates to a machine leased in 2005, the cost of which is capitalised in the company's accounts. The lease agreement states that the burden of wear and tear remains with the lessor.
6. The legal fees relate to the extension of the premises.
7. Capital allowances for the year are £7,272.

Requirement

Calculate the corporation tax liability for the year ended 31 March 2015 and show the dates on which the tax is payable.

Question 2.2

The profit and loss account of Zaco Ltd for the year ended 30 September 2014 is as follows:

	£		£
Salaries and wages	62,500	Gross profit	489,250
Rent and rates	5,400	Dividends (Note 6)	3,600
Repairs (Note 1)	16,100	Bad debts	300
Insurance	1,720	Profit on sale of fixed assets (Note 7)	15,200
Professional fees (Note 2)	1,600	Bank interest receivable	1,200
Depreciation	13,000	Property income	4,300
Audit fees	1,000		
Subscriptions (Note 3)	2,400		
Entertainment (Note 4)	600		
Staff award (Note 5)	1,000		
Discount allowed	320		
Bank interest	7,060		
Light and heat	21,250		
Profit	379,900		
	513,850		513,850

(Zaco Ltd has no subsidiaries.)

Notes
1. Repairs – includes improvements to offices of £5,200.
2. Professional fees – includes debt collection fees of £200, architects' fees re office improvements of £300.
3. Subscriptions – includes political donations of £750 and staff race sponsorship of £1,000.
4. Entertainment – this is made up as follows:

	£
Customer entertainment	450
Supplier entertainment	150
	600

5. Staff award – a special award of £1,000 was made to an employee who achieved first place in Ireland in his engineering examinations during the year.
6. Dividends – foreign dividends (net of 20% withholding tax) £3,600. Received on 31 August 2014 and meets one of the exemptions in Part 9A CTA 2009.
7. Profit on sale – indexation factor 0.035

Building	£
Cost June 2007	200,000
Proceeds July 2014	215,200
Profit on sale	15,200

8. The capital allowances (including balancing allowances and charges) are £9,846.
9. There are capital losses brought forward of £10,000.

Requirement

Calculate the company's corporation tax liability for the year.

Question 2.3

From the following information you are required to calculate the corporation tax liability of Alpha Ltd for the year ended 31 March 2015. Alpha Limited has two subsidiaries.

Profit and Loss Account

	£		£
Salaries and wages (Note 1)	71,300	Gross profit	600,000
Rent and rates (Note 2)	7,600	UK dividends (Note 14)	4,500
Repairs (Note 3)	18,500	Gain on sale of fixed assets (Note 15)	1,000
Insurance (Note 4)	1,350	Amortisation of grant (Note 16)	240
Loss on sale of investments (Note 5)	600	Interest on tax overpaid	475
Legal expenses (Note 6)	2,700	Royalties received (net of 20% tax)	2,500
Commissions	9,209	Rent received	6,000
Depreciation	13,260	Deposit interest (received gross)	1,500
Audit fees	1,550	Bad debts recovered	50
Subscriptions (Note 7)	3,400		
Discounts allowed	900		
Bank interest (Note 8)	3,300		
Other interest (Note 9)	7,000		
Light and heat	11,234		
Motor expenses (Note 10)	33,126		

continued overleaf

Sundry (Note 11)	3,740		
Entertainment			
Expenses (Note 12)	1,191		
Finance lease depreciation (Note 13)	1,700		
Net profit	424,605		
	616,265		616,265

Notes

1. Salaries and wages include £25,000 in respect of staff bonuses relating to the year ended 31 March 2015 which were paid in full by 31 March 2015.
2. Rent and rates include an amount of £1,000 received by the company which relates to part of the company's premises which has been let to a sub-tenant on a short-term basis.
3. Repairs include an amount of £15,000 for an extension to the factory premises.
4. Insurance includes an amount of £350 relating to the let premises.
5. Loss on sale of investments:

UK shares purchased 2003:	£
Cost	10,000
Proceeds (01/07/2014)	(9,400)
	600

6. Legal expenses:

	£
Debt collection	700
Extension to factory	2,000
	2,700

7. Subscriptions:

	£
Chamber of Commerce	450
Trade association	1,135
Political	1,815
	3,400

8. Bank interest – bank interest includes an amount of £1,500 relating to borrowings taken out to finance the extension to the factory premises.
9. Other interest is deemed to be trading loan relationship £7,000.
10. Motor expenses – the company leased six new motor cars on 1 April 2014. The retail price of each, at the time the lease contracts were entered into, was £26,000. All of the cars had CO_2 emissions greater than 130g/km.

The motor expenses can be analysed as follows:

	£
Leasing charges on leased cars	21,126
Running costs of leased cars	12,000
	33,126

11. Sundry:

	£
Interest on late payments of VAT	1,630
Parking fines	30
Christmas party	500
Gifts to customers (hampers)	541
General office expenses	1,039
	3,740

12 Entertainment includes an amount of £1,191 for hotel and accommodation for overseas customers

13. Finance lease depreciation relates to new machinery leased in 2005, the cost of which is capitalised in the company's accounts. The lease agreement states that the burden of wear and tear remains with the lessor.

14. UK dividends:

	£
Dividend on Bank of Ireland shares received 1 December 2014	1,800
Dividend from subsidiary received 1 April 2014	2,700
	4,500

15. Sale of fixed asset:

	£
Cost (July 2004)	4,000
Proceeds (January 2015)	5,000
Profit on sale	1,000

16. A grant of £1,200 was received on 2 April 2008 in respect of the factory extension. This is being amortised over a five-year period.

17. Capital allowances for the accounting period are £26,006.

18. The company has a trading loss of £20,000 carried forward from the year ended 31 March 2014.

19. There is a capital loss carried forward of £189 from year ended 31 March 2014.

Question 2.4

It is January 2016, and you are the newly appointed financial controller of a UK stand-alone company. When recruited, it was made clear to you that some of your duties would involve tax compliance in order to minimise the cost of taking professional advice. One of your first projects is to review the draft corporation tax computation for the year ended 31 March 2015 which was prepared by your predecessor.

The company, Comtech Limited, has its own Research and Development (R&D) department and, when reviewing the draft corporation tax computation, you noted that no claims for R&D tax relief have been made. You mention this in passing to the finance director who asks you to prepare a memo outlining the key aspects of the UK R&D tax relief scheme and the potential amounts that the company could claim tax relief on for the 2015 period only, including providing explanations of your calculations and the overall tax saving available.

Comtech's turnover for the year ended 31 March 2015 was £34.6 million (which equates to roughly €40 million) and it has 55 employees. Its balance sheet total was £48 million (roughly €55 million).

You have reviewed the draft computation and are satisfied that, aside from any potential claim for relief on R&D expenditure, no other adjustments to the draft taxable total profits figure of £3,428,925 is required. You also note that the company was in receipt of a non-group dividend totalling £75,000 during 2015.

The R&D team is tasked with developing new and innovative products for the company to bring to market so its work directly links to the trade of the company and, in its particular field, Comtech is considered a "blue skies" industry leader.

At a meeting with the head of the R&D department, it is established that the revenue costs of running the R&D department in 2015 were as follows:

	£
Gross wages	212,567
Redundancy payments	4,250
Employer's NIC	27,209
Pension scheme contributions	15,000
Company car benefit-in-kind	7,825
Consumable items	22,425
Power, water and fuel	8,762
Software	4,933
Rates	25,655
Professional fees*	12,250
	340,876

* During the period, the R&D department sub-contracted some of its work to a dedicated lab facility nearby at a cost of £12,250. The lab facility is not connected to the company.

Having reviewed all of the above costs you do not identify any tax disallowable items therein.

During the 2015 period a new R&D facility was built specifically for Comtech's R&D team. This included a building at a cost of £1.2 million (including land of £125,000) and several new pieces of high-tech plant and equipment costing £525,000. The overall cost of land and buildings in the company accounts is £10.2 million. In the draft computation, no capital allowances have yet been claimed on this expenditure.

Requirement

Prepare a memo to the finance director in which you:

(a) Outline the UK R&D regime including details of the amount of relief potentially available to companies and the conditions for claiming the relief.

(b) Assuming the activities of the R&D department qualify as R&D as defined by tax legislation, calculate the maximum amount of tax relief available to the company under the UK R&D regime. Outline for the finance director the tax saving to be achieved by making the R&D claim and any other relevant recommendations.

Income Tax on Annual Payments, Qualifying Charitable Donations and Loan Relationships

Learning Objectives

After studying this chapter you will have developed competency in the following:

Annual Payments
- A company can either make or receive an annual payment from which tax may or may not have been deducted.
- If a company makes an annual payment on which it has withheld income tax at the appropriate rate, it must pay it over to HMRC and complete the relevant form (CT61(Z)).
- If a company receives a payment from which an amount of income tax has been deducted, then the company is taxed on the gross amount. The tax withheld is relievable against either payments it has made from which it has withheld the income tax or, in the absence of such sufficient payments, the company's corporation tax payable for the accounting period.

Qualifying Charitable Donations
- A qualifying charitable donation (QCD) is deductible against total profits.
- These are deducted from the company's total profits for the period after any other relief from corporation tax other than group relief.
- The amount of the deduction is limited to the amount that reduces the company's taxable total profits for the period to nil.

Loan Relationships
- A loan relationship arises when a company lends or borrows money.
- Trading loan relationships are dealt with as trading income.
- A net credit on a non-trading loan relationship is taxable under the loan relationship provisions. A net debit (expense) on non-trading loan relationships creates a non-trading deficit.
- There are various means by which the company can relieve its non-trading deficit (loss).
- Certain costs of finance are tax deductible.

3.1 Annual Payments

3.1.1 Relevant Payments

A company must deduct income tax when making certain relevant payments. These payments include:

- Patent royalties where the recipient is not a UK company or payments to individuals.
- Annuities and annual payments where the recipient is not a UK company or payments to individuals.
- Debenture interest.
- Rents paid to non-residents in respect of property in the UK.

It should also be noted that a "close" company must self-assess tax liabilities in respect of any loans not in the ordinary course of business made to "participators" or associates, most commonly directors or shareholders and "relatives" thereof. This can result in the company having to make a tax payment to HMRC equivalent to 25% of the outstanding loan made during the accounting period. The tax will not fall due if the loan has been repaid, released or written off prior to the normal due date of payment of the mainstream corporation tax liability (namely nine months and one day after the end of the accounting period).

The following annual interest may be paid without deduction of tax:

- Interest paid to a bona fide bank or building society in the UK and other UK companies that carry on a trade of lending and satisfy certain conditions.
- Interest paid to a resident of a country with which the UK has a tax treaty that provides that withholding tax is to be reduced to nil, provided that clearance has been received from HMRC to make such gross payments.
- Annual payments made by a member of the group to another member of that group.
- Interest on loans for fixed periods of less than one year.

EU Interest and Royalties Directive

This Directive provides for the abolition of withholding tax on business interest and royalty payments made by a company in one Member State or Switzerland to its associated company resident in another Member State or Switzerland. It applies as long as the payment is made for the purposes of the trade carried on by the company through a permanent establishment in the State.

For the purposes of the Directive, the claimant and the payer must be 25% associates. A company will be regarded as an associated company of another company throughout an uninterrupted two-year period during which it controls not less than 25% of the voting power of the other company, or where a third company directly controls not less than 25% of the voting power in each company.

3.1.2 Payment of Tax Deducted from Annual Payments

Income tax at the standard rate of 20%, which has been deducted from relevant annual payments, must be paid over to HMRC.

As well as deducting basic rate tax from the relevant payments denoted above, building societies, banks and other deposit takers (including non-resident companies trading from a branch or agency in the UK and, in some cases, local authorities) are required to deduct income tax at the rate in force in the relevant year of assessment (currently 20%), from interest paid or credited to individual depositors. Those individuals who do not expect to have to pay tax can register to have their interest paid in full without deduction of income tax.

Any amounts so deducted must be paid over to HMRC using form CT61(Z). The form must potentially be completed a maximum of five times during an accounting period, namely on four defined quarter dates as well as the date coinciding with the end of the accounting period. Thus for a company with a year ended 31 March 2015, it could potentially have to complete CT61(Z) forms for the quarters ending 30 June 2014, 30 September 2014, 31 December 2014 and 31 March 2015. If the company has a year ended 31 January, then as well as the above four quarter dates, it would also potentially have to complete a form for the period ending 31 January for any relevant payments made in that month.

3.1.3   Credit for Tax Suffered on Annual Payments Received

Where, in an accounting period, a company receives a payment from which UK income tax has been deducted, the grossed-up amount is included within the company's corporation tax computation. For example, if patent royalties were paid net of tax, the grossed-up figure would be included within the trading income computation.

Where a company both makes and receives payments from which it respectively deducted income tax and had it deducted, then as well as completing the relevant CT61(Z) form for the period in which the various payments were made, the company must also consider the net income tax position at the end of the accounting period. If the tax suffered on income exceeds the tax deducted from amounts paid net, then this excess is reclaimed by subtracting it from the company's corporation tax liability.

3.2   Qualifying Charitable Donations

Qualifying charitable donations (QCDs) made by a company are allowed as deductions from the company's total profits in calculating the corporation tax chargeable for an accounting period under section 1300(5) CTA 2009. They are deducted from the company's total profits for the period after any other relief from corporation tax other than group relief.

The amount of the deduction is limited to the amount that reduces the company's taxable total profits for the period to nil. Any surplus is not available to carry forward and relief is effectively lost.

A payment made to a charity by a company is a qualifying payment if each of conditions A to F is met.

- Condition A is that the payment is a payment of a sum of money.
- Condition B is that the payment is not subject to a condition as to repayment.
- Condition C is that the company making the payment is not itself a charity.
- Condition D is that the payment is not disqualified by virtue of associated acquisition, etc. by the charity. Broadly, this means that the payment is conditional on an acquisition of property by the charity from the company or a person associated with the company or the payment is associated with such an acquisition, or is part of an arrangement involving such an acquisition. An acquisition by way of gift is ignored for the purposes of this condition.
- Condition E is that the payment is not disqualified as a distribution.
- Condition F is that the payment is not disqualified as a result of the payment being associated with a benefit.

There are two conditions for test F which, if either is met, mean that the restrictions on benefits associated with a payment to a charity are breached. The two conditions are:

1. a stepped scale, depending on the amount of each payment (Condition A) – the "benefit per payment" test; and
2. an overall monetary limit on benefits associated with the total of any payments to a single charity in the course of an accounting period – the "benefit per accounting period" test (Condition B). This is unrelated to the size of any particular payment.

Both these restrictions apply to any benefit "associated with" a payment.

3.3 Loan Relationships

3.3.1 General

A loan relationship arises when a company lends or borrows money, including issuing or investing in debentures or buying gilts. This can either be:

1. a creditor relationship (where the company lends or invests money); or
2. a debtor relationship (where the company borrows money or issues securities).

The following types of debt (not exhaustive) have always been included within loan relationships: bank loans and deposits, advances, mortgages, overdrafts, debentures and government stock.

A normal trade debt is however **not** a loan relationship, nor are, inter alia, finance leases, hire purchase agreements or loan guarantees. Prior to the introduction of IAS 39, the two accounting methods used were the authorised accruals approach (transactions allocated to the accounting period to which they accrued) and the mark-to-market basis (transactions allocated at their fair amount in each period – the amount that the company would expect to receive). These have now been aligned to the amortised cost basis and the fair value basis respectively.

However, from a corporation tax standpoint, it is imperative to distinguish whether a loan relationship is either trading or non-trading.

3.3.2 Treatment of Trading Loan Relationships

In making any distinction between a trade or non-trade loan relationships, it is assumed that the accounts have been prepared in accordance with the appropriate accounting standards and methods. This approach should mean that all credits and debits (both capital and revenue) have been properly brought into account in the corporation tax computation.

In essence, where a company either owes or is due monies for the purposes of its trade (other than those items mentioned above), then it is within the trading loan relationship rules. In this situation, any resultant credits and debits are included as trading receipts and expenses within the Trading Income computation. When one is dealing with the "lender company", it is very difficult for them to fall within the "trading loan relationship" regime unless the loans were entered into in the course of activities forming an integral part of its trade. The latter situation is only likely to be the case for companies in the financial sector.

3.3.3 Treatment of Non-trading Loan Relationships

If a loan relationship is not one to which the company is party for trade purposes, all credits and debits must be pooled together. For many companies, their only source of non-trading income will be bank interest receivable from investment of surplus funds. It should be noted that neither a UK nor an overseas property business is deemed to be "trading" for loan relationship rules. Non-trading loan relationship debits and credits are combined to result in a net deficit or surplus.

3.3.4 Relief for Non-trading Deficits

However, the company has a choice about how it uses the net deficit (loss) on non-trading loan relationships. Relief can be given when:

1. set-off against profits of the company of the same accounting period;
2. carried back and set against surpluses (if any) on non-trading loan relationships for the previous 12 months;
3. surrendered as group relief; or
4. any residual deficit not used in the above can be carried forward and set against non- trading profits in succeeding accounting periods.

The company must make a claim to utilise the deficit (loss). In the case of points 1, 2 and 4 above, the time limit is that the claim must be made within two years of the end of the accounting period, while for 3, the claim must be made at any time up to the first anniversary of the filing date for the corporation tax return.

Two important points to bear in mind are:

1. unlike for normal trading losses (see later), a company can make partial current year claims (possibly so as to preserve foreign tax that may have been suffered), i.e. the in-year set-off does not have to be automatically applied.
2. the carried forward deficit can be set against the company's non-trading profits for the following years (to include property income, net credits from non-trading loan relationships and chargeable gains) and not just surpluses on non-trading loan relationships. Once again, the company can disclaim sufficient of the carried forward deficit to preserve income that may have suffered a foreign tax credit.

3.3.5 Costs of Finance

Many costs associated with obtaining loan finance are deemed to be allowable debits in the case of both trading and non-trading loan relationships. Examples of such costs include arrangement fees with banks, legal fees on the transfer of a security and pursuing bad debts, and brokers' fees related to transactions in existing securities.

It is also worthwhile noting that the cost of abortive expenditure incurred in trying to bring a loan relationship into existence is also potentially allowable, provided the expense would have been allowable if the loan had been raised.

However, costs that are deemed not to be directly incurred in either bringing a loan relationship into existence (even if it transpires to be an abortive attempt), giving effect to or making payments under a loan relationship or related transaction, or pursuing payments due under a loan relationship, **are not deductible**.

As the accounting treatment for certain costs of finance may dictate that the interest is capitalised, perhaps incorporated within fixed assets, relief is obtained by adjusting the corporation tax computation for such items not charged through the P&L account. Care must be taken not to double count such relief when the underlying asset is eventually sold and/or during its life written off (through amortisation). Note that this treatment does **not** apply to interest charged to work in progress, as it will have already been included within the movement in this asset, year on year.

Questions

Review Questions
(See Suggested Solutions to Review Questions at the end of this textbook.)

Question 3.1

Spider Ltd has the following income/payments during the year to 31 March 2015:

	£
Accounting profits (after charging depreciation of £5,000)	96,000
Property income	17,000
Payment to British Red Cross	8,000

Requirement
Calculate the company's taxable total profits for the year ended 31 March 2015.

Question 3.2

During the year ended 31 December 2014, Venus Ltd had the following loan relationship transactions:

- Interest received from a bank deposit account: £15,000.
- A bank loan of £75,000, which at the bank's instigation of an early repayment agreement, was fully settled for £55,000 by 31 December 2014.
- Legal fees of £1,500 were incurred in connection with the above bank loan settlement.

Requirement
Calculate Venus Ltd's net non-trading loan relationship credit/deficit for the year ended 31 December 2014.

Question 3.3

Special rules apply to a company's 'loan relationships' for corporation tax purposes.

(a) Explain the term 'loan relationship'.
(b) Give examples of loan relationships.
(c) Briefly explain how the amount to be included in the corporation tax computation is calculated.

Question 3.4

During the year ended 31 March 2015, a manufacturing company had the following transactions in interest receivable and payable:

	£
Interest receivable:	
Customers charged interest for paying late	724
Bank deposit interest	6,233
Bond held with local council	775

Interest payable:

Bank overdraft	4,210
Mortgage on rental property	3,178
Bank loan for purchase of trading equipment	7,500
Bank loan to acquire shares in unconnected companies	555

Requirement

Calculate the amount of interest that should be included under non-trading loan relationships in the company's corporation tax computation for the 31 March 2015 accounting period end.

Corporation Tax Loss Relief

Learning Objectives

After studying this chapter you will have developed competency in the following:

- The utilisation of losses depends on the type of loss and when it was incurred.
- A single company trading loss must **first** be set-off against the total profits of the same accounting period.
- Any surplus **may** then be carried back to be offset against the total profits of the previous 12-month chargeable period (provided the trade was being carried on in that chargeable period). Finance Act 2009 temporarily extended the carry-back period to 36 months, subject to a cap of £50,000; this rule only applies to losses incurred in an accounting period ending between 23 November 2008 and 24 November 2010.
- Loss relief must first be used in the current accounting period **before** either carry-back or carry-forward and it is not possible to make partial claims. The current year loss must be used in full and it is only the balance which is available for carrying back or forward depending on the most tax-efficient utilisation of the unused losses.
- Unused losses not relieved in the current period and not carried back are then available to carry forward against the future profits of the same trade.
- The carried forward loss must be used against the first available future profits of the same trade on a sequential basis and, as above, there is no facility for making partial relief claims. It is important to note that this relief is only available where the **same** trade is being carried on in the future.
- Loss relief is "ring-fenced" in that there is a restriction on the losses incurred of previously non-resident companies and/or on former UK companies when they become non-resident.
- Capital losses may only be offset against capital gains.
- Qualifying charitable donations are deducted from total profits of the current accounting period in order to reduce this to nil. If they exceed total profits, the excess cannot be used to create a loss and they are effectively "lost".
- Losses arising from pre-trading expenses **can** be set-off against other profits of the company, and can be group relieved. These losses can also be carried forward against future income of the same trade.
- Unused trading losses of the final 12 months – referred to as terminal losses – may be carried back against trading income of the three preceding years, with the later years being considered first.
- Where there is a change of ownership of the company, the trading losses will not be available for carrying forward if there is a significant change in the nature or conduct of the trade.

4.1 Relief for Trading Losses in a Single Company

Trading losses are computed in the same way as trading income and the company must prepare its corporation tax computation in the normal way and forward its completed form CT600 (recording chargeable profits as NIL), statutory accounts and associated computational schedule to HMRC, similar to what is required if the company had made a trading profit.

A company which incurs a trading loss in an accounting period may obtain relief for the loss in several ways:

1. First by set-off against total profits in the same accounting period under section 37(3)(a) CTA 2010 (formerly section 393A(1) ICTA 1988);
2. By set-off against total profits in the immediately preceding accounting period of the previous 12 months (section 37(3)(b) CTA 2010 – formerly section 393A(1)(b) ICTA 1988).
3. By carry forward under section 45 CTA 2010 (formerly section 393(1) ICTA 1988) against future trading profits arising from the same trade.

CTA 2010 has effect for accounting periods ending on or after 1 April 2010 and requires a formal claim to be made for both (1) and (2). However, one should note that trading losses must first be used in the current period before carry-back or forward. By law, such claims must be made within two years of the end of the accounting period in which the loss occurs.

4.1.1 Carry Forward of Trading Losses

Trading losses of an accounting period can be carried forward, under section 45 CTA 2010, for set-off against future trading profits of the same trade. Whilst no formal claim is required to carry forward any trading loss (as this relief is given automatically), the company, when completing a corporation tax return, must state the amount of the loss to be carried forward.

In order to obtain loss relief in this fashion, the loss must have occurred when the company was within the charge to corporation tax. Thus, while a former non-resident company may well become UK resident **and** continue with the same trade as before, any loss incurred prior to coming within the charge to corporation tax will not be available for relief.

Thus, the crucial aspects with carry forward trading losses are that:

1. the losses must have been incurred when the company was within the charge to corporation tax;
2. they can only be set against future trading profits; and
3. the set-off can only be against profits of the same trade.

Provided the various conditions are satisfied, the carry forward loss is set against the first available profits. If there are not sufficient profits to use up the total losses, the excess is further carried forward to be set against the next available trading profits. There is no scope to have partial claims in respect of the carry forward losses and they must be used sequentially year on year until depleted.

This could create an issue where the company ceases to trade. This means there will then be no future profits against which to set the carried forward losses. Any balance of carried forward losses would thus be wasted.

There is, however, a special type of relief where trading losses are incurred in the last 12 months of trading. Losses in this period are known as "terminal losses", and there is a specific relief available to enable such losses to potentially be relieved.

Example 4.1

ABC Ltd, a UK company with no subsidiaries, has the following results for the year ended 31 March 2015.

	£
Trading income (as adjusted for tax purposes)	55,000
Net credit from loan relationships	2,000
Property Income	3,200
Chargeable gains	25,000
Qualifying charitable donations	(3,000)
Trading losses (of same trade) brought forward under section 45 CTA 2010	(70,000)

Solution

Corporation tax computation for ABC Ltd for the year ended 31 March 2015

	£	£
Trading income	55,000	
Less: trading losses c/fwd	(55,000)	
		0
Net credit from loan relationships		2,000
Property Income		3,200
Chargeable gains		25,000
Total profits		30,200
Qualifying charitable donations		(3,000)
Taxable Total Profits (TTP)		27,200
Corporation tax payable:		
£27,200 @ 20%		5,440
Due on or before 1 January 2016		

Loss Memo

Trading losses brought forward	70,000
Utilised (y/e 31/03/2015)	(55,000)
Carried forward (to set against future trading profits of the same trade)	15,000

If the trading profits of ABC Limited had been greater than £70,000 for the year ended 31 March 2015, all of the losses brought forward would have been utilised.

If ABC Ltd had made no trading profit (i.e. it either broke even or made a loss), then the brought forward trading losses would have been carried forward to the year ended 31 March 2016 to be set against any potential trading profits of that year, provided the same trade was being carried on. This process would be continued until either all of the losses had been utilised or the company ceased trading.

4.1.2 Relief by Set-off against Total Profits of the Same Accounting Period

Before carrying forward the trading loss of an accounting period, the company must set a current period trading loss against the total profits of the same accounting period, under section 37(3)(a) CTA 2010.

Example 4.2

Jones Limited has the following income for the year ended 31 December 2014. Jones Limited does not have any subsidiaries.

	£
Trading income losses	(10,500)
Net credit from loan relationships	5,000
Property income	4,300
Chargeable gains	7,200
Qualifying charitable donations	(2,500)

Solution

	£
Net credit from loan relationships	5,000
Property income	4,300
Chargeable gains	7,200
Profits	16,500
Trading loss of same accounting period (under section 37(3)(a))	(10,500)
	6,000
Deduct qualifying charitable donations	(2,500)
Taxable total profits (TTP)	3,500

	£
Corporation tax payable	
TTP £3,500 @ 20%	700

Corporation tax due on or before 1 October 2015.

4.1.3 Relief by Set-off against Total Profits of the same Accounting Period followed by Carry-back against Total Profits of the Previous 12 Months

Where a company has incurred a trading loss which exceeds the total profits of the same accounting period, and it has made a claim (mandatory) against these total profits under section 37(3)(a) CTA 2010, the company can then elect to carry the "excess" back to set against the total chargeable profits of the previous 12 months, under section 37(3)(b) CTA 2010. To obtain this relief, the company must have carried on the same trade in the previous 12 months. The relief for the trading loss must be taken in this strict order (i.e. against profits of the same accounting period first). Any excess losses after in-year offset can be either carried back or forward (as previously described).

There is no facility to make a partial claim of the trade losses incurred.

It must be stressed again that the carry-back facility is **only available** after the total profits of the same accounting period have been depleted and there is no scope to make a claim to relieve only part of the loss.

Either of the above claims must be made within two years of the end of the accounting period in which the loss was incurred.

Example 4.3

Apple Ltd, a single company, has the following results for the accounting periods ended 31 March 2013 through to 31 March 2015. It has carried on the same trade throughout and there has been no change of ownership.

Year ended	31 March 2013	31 March 2014	31 March 2015
	£	£	£
Trading income	10,000	(16,500)	7,600
Property income	4,000	2,700	3,850
Chargeable gains	6,750	8,300	–

Show the various options that are open to Apple Ltd to utilise its trading losses of £16,500 for the accounting period ended 31 March 2014.

Solution

(a) It must first utilise as much of the loss as possible (£11,000) against the company's total profits of the same period and then either carry the balance (£5,500) back to the previous 12-month period to set against the total profits of that period (namely the £20,750 in the year ended 31 March 2013).

Or

(b) It could elect to carry forward the remaining £5,500 to set against the future profits of the same trade (i.e. the £7,600 in the year ended 31 March 2015) by not choosing to carry-back.

The company's method of choice will depend on the specifics of the original assessable profits. In commercial terms, the company may more than likely adopt the carry-back option (because the results of the future period may not be known for some considerable time). However, from a student perspective, one must be aware of all potential options available to the company.

Finally, the carry-back of trading losses to the previous 12-month period in some circumstances could substantially reduce the company's corporation tax liability for that period, and possibly even wipe it out completely. In this situation, the company may decide not to make any payment for that year. However, the company will still be charged **interest** on the unpaid liability from its normal due date (usually nine months and one day from the end of the accounting period) until the due date of the loss period.

Example 4.4

Zanny Limited had an accounting year end of 30 September. Its corporation tax profits for the year ended 30 September 2014 were £125,000, and it had a corporation tax liability of £25,623. In the first four months of 2015, the company suffered a major downturn in trading activity and it had projected trading losses for the following year to 30 September 2015 of £180,000. The company had no other income and decided that it would thus not need to make the payment of £25,623 on 1 July 2015. In due course, the company carried back its 2015 trading losses and wiped out the 2014 profits of £125,000. However, HMRC will still charge interest on the corporation tax liability from 1 July 2015 to 1 July 2016 – the effective date of the loss carry-back.

4.1.4   Temporary Extension of Carry-back Period

Legislation was introduced in Finance Act 2009 to provide a temporary extension to the trading loss relief rules. Where a trading loss arose in respect of an accounting period ended after 23 November 2008 but before 24 November 2010, the operation of section 393A ICTA 1988 and section 37(3)(b)

CTA 2010 are amended to enable the company to set the loss against its profits of the same period and **then** its profits for the **preceding three years**.

The loss must be **carried back in order** so that it is set against the profits of the most recent year first. The existing rules relating to the carry-back of a loss to the preceding year also apply to the carry-back of a loss to the second and third years with one exception; whereas the amount of the loss that can be carried back one year is not subject to a cap, the amount of the loss which can be carried back to the second and third years is restricted to:

- £50,000 for losses incurred in accounting periods ending after 23 November 2008 and before 24 November 2009; and
- £50,000 for losses incurred in accounting periods ending after 23 November 2009 and before 24 November 2010.

This means that, if a company has two loss-making accounting periods ending within the period between 23 November 2008 and 24 November 2009, or 23 November 2009 and 24 November 2010, the total extended loss relief is limited to £50,000. If a company has a relevant accounting period which is less than 12 months long, the limit is reduced by dividing the number of days in the relevant accounting period by 365.

Example 4.5

Eclipse Limited makes a loss of £60,000 in its accounting period from 1 January to 31 October 2010. What is the maximum amount of the loss which can be carried back to its accounting periods ended 31 December 2009 and 31 December 2008?

Limit on extended loss carry-back = £50,000 × 304/365 = £41,644.

4.2   Relief for Qualifying Charitable Donations

Qualifying charitable donations (QCDs) are allowed as deductions from a company's total profits and are deducted **after** any other relief from corporation tax other than group relief. Any excess cannot be relieved by carry-back or forward but may be available for group relief, subject to the group relief rules for these amounts in CTA 2010. This is dealt with in more detail in **Chapter 9**.

Reliefs, such as trading losses carried back, are given prior to any deduction of QCDs, and this may result in the company's QCDs being wasted as it is not possible to choose how much of a loss is to be carried back and partial claims are not possible.

For accounting periods ending before 1 April 2010, donations and gifts to charities not related to a company's trading activities were known as non-trade charges.

4.3   Pre-trading Expenditure

If a company incurs expenditure within seven years of commencing to trade and the debit would otherwise have been allowable if incurred in a period since trading commenced, then the company may treat the debit as a trading expense of that later year. Note that any interest that a company incurs before trading commences would ordinarily be deemed to be a non-trading deficit. However, such deficits can only be utilised by carry-forward for set-off against future non-trading income. HMRC allows a company to elect, within two years of the end of the accounting period in which the non-trade debit arose, that such interest is not to be treated as a non-trading deficit but rather as a trading expense once trade commences; this is also subject to a seven-year time limit.

If these expenses exceed the company's trading income, resulting in a loss, this loss **can** be set-off against other profits of the company, and it can be group-relieved. It can also be carried forward against future income of the same trade.

4.4 Relief for Loss on Cessation (Terminal Losses)

It is possible that a company may have to cease trading as a result of a downturn in its trading activities. Thus, a company may have had a few years of trading losses, and it will obviously not have any future profits from the same trade against which to set any such losses. It is also unlikely that a company will cease trading exactly on its former accounting year end.

The losses available for relief on cessation are known as "terminal loss relief".

A terminal loss is the loss relevant to the last 12 months of trading. Where the date of cessation coincides with the company's year end, the terminal loss will be the whole of that period's loss. Where the cessation date is not co-terminous with the company's accounting date, the 12-month period will be the last period (if less than 12 months) plus the relevant proportion of the preceding accounting period. Thus, if a company which has always had 30 September as its accounting year end ceased on 31 March 2015, then the terminal loss would comprise the loss of the six months to 31 March 2015, plus 6/12 of the loss (if any) of the accounting year ended 30 September 2014.

Instead of the normal carry-back period of 12 months, terminal losses can be carried back for 36 months, provided the same trade was being carried on during that time.

4.5 Restriction of Trading Losses

Losses forward and back are potentially valuable. If a company makes profits from the trade, it will not pay corporation tax on those profits until all losses forward are utilised. Equally, another company may find it attractive to buy a company, ensure that the company's trade is profitable when the new shareholder is running it (e.g. by transferring in some business) and thereby have losses to offset against trading profits and thus reduce tax.

There are anti-avoidance rules that limit the ability to do this type of planning. There are provisions to disallow the carry forward of trading losses incurred before **a substantial change of ownership of a company's shares**. The disallowance will apply if there is a change in the ownership of a company and either:

1. there is a major change in the nature or conduct of a trade carried on by the company within any period of three years in which the change of ownership occurs; or
2. at **any** time after the change in ownership, the scale of the activities in a trade carried on by the company has become small or negligible (and before any significant revival of the trade).

(Sections 673–675 CTA 2010, previously sections 768 and 768A ICTA 1988, apply.)
The provisions were introduced with the intention of attacking the practice of purchasing shares in a company to obtain the benefit of accumulated losses.

In applying the provisions to the accounting period in which the change of ownership occurs, the part of the period occurring before the change of ownership and the part occurring after the change are treated as separate accounting periods. Apportionments are to be made on a time basis except where, to HMRC, it appears that that method would work unreasonably or unjustly.

A "major change in the nature or conduct of the trade" includes:

(a) a major change in the type of property dealt in, or services or facilities provided in, the trade; or

(b) a major change in customers, outlets or markets of the trade.

Such a change will be regarded as occurring even if the change is the result of a gradual process which began outside the three-year period.

There have been a number of cases which dealt with the meaning of a "major change in the conduct of the trade" which provide some guidance on how these rules are to be interpreted and applied in practice.

Cases where it was held that there had been **no major change** in the nature or conduct of the trade, include:

1. A company, which had sold its products directly to customers, mainly wholesalers, then commenced to do the same through distribution companies.
2. A company ceased to slaughter pigs and manufacture meat products and, for a temporary period of 16 months, distributed the same products manufactured by its parent company. After the 16-month period, it recommenced slaughtering and manufacturing meat products.
3. A company operating a dealership in one make of vehicle switched to operating a dealership in another make which served the same market.

Cases where it was held that there had been a **major change** in the nature or conduct of the trade, include:

1. A company which carried on a business of minting coins and medallions from precious metals purchased its principal supplier's entire stock of gold and then purchased gold directly from wholesalers. This resulted in substantial increases in stock levels.
2. A company, which operated a retail chain of shops, changed its promotional policy by discontinuing the issue of trading stamps and reducing prices. The change resulted in a substantial increase in turnover.
3. A company changed from providing a service to being instead a primary producer.

There are rules for determining whether there has been a change in ownership and generally these are such as to ensure that, if there is a new person or persons controlling the company, then there is a change of ownership. These rules also apply, since 2005, to excess non-trade debits.

4.6 Property Losses

The income from letting of UK land and property is taxed on companies as property income.

If the company has property losses, the utilisation of such losses is not ring-fenced. Property losses are first set against the company's total profits for the same accounting period. Any excess is then carried forward and deemed to be a property loss of the next accounting period and is thus available for set-off against the total profits (of all descriptions). However, the property trade must still be carried on in the next accounting period. This process is continued until either:

▪ the property loss is used up; or
▪ the property business ceases.

Losses from a property business are very flexible. However, they **cannot** be carried back.

If a loss still remains after the cessation of the property business, the residue is deemed to be management expenses and carried forward for future relief as excess management expenses but only if the investment business continues.

As with trading losses, there is a restriction on the availability of carry-forward property losses where the change of ownership conditions apply (as set out in **Section 4.5**).

From April 2011, loss relief may only be set-off against income from the same furnished holiday letting (FHL) business. UK losses can relieve UK FHL income only and similarly with the EEA losses. Group relief of FHL losses is never available.

4.7 Capital Losses

As stated above, a company is charged to corporation tax on its chargeable gains. The quantum of chargeable gains is reduced by any capital losses of the same period as well as any unrelieved capital losses brought forward. Capital losses can only be set against chargeable gains of the current period or carried forward to set against future chargeable gains. It is not possible to carry-back capital losses or to set such losses against other income, except in certain circumstances. For example, an investment company may claim relief against income for capital losses arising on the disposal of subscribed for shares in unquoted qualifying trading companies. The above income is prior to deduction of management expenses and charges. The capital losses are relieved against income of the same accounting period and any excess can be set against income of the previous 12 months. This relief is known as "share loss relief against income", the conditions for which are set out in detail in Part 4, Chapter 5 CTA 2010.

Capital losses, unlike trading losses, excess property losses, non-trading deficits and excess charges on income, **cannot** be group-relieved. However, a group can achieve a similar result by netting off its gains and losses by utilising the election in section 171A TCGA 1992 dealt with in **Chapter 10**.

Where a share disposal by an investing company meets the conditions for Substantial Shareholdings Exemption, where one trading company (or holding company of a trading group) holds at least 10% of the share capital of another such company and is also entitled to at least 10% of the profits and assets available for distribution **and** has so held the shares for at least 12 months), the disposal of such shares is deemed **not to be a chargeable gain**. Thus, in the circumstances where a capital loss would otherwise arise, no capital loss is created for the investing company.

4.8 Summary: Choice of Loss Relief and Non-trading Losses

4.8.1 Loss Relief

If a company incurs a trading loss, it will have a variety of choices as to how best to relieve this loss. Given that it must first use the losses against other income and gains of the same period, the company could carry the loss forward to set against future trading profits of the same trade or perhaps the total profits of the previous 12 months.

The choice of which loss relief to avail of will depend on a variety of factors including, *inter alia*:

1. the likelihood that the company will have future profits in the same trade and the quantum thereof;
2. the rates of corporation tax;
3. the possibility that QCDs may be unrelieved;
4. the company's cash flow position; and
5. the company's overriding desire to maximise the tax saved as a result of the loss claim.

4.8.2 Non-trading Losses

A company can incur non-trading losses in any of the following situations:

1. Losses from miscellaneous income
Such losses are first relieved against other miscellaneous income of the same accounting period, and then against the miscellaneous income of future periods; hence, their use is quite restrictive.

2. Non-trading losses on intangible fixed assets
A company which incurs a non-trading loss on intangible fixed assets in an accounting period may claim all or part of the loss against the company's total profits for that period, or it might group-relieve (see later) the loss. Any part that is not so utilised is carried forward and treated as non-trading expenditure of the next accounting period.

3. Net debits on non-trading loan relationships
If a company incurs a deficit on its non-trading loan relationships, then it can be relieved by:

(a) set-off against the total profits of the company in the current period (after deducting any trading losses forward but before deducting current year trading losses and QCDs);
(b) surrendered by way of group relief (see **Chapter 9**); or
(c) set-off against the company's non-trading loan relationship income of the previous 12 months.

4. Losses from property income
Property losses may be set against the company's total profits for the accounting period in which the loss occurs. Any unused relief is then available to be carried forward and set against the company's total profits in future periods (provided the property business has not ceased), or it may be group-relieved (again see **Chapter 9**).

5. Capital losses
A company's capital losses are first set against its chargeable gains of the same accounting period and any unused amount is carried forward to set against the chargeable gains of subsequent accounting periods. Capital losses **cannot** be either group-relieved **or** set against any other form of income.

Unlike for individuals, companies are not entitled to an annual exemption and thus there is no need to restrict capital losses brought forward. Nor is there the facility to carry back capital losses.

Finally, be aware of the potential anti-avoidance restriction in relation to carry-forward/carry-back of certain losses where there is a change in ownership of a company – see **Section 4.5**.

Questions

Review Questions
(See Suggested Solutions to Review Questions at the end of this textbook.)

Question 4.1

Using the figures given below for Enya Ltd, show how the property (property income) and trade losses may be used. Ignore the extended 36-month loss carry-back rules introduced by Finance Act 2009.

		Rents	Trading profits/(losses)	Income from loan relationships
		£	£	£
y/e	31/03/2012	50,000	600,000	100,000
y/e	31/03/2013	(40,000)	700,000	50,000
y/e	31/03/2014	60,000	(1,300,000)	100,000
y/e	31/03/2015	80,000	100,000	35,000

Requirement
Calculate the taxable profits for each year, showing the loss relief claimed and a loss memorandum showing the loss carried forward at 1 April 2015.

Question 4.2

Hells Bells Ltd shows the following results:

	Year ended 31 March 2014	Nine months ended 31 December 2014
	£	£
Trading profit/(loss)	167,000	(190,000)
Rents	4,000	(4,000)
Chargeable gains/(losses)	(19,000)	10,000
Net credit from loan relationships	10,000	20,000

Requirement
Calculate the corporation tax payable for each accounting period claiming the earliest possible relief for losses.

Question 4.3

Monk Ltd, a manufacturing company, prepares annual accounts to 31 March each year. Recent results were as follows:

| | Year Ended 31 March | |
| | 2014 | 2015 |
	£	£
Adjusted trading profit/(loss) (Note 1):		
(before capital allowances)	360,000	(310,000)
Capital allowances	20,000	90,000
Bank deposit interest	5,000	30,000
Property income	15,000	20,000
Capital gains as adjusted for CT	12,000	126,000

The following additional information is available:

1. Monk Ltd has an agreed unutilised trading loss forward from the year ended 31/03/2013 of £20,000.
2. The company wishes to claim the loss reliefs available so as to maximise the benefit of the losses.

Requirement

Compute the corporation tax payable for each of the above years and indicate the amount (if any) of unutilised losses available for carry forward to year ending 31 March 2016.

Distributions and Dividend Withholding Tax

5.1 Distributions

5.1.1 Distributions Paid by UK Companies

For corporation tax purposes, no deduction is allowed in computing income from any source in respect of dividends or other distributions. When doing a computation for a trading company, one always starts with "profit (or loss) before taxation" and, therefore, there is no need to adjust for dividends as they will generally not have been deducted at that stage. Regarding other distributions, such as certain interest paid to directors by close companies, the interest will have been expensed in the P&L and, therefore, it will have to be added back. This generally applies where, for example, the interest has been paid in excess of a normal commercial rate.

One also needs to watch out for dividends paid on preference shares. For accounting purposes, these are treated as "share interest" and will already have been deducted from the profit or loss before tax so must always be added back.

5.1.2 Distributions Received by UK Companies

For corporation tax purposes, the distribution rules apply whenever cash or assets are passed to the company's members. However, where the payment relates to a member's services to a company, it may fall to be chargeable as employment income.

Distributions can take a variety of forms and include:

1. Dividends paid by a company, including a capital dividend (but not stock dividends or dividends paid by building societies).
2. Redemption of bonus securities or redeemable shares.
3. Any distribution out of assets in respect of shares, except any part of which represents a repayment of capital.

4. Sale of assets by a company at undervalue or purchase of assets by a company at overvalue from a shareholder.
5. A bonus issue subsequent to a repayment of share capital (other than fully paid preference shares).
6. Interest payments in excess of a normal commercial rate of return may be treated as a dividend.
7. Certain expenses incurred by a close company in the provision of benefits for a non-working participator or a non-working associate of a participator will be treated as a distribution. If the participator is also a director or an employee, the expenses will be treated as remuneration and will be assessed under the benefit in kind rules.

The rules on the taxation of dividends and other distributions **received** by UK companies were amended by Finance Act 2009 with effect from 1 July 2009.

5.1.3   Distributions Received by UK Companies – on or After 1 July 2009

From 1 July 2009, the **basic principle** is that all dividends and other income distributions received by UK companies are **taxable**, regardless of the residence of the payer of the dividend.

However, due to a wide range of exemptions, **in practice**, both UK and non-UK dividends received on or after 1 July 2009 are **exempt** from corporation tax.

Note that these changes mean that **all** dividends received from non-group companies (whether resident in the UK or not) are now franked investment income (FII) and must be taken into account when calculating the **rate** of corporation tax payable by the company.

5.2   Winding up Distributions

Distributions in a winding up situation are not income distributions, but rather are dealt with under the CGT regime.

Since 6 April 1999, there is no liability to corporation tax if a company makes a distribution payment.

5.3   Exempt Distributions

Some transactions, mainly dealing with situations where a company is being reorganised or wound-up, are exempted from the overall distribution rules. These would include:

1. Company purchase of its own shares – however, if conditions for CGT treatment are not met, this will be treated as an income distribution.
2. Distributions on a winding up situation of less then £25,000 after 1 March 2012.
3. Demergers.

There are clearance procedures in place and the company can apply to avail of this treatment.

Questions

Review Questions

(See Suggested Solutions to Review Questions at the end of this textbook.)

Question 5.1

Ice Sculptors Ltd received £475,000 of dividend income from Ice Sculptors Ireland Ltd, a non-UK tax resident company, net of overseas withholding tax of 10%. The dividend was received in September 2014, as part of its 31 December 2014 accounting period end.

Ice Sculptors Ltd is able to secure control by virtue of powers conferred by the articles of association so that the affairs of Ice Sculptors Ireland Ltd are conducted in accordance with its wishes.

Requirement

Advise your client whether the receipt of the above dividend is subject to UK corporation tax during the accounting period ended 31 December 2014. Assume Ice Sculptors Ltd is a large company for these purposes.

Question 5.2

Outline in detail the UK dividend exemption rules that apply from 1 July 2009.

Question 5.3

Distributions paid by a company can take many forms. Name the types of company transactions that are regarded as distributions.

Close Companies

6.1 Meaning of Close Company

A close company is one which is under the control of:

- five or fewer participators; or
- any number of participators who are also directors.

A company will not be a close company if it is non-UK resident. Control is the ability to exercise, or entitlement to acquire, direct or indirect control over the company's affairs, including the ownership of over 50% of the company's share capital, voting rights, distributable income or assets in the event of the winding up of the company.

Many UK private companies are close companies, whereas publicly quoted companies tend not to be close companies. As many private companies are close companies, the specific tax provisions that relate to close companies must be considered.

6.2 Definitions

These definitions are based on those in Part 10 CTA 2010, which are broadly similar to the previous legislation applicable for accounting periods ending on or before 31 March 2010 in Part XI ICTA 1988.

6.2.1 Participator

A participator is any person having a share or interest in the capital or income of the company and also includes:

1. a person who possesses or who is entitled to acquire share capital or voting rights in the company;

2. a "loan creditor" of the company (this is a creditor to the company because of money lent to the company or a capital asset sold to the company. A normal bank would not, however, be regarded as a loan creditor);
3. any person who has a right, or is entitled to acquire a right, to a share in the distributions of the company including any amounts payable to loan creditors by way of premium on redemption; and
4. any person who is entitled to secure that income or assets, either at present or in the future, will be applied directly or indirectly for his benefit.

Future entitlement includes anything which the person is entitled to do at a future date or will at a future date be entitled to do.

6.2.2   Control

A person is regarded as having control of a company if he exercises, is able to exercise, or is entitled to acquire direct or indirect control over the company's affairs and, in particular, if the person possesses or is entitled to acquire:

1. more than 50% of the company's issued share capital;
2. more than 50% of the company's voting share capital;
3. more than 50% of the company's income if it were distributed (excluding rights as a loan creditor); or
4. more than 50% of the company's assets in a winding up.

Importantly, if two or more persons together satisfy any of the conditions, they are deemed to have control. Therefore, in determining if an individual satisfies any of the above tests, the rights and powers of his associates and any company over which he, or he and his associates, have control, are attributed to him.

6.2.3   Associate

An associate of a participator means:

1. A relative of the participator (i.e. spouse or civil partner, parent or remote forebear, child or remoter issue, brother or sister).
2. A partner of the participator.
3. A trustee of a settlement established by the participator or a relative.
4. If the participator has an interest in any shares or obligations of a company which are subject to any trust, the trustees of any settlement concerned.

6.2.4   Director

In order to be regarded as a director, a person need not actually have the title director. A director includes a person:

1. occupying the position of director by whatever name called,
2. in accordance with whose directions or instructions the directors are accustomed to act,
3. who is a manager of the company or otherwise concerned in the management of the company's trade or business and who as beneficial owner is able to control at least 20% of the company's ordinary share capital (either directly or indirectly).

Example 6.1

Shares in Alphabet Ltd, a UK resident company, are held as follows:

	Status	Shareholding
Mr A	Director	10%
Mrs A		2%
Mrs C (Mr A's aunt)		2%
Mrs B		10%
B Ltd (Shares in B Ltd held 50% each by Mr and Mrs B)		5%
Mr J (Mrs B's cousin)		4%
Mr D	Director	10%
Mrs D		2%
Ms D (Mr and Mrs D's daughter)		2%
Mrs E (Mr D's sister)		2%
Mr F		6%
Mr G		5%
Other shareholdings		
(unrelated parties all holding < 5%)		40%
		100%

Is Alphabet Ltd under the control of five or fewer participators?

Shares held by Mr A:		
Mr A	10%	
Mrs A	2%	12%
Shares held by Mrs B:		
Mrs B	10%	
B Ltd	5%	15%
Shares held by Mr D:		
Mr D	10%	
Mrs D	2%	
Ms D	2%	
Mrs E	2%	16%
Mr F		6%
Mr G		5%
		54%

In determining the shares controlled by each participator, shares held by associates are included. While spouses, children, siblings and parents are included as associates, shares held by cousins or aunts are not included.

Alphabet Ltd is under the control of five or fewer participators and is, therefore, a close company.

6.3 Excluded Companies

Certain companies who would be regarded as close companies under the above definitions are not regarded as close companies. These include:

1. A company not resident in the UK.
2. A registered industrial and provident society.
3. A building society.
4. A company controlled by or on behalf of the Crown and not otherwise a close company.
5. A company controlled by or on behalf of:

    (a) a Member State of the EU; or
    (b) the government of a country with which the UK has a double taxation treaty and which is not otherwise a close company.

6. A company which is controlled by a company which is not a close company or by one or more companies which are not close companies and the company could only be regarded as close if one of these companies were included in the five or fewer participators.
7. Registered pension schemes: If shares in a company are held on trust for a registered pension scheme, the persons holding the shares are to be treated as the beneficial owners of the shares and, in that capacity, as a company which is not a close company. However, this exemption does not apply if the scheme is established wholly or mainly for the benefit of directors, employees, past directors or past employees of a company (as specifically defined) or dependants of an individual holding the shares beneficially.
8. "Public" companies: For this purpose, a company is regarded as a public company if the following two tests are satisfied:

    (a) at least 35% of the voting share capital is held by "the public"; and
    (b) these shares are quoted on a recognised stock exchange, and in the previous 12 months there have been dealings in those shares on the stock exchange.

In this context "the public" does not include:

- directors or their associates;
- a company under the control of directors and or their associates;
- an associated company of the company;
- a fund for the benefit of employees or directors (past or current); or
- a principal member, which means a person who holds more than 5% of the voting share capital and who is one of the five largest shareholders. In determining a principal member's shareholding, shares held by an associate are taken into account.

6.4   Consequences of Close Company Status

A company controlled by a small group of persons may arrange its affairs to enable those persons to avoid income tax. The rationale for the special tax rules for close companies is to deal with the fact that closely held companies generally can take decisions in such a way as to minimise tax. These would not be feasible for a publicly quoted company. Legislation to prevent this form of avoidance was first introduced as long ago as 1922 but, since 1965, the counter measures have been provided by the "close company" provisions.

Without close company rules, it is possible that more individuals would incorporate. The top income tax rate is currently 45% (plus either employee's NIC or self-employed Class 2 and Class 4 NIC), while the corporation tax rate currently lies between 20% and 21%. Therefore, incorporation could possibly save money. However, the close company status provisions may make incorporation significantly less attractive, as they:

▧ extend the meaning of "distributions" to encompass certain benefits which may be disguised distributions of profit to the shareholders or their families;

▧ impose tax in respect of certain loans made to shareholders, etc. which could in practice represent the extraction of profits without the payment of tax by the shareholders, etc. (these loans are grossed up and corporation tax at 25% on the grossed-up amount is payable by the close company); and

▧ impose certain restrictions on close companies which are close investment holding companies.

The detailed operation of these negative consequences is set out in **Chapter 7**.

Questions

Review Questions
(See Suggested Solutions to Review Questions at the end of this textbook.)

Question 6.1

X Ltd has 1,000 issued shares of £1, held as below:

Trustees of A's settlement	449
Mrs A (settlor)	60
Ten other shareholders	491
Total issued ordinary shares	1,000

The ten shareholders are not associated with each other or with A or Mrs A and none of them hold more than 50 shares.

Requirement
Determine if X Ltd is a close company.

Question 6.2

In a trading company, issued ordinary shares carry one vote each but 'A' ordinary shares do not confer any voting rights. The shareholders are as below:

	Ordinary shares	'A' ordinary shares
A	280	
Wife of A	100	
B (brother of A)	10	
Trustees of A's settlement	40	
Company X (controlled by A)	80	
	510	
Mrs C (daughter of B)	20	
10 other equal holdings	470	500
Total issued shares	1,000	500

The shares carry equal rights to dividend.

Requirement
Determine if the company is a close company.

Question 6.3

The authorised and issued share capital of Company Y is £1,000 in the form of 1,000 ordinary shares of £1 each, held as below.

A	200
B	100
C	50
D	50
E	40
Company Z	99
Other shareholders	461
Total issued ordinary shares	1,000

A, B and C are directors.

The issued capital of Company Z is £100 in the form of 100 ordinary shares of £1 each, held by:

F (son of E)	60
G	40
Total issued shares	100

The shareholders in Company Y, other than Company Z, are all individuals and none are related or otherwise associated. No 'other shareholder' holds more than 50 shares.

Requirement
Determine if the company is a close company.

Close Companies: Disadvantages

Learning Objectives

After studying this chapter you will have developed competency in the following:

Tax Treatment of Expenses Paid to Participators and their Associates

■ Benefits in kind provided by a close company to its participators (or their associates) are generally regarded as distributions (it should be noted that a benefit in kind to a participator is not treated as a distribution if it is already assessable as employment income). The cost to the company of providing the benefit is disallowed in computing its corporation tax liability. Furthermore, the company is deemed to have made a distribution equal to the amount that would fall to be assessed on an employee or director earning at least £8,500 per annum **and** the recipient of the benefit is taxed as if they have received a dividend of the same amount. This applies to payments to non-working participators or non-working associates which cannot be classed as employment income.

Loans to Participators and their Associates

■ Where a company makes a loan to a participator/shareholder or associate which is not in the ordinary course of business, it must also make a payment to HM Revenue & Customs (HMRC) equal to 25% of the outstanding loan or advance made during the year. This tax need **not** be paid where the loan has been repaid, released or written off within nine months and one day following the end of the accounting period, which is the due date for the payment of the company's corporation tax liability. Where the repayment, release or write-off occurs at any point later than the due date, HMRC will repay the tax on the due date for payment of corporation tax of the accounting period in which the repayment, release or write-off took place.

■ There is an exception for small loans, i.e. loans of £15,000 or less to employees/directors who work full-time in the company or associated company and who do not own more than 5% of the shares.

■ The receipt of the loan has no initial consequences for the shareholder. However, if it is at a preferential rate, which it typically is, the income tax benefit in kind rules will apply to either treat the interest below HMRC's official rate for beneficial loans as a benefit in kind (if the participator/associate is also an employee or director earning >£8,500 (including the value of the benefit), which is assessable as employment income) or as a distribution under the rules outlined above.

Repayment or Write-off of Loans to Participators

■ For as long as the loan is on the balance sheet of the company, the corporation tax payment made to HMRC stays with HMRC. There are two possible ways of the loan ceasing to be on the balance sheet, namely:
- the loan is written off; or
- the shareholder repays the loan.

■ If the loan is written off, the shareholder receives income treated as a distribution net of the 10% tax credit. This charge takes precedence over any employment income charge. For debts released or written off after 24 March 2010, the company is not allowed a deduction for the loan written off, i.e. it must be added back. Prior to that date, the tax treatment would have been to add the loan write-off back, and then treat the relevant amount as a non-trade debit. However, the company is entitled to reclaim the corporation tax paid on the loan and HMRC will repay the tax as noted for the treatment of loans repaid.

■ If the shareholder repays the loan, HMRC repays the tax, which can be in stages. Depending on the timing of the repayment, the company will either:

- complete an amended return for the accounting period in which the loan was made (provided the amended return is submitted within the 12-month period); or
- in all other cases, Schedule 1A TMA 1970 applies and relief is given by discharge or repayment. HMRC will generally accept a claim via letter if all the appropriate details are set out.

Personal Service Companies/Managed Service Companies/IR35

■ These are mainly professional services companies, where individuals provide their services through a company.

■ IR35 rules came into effect as from 6 April 2000 and were extended again as from 9 April 2003.

■ The thrust of the legislation is to prevent individuals from avoiding paying tax and National Insurance Contributions (NICs) by providing services through an intermediary, i.e. the company. This would otherwise be achieved by the individual taking dividends from the company which, in some circumstances, is more tax-efficient than taking a salary.

■ The anti-avoidance legislation results in workers, who would otherwise be treated and taxed as employees if they were engaged directly, no longer being able to avoid paying tax and NICs on any payments of salary by using a service company. IR35 rules effectively "unwind" the potential third party "sham", where an individual performs services for another person and such services, if performed under a contract between the two, would suggest that the individual was in fact employed, are "packaged" as arrangements with a third party.

■ If it is established on the facts that IR35 rules apply, then a deemed salary payment, subject to tax under PAYE, may fall to be made by the worker on 5 April at the end of the financial year.

■ Managed service companies (MSC) are, in essence, multi-person personal service companies. Typically in MSCs, otherwise unrelated workers all become worker-shareholders of the MSC, with each worker having a different class of share. This allows for different dividend payments to be made to each worker, the payments typically being in line with the level of time worked for the end client by that particular worker. The payment of a dividend obviously avoids the payment of NIC. Care is also normally taken to ensure that the "profits" of the company remain within the small profits rate.

▨ FA 2007 deemed that, where individuals provide their services through MSCs, the income is to be treated (if not already done so) as employment income. These changes mean that HMRC no longer has to rely on the IR35 legislation to ensure that MSCs properly operate the deduction of tax and NIC from this "employed income" in accordance with PAYE regulations.

7.1 Disadvantages of Close Company Status

The disadvantages of close company status are as follows:

1. Certain **expenses** for participators and their associates are treated as distributions.
2. **Interest** payments made by the company to participators/associates of participators which are in excess of a normal commercial rate of return may be treated as a dividend. Similarly, interest payments by participators/associates to companies on overdrawn loan accounts which are below the normal commercial rate may be classed as a distribution or a benefit in kind.
3. There is a potential tax payable by close companies when making **loans** to participators or their associates.
4. Loans to participators or their associates which are subsequently **written off** will be assessable to income tax in the hands of the individuals.

We will now examine each of the above.

7.2 Certain Expenses for Participators and their Associates

Any expenses incurred by a close company in providing benefits or facilities of any kind for a non-working participator or a non-working associate of the participator will be treated as a distribution. Where an item is treated as a distribution, the expense will be disallowed in the company's corporation tax computation.

The following expense payments are not treated as distributions:

1. Any expense made good to the company by the participator.
2. Any expense incurred in providing benefits or facilities to working directors or employees as such expenses are already assessable as benefits in kind.
3. Any expense incurred in connection with the provision for the spouse, children or dependants of any director or employee of any pension, annuity, lump sum or gratuity to be given on his death or retirement.

The legislation also contains anti-avoidance measures to counter two or more close companies from arranging to make payments to one another's participators.

Example 7.1
Mr A holds 2% of the ordinary share capital of X Ltd, a close company. Mr A is not an employee or director of X Ltd.
X Ltd pays the rent on Mr A's house of £3,000 per annum. The amount is charged each year in X Ltd's accounts under rental expenses.
As X Ltd is a close company and Mr A is a participator, the expense will be treated as a distribution. Accordingly, the £3,000 will be disallowed to X Ltd in arriving at its profits assessable to corporation tax and will also be treated as a distribution in the hands of Mr A.

7.3 Loans to Participators and their Associates

Where a close company makes a loan to an **individual** who is a participator or an associate of a participator, the company will be required to pay tax in respect of the amount of the loan grossed up at the standard rate (i.e. 25%) as if that grossed-up amount were an annual payment (section 455 CTA 2010, formerly section 419 ICTA 1988). A close company is regarded as making a loan to any person who incurs a debt to the company or where a debt due from a person to a third party is assigned to the company.

There are **three exceptions** to the above, with the following **not** treated as loans to participators:

1. Where the business of the company is or includes the lending of money and the loan is made in the ordinary course of that business.
2. Where a debt is incurred for the supply of goods or services in the ordinary course of the business of the close company, unless the credit given exceeds six months or is longer than the period normally given to the company's customers.
3. Loans made to directors or employees of the company (or an associated company) if:
    (a) the amount of the loan, together with all other loans outstanding made by the company (or its associated companies) to the borrower (or his spouse), does not exceed £15,000; **and**
    (b) the borrower works full-time for the company; **and**
    (c) the borrower does not have a "material interest" in the company or an associated company – a person has a material interest if he, either on his own or with any one or more of his associates, or if any associate(s) of his with or without any such other associates, is the beneficial owner of, or is able to control, directly or indirectly more than 5% of the ordinary share capital.

It should be noted that, in relation to (3)(c), if the borrower subsequently acquires a material interest, the company will be required to pay corporation tax in respect of all the loans outstanding from the borrower at that time.

When the loan or part of the loan is repaid by the participator (or associate), the tax or a proportionate part of it will be refunded to the company provided a claim is made within four years of the end of the financial year in which the repayment is made or the release or writing off occurs. However, the tax will not be refunded with interest.

Example 7.2
ABC Ltd, a close company, made interest-free loans to the following shareholders in the accounting period to 31 March 2015.

	£
Mr A (director owning 10% of the share capital)	16,000
Mr B (director owning 4% of the share capital)	10,000
Mr C	8,000

What are the tax consequences for the company, assuming that no other loans had been made to the three individuals in the past? You may also assume that Mr A and Mr B work full-time for the company.

continued overleaf

Solution

The company will be required to pay corporation tax in respect of the loans to Mr A and Mr C at 25% of the outstanding amount, calculated as follows:

	£
Mr A	16,000
Mr C	8,000
	24,000 × 25% = £6,000

The loan to Mr B is not subject to this provision as Mr B:

1. is a director who works full time, and

2. does not have a "material interest" in the company, and

3. the loan is less than £15,000.

This tax of £6,000 must be paid over to HMRC on or before 1 January 2016 (nine months and one day after the accounting period end). The tax will be repaid (or partially repaid) by HMRC nine months and one day after the end of the accounting period in which the loans have been repaid (or partially repaid) by the shareholders.

Finance Act 2013 saw the introduction of anti-avoidance provisions to deny the various means by which close companies could bypass the existing rules. Three changes to the rules were introduced:

1. To put beyond doubt that loans to various intermediaries are within the scope of the charge. This sought to address arrangements using perceived loopholes in the legislation by making loans and other payments to participators via intermediaries such as limited liability partnerships (LLPs), partnerships and trusts in which the close company and at least one participator in the close company are members, partners or trustees.

2. To address certain arrangements where value is extracted from a close company and an untaxed benefit is conferred on an individual participator (or associate) other than by way of a loan or advance.

3. To ensure the repayment rules are reinforced so relief is only given for genuine repayments thereby dealing with the scenario whereby the loan is repaid and shortly thereafter drawn down again.

These measures are effective from 20 March 2013.

7.4 Write-off of Loans to Participators

Where a company makes a loan to a participator and subsequently releases or writes it off, the shareholder is deemed to receive income at the time of writing off the loan as a debt is released. The participator will be treated as though his total income for the year in which the release or writing off occurs were increased by the amount released or written off, grossed up at 10/9 for the notional tax credit on dividends.

However, the corporation tax already paid by the company is not available for offset against any additional tax arising in the hands of the individual nor is the notional tax credit. The company can, however, reclaim the corporation tax paid subject to the procedure, conditions and time limits for same already outlined.

Example 7.3

Assume that in the previous example Mr A repays his loan of £16,000 on 1 February 2016 and at the same time the company writes off the loan to Mr C.

What are the tax consequences for the company and the shareholders?

Company

The company will be repaid the tax on Mr A's loan, i.e. £4,000 (25% × £16,000) but only after 1 January 2017, i.e. nine months and one day after the end of the accounting period in which repayment occurred (being 31 March 2016).

Shareholders:

There are no tax consequences for Mr A.

Mr C, however, will be assessed as receiving the distribution net of the 10% tax credit, i.e. gross distribution income of £8,000 × 10/9 = £8,889. This amount will be subject to income tax at the dividend rate, and this charge will take precedence over any employment income tax charge. Tax will also be repaid on Mr C's loan.

7.5 Indirect Loans and Anti-avoidance

Indirect loans also fall to be treated in the same manner as "loans to participators". Hence the taxpayer cannot circumvent the potential charge to tax under section 455 CTA 2010 via the interposition of a third party. Section 459 CTA 2010 is an anti-avoidance clause which effectively brings the tax charge into play whenever a loan is made to a participator by a third party, which is either directly or indirectly financed by the participator's close company. Furthermore, loans to a participator by a company controlled by a close company, are also deemed to fall foul of the above anti-avoidance legislation.

7.6 Close Investment Holding Companies

Where a close company is non-trading or lets property to connected parties, the company may well be a close investment holding company. Such a company will **be liable to pay corporation tax at the main rate irrespective of its level of profits**.

A company is connected with another company if:

1. the same person has control of both, or a person has control of one and persons connected with him have control of the other; or
2. if a group of two or more persons has control of each company.

However, if throughout the period a close company exists wholly or mainly to:

(a) carry on a trade on a commercial basis, **or**
(b) to make investments in land or interests in land where the land is intended to be let to unconnected persons,

then it will not be a close investment holding company.

Questions

Review Questions
(See Suggested Solutions to Review Questions at the end of this textbook.)

Question 7.1

Requirement

(a) State the tax effect on a close company arising out of a loan made to a participator in that company. Indicate the circumstances in which the loan would have no tax consequences for the company.

(b) Size Ltd is a close single company and has the following adjusted profits for the year ended 31 December 2011:

	£
Property income (not rented to connected parties)	30,000
Trading income	100,000
Deposit interest	3,000
	133,000

Calculate its corporation tax liability for the year ended 31 December 2011.

Question 7.2

Close Ltd is a family-owned distribution company with no associated companies. Results to 31 December 2014 are as follows:

	£	£
Gross profit	50,000	
Other income (Note 1)	10,000	
		60,000
Depreciation	15,000	
Salaries	10,000	
Rent and rates	1,000	
Sundry (Note 2)	1,100	(27,100)
Net profit		32,900

Notes

1. Other income:

	£
Bank interest	8,500
Capital grants	1,500
	10,000

2. Sundry:

	£
Miscellaneous office expenses	300
Expenses of majority shareholder's brother Y who does not work for Close Ltd paid to him on 01/07/2014	800
	1,100

Capital allowances due are £4,000.

Requirement
(a) Compute the corporation tax payable.
(b) Explain the tax treatment of the expenses paid for Y.

Question 7.3

Maxi Ltd, a family-owned company with no associated companies, deals in farm machinery. The results for the year ended 31 March 2015 were as follows:

	£	£
Sales		6,300,000
Opening stock	1,100,000	
Purchases	5,650,000	
	6,750,000	
Closing stock	1,450,000	
		(5,300,000)
		1,000,000
Less: Expenses		
Administration	220,000	
Financial	200,000	
Distribution and sales (Note 1)	270,000	
Depreciation	100,000	(790,000)
Trading profit		210,000
Loss on sale of plant (Note 4)	(20,000)	
Profit on sale of building (Note 2)	1,480,000	
Rents (Note 3)	200,000	
		1,660,000
Net profit		1,870,000

The directors have a policy of not paying dividends.

Notes

1. The following items were included in distribution and sales:

	£
Entertainment	
Entertaining customers	6,000
Entertaining suppliers	5,000
Staff Christmas party	10,000
Christmas gifts for suppliers	900
Cost of MD attending trade fair in London	850
	22,750

2. The building, which was sold in October 2014, had been acquired in 1970 for £2,000. It was valued at £50,000 on 31 March 1982. The building was located on a site on which planning permission had been granted for the construction of a shopping centre. Proceeds received for the building were £1.5 million. Legal fees of £18,000 were incurred in connection with the disposal. Indexation allowance from March 1982 to the date of sale was 110%.

3. On 1 June 2014, the company re-let its investment property under a 20-year lease. A premium of £50,000 was received on the sub-letting. This premium is included in property income in the profit and loss account.

4. Total capital allowances, including balancing allowances and charges, for the year were agreed at £50,000.

Additional information

In June 2014 the managing director (and principal shareholder) borrowed £550,000 from the proceeds from the sale of the building to purchase a new residence for himself in his own name.

Maxi Ltd has £210,000 of trading losses forward at 31/03/2014.

Requirement

Calculate the corporation tax payable by Maxi Ltd.

Note: the CGT consequences arising from the granting of the lease may be ignored.

Question 7.4

Servisco Ltd, a closely held firm of management consultants, had the following income for the year ended 31 March 2015:

	£
Professional income	430,000
Property income	100,000
Bank deposit interest	50,000
Chargeable gains before adjustment	86,400

The company had a loss forward of £9,000 on its professional activities from the year ended 31 March 2014.

The company received dividends of £17,500. £10,000 of these dividends were from another UK company in which Servisco has a minor shareholding. The remaining £7,500 gross dividend was from a company resident in the Republic of Ireland, in which Servisco Ltd holds 7.5% of the shares, and was received on 1 April 2014.

Requirement

Compute the company's corporation tax liability for the year ended 31 March 2015.

Question 7.5

Machinery Ltd was incorporated in the UK on 1 June 1970 and since that date has been engaged in providing machinery to companies.

The founder members of the company were Mr Vincent Duffy and his wife Julie and the company was formed to take over their existing business which they previously conducted in partnership. Mr and Mrs Duffy have actively encouraged members of their immediate family and other relatives to take up employment within the company and have endeavoured to ensure that the control of the company remains, as far as possible, within the family.

The company's profit and loss account for the year ended 31 March 2015 showed the following results:

		£	£
Sales			1,660,000
Stocks at 31/03/15		450,000	
Stocks at 01/04/14		(360,000)	(90,000)
			1,750,000
Purchases			(805,000)
Gross profit			945,000
Less:	Depreciation	59,790	
	Rent	79,710	
	Light and heat	17,500	
	Distribution costs	39,000	
	Bank and loan interest	65,000	
	Motor expenses (all vans)	44,300	
	Sundry expenses	13,000	(318,000)
	Net profit from trading		626,700
Add:	Bank deposit interest	10,000	
	Rents from let property		
	(after allowable deductions)	50,000	60,000
	Profit for year		686,700

The shareholdings and loans made to the company as at 31 December 2014 were:

	Ordinary £1 shares	Loans made (@ interest rate)	Interest paid £
V. Duffy (director)	3,000	£4,000 @ 15%	600
Mrs J. Duffy (director)	1,250	£5,000 @ 12%	600
Trustees of settlement made by V. Duffy	2,900	£5,000 @ 15%	750
Executors of the will of J. Duffy deceased (father of V. Duffy)	2,000	£5,000 @ 15%	750
D. O'Connell (director)	2,750	£5,000 @ 15%	750
Mrs K. Moran (aunt of V. Duffy)	500	–	–
L. T. Smith (director)	2,100	£10,000 @ 13.21%	1,321
Louise Hare (company secretary)	3,000	£3,000 @ 12%	360
Paul Hare (husband of V. Duffy's sister)	2,500	£3,000 @ 9.3%	279
	20,000		5,410

Notes
1. V. Duffy is an executor of his father's will.
2. The loan interest was paid in addition to bank interest of £59,590, thus reconciling with the amount shown in the P&L Account.
3. For the accounting period ended 31 March 2015, capital allowances were £10,700.
4. None of the shareholders are related except as shown above.
5. The share capital at 1 April 2014 was the same as at 31 March 2015.
6. The commercial rate of return is deemed to be 6%.

Requirement
You are required to compute the corporation tax liability of the company for the accounting year ended 31 March 2015.

Question 7.6

Tax Advisors Ltd, a professional services company, had the following sources of income and charges for the year ended 31 December 2014:

	£
Trading income	100,000
Interest income	100,000
Qualifying charitable donations paid	(60,000)

Requirement
Calculate the corporation tax payable by Tax Advisors Ltd in respect of the above figures.

Non-resident Companies

Learning Objectives

After studying this chapter you will have developed competency in the following:
- A company will be non-UK resident if it is centrally managed and controlled outside the UK. A company incorporated in the UK is, *prima facie*, resident in the UK.
- A non-resident company is liable to corporation tax if, and only if, it carries on a trade in the UK through a permanent establishment (PE).
- Income from any property or rights used by, or for, the PE is chargeable.
- Gains on disposal of assets situated in the UK and used for the purposes of the trade of the PE are chargeable.

8.1   Introduction

You will recall from **Chapter 1** that a company which is centrally managed and controlled in the UK is UK tax resident. In addition, a UK incorporated company is automatically regarded as resident in the UK.

If a non-UK resident company were to move its central management and control to the UK, it would thus become UK resident. However, the jurisdiction of its incorporation may determine that it remains also resident in that other country. In this situation, the company becomes a dual-resident company, and the relevant double taxation treaty and any specific tiebreaker clause need to be examined in such situations.

In particular, there are certain important restrictions in the case of dual-resident non-trading (investment) companies.

A company that is regarded as resident in another country under the terms of a double taxation treaty may have its income exempt from UK corporation tax.

However, normally a non-resident company not carrying on a trade in the UK will be chargeable to income tax at the basic rate on any of its UK income. If tax has been deducted at source from such income, the tax payable is limited to that amount.

Most companies in the UK are UK resident and, therefore, are liable to UK corporation tax on all their profits, irrespective of where the income arises or wherever the assets (subject to chargeable gains) are situated. This is the case whether or not such income or gains are remitted to the UK.

8.1.1 UK Multinationals

Where a UK company expands into international markets, it will generally establish a separate subsidiary company in the foreign country. Often the foreign subsidiary is managed and controlled in that foreign country and is, therefore, not UK resident. Such foreign subsidiaries of UK companies are non-resident in the UK and are only liable to UK corporation tax on the profits as detailed above. However, these foreign subsidiaries typically do not generate UK profits (as they are established to generate foreign profits) and, therefore, no UK tax is payable by the foreign subsidiary. Foreign tax is likely to arise in the overseas jurisdiction. However, the UK parent may be subject to UK corporation tax on the income profits of the foreign subsidiary under the Controlled Foreign Companies legislation (see **Section 8.6**).

Alternatively, the UK company may establish a branch in the foreign country. The profits of the foreign branch will be included with the year end results for the UK company and are chargeable to UK corporation tax. The foreign branch profits may or may not be assessed to tax in the foreign country, depending on the taxation rules in the foreign country. Where foreign tax is payable, this will normally be available for deduction by credit relief against the element of the UK corporation tax assessed on the branch profits. Legislation was introduced in Finance Act 2011 to exempt the profits of foreign branches of UK-resident companies from corporation tax, therefore precluding the need for credit relief to prevent double taxation. Companies are able to opt into this exemption regime, and any such election is irrevocable. This amendment has effect for accounting periods commencing on or after 19 July 2011, the date of Royal Assent to Finance Act 2011.

8.1.2 Foreign Investment into the UK

Where a foreign company establishes an operation (e.g. factory in the UK), the operation will be run by a company in the multinational group. This company is normally a UK-resident company established specifically to run the UK operation. Sometimes, for international tax planning reasons, a non-resident company is used. Where a non-resident company runs the UK operation, its liability to UK corporation tax is as set out above.

8.2 Non-resident Companies Charge to Tax

A non-resident company is chargeable to UK corporation tax if it carries on a trade in the UK through a PE. Prior to 1 January 2003, non-resident companies were assessed to UK corporation tax if they had a "branch or agency" in the UK. Whilst a PE may indeed be a branch or agency, the definition has now taken on a wider meaning. A PE is a fixed place of business through which the business of the company is wholly or partly carried on; **or** it can be where an agent has, and exercises, authority to do business on behalf of the company. Examples of a fixed place of business include a branch, workshop, factory or office.

If the non-resident company does carry on a trade in the UK through a PE, corporation tax will be charged on:

1. any trading income arising directly or indirectly through or from that PE;
2. any income, wherever arising, from property or rights used by, or held by or for that PE, e.g. income from patent rights held by the branch; and
3. chargeable gains accruing on assets situated in the UK used for the purpose of the trade of the PE.

Income from sources *within* the UK which are not subject to corporation tax (because it is not attributable to a trade in the UK through a PE) will instead be subject to *income tax*.

Therefore, the difference between a non-resident and a resident company is that any profits not attributable to the UK branch, e.g. foreign interest and foreign trading income, are not liable to UK tax.

Note: profits are either liable or not liable. There is no remittance basis concept.

8.3   Dividends and Other Distributions Received

Prior to 1 July 2009, dividends paid by foreign companies to UK companies were chargeable to UK corporation tax (as "miscellaneous income") in the hands of the recipient. Such foreign dividends generally had tax withheld (withholding tax) by the foreign company. A company was able to obtain double taxation relief (DTR) for overseas withholding tax and, provided its investment in the foreign company was sufficiently large, for underlying tax.

8.4   Capital Gains

In relation to capital gains, there is a charge to corporation tax on a non-resident company carrying on a trade in the UK through a PE on chargeable gains accruing on the disposal of assets in the UK which, at or before the time when the chargeable gain accrued, were used in or for the purposes of the trade of the PE.

When a company becomes non-UK resident, it ceases to be chargeable to corporation tax. There will thus be a cessation of an accounting period, with the ensuing potential balancing adjustments for capital allowances purposes. In this situation, it must notify HMRC of the date that it intends to become non-resident. It must also provide a statement of all amounts owing and how, and when, it will make the relevant payments.

The company's UK departure will also create a potential "exit charge", as it will be deemed to have disposed of all its chargeable assets at market value. The resultant chargeable gains will fall to be taxed on the company at that point. This is also the situation where a company becomes treaty non-resident.

Postponement of the "exit charge" may take place where:

1.   the assets are "foreign assets", i.e. assets situated outside the UK used for the trade carried on outside the UK; **and**
2.   the company is a 75% subsidiary of a UK resident company (i.e. the principal company remains UK resident) and both companies make the relevant election.

The "postponed" gain falls to be taxed on the UK-resident company if the asset is disposed of within six years of the company becoming non-resident or the company ceases to be a 75% subsidiary. The postponed gain is computed by aggregating the chargeable gains and setting off the allowable losses on the relevant assets to arrive at a single chargeable gain. The gain will also crystallise if the UK resident principal company becomes non-resident.

8.5   Foreign Tax Credit

From 1 July 2009, the rules outlined below apply **only** where the dividend received by the UK company does **not** qualify for one of the exemptions. This will be rare.

8.5.1 Withholding Tax

The general principle is that relief is available for overseas tax suffered on dividends (and indeed PE's profits and interest) up to the amount of the UK corporation tax attributable to that income (applying the company's effective tax rate).

Where a foreign company paid a dividend of £75,000 to a UK company and it had withheld tax of £25,000, it is the grossed-up figure of £100,000 which is to be included within the taxable total profits. If the company's effective tax rate was, say 22%, then the DTR would be restricted to the lower of:

1. the foreign tax suffered (i.e. £25,000); and
2. the UK tax on the foreign income (i.e. 22% of £100,000 = £22,000).

In this scenario, DTR would be restricted to £22,000 and £3,000 would be excess foreign tax. If the company's effective tax rate had been 27%, then DTR would be £25,000 (being less than £27,000).

For any dividends paid prior to 1 July 2009, if the company had eligible unrelieved foreign tax (EUFT), the company was able to "pool" together all foreign dividends and set the excess foreign tax on dividends against UK corporation tax on other foreign dividends. This was known as "on-shore pooling" and was achieved by either:

1. setting off excess foreign tax in the current period;
2. carrying back for three years on a "last in first out" basis;
3. carrying forward indefinitely; or
4. surrendering to another group company.

It should be noted that, where the excess foreign tax was carried either backwards or forwards, it was set against the UK corporation tax on foreign dividends (except for dividends paid by controlled foreign companies (CFC) or dividends where the underlying tax has been capped).

The on-shore pooling rules have no effect after 1 July 2009 because after that date, as a general rule, foreign dividends are no longer taxable. Therefore, there can be no claims to EUFT for dividends paid after that date, nor can such dividends generate EUFT to carry back to earlier periods.

8.5.2 Underlying Tax

Where a UK company owns more than 10% of an overseas company's equity and receives a dividend from such a company, the UK company will be able to obtain relief for the tax attributable to the relevant profits out of which the dividend was paid. Such tax is known as **underlying tax**.

The underlying tax is calculated by multiplying the gross dividend income by the foreign tax paid and dividing by the relevant profits (the profits available for distribution in the company accounts).

8.5.3 Credit Relief

The "credit relief" available to a company is restricted to the lower of:

1. the overseas tax paid; or
2. the UK corporation tax on the gross dividend.

Unrelieved tax credits on such dividends may be eligible for relief by:

(a) carry-back to the previous three years;
(b) carry-forward to the next accounting period; or
(c) in a group situation, through use of the "mixer cap".

8.6   Controlled Foreign Company (CFC)

A controlled foreign company (CFC) is a company which

1.   is resident outside the UK; and
2.   is controlled by persons resident in the UK; and

This is to help prevent companies accumulating income in a foreign country where the tax paid is significantly lower than the amount which would have to be paid by a UK company.

After an extended period of consultation, the Government published via Finance Act 2012 the new controlled foreign companies (CFC) rules.

It was considered that the previous rules required revision to enhance the attractiveness of the UK as a holding location for multinational business whilst at the same time protecting the UK corporate tax base.

The new rules are very different to those they replaced and are for the first time based on the principle that overseas activities are not taxed in the UK unless there is an artificial reduction of the UK tax base. Also, should a company come within the regime, the legislation will address only those profits which have been artificially diverted from the UK rather than being "all or nothing".

The main changes in the new legislation include:

1.   The introduction of a "gateway test" which defines the chargeable profits that are subject to the CFC regime. The business profits of a foreign subsidiary are outside the scope of the new CFC regime if they meet the specified conditions set out in a "gateway". This test seeks to address instances where there is a significant distortion between business activities undertaken in the UK and the profits arising from those activities being allocated outside the UK.
2.   "Safe harbours" for the gateway conditions are provided covering general commercial business, incidental finance income and some sector specific rules. A foreign subsidiary can rely on these safe harbours to show that some or all of its profits are outside the regime's scope.
3.   As an alternative to the gateway, the regime also provides a number of entity exemptions for CFCs. Where a CFC satisfies an entity level exemption, no CFC charge is imposed in relation to any of its profits. The exemptions are:

    (a)   Low profits exemption – the adjusted accounting profits of the CFC do not exceed £50,000 or do not exceed £500,000 and the profits representing non-trading income do not exceed £50,000.
    (a)   Low profit margin exemption – the exemption is available to a CFC where its profit margin is less than 10%.
    (a)   Excluded territories – companies resident and carrying on what are considered to be acceptable activities in certain territories are excluded. Broadly this is intended to cover any CFCs that pay foreign tax of at least 75% of the tax that they would have paid were they resident in the UK.

These rules apply to accounting periods of CFCs beginning on or after 1 January 2013 (with the previous rules applying to any earlier periods).

Questions

Review Questions
(See Suggested Solutions to Review Questions at the end of this textbook.)

Question 8.1

In July 2014 Medtech Ltd, a UK resident company with a 30 June accounting period end, entered into a joint venture in Cyprus by purchasing a 48% holding in MedAssist Ltd, a company involved in the wholesale and distribution of pharmaceutical products. MedAssist also has a 30 June accounting period end.

One of the reasons Medtech invested in MedAssist was the low rate of corporation tax in Cyprus (currently 10%). The other 52% of the shares in MedAssist are held by Medservices SA, a Portuguese company. Medtech has used MedAssist for the distribution of their own products in the past which is how they became aware of this investment opportunity.

Requirement
Outline the rationale for the controlled foreign company (CFC) rules, assess if MedAssist Ltd is a CFC and consider if a CFC charge will arise on the basis of the above information.

Question 8.2

Hulk Ltd, a UK resident company, owns 46% of the ordinary share capital of Black Widow Co. Black Widow Co. is German resident. The remaining 54% shares in Black Widow Co. are held by a French tax resident company, Hawk Eye Srl.

For the year ended 31 March 2015, Black Widow Co. has profits, calculated in accordance with UK tax rules, of £1,500,000, of which 75% is regarded as having been artificially diverted from the UK. Unfortunately, none of the controlled foreign company (CFC) exemptions are available to Black Widow Co.

Black Widow Co. has suffered tax in its country of residence of £150,000. Hulk Ltd's accounting period end is also 31 March.

Requirement
(a) Determine if Black Widow Co. is a CFC.
(b) Calculate the CFC charge for the year ended 31 March 2015 on the basis of the above information. Who is responsible for paying the charge and how is it reported to HMRC?

Group Relief
and Consortia Relief

Learning Objectives

After studying this chapter you will have developed competency in the following:
- The distinction between associated companies, 75% subsidiaries, consortia and capital gains tax groups.
- The most important relief is loss relief, i.e. if one company in a group has a loss, it can be utilised by another group member.
- The types of losses that may be group-relieved are:
  - trading losses;
  - losses from a UK property business;
  - non-trading deficits on loan relationships;
  - non-trading losses on intangible fixed assets;
  - excess capital allowances;
  - qualifying charitable donations; and
  - management expenses.
- No other losses may be grouped.
- Only losses of the current year may be group-relieved.
- A surrendering company may group-relieve trading losses, excess capital allowances and non-trading loan relationships deficits before setting it against its own other profits for the period of the loss.
- The profits of a claimant company against which a surrendered loss may be set is after deducting the amount of the claimant company's own current year losses or those brought forward from previous years.
- Both companies must be members of the group throughout the corresponding accounting period; otherwise, apportionment will apply.
- "Qualifying overseas losses" may be surrendered for group relief purposes following the decision in the Marks & Spencer case and subsequent legislative changes in the UK.
- A consortium-owned company (linked or unlinked) can surrender/claim losses in proportion to the stakes of the members of the consortium. Unlike the normal situation, the amount of losses available for surrender by a consortium-owned company must be reduced by any potential claim it could have made against its other current period profits.
- The applicable anti-avoidance rules.
- The tax treatment of intragroup payments.

9.1   Introduction

For corporation tax purposes, the percentage shareholding that one company has in another determines the taxation consequences.

The main types of relationship for tax purposes (based on the degree of share ownership) are:

1. Associated companies
2. 75% subsidiaries
3. Consortia
4. Chargeable gains tax groups

9.1.1   Associated Companies

For corporation tax purposes, two companies are "associated" with each other if one is under the (direct or indirect) control of the other, or both are under the control of the same person or persons (including companies).

As previously outlined, the number of associated companies can determine the limits to be applied for the small profits rate and marginal relief, irrespective of where the companies are resident, the only exception being that associated companies which are dormant are not included for the purposes of this calculation.

Control (in the above context) is the entitlement to more than 50% of the share capital, or voting rights, or income or net assets on a winding up.

A company is another company's associated company in an accounting period if it is an associated company for **any part** of the accounting period. This rule applies to each of two or more associated companies even if they are associated companies for different parts of the accounting period.

9.1.2   Group Relief

While associated companies are based on more than 50% shareholding/control, special rules apply to situations where the share ownership reaches 75%.

For corporation tax purposes, two companies are members of a "group" for group relief purposes where one is a 75% subsidiary of the other, or both are 75% subsidiaries of a third company. In this context, for one company to be a 75% subsidiary of another, the holding company must have at least 75% of the ordinary share capital. However, if the company is not also entitled to at least 75% of the distributable income of the subsidiary **and** entitled to at least 75% of the net assets of the subsidiary on a winding up, group relief may be denied when there are unusual financing structures in a subsidiary so that, for example, the parent is entitled to less than 75% of profits.

For two companies to be in a group, there has to be a 75% effective interest. Hence, if company H owns 90% of company A, which in turn owns 80% of company B, then B **is not** in a group with H as H only has an effective interest of 72% of B (being 90% of 80%). Nevertheless, A and B **are** in a group for group relief purposes.

However, it should be noted that the group relief rules **cannot** be circumvented by trying to use company A as a conduit (for example, if B transferred losses to A, which in turn A then transferred to H).

As in the case of associated companies, a group relief group may include non UK-resident companies. Furthermore, while losses may generally only be surrendered between UK-resident companies, group relief can, in certain circumstances, be available to UK branches or permanent establishments of overseas companies.

9.1.3 Consortium Relief

A company is owned by a consortium if:

1. at least 75% of its ordinary share capital is owned by companies (known as members of the consortium), none of whose shareholding is less than 5%, and each member of the consortium is entitled to at least 5% of any profits available for distribution and at least 5% of any assets on a winding up; **or**
2. if a trading company is a 90% subsidiary of a holding company and is not a 75% subsidiary of any company apart from the holding company and, as a result of (1), the holding company is owned by a consortium, then that trading company is also owned by the consortium.

CTA 2010 extended the availability of consortium relief to the situations in (2). It also should be noted that, although a consortium can be established with non-UK resident companies, losses generally cannot be surrendered to or from a non-UK resident entity.

9.1.4 Capital Gains Tax Groups

Companies are in a capital gains tax group (CGTG) if, at each level, there is a 75% holding and the top company has an effective interest of at least 51% in the group companies. Compare this with the effective 75% interest required for "group relief groups".

Thus, if company S holds 80% of company T, which in turn holds 80% of U, which in turn holds 80% of V, which in turn holds 80% of W, then:

S, T, U and V are in a CGTG (since S has an effective 51.2% interest in V, being 80% × 80% × 80%).

However, S only has a 40.96% effective interest in W (80% × 80% × 80% × 80%), so W is not part of this CGTG.

Any intragroup transfers of chargeable assets within a CGTG must be made on a no gain/no loss basis. This facility also extends to the intangible assets regime in that intangible assets can be transferred between members of a CGTG without a trading profit or loss arising.

Capital losses cannot be surrendered to other group companies. However, it is possible to elect to 'transfer' capital gains within groups so as to best utilise capital losses elsewhere. This could also achieve a lower rate of corporation tax, for example, if there are companies within the group with sufficient profits to allocate all or a partial amount of the capital gain so as to utilise the remainder of the small company band.

If a company leaves a group while it still retains an asset transferred to it within the previous six years on a no gain/no loss basis, then the departing company is treated as having crystallised a disposal, as at the date of the original transfer, by the deemed sale and reacquisition at its then market value. The consequent chargeable gain/(loss) is computed in the normal way (up to the date when the transfer took place) but is brought into the departing company's corporation tax computation for the accounting period in which it leaves the group. Similar provisions apply in respect of previously transferred intangible assets. The above provisions **do not apply** if a company leaves a group only as a result of another group company ceasing to exist.

Non-UK resident companies are included within a CGTG and, provided there is no loss to HMRC, the no gain/no loss transfer is possible within a worldwide group of companies (for example, it may be possible to make a no gain/no loss transfer to a non-UK resident company with a branch or agency in the UK).

9.2 Intragroup Payments

Certain payments made by companies are generally required to be made under deduction of income tax at the standard rate (i.e. if not paid to a company).

A UK company is not required to deduct tax at source from intragroup interest and royalty payments where the other company is either:

1. UK resident; or
2. if non-resident, the company operates a UK PE.

See **Chapter 3** for more details.

9.3 Loss Relief – Groups and Consortia

9.3.1 Introduction

The group relief provisions mean that companies within a 75% group (as defined above) can transfer trading losses to other group companies within the group, so as to set these against taxable profits and reduce the group's overall corporation tax liability.

Generally, losses may only be surrendered between UK-resident companies; although, in certain circumstances, group relief is available to UK branches of overseas companies.

9.3.2 Losses which may be Group-relieved (section 99 CTA 2010; previously section 402 ICTA 1988)

The following types of loss may be group-relieved:

1. trading losses;
2. excess capital allowances;
3. non-trading deficits on loan relationships;
4. amounts allowable as a qualifying charitable donation;
5. a UK property business loss;
6. excess management expenses of investment companies; and
7. non-trading loss on intangible fixed assets.

If the surrendering company surrenders relevant amounts in categories 4–7, the amount surrendered is treated as consisting of: qualifying charitable donations, followed by UK property losses, then excess management expenses and, finally, non-trading losses on intangible fixed assets. These items **must** be surrendered in that specific order.

There is also a further test for the above loss types: the total of the relevant amounts **must exceed** the surrendering company's "gross profits" for the surrender period. In this context, "gross profits" is not the same as the accounting term in a set of accounts; here "gross profits" means taxable profits for that period **before** group relief **or** any deduction in respect of losses, allowances or other amounts of any other period or a deduction by virtue of other amounts carried forward (**except** excess management expenses of prior periods treated as occurring in the next period).

Only current period losses may be group-relieved.

Losses in the above categories can only be utilised against profits of a corresponding accounting period. Thus, where the surrendering and claimant company's accounting periods are not coterminous, **both** the profits and losses have to be apportioned so that **only** the results of the **overlap** period are taken into account. The apportionment is generally calculated on a time basis, unless another method provides a more just and reasonable result.

9.3.3   Method of Relief

The amount of the group relief is as follows:

1. an amount equal to the surrendering company's surrenderable amounts for the surrender period; or
2. if the claim is in relation to only part of those amounts, an amount equal to that part.

However, the surrenderable amount is limited to the lower of:

1. the unused part of the surrenderable amounts (as calculated by the surrendering company); or
2. if less, the unrelieved part of the claimant company's available total profits of the claim period.

Surrendering Company
The unused part of the surrenderable amounts is the amount equal to:

- the surrenderable amount for the overlapping period; less
- the amount of prior surrenders for that period.

To determine the surrenderable amount for the overlapping period:

- take the proportion of the surrender period included in the overlapping period; and
- apply that proportion to the surrenderable amounts for the surrender period.

The surrendering company is given a certain flexibility as regards both the method of relief and the amount to be relieved. To this extent, it may surrender losses **before** setting them against its other profits for the period of the loss (perhaps to relieve profits being charged at a higher effective corporation tax rate elsewhere in the group) **and** it can choose the quantum of its losses that it wishes to surrender. The overriding aim is, where possible, to bring the taxable total profits down to the lower limit for the small profits rate.

Claimant Company
The claimant company must calculate the unrelieved part of its available total profits of the claim period. "Available total profits" are total profits after all possible deductions for the current period **except** amounts carried back from later periods **less** the amount of previously claimed group relief for that period.

The claimant company may claim all or part of the surrendering company's surrenderable amounts. The claimant company is therefore assumed to use its own current year losses or losses brought forward to determine the maximum amount of group relief it may claim. This is a theoretical calculation as HMRC is effectively restricting the availability of the losses to be claimed.

So, the profits available for offsetting group relieved losses are calculated **after all other reliefs for the current period are claimed**, including non-trading deficits on loan relationships and charges. However, group relief is given **before** relief for any amounts brought back from later periods.

Example 9.1

The following companies are in a group:

Company	Accounting period	
A	12 months to 31/12/14	Profit £72,000
B	6 months to 30/6/14	Profit £5,000
C	12 months to 30/9/14	Loss £120,000

Company B claims from company C, which has not previously surrendered any of its losses.

C's "unused part of the surrenderable amount for the overlapping period" is the same as its "surrenderable amount for the overlapping period". This is because there have been no prior surrenders of C's losses. It is:

$$6/12 \times £120,000 = £60,000$$

B's "unrelieved part of the claimant's total profits for the overlapping period" is also the same as its "total profits for the overlapping period". This is because it has made no prior claims. It is:

$$6/6 \times £5,000 = £5,000$$

The amount that can be surrendered/claimed is the smaller of these. It is £5,000.
A then claims from company C, which has made a prior surrender. The calculations are as follows:
The overlapping period is nine months ended 30/9/14.
C's "surrenderable amount for the overlapping period" is:

$$9/12 \times £120,000 = £90,000$$

C's "unused part of the surrenderable amount for the overlapping period" is this amount less the "amount of any prior surrenders attributable to the overlapping period".

Step 1

B's claim from C involves part of C's surrenderable amount for the accounting period ended 30/09/14.

Step 2

The amount of B's claim, £5,000, is treated as being for the overlapping period in that claim, which is six months ended 30/6/14.

The common period of the overlapping periods in B's claim and A's claim is six months ended 30/6/14. The whole of the £5,000 is apportioned to that common period.

Step 3

The total, £5,000, is the "amount of any prior surrenders attributable to the overlapping period".

So C's "unused part of the surrenderable amount for the overlapping period" is £90,000 less £5,000 which is £85,000.

A's "unrelieved part of the claimant's total profits for the overlapping period" is the same as its "total profits for the overlapping period". This is because it has made no prior claims. It is:

$$9/12 \times £72,000 = £54,000$$

If there was another company in the group and A had already claimed group relief from this company for the same overlapping period, the amount of this would have to be deducted from the £54,000.

However, there have been no prior claims and, therefore, the amount that can be surrendered/claimed is the smaller of £85,000 and £54,000, which is £54,000.

Method of Claim

A claim for group relief is generally made on the claimant company's tax return, but there must also be a notice of consent given by the surrendering company. In order to amend a claim, the claimant company must withdraw the original and submit a new claim. All such claims must be made no later than:

1. the first anniversary of the filing date; or
2. 30 days after either the completion of an enquiry into the return, or the amendment of a self-assessment or settlement of the appeal against an amendment.

There is also the facility for group-wide claims/surrenders to be made. It should be noted that no payment is required by the claimant company to the surrendering company in respect of the group relief transferred. However, any such payment, up to the level of the actual loss surrendered, is ignored for corporation tax purposes.

See **Example 9.2** for a detailed example of how to calculate this.

9.3.4 Examples

Example 9.2

A Ltd owns 80% of B Ltd. The following are the results for the year ended 31 December 2014:

	A Ltd	B Ltd
	£	£
Relevant trading income/(loss)	10,000	(25,000)
Net credit on loan relationships	8,000	6,400

Calculate the corporation tax payable by each company.

	£	£
B Ltd		
Trading income		–
Net credit on loan relationships		6,400
Loss relief (section 37 CTA 2010)		(6,400)
Taxable total profits (TTP)		NIL
A Ltd		
Trading income	10,000	
Net credit on loan relationships	8,000	
Total	18,000	
Group relief (section 99 CTA 2010)	(18,000)	
TTP	NIL	

Loss Memo		£
Relevant trading loss for y/e 31/12/2014		25,000
Utilised by way of:		
section 37 against B Ltd		(6,400)
section 99 against profits of A Ltd		(18,000)
Losses to be carried forward under section 45		
against B Ltd's future profits of the same trade		600

Example 9.3

C Ltd owns 90% of D Ltd and 90% of E Ltd. The following are the results for the year ended 31 March 2015.

	C Ltd	D Ltd	E Ltd
	£	£	£
Relevant trading income/(loss)	300,000	90,000	(353,000)
Net credit on loan relationships	6,000	12,000	23,000
Property income	30,000	10,000	18,000
Chargeable gain	110,000	–	–
Qualifying charitable donation	(5,000)		

It is not expected that E Ltd will be profitable in the near future.

Calculate the corporation tax payable by each company after maximum utilisation of any group relief available.

Solution

Upper and lower limits for the small profits tax rate are £500,000 and £100,000.

This is because C Ltd has two associated companies.

In questions of this type, one should begin by looking at the position in the absence of any group relief.

	C Ltd	D Ltd	E Ltd
	£	£	£
Trading income income/(loss)	300,000	90,000	
Net credit on loan relationships	6,000	12,000	23,000
Property income	30,000	10,000	18,000
Chargeable gain	110,000	–	–
Qualifying charitable donations	(5,000)		
TTP	441,000	112,000	41,000
Corporation tax rate	marginal	marginal	20%

The aim is to try to reduce, as far as possible, the profits of each company down to the level of the lower limit (here £100,000).

	C Ltd	D Ltd	E Ltd
	£	£	£
TTP (before group relief)	441,000	112,000	41,000
Less section 99 CTA 2010	(341,000)	(12,000)	
TTP	100,000	100,000	41,000
Corporation tax rate @ 20%	20,000	20,000	8,200

Example 9.4: Corresponding Accounting Period

F Ltd owns 100% of G Ltd. F Ltd's results for the year ended 31 August 2014 show a trading loss of £12,000 and it has no other income.

G Ltd has had the following results for the two years ended 30 November 2013 and 2014:

	Year ended	
	30 Nov 2013	**30 Nov 2014**
	£	£
Trading income	16,000	10,000

Solution

For the year ended 30 November 2013, the overlap period would be 01/09/2013 to 30/11/2013 (although technically apportionment should be in days, we shall work in months for simplicity).

	£
G Ltd (profits 3/12 of £16,000)	4,000
F Ltd (losses 3/12 of £12,000)	(3,000)

Thus G Ltd could make a group relief claim for £3,000 against its profits.

For the year ended 30 November 2014, the overlap period would be 01/12/2013 to 31/08/2014.

	£
G Ltd (profits 9/12 of £10,000)	7,500
F Ltd (losses 9/12 of £12,000)	(9,000)

Thus G Ltd could make a group relief claim for £7,500 against its profits.

The unutilised loss of £1,500 (£12,000 − £3,000 − £7,500) is available for relief in the normal way (either carry back/carry forward, etc.).

9.3.5 Qualifying Group

To avail of group relief, the profit-maker must be in the same "75% group" as the loss-maker. This condition is satisfied in relation to two companies if one company holds, directly or indirectly, not less than 75% of the ordinary share capital of that company, or both companies are 75% subsidiaries of a third company. To establish the 75% relationship, shares held in a share dealing capacity either directly or indirectly are ignored.

A company may establish the 75% holding by aggregating any ordinary shares held directly in that company and also those held indirectly through the medium of a third company. This is illustrated further in the following examples of qualifying loss groups.

Examples of Qualifying 75% Loss Group for UK Group Surrenders

1. The loss-maker is a 75% subsidiary of the profit-maker, or vice versa:

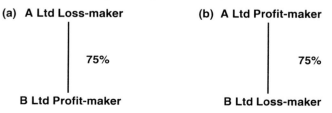

2. Both are 75% subsidiaries of a third company:

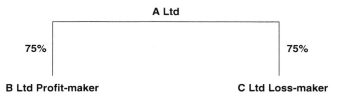

3. Establishing a 75% relationship through the medium of a third company – A Ltd owns 100% of C Ltd and 50% of B Ltd and C Ltd also owns 30% of B Ltd.

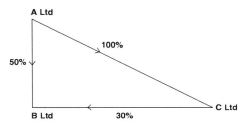

A, B and C Ltd are all members of the same 75% loss group.

For the purposes of the 75% test, an equity holder is defined as any person or company holding "ordinary shares" or a loan creditor of the company in relation to a loan other than a normal commercial loan. "Ordinary shares" is defined as shares other than restricted preference shares. Generally this is all the issued share capital (by whatever name called) of the company, other than capital where the holders have a right to a dividend at a fixed rate but have no other right to share in the profits of the company.

9.3.6 General Conditions

1. In a qualifying group, relief may be passed upwards, downwards or sideways.
2. It is permissible for two or more profit-makers to avail of relief from any one loss-maker.
3. It is not necessary for the profit-maker to make a claim for the full amount of the loss-maker's loss, i.e. the claim may be tailored to suit the individual company's needs. It is not necessary for the profit-maker to make a payment to the surrendering company when claiming group relief.
4. Even though the relationship between the companies is less than 100%, say 80%, all of the loss may be grouped.
5. There is no rule in group relief which requires that losses of the surrendering company must first be applied in reducing other profits arising in the accounting period of the loss. The surrendering company may, accordingly, choose to be liable to corporation tax on any non-trading income or gains of the period while surrendering the full amount of the loss sustained in the period.
6. It is vital to remember that, before availing of group relief, the profit-maker concerned must claim all other relief, except set-off of losses for a subsequent accounting period and terminal relief. Thus, while excess capital allowances, excess management expenses and qualifying charitable donations of the loss-maker are available for set-off against the profit-maker's total profit, it is the profit-maker's total profit after all claims have been made for such items in the accounting period, as well as unutilised losses and capital allowances coming forward from a previous accounting period and any losses incurred and capital allowances claims for the current accounting period, for which group loss relief is being claimed.

7. Group relief is only available where the accounting period of both the loss-maker and profit-maker corresponds wholly or partly. Where they correspond partly (overlap period), the relief is restricted on a time-apportionment basis.
8. The profit-maker must lodge a formal claim to avail of group relief from the loss-maker within two years of the end of the loss-maker's accounting period.
9. The loss-maker must give formal consent for the surrender of the loss.
10. Shares held as trading stock (i.e. by share dealing companies) are excluded for the purposes of calculating the necessary shareholding relationship.
11. Payments to the loss-maker by the profit-maker for availing of the losses are ignored for corporation tax purposes, provided they do not exceed the amount of the loss surrendered, i.e. no tax deduction is available to the profit-maker in respect of the payment and the receipt by the loss-maker is not taxable.

9.3.7   EU Loss Relief

Following the ECJ decision in *Marks & Spencer v. Halsey,* and with effect for accounting periods beginning on or after 1 April 2006, a "qualifying overseas loss" may be surrendered for group relief purposes. For this to occur, the surrendering company must be resident in (i.e. chargeable to tax under the laws of) an European Economic Area (EEA) territory, and it must be:

1. a 75% subsidiary of a UK resident claimant company; or
2. both the claimant and surrendering company are 75% subsidiaries of a third company that is itself UK resident.

For a company to be chargeable to tax in an EEA territory, it must either be:

1. resident in the territory; or
2. carry on a trade in any EEA territory through a permanent establishment.

If the 75% relationship is met, an overseas loss of a non-resident company is available for surrender as group relief provided certain conditions are met, mainly ensuring that the loss and its quantum are of a kind that would have been available if the company had been UK resident and also ensuring that such a loss has not already been relieved in some fashion, particularly in the overseas territory.
Note: the terms of this relief are very restrictive, and the foreign company must have exhausted all possibility of using the losses in its own territory. Generally, this relief will only be available where the trade of the foreign company has ceased and is discontinued.

9.3.8   Consortium Relief

These rules are best demonstrated by the diagrams below.
    If the shares in a single company (C) are held by other companies (M1, M2, etc.), C may be a "company owned by a consortium". In that case, losses of C may be set-off against the profits of M1, M2, etc. and the losses of M1, M2, etc. may be set-off against the profits of C.

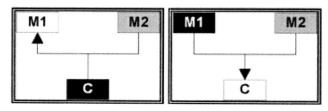

If C is also a member of a group (with its subsidiary S), it may be possible for losses to flow between members of the group and M1, M2, etc. and, if M1 is a member of a group (with its parent, P), it may be possible for losses to flow between members of that group and C.

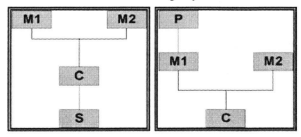

Consortium relief is available as a result of the existence of either:

1.   a consortium, not involving a "link" company; or
2.   a consortium involving a "link" company.

There is also a requirement that the companies concerned are "UK related", meaning either a UK resident or a non-UK-resident company carrying on a trade in the UK through a PE. For accounting periods commencing on or after 12 July 2010, the rules were extended to allow any company established within the EEA to be a link company.

Sections 132 and 133 CTA 2010 allow claims involving companies owned by a consortium. It is based on section 402 ICTA 1988. Group relief may go 'upwards' from a company owned by a consortium to a member of the consortium as follows:

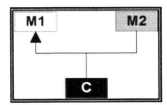

Group relief may also go 'downwards', from a member of a consortium to a company owned by the consortium.

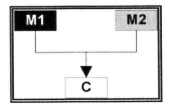

As stated above, a company is owned by a consortium:

1.   if at least 75% of its ordinary share capital is owned by companies (known as members of the consortium), none of whose shareholding is less than 5%, and each member of the consortium is entitled to at least 5% of any profits for distribution and at least 5% of any assets on a winding up (this is known as consortium condition 1); **or**
2.   if a trading company is a 90% subsidiary of a holding company and is not a 75% subsidiary of any company apart from the holding company and, as a result of 1, the holding company is

owned by a consortium, then that trading company is also owned by the consortium (these situations are known as consortium conditions 2 and 3). This is demonstrated in the following diagram:

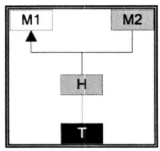

Consortium relief is a loss relief that is available where:

(a) the surrendering company is a trading company (or a holding company) owned by a consortium and **the claimant company belongs to the consortium and vice versa** the claimant company is a trading company (or a holding company) owned by a consortium and **the surrendering company belongs to the consortium; or**

(b) the surrendering company is a trading company or a holding company owned by a consortium, and the claimant company is not a member of the consortium but the claimant company is a member of the same group of companies as a third company ("the link company") and the link company is a member of the consortium (and vice versa).

The following diagrams best denote those situations covered by (b):

Relief may go upwards from company C, owned by a consortium, to company P, which is in the same group as the link company (L).

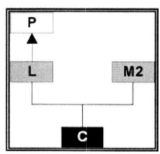

Relief may go downwards from company P, which is in the same group as the link company (L), to company C owned by the consortium.

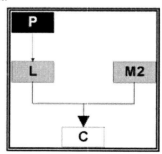

Claims under Consortium Condition 1

If a claimant company makes a claim for group relief based on consortium condition 1, and it is the surrendering company that is owned by the consortium, then the group relief to be given on the claim is limited to the ownership proportion of the surrenderable amount for the overlapping period. This is the same as the calculation at **Section 9.3.3**.

The ownership proportion is the same as the lowest of the following proportions:

1. the proportion of the ordinary share capital of the surrendering company that is beneficially owned by the claimant company;
2. the proportion of any profits available for distribution to equity holders of the surrendering company to which the claimant company is beneficially entitled;
3. the proportion of any assets of the surrendering company available for distribution to such equity holders on a winding up to which the claimant company would be beneficially entitled; and
4. the proportion of voting rights and the extent of control the claimant company holds.

If the claimant is owned by the consortium, then the group relief to be given on the claim is limited to the ownership proportion of the claimant company's total profits of the overlapping period. This is also calculated as shown in **Section 9.3.3**.

The ownership proportion is the same as the lowest of the following proportions:

1. the proportion of the ordinary share capital of the claimant company that is beneficially owned by the surrendering company;
2. the proportion of any profits available for distribution to equity holders of the claimant company to which the surrendering company is beneficially entitled;
3. the proportion of any assets of the claimant company available for distribution to such equity holders on a winding up to which the surrendering company would be beneficially entitled; and
4. the proportion of voting rights and the extent of control the claimant company holds.

If one is dealing with the case where a trading company (T) is indirectly owned by a consortium through a holding company (H), the various proportions referred are calculated by reference to the consortium member's (M1's) interest in H:

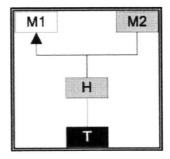

Claims under Consortium Conditions 2 and 3

If one is dealing with a claim by a company that is a member of the same group as the link company for relief from a company owned by the consortium, the position is as follows:

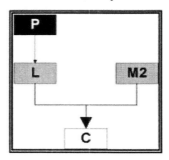

The overlapping period for the claim is still determined by reference to the accounting periods of the actual claimant company (P) and the surrendering company (C). However, for the purposes of the relief, the link company (L) is treated as if it were the claimant. So the "applicable proportion" of the surrenderable amounts is based on L's interest in C in the overlapping period.

If one is dealing with a claim by a company owned by a consortium for relief from a company that is a member of the same group as the link company, the position is as follows:

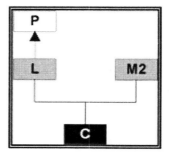

The overlapping period for the claim is also determined by reference to the accounting periods of the claimant company (C) and the actual surrendering company (P). Again the link company (L) is treated as if it were the surrendering company. So in this example the "applicable proportion" of C's profits is based on L's interest in C in the overlapping period.

Note: however, unlike the group relief provisions, a loss made by a consortium-owned company **must be first reduced** by any potential claim it could make against its own other income before it can determine the amount of loss that may be surrendered as consortium relief.

Example 9.5 (This example is for illustrative purposes only.)
H Ltd owns 65% of K Ltd, I Ltd owns 25% of K Ltd and J Ltd owns 10% of K Ltd. Thus K Ltd is a consortium-owned company whose consortium members are H Ltd, I Ltd and J Ltd.
The results for the year ended 31 March 2015 were as follows:

	H Ltd	I Ltd	J Ltd	K Ltd
	£	£	£	£
Trading income	190,000	80,000	1,000	(63,000)
Net credit on loan relationships				13,000

No dividends have been paid or received.

Calculate the corporation tax liability for all four companies assuming that K Ltd does not make any claim to set-off its loss against other income of the same period (section 37 CTA 2010).

Solution

Even though K Ltd is **not** making a claim under section 37, for consortium relief purposes the amount available for surrender **must** be reduced by the potential claim.

Thus, the consortium relief that may be claimed by H Ltd, I Ltd and J Ltd is:

H Ltd	The lower of:	
	(£63,000 − £13,000) × 65% = £32,500	
	£190,000 × 65% = £123,500	£32,500
I Ltd	The lower of:	
	(£63,000 − £13,000) × 25% = £12,500	
	£80,000 × 25% = £20,000	£12,500
J Ltd	The lower of:	
	(£63,000 − £13,000) × 10% = £5,000	
	£1,000 × 10% = £100	£100

Thus H Ltd's corporation tax liability is (note that it has one associated company):

	£
Profits	190,000
Consortium relief	(32,500)
Taxable total profits (TTP)	157,500
Corporation tax:	
£157,500 @ 21%	
Less marginal relief: 33,075	
$(750,000 - 157,500) \times \dfrac{157,500}{157,500} \times 1/400$	(1,481)
Liability (due on or before 1 January 2016)	31,594
I Ltd's corporation tax liability:	£
Profits	80,000
Consortium relief	(12,500)
TTP	67,500

continued overleaf

	£
Corporation tax:	
£67,500 × 20% (due on or before 1 January 2016)	13,500
J Ltd's corporation tax liability:	
Profits	1,000
Consortium relief	(100)
TTP	900
Corporation tax:	
£900 × 20% (due on or before 1 January 2016)	180

K Ltd has unused losses to use in the current period and then carry forward of £17,900 (being £63,000 − £32,500 − £12,500 − £100).

9.4 Worldwide Debt Cap

Legislation was introduced in Finance Act 2009 to cap the tax deduction for finance expenses payable by the UK members of a worldwide group of companies. This applies to accounting periods beginning on or after 1 January 2010. The function of the debt cap is to restrict the tax deduction for interest and other finance expenses in respect of excessive debt owed by UK members of a large group by reference to the group's consolidated finance costs.

9.4.1 Who Does it Apply to?

The debt cap rules apply to large groups of companies where at least one of the group members is either a company resident in the UK for corporation tax purposes, or has a permanent establishment carrying on a trade in the UK known as a 'relevant group company'. A group will be large if at least one member has 250 staff, turnover of at least €50 million and/or a balance sheet total of at least €43 million.

9.4.2 The Gateway Test

The debt cap rules will only apply if the "gateway test" is satisfied. This test is met where the UK net debt of the group exceeds 75% of the worldwide gross debt of the group, subject to two exclusions where:

1. the net debt is less than £3 million; and
2. the company is dormant.

9.4.3 Corporation Tax Disallowance

Where the gateway test is satisfied, it is then necessary to determine if any of the corporation tax deduction is to be disallowed.

The debt cap operates by disallowing the costs of net financing costs by relevant UK companies where the finance expenses on this borrowing exceeds the gross worldwide external group finance cost, i.e. the excess UK financing costs are disallowed.

Questions

Review Questions
(See Suggested Solutions to Review Questions at the end of this textbook.)

Question 9.1

B Ltd has the following results for year ended 31 March 2015:

	£
Tax-adjusted trading profits (i.e. after current year capital allowance claim)	170,000
Bank deposit interest	4,000
Property income	20,000

Unutilised trading losses brought forward from the year ended 31 March 2014 amount to £16,000. Z Ltd is a 100% trading subsidiary of B Ltd. During the year ended 31 March 2015, it incurred tax-adjusted trading losses of £96,000. It also had taxable interest income of £20,000.

Requirement
Compute B Ltd's corporation tax liability for the year ended 31 March 2015 after allowing for any group relief for losses of Z Ltd.

Question 9.2

A Ltd owns 80% of B Ltd's issued share capital and 75% of C Ltd's issued share capital. Results for year ended 31 March 2015 were:

	A Ltd	B Ltd	C Ltd
	£	£	£
Trading profit/(loss)	(90,000)	56,000	48,000
Net credit from loan relationships	1,000	2,000	3,000
Property income	20,000	25,000	2,000
Trading losses forward	(4,000)	–	(26,000)

Requirement
Calculate the corporation tax payable by each company for the year ended 31 March 2015.

Question 9.3

Queen Ltd has two wholly-owned subsidiaries, Pawn Ltd and Rook Ltd. All three are trading companies. Accounts for the year to 31 March 2015 show the following results:

	Queen Ltd	Pawn Ltd	Rook Ltd
	£	£	£
Gross operating profit	297,463	81,000	47,437
Less: Depreciation	12,000	10,000	16,000
Entertaining (customers)	1,350	1,200	1,650
Administration	73,650	61,110	107,373
Interest	11,150	10,720	3,000
	98,150	83,030	128,023
Net profit/(loss) before investment income	199,313	(2,030)	(80,586)

Notes

1. Rook Ltd was incorporated and commenced to trade on 1 April 2014.
2. (i) Interest is analysed as follows:

	Queen Ltd	Pawn Ltd	Rook Ltd
	£	£	£
Accrued 1 April 2014	(1,250)	–	–
Paid	10,000	9,000	2,750
Accrued 31 March 2015	2,000	1,720	250
Interest on overdue PAYE	400	–	–
	11,150	10,720	3,000

   (ii) Pawn Ltd has used its loan to purchase 7% of the share capital of Bridge Ltd, whose income consists mainly of property income from commercial properties. The interest paid by Queen and Rook is trade-related, unless otherwise identified.

3. (i) On 1 September 2014, Queen Ltd received a dividend of £9,000 from a French company in which it has a 20% shareholding. This dividend has not been included in the profit figures above.
   (ii) Queen Ltd also received deposit interest gross of £23,846, which is not included in the profit figures above.

4. Capital allowances

	Queen Ltd	Pawn Ltd	Rook Ltd
	£	£	£
	7,375	3,000	5,627

5. Pawn Ltd had trade losses brought forward of £80,000 at 1 April 2014. Queen Ltd intends to pay a dividend of £10,000 on 9 June 2015.

Requirement
(a) Compute the corporation tax liabilities (if any) of each of the three companies for the year ended 31 March 2015 on the assumption that all available reliefs are claimed to the benefit of the group as a whole.
(b) State the tax consequences for the company of paying the dividend of £10,000.
(c) State the amount of any losses available to carry forward at 31 March 2015 for each company.
(d) State the due date of payment of any corporation tax payable.

Company Chargeable Gains

Learning Objectives

After studying this chapter you will have developed competency in the following:

- Most gains are liable to corporation tax.
- There is a very important exemption from corporation tax on gains on disposal of certain shareholdings. There are a number of conditions, the most important being that the selling company owns at least 10% of the shares, the shares have been held for at least a year and the shares are in a trading company or the holding company of a trading group. This is known as the Substantial Shareholdings Exemption (SSE).
- Companies are in a capital gains tax group (CGTG) if, at each level, there is a 75% holding **and** the top company has an effective interest of at least 51% in the group companies. Compare this with the effective 75% interest required for "group relief groups".
- The main benefit of the CGTG rules is that assets may be transferred from one group member to another without triggering a chargeable gain, i.e. it will be deemed to have been on a no gain/no loss basis. There is a special rule where the asset is trading stock for one of the group companies.
- When the asset is sold outside the group, the base cost is the original cost to the first member of the group to own the asset.
- Where a member of a group leaves the group with an asset that it had acquired from another group member, then the company leaving the group is liable to corporation tax on the gain not triggered when the asset was originally transferred to it.
- While capital losses cannot be group relieved, two members of a CGTG can elect that an asset that has been disposed of outside the group is treated as if it had been transferred between them immediately before the disposal.
- Rollover relief is available in a CGTG.
- There is a range of anti-avoidance rules in relation to pre-entry losses, companies transferring their residence out of the UK and gains realised by certain non-resident companies.
- Companies pay corporation tax on their chargeable gains at the same rate as their trading profits and other income. The chargeable gains are computed in accordance with the usual CGT principles that apply for individuals, except that the company is not entitled to any annual exemption but is entitled to indexation.

■ All companies under common control are "connected persons" for chargeable gains purposes.

■ A company's chargeable gains are reduced by allowable capital losses of the same period and any unrelieved capital losses brought forward from previous accounting periods. Capital gains can also be relieved by current period losses or group relief. Capital losses may only be set against capital gains of the current year or carried forward to set against future capital gains.

■ It should be noted that, in relation to capital losses, they:
  ● cannot be carried back;
  ● cannot be group relieved; and
  ● cannot be offset against trading or other income (except for losses of investment companies on shares in qualifying unquoted trading companies).

10.1 Chargeable Gains Liable to Corporation Tax

10.1.1 UK Resident Companies

Such companies are liable to corporation tax in respect of all capital gains wherever arising. Thus gains on disposal of foreign assets by a UK resident company are liable to UK corporation tax.

10.1.2 Non-resident Companies

A non-resident company is only liable to corporation tax if it carries on a trade in the UK through a PE. The chargeable gains which are assessable are those accruing on the disposal of assets situated in the UK used for the purposes of the trade of the PE.

10.2 Exemption from Tax on Disposal of Certain Shareholdings

There is an exemption from corporation tax for any gain arising when a trading company (or member of a trading group) disposes of the whole or any part of a substantial shareholding in another trading company (or indeed in the holding company of a trading group). The exemption is known as the Substantial Shareholdings Exemption (SSE).

SSE applies not only to actual disposals of shares but also to other types of disposal for capital gains purposes. These include certain deemed disposals and capital distributions on the liquidation of a subsidiary company.

The Main Exemption
The SSE legislation is set out in Schedule 7AC Taxation of Chargeable Gains Act (TCGA) 1992. It contains a main exemption and two secondary exemptions.

The main exemption is contained in Schedule 7AC paragraph 1. It states that a gain accruing to a company (the "holding company") on a disposal of shares in another company (the "subsidiary") is not a taxable gain if the requirements in relation to the following are met:

1. the substantial shareholding;
2. the holding company; and
3. the subsidiary.

This is subject to an overriding anti-avoidance provision contained in paragraph 5 of the Schedule.

Substantial Shareholding

The first requirement, in paragraph 1, in relation to the shareholding itself is that the holding company must have held a "substantial shareholding" in the subsidiary throughout a 12-month period in the two years before the disposal takes place.

The meaning of "substantial shareholding" in this context is set out in paragraph 8 and is a holding of shares in the subsidiary company by virtue of which the holding company:

1. holds at least 10% of the company's ordinary share capital;
2. is beneficially entitled to at least 10% of the profits available for distribution to equity holders of the company; and
3. would be beneficially entitled on a winding-up to at least 10% of the assets of the company available for distribution to equity holders.

As only a 10% holding of shares is required, it is not technically correct to use the terms "holding company" and "subsidiary". The legislation uses the terms "the investing company" and "the company invested in". For ease of understanding, this section will continue to refer to holding companies and subsidiaries, but bear in mind that only a 10%, not a 50%, shareholding is required to qualify for SSE.

Holding Company

The requirements which the holding company itself must meet are contained in paragraph 18. In order to qualify, the holding company must:

- have been a sole trading company or a member of a "trading group" throughout the "qualifying period"; and
- be a sole trading company or a member of a trading group immediately after the time of disposal.

The "qualifying period" referred to in (a) is generally the 12 months prior to the date of disposal.

The terms "trading company" and "trading group" require some consideration. Paragraph 20 states that a trading company means a company carrying on trading activities whose activities do not include, to a substantial extent, non-trading activities.

A "trading group", under paragraph 21, is a group:

- one or more of whose members carry on trading activities; and
- the activities of whose members, taken together, do not include to a substantial extent activities other than trading activities.

SSE will not be available if HMRC can show that there is a substantial element of non-trading activities in a company or group. "Substantial" for these purposes is not defined in the legislation, but it is generally taken to be 20% and this can relate to a percentage of turnover, assets or management time. This is the same test as is used for section 165 TCGA 1992, holdover relief and section 169H TCGA 1992, entrepreneurs' relief.

"Trading" groups often assume that there will be no difficulty in falling below the 20% test when looking at non-trading activities. The problem is that HMRC's interpretation of "non-trading activities" may differ from that of the group or its advisors. Non-trading activities can include items such as the making of intercompany loans.

It can be difficult to meet the requirement at paragraph 18(1)(b) that the holding company be a trading company or a member of a trading group immediately after the time of the disposal.

Subsidiary Company

Paragraph 19 states the requirement for the company being sold. It must:

1. have been a "qualifying company" throughout the 12 months prior to the disposal; and
2. be a qualifying company immediately after the time of the disposal.

A "qualifying company" is a trading company or the holding company of a trading group or subgroup. The same definitions of trading company and trading group discussed above apply.

There is no requirement for the subsidiary company to be UK resident.

Example 10.1

Holdco Ltd owns 100% of the shares in Tradeco Ltd, a qualifying trading company. Holdco Ltd is a holding company with no other investments and has held the shares for five years. Holdco sells the shares in Tradeco Ltd to a third party, realising a gain of £10 million.

Before the disposal, Holdco Ltd is a member of a qualifying trading group that meets the minimum shareholding and minimum holding period conditions. However, Holdco Ltd does not meet the condition at paragraph 18(1)(b), as after the disposal its only asset will be the cash received on the sale.

Holdco Ltd is therefore unable to claim the main exemption in paragraph 1 of Schedule 7AC TCGA 1992.

In the circumstances of this example, the gain on the disposal will benefit from SSE only if the conditions for one of the secondary exemptions are met.

Example 10.2

Owner Ltd, a UK trading company, has owned 100% of Irish Ltd, a trading company resident in the RoI, for the last 10 years. Acquisition Ltd wishes to acquire Irish Ltd. This disposal by Owner Ltd will generate a profit of £5 million. Due to the availability of SSE, Owner Ltd will pay no corporation tax on this gain.

Conversely, if Owner Ltd incurred a capital loss on the disposal, this is not a qualifying capital loss for corporation tax purposes and is thus disregarded as a loss.

10.3   Method of Taxation

Where, for an accounting period, chargeable gains accrue to a company, the chargeable gain is calculated by comparing the gross sale proceeds, net of incidental costs of sale, with the allowable items of expenditure, to include the original cost of the asset (or 31 March 1982 value if held at that time), any enhancement expenditure and any incidental costs of acquisition. As well as the allowable expenditure, a company may also deduct an "indexation allowance". This allowance is intended to reflect the "time value of money" associated with the allowable costs and is calculated by reference to the period of ownership (or 31 March 1982 if owned at that date) up to the date of sale. Unlike for individuals, indexation is **not** frozen at 6 April 1998.

Example 10.3

X Ltd prepares accounts to 31 March each year. In the year ended 31 March 2015, the trading profit was £20,000. During that year, the company sold an asset for £17,000 which it had bought the previous year for £10,000. The indexation factor was a figure of 0.04. The company had a capital loss brought forward of £1,000.

X Ltd year ended 31 March 2015

	£	
Trading profit	20,000	
Chargeable gain (Note)	5,600	
Taxable total profits	25,600	

		£
£25,600 @ 20%		5,120

Note:

   Chargeable gain

	£	£
Proceeds		17,000
Cost	10,000	
Indexation (0.04 × £10,000)	400	
		(10,400)
Gain		6,600
Capital loss b/fwd		(1,000)
Chargeable gain		5,600

10.4 Capital Gains Tax Group: Introduction

A company may be part of a group for CGT purposes – a capital gains tax group (CGTG). This can give important benefits to the companies within the group, namely that assets can be transferred from one group company to another without triggering a chargeable gain, i.e. on a no gain/no loss basis.

What is the definition of a CGTG? **Companies are in a CGTG where:**

1. at each level, there is a 75% holding; and
2. the top company has an effective interest of at least 51% in the group companies.

A company is an effective 75% subsidiary of another company (the parent) if:

1. the company is a 75% subsidiary of the parent, i.e. the parent owns, directly or indirectly, not less than 75% of its ordinary share capital;
2. the parent is beneficially entitled to not less than 75% of any profits available for distribution; and
3. the parent would be beneficially entitled to not less than 75% of the assets of the company available for distribution on a winding up.

(In the examples that follow, it should be assumed that a company is entitled to the same percentage of profits and assets as its shareholding percentage, e.g. where the example indicates 75% shareholding, it should be assumed that there is an entitlement to 75% of profits and assets also.)

Previously, the capital gains reliefs (transfer of asset without triggering a chargeable gain) for groups only applied to UK resident companies.

Now the reliefs can also apply to assets situated outside the UK and which are used in or for the purposes of a trade carried on outside the UK **and** the company is a 75% subsidiary of a UK resident company.

Example 10.4

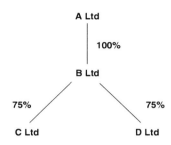

A, B, C and D form a capital gains group.

If A, C and D are UK resident and B is non-resident in the UK (and has no branch in the UK), A, B, C and D still form a capital gains group but the reliefs applying on transfer of assets between group members only apply to transfers between A, C and D. However, if B had a UK branch and if the asset **was** situated in the UK and used by the UK branch, then a transfer of the asset between B and A, C or D would qualify.

The distinction between a group for loss relief purposes and for CGT purposes is that the top company **must have effective** 75% interest for **group relief** purposes (only require effective 51% for CGTGs).

Example 10.5

X Ltd takes over 80% of the ordinary share capital of A Ltd. The new structure is as follows:

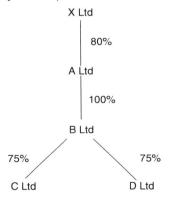

While X does not directly or indirectly own 75% of the ordinary share capital of C or D Ltd, all the companies X, A, B, C and D are members of the one CGTG. This is because B, C and D are clearly 75% subsidiaries of A, and A itself is an effective 75% subsidiary of X. It should be noted, however, that all of the above companies do not form a single group for loss relief purposes, i.e. X, A, B, and A, B, C, D groups form separate groups for loss relief purposes, i.e. X is not common to both these groups.

A company can only be a member of one group. Where the conditions qualify so that it would appear that a company could be a member of two or more groups, it is the link to the principal company that determines to which group it belongs.

Example of group structures incorporating non-resident companies:

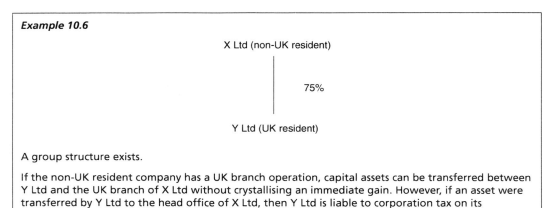

Example 10.6

X Ltd (non-UK resident)

75%

Y Ltd (UK resident)

A group structure exists.

If the non-UK resident company has a UK branch operation, capital assets can be transferred between Y Ltd and the UK branch of X Ltd without crystallising an immediate gain. However, if an asset were transferred by Y Ltd to the head office of X Ltd, then Y Ltd is liable to corporation tax on its chargeable gain.

10.5   Disposal of Capital Assets Within a Capital Gains Tax Group

In general, a transfer of an asset from one member of the group to another is deemed to be for a consideration of such amount that neither a gain nor a loss accrues.

The group is effectively treated as one taxpayer so that a chargeable gain does not arise until the asset is sold outside the group or the company holding the asset leaves the group.

The same rule applies to transfers of capital assets between UK branches of EU resident companies.

Example 10.7: UK-resident companies

X Ltd owns a building which it bought for £1 million, nine months ago. It disposes of it to its parent Y Ltd when it is worth £1.525 million. Indexation for the nine months is a figure of 0.225. Therefore, a gain of £0.3 million arose. Normally this gain would be adjusted and included in the profits of X Ltd. However, this rule ensures that the asset moves at no gain/no loss, i.e. its indexed cost of £1.225 million. Consequently, X Ltd has no chargeable gain and Y Ltd's base cost is £1.225 million. The above unrealised gain falls on the principal company.

Relief for sales between group companies is granted automatically and is compulsory.

10.5.1   Capital Losses

As denoted in **Chapter 9**, capital losses cannot be included in a group relief claim. However, members of a CGTG can elect that an asset which has been disposed of outside the group be treated as if it had been transferred between them immediately before its "outside" disposal. In this situation, the actual disposal is deemed to have been made by the transferee company. This would be beneficial in the circumstances where the transferee company had capital losses of its own available for offset against the deemed chargeable gain or if there were other companies in the group who had not fully utilised the small company band or indeed current year losses unused in other companies. Such an election must be made within two years of the end of the accounting period in which the disposal took place and can be for a percentage of the gain if required.

Prior to the introduction of the above, if one member of a group had a capital loss which it was unable to utilise, and another company in the group wished to sell an asset (to a third party) which would crystallise a chargeable gain, then to utilise the loss, the asset had first to be sold to the group company holding the loss and then sold by that company to the third party.

Thus, the aim should be to ensure that **"net" chargeable gains arise in the company subject to the lowest rate of corporation tax.**

10.5.2 Pre-entry Losses

In the past, companies who anticipated a future gain on the disposal of an asset would acquire a company with capital losses forward. The asset with the gain would be transferred, before the sale, into the company with the losses forward so that the losses forward could be used to shelter the gain. The term "pre-entry losses" refers to losses accruing to the company before entry to the group as well as the potential unrealised losses on the sale of that company's assets. Anti-avoidance provisions were introduced to prevent use of such pre-entry losses. While the provision ensures that these losses cannot be used subsequently by a group which had no previous commercial connection with the company when those losses accrued, that company will be allowed to use those losses itself in the same way that it could have had it never entered the group.

What is a Pre-entry Loss?
The term applies to losses:

- which have arisen in a company prior to it becoming a member of the group, and
- the pre-entry proportion of a loss arising on an asset held at the date a company became a member of a group (even though the loss is crystallised after it became a member). Note that these rules were removed by Finance Act 2011 (see below).

Where a pre-entry asset is sold at a loss after a company joins a group, the pre-entry proportion of the loss is found by calculating the sum of the proportion for each item of allowable expenditure. The proportion for each item of allowable expenditure is given by the formula:

$$A \times (B/C) \times (D/E)$$

where A is the total loss, B the item of allowable expenditure, C the sum of all items of allowable expenditure, D the period from when the expenditure was incurred up to joining the group and E the period from when the expenditure was incurred up to the disposal date.

If the company which joined the group makes an election within two years of the end of the accounting period of the eventual disposal, the above computation is set aside and the pre-entry loss is the lower of:

- a loss calculated with reference to the market value at the date on which the company became a member of the group; and
- the amount of the actual loss which arose on disposal.

Pre-entry Loss Before Joining the Group: Gains from which it is Deductible
Pre-entry losses which actually accrued to the company before it joined the group can be set against:

1. gains on assets disposed of after entry but which were held by the company before entry;
2. a gain arising on the disposal of an asset which was acquired from a non-group member and which has been used for the purpose of the company's trade; or
3. gains on assets disposed of before joining the group.

Loss on Pre-entry Asset: Gains from which it is Deductible
The loss on a pre-entry asset must be split between that part which is pre-entry and can only be offset against the gains specified in the previous paragraph, and that part which is post-entry and can be offset under the normal rules.

Example 10.8
Sing Ltd joined a group, Arkways Ltd, on 1 July 1997. Sing Ltd had purchased land on 1 September 1991 for £800,000 and had spent a further £200,000 on enhancement on 1 August 1994. The land was worth £650,000 as at the date of joining the group. Sing Ltd sold the land on 1 December 2014 for £500,000. Calculate the pre-entry proportion of the capital loss.

Solution
The overall allowable loss would be:

	£	£
Proceeds		500,000
Cost	800,000	
Enhancement	200,000	
		(1,000,000)
Allowable loss		(500,000)

The pre-entry proportion (in the absence of an election):

500,000 × (800,000/1,000,000) × (70/279)	100,358
500,000 × (200,000/1,000,000) × (35/244)	14,344
	114,702

If the land had been sold when Sing Ltd joined the group, then the allowable loss would have been:

	£
Proceeds	650,000
Cost	800,000
Enhancement	200,000
	(1,000,000)
Allowable loss	(350,000)

Thus, with an election, the pre-entry proportion of the loss would be the lower of £350,000 or £500,000 (the actual loss), i.e. £350,000.

As the company wishes to have the **lowest** possible pre-entry proportion, the company would **not** therefore make the election and the pre-entry loss would be £114,702.

The remainder of the actual loss £385,298 (£500,000 − £114,702) is available to set against all capital gains made by Sing Ltd in the same or later accounting periods, without any further restriction.

Pre-entry Capital Losses after a Change of Ownership

Legislation was introduced in FA 2011 simplifying the rules for the treatment of pre-entry capital losses after a company that is or has been a member of a group changes ownership. This removed the pre-entry loss rules which restricted relief for unrealised capital losses realised after the change of ownership. Restrictions on relief for capital losses realised before the change of ownership are still applicable. The amendments made affect pre-entry losses, regardless of whether the loss accrued before commencement of this amendment (19 July 2011) or whether the company which accrued the loss became a member of the relevant group before commencement (19 July 2011).

10.5.3 Transfer of Trading Stock

An asset can be held as a capital asset by one company and as trading stock by another company. For example, one company within a group could hold land as a capital asset as it is a property investment company, while another company could hold it as stock because it is a property dealing company. Therefore, there are special rules for dealing with the situations where an asset is transferred within a group and one company holds it as stock, while the other holds it as a capital asset.

Sold by a Company that Holds it as Capital to a Company that Holds it as Stock

This is dealing with the situation where a company disposes of an investment (held as capital) to a group member that deals in that type of asset (and hold it as stock). Where a member of a group of companies acquires as trading stock an asset from another member in whose hands the asset was not trading stock, the member acquiring the asset is to be treated as having acquired it otherwise than as trading stock and as having immediately appropriated it to use as trading stock.

The result is that the company disposing of the asset is treated as having made neither a gain nor a loss on the disposal and the company acquiring the asset is treated as having:

- acquired it at the price at which the other company acquired it; and
- immediately disposed of it at market value with the resultant charge to tax on the chargeable gain.

Note that the transferee adopts the transferor's asset base cost and indexation.

However, the acquiring company is given the option of bringing the asset (now trading stock) into its trading account at its market value as reduced by the chargeable gain. Effectively, the actual profit on the disposal would then be a profit on income account. It will do so by making an election under section 161(3) TCGA 1992.

As there is the potential here to turn a capital loss into a trading loss, such a loss would only be allowed if there is a true trading intention.

Example 10.9

Investment Ltd transfers a fixed asset to Stock Ltd in December 2004. It had purchased this asset in May 2000 at a cost of £50,000. In December 2004, the market value of the asset was £70,000 and the indexation over this period was £6,000. Stock Ltd had appropriated the asset to its trading stock. In November 2014, Stock Ltd sold the asset for £90,000.

If no election is made

Stock Ltd will have both a chargeable gain (at the date it transferred the asset to trading stock) and a trading profit in November 2014.

	£	£
Chargeable gain		
Deemed proceeds (market value)		70,000
Cost	50,000	
Indexation	6,000	
		(56,000)
Chargeable gain		14,000
Trading profit		
Sale proceeds		90,000

continued overleaf

Base (deemed cost)		(70,000)
Trading profit		20,000
With an election (under section 161(3), TCGA 1992)		
Proceeds (in November 2014)		90,000
Cost	50,000	
Indexation	6,000	(56,000)
Trading profit		34,000

Sold by a Company that Holds it as Stock to a Company that Holds it as Capital

Where a group company transfers an asset which it has held as trading stock to another group company which is to hold it as an asset, then the transferor is deemed to have made a trading profit based on the difference between the market value at the date of the transfer and its original cost, while the transferee company will crystallise a potential chargeable gain when it onward sells the asset outside the group. The gain will be calculated in the normal way as being the difference between the actual proceeds (less incidental costs of sale) and its deemed cost (market value at transfer) plus indexation from the date of transfer.

10.5.4 Rollover Relief

Provided certain conditions are fulfilled, a company may claim that a chargeable gain arising on the disposal of a business asset (the "old asset") may be "rolled over" against the cost of acquiring a replacement business asset (the "new asset").

In this scenario, the disposal of the old asset is deemed to give rise to neither a gain nor loss and the cost of the new asset is reduced by the actual gain that would have arisen but for the rollover relief. In essence, the chargeable gain is "deferred" until such time as the new asset is disposed of (subject to the possibility of a further rollover claim being available).

Full rollover relief is only available provided **all of the disposal proceeds** (not just the chargeable gain) are applied in acquiring the new asset. Any proceeds not re-invested fall to be taxed immediately (provided the amount retained is less than the gain) and the cost of the new asset is reduced by the amount of the gain which was not immediately chargeable.

The conditions which must be satisfied in order for a company to make a rollover claim are:

1. both the old and new asset must be within the same class of assets (see below);
2. the old asset must have been used only for trade purposes throughout the period of ownership and the new asset must be used only for trade purposes; and
3. the new asset must be acquired during the period beginning one year before and ending three years after the date of disposal of the old asset.

The classes of assets include, *inter alia*:

(a) land, buildings and fixed plant and machinery;
(b) ships, aircraft and hovercraft;
(c) satellites, space stations and spacecraft;

Legislation included in FA 2012 allows the Treasury to add or amend existing classes of qualifying assets provided in section 155 TCGA 1992 by statutory instrument rather than by primary legislation ensuring swifter updates to the list as required.

However, for companies (unlike individuals), the list does **not** include **goodwill** or **quotas** as these assets are incorporated within the intangible assets regime for companies.

10.5.4 Holdover Relief

Where the new asset is a "depreciating asset" (an asset with an expected life of 60 years or less at the time of acquisition), the chargeable gain arising on the disposal of the old asset **cannot** be rolled over and is **not** deducted from the cost of the new asset. Instead, the chargeable gain is "held over" or "temporarily deferred" until it becomes chargeable (crystallises) on the earliest of the following three dates:

1. the date on which the new asset is disposed of;
2. the date on which the new asset ceases to be used in the trade; or
3. the 10th anniversary of the acquisition of the new asset.

It should be noted that, if a company were to purchase a non-depreciating asset (within the relevant class) prior to the expiration of the earliest of the above three dates, then it could "convert" the temporary "held-over" gain into a "rolled-over" gain by making a claim to do so.

Rollover relief is also available within a CGTG. If a group member disposes of an asset which is eligible for capital gains rollover (or indeed holdover) relief, then it can treat all the group members as a single entity for claiming such relief (provided, of course, that all relevant conditions are met).

Thus, if other group members acquire a relevant asset within the qualifying period (one year before the disposal or three years afterwards) then the company making the disposal may match the acquisition for rollover/holdover relief purposes.

For it to be effective, both the acquiring company and the disposing company must make the claim.

It should be noted that assets transferred intragroup on a no gain/no loss basis *are not available* to be matched for rollover/holdover relief purposes.

10.6 Disposal of Capital Assets Outside the Group

If there is a disposal of an asset by a member of a group to a person outside the group, and the asset had been acquired by the company making the disposal from another group member, **then the period of ownership for the purpose of both indexation relief and determining the appropriate rate of tax to be applied to the gain (currently there is only one rate) is arrived at by reference to the length of time the asset had been owned by the group as a whole.** Of course, if the asset had originally been acquired prior to 31 March 1982, then the market value at that date will form the base cost for indexation purposes, and indexation will run from 1 April 1982 to the date of sale.

Example 10.10

A Ltd and Y Ltd are UK resident members of a capital gains group. Both companies prepare accounts to 31 December each year. Y Ltd acquired an asset in 1973 at a cost of £10,000 and transferred it to A Ltd in August 1984. On 31 December 2014, A Ltd sold the asset to a non-group company for £200,000. The market value of the asset at 1 April 1982 was £60,000. Indexation factor is 1.80.

When the asset was disposed of by Y Ltd to A Ltd in 1984, no gain arose to Y Ltd.

continued overleaf

A Ltd has a disposal in the year ended 31 December 2014 of an asset with a base cost of £60,000 (i.e. 31 March 1982 valuation).

Computation of A Ltd's liability:

	£	£
Proceeds		200,000
Base cost (MV at 31/3/1982)	60,000	
Indexed at 1.80	108,000	
		(168,000)
Chargeable gain		32,000

10.7 Company Leaving Group: Anti-avoidance Measure

Where a company ceases to be a member of a group of companies within six years of an intragroup transfer, a chargeable gain arises on retained assets that were acquired, on a no gain/no loss basis, from other group members within the previous six years.

The chargeable gain is calculated by deeming that the asset was, in effect, sold and immediately re-acquired by the company leaving the group at its market value at the time of its original acquisition from the other member of the group, i.e. **the gain arising on the original transfer between the group members is triggered**. Indexation relief is applied by reference to that date and not by reference to the date the company actually leaves the group. It should be particularly noted that the gain and corresponding **liability is that of the company leaving the group.** Whilst the gain is calculated as at the date of the original intragroup transfer, it is charged in the accounting period in which the company leaves the group. The cost of future disposals of the assets in question by the company leaving the group will, of course, be the market value attributed to the earlier transfer.

The company leaving the group and the group member from whom the asset was acquired may jointly elect that the capital gain be treated as that of the latter group member. If the relevant conditions are met then, if qualifying, the asset will be available for rollover relief.

Example 10.11

Groups Ltd acquired a freehold property for £100,000 in 1990. In December 2007, when the market value of the property was £460,000 and indexation to date was £26,000, Groups Ltd transferred the property to another CGTG member, Just Ltd, for £375,000. Just Ltd leaves the group on 1 June 2014. Both companies prepare accounts to 31 July.

Calculate the chargeable gains arising in respect of the above transactions.

Solution

2007: No chargeable gain arises as the transfer was to another group member on a no gain/no loss basis.

2014: Gain on Just Ltd would be calculated as:

	£	£
Gross proceeds (market value)		460,000
Cost	100,000	
Indexation	26,000	
		126,000
Chargeable gain		334,000

continued overleaf

This is chargeable on Just Ltd in the year ended 31 July 2014. Note that £375,000 is irrelevant.

If Just Ltd purchased another qualifying asset within the correct timeframe, then it would be able to avail of rollover relief (provided all relevant conditions are satisfied).

Alternatively, both Groups Ltd and Just Ltd could elect that the chargeable gain would be that of Groups Ltd. Once again, the latter company may be able to make a rollover claim provided all relevant conditions are met and the new asset is a qualifying asset.

10.7.1 Finance Act 2011 Changes

Legislation was introduced in FA 2011 to simplify the rules for the calculation of chargeable gains degrouping charges for companies. The measures have effect where companies leave a group on and after the date that FA 2011 received Royal Assent (19 July 2011).

FA 2011 made changes to the way that most degrouping charges are computed in section 179 TCGA 1992. Where a company leaves a group as a result of a disposal of shares by a group company, any degrouping charge will be made by way of an adjustment to the consideration taken into account for calculating the gain or loss on the disposal of shares. A consequence of this is that any exemption or relief that may apply to the share disposal, such as the SSE, will also apply to the degrouping charge.

A provision was also introduced to allow a reduction in the amount of a degrouping charge where it is just and reasonable to do so, taking into account the amount of share capital of the companies being sold, and the circumstances under which the company leaving the group acquired the asset which gives rise to the charge.

Changes were also made to clarify the circumstances when the associated companies' exception applies. The revised exception ensures no chargeable gains degrouping charge is made in respect of an asset that has been transferred between two companies belonging to the same sub-group if those companies leave the group together.

The facility to roll over a degrouping charge on the acquisition of a replacement asset under section 179B and Schedule 7AB TCGA 1992 was repealed, as was section 179A TCGA 1992, which allowed a degrouping charge to be transferred between group companies. To replace this, a minor amendment was made to section 171A TCGA 1992 (election to re-allocate gain or loss to another member of the group) so that it can also apply to a standalone degrouping gain or loss.

10.8 Limits on Certain Losses/Gains

There are anti-avoidance provisions designed to prevent the creation of artificial CGT losses within a group of companies.

Under the CGT transfer of assets provisions, it is possible for assets to be moved within a group without creating CGT liabilities. In these circumstances, it would be possible for a parent company to transfer all the capital assets from its subsidiary to itself without triggering any liability, while at the same time ensuring that the value of its shareholding in the subsidiary is substantially reduced. Similarly, if the parent company received substantial dividends from its subsidiary, the parent company would have reduced the value of the subsidiary but would not be taxable on the dividends.

If a shareholder exercises his control over the company, so that value passes out of that person's shares or those of a connected party, a disposal is deemed to have taken place at market value. Likewise, a loss of disposal arising in this situation will not be an allowable loss.

Similar rules apply for intangible assets.

10.9 Company Ceasing to be Resident

10.9.1 Overview

This legislation is concerned with countering a possible tax avoidance scheme whereby a company would dispose of assets **after** ceasing to be resident in the UK and thus **potentially** avoid any liability to corporation tax in respect of chargeable gains.

10.9.2 Deemed Disposal of all Assets

HMRC imposes an exit charge on companies that change residence from the UK to another jurisdiction. A change of residence by a company ("the relevant company") is to be treated as a disposal and re-acquisition of all assets of the company at their market value on the date of the change of residence ("the relevant time"). This procedure results in a charge to corporation tax in respect of any chargeable gains, net of any losses that may have accrued in respect of such assets. Some of these assets could be shares that would, under normal rules, qualify for the exemption on disposal of certain shareholdings (SSE) outlined above. Deemed disposals under this anti-avoidance law cannot qualify for the exemption.

10.9.3 Exceptions to Exit Charge

The provision does not apply where the assets continue to be used in the UK by a branch or agency of the migrating company (i.e. they are still within the charge to UK corporation tax).

10.9.4 Postponement of Exit Charge

The law provides for a possible postponement of the charge to this exit tax on "foreign assets" situated outside the UK which are used in or for the purposes of a trade carried on outside the UK and where a parent company of the migrating company remains UK resident, i.e. the gain on such assets may be postponed where:

- immediately after the change of residence, the migrating company is a direct 75% subsidiary of another company (referred to as "the principal company");
- the principal company remains a UK resident company; and
- both companies jointly elect in writing to HMRC within two years of the change in residence.

This postponed charge is crystallised if:

- a relevant asset is disposed of within six years of the relevant date of exit and a gain would have accrued on the deemed disposal of the relevant asset at the relevant date;
- the migrating company ceases to be a direct 75% subsidiary of the principal company;
- the principal company ceases to be resident in the UK; or
- the principal company disposes of any of the ordinary shares of the subsidiary.

10.9.5 Exit Charge Deferral

FA 2013 introduced provisions to assist in minimising the relative cash flow disadvantage associated with the transfer of a company's place of management to another EU or European Economic Area (EEA) Member State, when compared to an equivalent intra-UK transfer.

There are two new proposals for deferring payment of the exit charges. Both are optional and are designed to allow, by election, the deferred payment of exit charges subject to certain conditions to ensure that HMRC will receive full payment over time. The tax is calculated at the time of exit under both options and interest accrues on any tax postponed.

The two options are:

1. a straightforward instalment basis whereby the exit tax is spread over a period of six years, thereby minimising the administrative burden upon the company; and
2. the realisation basis which is more directly related to the economic life of assets and the tax is paid in tandem with asset realisations. Companies would be obliged to provide HMRC with an annual statement identifying the realisations of assets in that period and the tax payable in respect of those sales.

These provisions apply retrospectively to allow companies to opt for deferred payment arrangements in respect of exit charges arising on or after 11 December 2012.

Questions

Review Questions
(See Suggested Solutions to Review Questions at the end of this textbook.)

Question 10.1

It is April 2015 and a longstanding client comes into your office to discuss a recent transaction. Paul Kelly is the managing director of Kelly Cars Group Limited, a UK company that holds 100% of the shares in Kelly Luxury Cars GmbH and has done since 2002. Kelly Luxury Cars GmbH is a German company specialising in sourcing and importing luxury cars from Europe for wealthy customers. Both companies have always been trading companies.

Kelly Cars Group Limited sold 95% of the shares of Kelly Luxury Cars GmbH on 25 June 2014 for a significant profit and is using the proceeds obtained to invest in its own future trading activities. The new owners of Kelly Luxury Cars GmbH continued with the existing trade of the company when they bought the shares.

Kelly Cars Group Limited held onto the remaining 5% of the shares for sentimental reasons. However, the company has now been approached by the same buyers and is in negotiations to sell the remaining 5% by the end of May 2015.

Requirement
Explain, with supporting analysis, whether the sale of the 95% shareholding in Kelly Luxury Cars GmbH in June 2014 qualified for substantial shareholdings exemption (SSE). Advise whether the sale of the remaining 5% (for a profit) in May 2015 will qualify for SSE.

If the remaining 5% is to be sold at a loss, consider what recommendation you might make to the company.

Question 10.2

You are a tax senior in a mid-sized Belfast practice. One of the clients recently assigned to you is the Solar Group ("Solar"). Solar is a trading company that has four wholly owned trading subsidiaries – Neptune Ltd. ("Neptune"), Venus Ltd. ("Venus"), Saturn Ltd. ("Saturn") and Mercury Ltd. ("Mercury"). At a recent meeting with the managing director you discussed the group's tax affairs. The managing director is keen for the group's corporation tax affairs to be finalised as soon as possible and is anxious to know what the group's liability is for the year ended 31 March 2015. All companies in the group prepare accounts to 31 March and none paid tax in instalments in 2014.

During the year ended 31 March 2015, Solar and its subsidiaries had the following results:

- Solar made a trading profit of £67,550 and has unused capital losses carried forward from earlier years of £375,000.
- Neptune made a trading profit of £47,087. At 31 March 2014 it had trade losses available to carry forward of £75,000.
- Venus made a trading profit of £72,680 and also made a capital gain of £55,260. At 31 March 2014 it had capital losses to carry forward of £47,000.
- Saturn made a trading profit of £112,559, as adjusted for tax purposes, before deducting capital allowances. The capital allowances for the period are £29,766.
- Mercury made a trading loss of £9,236 before deducting capital allowances of £37,257. At 31 March 2014, the company had trade losses available to carry forward of £27,073, together with capital losses available to carry forward of £35,000.

You have been provided with the following additional information:

(a) You have been advised that it is the intention to sell Saturn and an offer of £300,000 has been received from an interested party, Y Ltd. It is almost certain that this offer will be accepted within the next week. Y Ltd intends to inject additional funding into Saturn to assist them in purchasing additional freehold property and fixed plant and machinery and so expand Saturn's trade.

    The original cost of Solar's investment in Saturn in June 1996 was £55,000. Indexation allowance from 1996 to now is 65%. The principal assets of Saturn are its freehold property and goodwill which has been created over a number of years. The property was originally bought by Solar in 1980 for £40,000 and transferred to Saturn in March 2007 when its value was £230,000.

    Its current value is £350,000 and, in March 1982, the property was worth £50,000. Indexation allowance from 1980 to 2007 is 100%, from 1982 to 2007 is 107% and from 1982 to now is 122%.

(b) Due to Neptune's continued expansion, it requires larger business premises. Solar therefore plans to transfer to Neptune a suitable freehold property that it no longer requires and which it currently rents out. If sold to an unconnected third party, a capital gain of £100,000 would arise.

    Neptune, in turn, proposes to sell the property it currently occupies outside the group. This property was acquired from Solar 10 years ago. X Ltd, an unconnected third party, has been identified as a possible purchaser. A capital gain of approximately £150,000 will be realised from the sale.

(c) You have also been advised that, as part of the future marketing strategy of the group, it has been decided to acquire a new company, Mars. Mars has significant trading losses in excess of £500,000, which are proving attractive to the Solar Group. The board intends to focus on substantially different products aimed at new customer types and markets.

Requirement

The board of directors would like you to draft a report providing information on the following specific areas:

(a) The group's corporation tax liability for the year ended 31 March 2015, making use of all available claims and elections and advising on the due date for payment of any tax liabilities arising.

(b) Advice in relation to the tax implications of the proposed sale of shares in Saturn, in particular:
  (i) the amount of the capital gain arising in respect of the sale of Solar's shareholding in Saturn and whether the substantial shareholdings exemption will be available;
  (ii) any other tax implications arising from Saturn leaving the group.

(c) Advice in relation to the proposed transfer of the freehold property from Solar to Neptune and the sale by Neptune of its current property, in particular:
  (i) the tax implications arising out of the proposed transfer as part of Neptune's expansion plans;
  (ii) mitigating the gain arising on the sale of Neptune's property.

(d) Acquisition of Mars – advise the board on the availability for relief after acquisition of the trading losses that exist in this company.

Question 10.3

Pharma Research Group ("PRG") is the holding company of a group of companies, is Australian tax resident and holds 100% of the shares in each of two subsidiary companies, Pharma Research Ireland Limited ("PRI") and Pharma Research UK Limited (PRUK). The two subsidiaries are incorporated and tax resident in the UK.

PRG is a global service provider of cost-effective and comprehensive pharmaceutical products with operations in the USA, Ireland, the UK and Europe.

For some reason, when PRI was set up, it was incorporated in the UK even though this company does not have any UK customers or any trading presence in the UK, though the board does currently hold its meetings in London. All UK customers are serviced through PRUK.

PRI is extremely profitable and as it is UK incorporated, it is automatically UK resident, and is therefore subject to UK corporation tax (in addition to corporation tax payable in Ireland, where it has a permanent establishment).

There is no commercial reason for the company to be UK resident. It currently has a branch operation in Dundalk and because of this the board of directors is considering migrating the residence of the company to Ireland from 1 December 2015 in order to operate out of that branch, as the company's entire customer base is Irish and there is a clear strategic fit with Ireland.

The company have already looked at the residence issue in depth and while the company would be dual resident in both the UK and Ireland, under the tie-breaker clause in the UK and Ireland double taxation agreement, PRI would be deemed to be solely Irish resident for tax. The board is aware that future meetings will have to be held in Ireland if the company is to successfully migrate, so proving Irish tax residency won't be an issue.

Requirement

The board has asked you to address the potential exit charges and other relevant corporation tax issues that could arise if this migration went ahead and the date these would be required to be paid. To assist with this, see the company's most recent statement of financial position below.

You should assume that the rates of corporation tax in FY 2015 are the same as those in FY 2014 and that the statement of financial position (SFP) of PRI is representative of its SFP as at the planned date of migration on 1 December 2015. PRI's normal accounting period end is 1 September. Assume an indexation factor of 270.0 for the month of December 2015.

Statement of Financial Position – Pharma Research Ireland Limited as at 30 September 2015

Assets	£
Non-current assets:	
Property – original cost*	130,000
Plant and machinery**	43,000
	173,000
Current assets:	
Inventories***	15,000
Cash	527,000
Trade receivables	55,000
	597,000
Total assets	770,000
Equity and Liabilities:	
Share capital	100,000
Retained earnings	472,000
Total equity	572,000
Non-current liabilities:	
Long-term borrowings	88,000
Current liabilities:	
Trade and other payables	83,000
Current portion of long-term borrowings	12,000
Current tax payable	15,000
Total current liabilities	110,000
Total liabilities	198,000
Total equity and liabilities	**770,000**

* Purchased 1 March 2003, current market value of £1,500,000.

** Market value of £82,000 though no single item has an original cost or a current market value greater than £6,000.

*** Inventories have a market value of below accounting cost.

The trade of the company commenced on 1 March 2003 and goodwill has been valued at £300,000.

Companies in Liquidation

Learning Objectives

After studying this chapter you will have developed competency in the following:

- The responsibilities of a liquidator in a liquidation in the context of corporation tax.
- HMRC's position as an unsecured creditor of the company in liquidation.

11.1   Liquidation/Winding Up of a Company

When a company becomes **insolvent**, there are various courses of action that it can take. There are essentially four methods which can be adopted, which are not necessarily mutually exclusive:

1. Compulsory winding up by a court.
2. Voluntary winding up initiated by the creditors.
3. Voluntary winding up initiated by the secured creditors, such as a bank.
4. The court could make an administration order.

When a company commences to be wound up, it ceases to be the beneficial owner of its assets and the custody and control of those assets pass to the liquidator.

A company may also be put in liquidation when it is **solvent**. This route may be desirable for the shareholders in group reconstructions or if the shareholders simply wish to extract their capital from the solvent company.

11.2   Status of Liquidator

A liquidator is neither an agent of the company nor of the creditor. Furthermore, he is not an officer of the company.

Prior to liquidation, a company is both the legal and beneficial owner of its assets. When the company is put into liquidation, it ceases to be the beneficial owner and it no longer retains control of the assets. The liquidator holds the assets for the purposes of distributing them, or what remains of them, to the ultimate beneficial owners.

11.3 Corporation Tax Consequences of a Liquidation

11.3.1 Liquidator's Responsibilities

A company is chargeable to corporation tax on profits arising in the winding up of a company. During the course of the winding up, the liquidator has the responsibility of accounting for corporation tax on income received and on capital gains arising on disposal of chargeable assets. Therefore, the liquidator must pay the corporation tax by the due date and submit any corporation tax returns. It should be noted that profits during the winding-up remain chargeable to corporation tax on the company **and not** on the liquidator.

11.3.2 End of an Accounting Period for Corporation Tax

When a company commences to be wound up, an accounting period ends and a new one begins; thereafter an accounting period may not end otherwise than on the expiration of 12 months from its beginning or by the completion of the winding up. The ending of an accounting period can affect the following:

- the due date for payment of corporation tax;
- the date the company's corporation tax return must be submitted; and
- the extent to which trading losses may be offset against the total profits of the immediately preceding period, or against a fellow group member's total profits on a claim to group relief.

11.3.3 Ranking of Creditors and Revenue Priority

On the occasion of a company being put into liquidation, the ranking of creditors in respect of payments due to them is as follows:

1. secured creditors under fixed charges
2. all costs, charges and expenses properly incurred in the winding up
3. remuneration and expenses of the liquidator
4. preferential creditors (employee arrears of pay and holding pay, up to four months)
5. floating charges
6. unsecured creditors (including PAYE, NIC, VAT)
7. shareholders.

Corporation tax arising prior to the appointment of the liquidator is an unsecured claim; after his appointment, it is an administration or liquidation expense and, strictly speaking, must be paid ahead of the liquidator's remuneration.

11.3.4 ESC C16

Where a company has ceased business it may ask the Registrar of Companies to strike it off. Prior to 1 March 2012, the company could apply to HMRC for Extra Statutory Concession C16 to apply. ESC C16 was a concession granted by HMRC that allowed the directors of a company to effectively wind up a solvent company themselves without appointing a liquidator and pass the surplus funds to the shareholders as capital receipts rather than dividends. This was a very valuable relief as the capital gain would suffer a maximum tax charge of 28%, with the possibility of a 10% charge if entrepreneurs' relief was available, compared to a charge of up to 30.56% on the net amount received should it be treated as an income distribution for a 45% taxpayer (see **Chapter 12**).

From 1 March 2012, ESC C16 has now been enacted in legislation and as such it is no longer a relief that needs to be applied for. The legislation has introduced a £25,000 cap whereby any distributions which are made on or after 1 March 2012 in anticipation of a dissolution and which exceed £25,000 will be subject to income tax and not CGT.

11.3.5 Other Matters

During the liquidation period, it is unlikely that the company will be carrying on a trade. Hence, this will more than likely mean that the liquidator's costs will **not** be relievable (unless they can form part of the incidental costs of disposal).

Another important point to look out for is that a close company in liquidation **may** fall to be treated as a close investment holding company (CIHC) (subject to meeting the usual conditions) with the resultant impact of **not** being able to avail of the small profits rate. Nevertheless, a company will not fall to be treated as a CIHC in the accounting period immediately following the commencement of a winding-up if it were **not** a CIHC in the accounting period immediately before liquidation commenced. However, in practical terms, a company may not be able to avail of this relief if there is a very short gap between the end of a period in which a company was not a CIHC and the commencement of winding up. Care must be taken to ensure, as far as possible, that the company can avail of the above relief, where applicable.

Any distributions to shareholders during the liquidation are capital distributions. This means that they are subject to CGT in the hands of individual shareholders. In the hands of corporate shareholders, the distributions received during the winding up period will be treated as chargeable gains and it is possible that SSE will be available.

Question

Review Question
(See Suggested Solution to Review Questions at the end of this textbook.)

Question 11.1

It is early July 2014 and you are Steven James, a recently qualified Chartered Accountant working in the tax department of Mason & Co, a small two-partner accounting firm in Bangor. John Mason, the managing partner of the firm, calls you into his office.

"Steven, tomorrow morning I'm going out to meet with one of our larger clients, Kay & Sons Ltd, and I need your help to prepare for the meeting. James Kay, the controlling shareholder of the company, is just off the phone with me and he has provided me with a list of issues he'd like to discuss, though I'd like you to look at one specifically.

"The main business of the company is property dealing and development. However, as I'm sure you can appreciate, James and his fellow shareholders have become somewhat disenchanted with the property business after the bottom fell out of the market in 2008. They have spent the last few years selling off what was left of their property and land banks and they feel that they are now in position to cease the trade and liquidate the company. Luckily for them, they were not holding too much property as stock when the market fell and what was still in hand was not too highly geared. The shareholders should therefore still see a reasonable return on their investment given the high cash balance in the company. The company should make a distribution to them in the region of £1,000,000."

Requirement

Address the tax implications of the company entering into voluntary liquidation on 1 August 2014 and outline the tax treatment of the individual shareholders with regard to the liquidation. You should assume that the company's normal accounting period end is 31 March.

Taxation of Directors/Shareholders

Learning Objectives

After studying this chapter you will have developed competency in the following:

- Explain and calculate taxes arising for company directors as a direct result of holding a directorship.

12.1 Introduction

Many UK companies, particularly in Northern Ireland, are family-owned and managed. In family companies, the directors are also likely to be shareholders. As a consequence of this, directors of family companies tend to have control over their own remuneration packages, and should consider the tax effects of such packages on both the company and on themselves.

Legislation has been put in place to prevent directors from arranging their remuneration in such a way as to avoid taxation. One example of this is in relation to National Insurance contributions (NICs). As students know from their CAP 1 studies, Class 1 NICs are calculated by reference to the earnings period. This means that an employee in receipt of a monthly salary has their NICs calculated for each month in isolation (in contrast to the calculation of their income tax liability, which is carried out on a cumulative basis).

Example 12.1

Rhonda's gross monthly salary for 2014/15 is £2,000. In March 2015, she receives a bonus of £5,000 on top of her normal salary. The primary Class 1 NICs are calculated as follows:

April 2014 – February 2015	£
Gross salary	2,000
Less primary threshold	(663)
Earnings on which NICs are due	1,337
Class 1 NICs due @ 12%	160

Monthly NICs liability for the 11 months from April to February is, therefore, £160. So the total for the period is £160 × 11 = £1,760.

continued overleaf

March 2015	
	£
Gross salary	2,000
Bonus	5,000
Total earnings for period	7,000
Class 1 NICs due (£3,488 − £663) @ 12%	339
Class 1 NICs due (£7,000 − £3,488) @ 2%	70
Total Class 1 NICs due	409
Rhonda's total annual NICs are therefore £1,760 + £409 = £2,169	

As can be seen from this example, Rhonda's NIC liability in March 2015 is increased as the gross earnings for that period are in excess of the upper earnings limit for the month of £3,489. This is something that could be exploited by directors with control over their remuneration, as they could structure their salary in such a way as to utilise the upper earnings limit to restrict their exposure to primary Class 1 NICs.

For this reason, directors are subject to the annual earnings basis for the purposes of calculating their primary Class 1 NICs liability. This has the effect of calculating their NICs on a cumulative basis, so that they only benefit from the lower 2% rate of NICs when their total annual salary (including bonuses and other similar payments) exceeds the upper earnings limit.

Example 12.2

Using the same details as above, this time assume Rhonda is a director and so subject to the annual earnings basis. The primary Class 1 NICs are calculated as follows:

April 2014 – March 2015	
	£
Gross annual salary (£2,000 × 12)	24,000
Bonus in March 2015	5,000
Total annual earnings	29,000
Less primary threshold	(7,956)
Earnings on which NICs are due	21,044
Class 1 NICs due @ 12%	2,525

Note: none of the earnings have been charged at 2% as the annual earnings are less than the annual upper earnings limit of £41,865. As a result, the total NICs charge for the year has been increased by £356.

12.2   Tax on Remuneration

As stated above, when a director who is also a shareholder of a company is planning their own remuneration strategy, they will want to consider the taxation impact on both the company and themselves. There is no point in saving £3,000 in income tax on profits extracted if the company is exposed to an additional corporation tax liability of £5,000 as a result.

The first consideration when developing a remuneration strategy is the level of profits to be extracted. It may be more tax-efficient to retain most of the profits within the company, where they will be subject to corporation tax at a maximum rate of 21%, rather than extracting them and exposing them to income tax at rates of up to 45%. FA 2009 announced an additional 50% rate of income tax for incomes exceeding £150,000 for the tax year 2010/11, resulting in three rates of income tax, depending on income levels, of 20%, 40% and 50%. This additional rate was enacted by FA 2010. It has since been legislated in FA 2012 that the additional rate of income tax is reduced from 50% to 45% from 6 April 2013. Income tax rates are an annual tax and, therefore, rates are not enacted in advance and can be revised annually. Also, if profits are retained, this will increase the value of the company, and so the value of the shareholdings in the company. This will increase any chargeable gain on the future disposal of those shares, but such a disposal could qualify for entrepreneurs' relief (see **Chapter 18**) and/or be exposed to lower CGT rates.

However, it will be the case that most directors will need to extract some level of profit to fund their living expenses, and the rest of this section will consider the various ways in which this may be achieved.

12.2.1 Salary or Dividend

When profits are extracted by way of salary, NICs will be charged at the secondary rate (currently 13.8%) on the company and at the primary rate (currently 12%) on the recipient (2% on earnings in excess of upper earnings limit). The recipient will also be exposed to an income tax charge at up to 45% of the gross salary. The total cost of the salary, i.e. gross salary plus secondary NICs, will be an allowable deduction for corporation tax purposes.

When profits are extracted by way of dividends, then no NICs are payable by either the company or the recipient. Income tax is restricted to a maximum of 37.5%, and the top effective rate of tax (after taking the notional tax credit attaching to dividends into account) is 30.56% (see below). However, dividends are not an allowable deduction for corporation tax purposes, as they must be paid out of the distributable reserves of the company.

Example 12.3: Effective Rates of Tax on Dividend Payments

UK dividends have a 10% notional tax credit attached. Generally when dividends are being determined, a net dividend is decided upon and this amount is "grossed up" at 100/90. The appropriate rates available for dividends are applied to this grossed-up amount and the resulting liability is reduced by the 10% notional tax credit.

Ethan is the sole shareholder of Tempest Ltd. He wishes to withdraw £9,000 from the company by way of dividend. There are sufficient distributable reserves.

		£
Net dividend		9,000
Gross dividend	(9,000 × 100/90)	10,000
Notional tax credit	(10,000 × 10%)	1,000

It is the gross dividend that will be included in Ethan's tax computation for the purposes of determining his marginal tax rate. (Note that dividend income is taxed as the top slice of income.) The effective rate of taxation applied to this dividend will depend on his marginal rate of income tax:

continued overleaf

	Basic rate taxpayer	Higher rate taxpayer	Top rate taxpayer
Marginal income tax rate	20%	40%	45%
Dividend rate	10%	32.5%	37.5%
	£	£	£
Gross dividend	10,000	10,000	10,000
Tax @ dividend rate	1,000	3,250	3,750
Less: notional tax credit	(1,000)	(1,000)	(1,000)
Tax payable on dividend	Nil	2,250	2,750
Effective tax rate	Nil	25%	30.56%

The effective tax rate is calculated with reference to the net dividend. The net dividend is £9,000.

The tax charge on this dividend if Ethan is a higher rate taxpayer is £2,250.
The effective tax rate is therefore (2,250/9,000) × 100 = 25%.
The tax charge on the dividend if Ethan is a top rate taxpayer is £2,750.
The effective tax rate is therefore (2,750/9,000) × 100 = 30.56%.

These effective rates are regularly used by practitioners when referring to the tax charged on dividends and it is important to understand them.

When determining the most tax-efficient method of profit extraction, the effect of corporation tax and NICs must therefore be considered. As dividends are not deductible for corporation tax purposes, this means that they are not automatically more tax-efficient than salary payments.

Example 12.4

Rory is the director/shareholder of Mill Ltd. The company's taxable profit for the year ended 31 March 2015 is £600,000 and Rory would like to extract £50,000 by way of either a bonus or dividend. Mill Ltd has no associated companies and Rory's salary from the company is £150,000 in the 2014/15 tax year. (*Note:* no personal allowance is available to Rory as his income is in excess of £120,000).

Extraction by way of bonus:

Mill Ltd		£	£
Profits			600,000
Less: remuneration			(50,000)
Taxable total profits (TTP)			550,000
Corporation tax:	£300,000 @ 20%	60,000	
	£250,000 @ 21.25%	53,125	
		113,125	(113,125)
Profits after tax			436,875
Secondary NICs	£43,937 @ 13.8%	6,063	
Total tax charge		119,188	

continued overleaf

Rory

Gross salary			43,937
Primary Class 1 NICs	£43,937 @ 2%	879	
Income tax	£43,937 @ 45%	19,772	
Total tax/NICs		20,651	(20,651)
Income after tax			23,286
Total tax		139,839	
Retained profits			460,161
Effective rate of tax	(139,839/600,000) × 100		23.31%

Extraction by way of dividend:

Mill Ltd

TTP			600,000
Corporation tax:	£300,000 @ 20%	60,000	
	£300,000 @ 21.25%	63,750	
Total tax charge		123,750	(123,750)
Profits after tax			476,250
Profits after dividend	£476,250 − £50,000		426,250

Rory

Net dividend			50,000
Gross dividend	£50,000 × 100/90	55,556	
Income tax:	£55,556 @ 37.5%	20,833	
Less notional tax credit	£55,556 × 10%	(5,556)	
Total tax charge	(NB: same as £50,000 @ 30.56%)	15,277	(15,277)
Income after tax			34,723
Total tax		139,027	
Retained profits			460,973

The effective rate of tax ((139,027/600,000) × 100) is 23.17%

As can be seen from the above example, where a company is paying corporation tax at the marginal rate and the director is paying tax at the top rate, salary may be more tax-efficient. However, it is generally the case that, where a company is paying corporation tax at the small profits rate (20%), dividends tend to be more tax-efficient, especially where the profits extracted are relatively modest.

Example 12.5

Thomas is the director/shareholder of Soap Ltd. The company's taxable profit for the year ended 31 March 2015 is £300,000 and Thomas would like to extract £40,000 by way of either a bonus or dividend. Soap Ltd has no associated companies and Thomas's salary from the company is £50,000 for the 2014/15 tax year.

Extraction by way of bonus:

Soap Ltd		£	£
Profits			300,000
Less: remuneration			(40,000)
TTP			260,000
Corporation tax	£260,000 @ 20%	52,000	(52,000)
Profits after tax			208,000
Secondary NICs	£35,149 @ 13.8%	4,851	
Total tax charge		56,851	

Thomas			
Gross salary			35,149
Primary Class 1 NICs	£35,149 @ 2%	703	
Income tax	£35,149 @ 40%	14,060	
Total tax/NICs		14,763	(14,763)
Income after tax			20,386
Total tax		71,614	
Retained profits			228,386
Effective rate of tax	(71,614/300,000) × 100		23.87%

Extraction by way of dividend:

Soap Ltd			
TTP			300,000
Corporation tax	£300,000 @ 20%	60,000	(60,000)
Profits after tax			240,000
Profits after dividend	£240,000 − £40,000		200,000

Thomas			
Net dividend			40,000
Gross dividend	£40,000 × 100/90	44,444	
Income tax	£44,444 @ 32.5%	14,444	
Less: notional tax credit	£44,444 × 10%	(4,444)	
Total tax charge	(NB: same as £40,000 @ 25%)	10,000	(10,000)
Income after tax			30,000
Total tax		70,000	
Retained profits			230,000

The effective rate of tax ((70,000/300,000) × 100) is 23.33%.

As can be seen from the above examples, it will be necessary to carry out detailed calculations to determine the most tax-efficient method. This is especially important where profits/income straddle tax rate bands. The following should also be considered:

1. Dividends are not earnings and so the level of tax-relievable pension contributions that a director may make will be restricted if their remuneration is mainly in the form of dividends (contributions of up to £3,600 may be made irrespective of earnings). It may be possible to reduce the impact of this restriction on the growth of a pension pot by making a company contribution on behalf of the director. Indeed, this can be a very tax-efficient form of remuneration for directors/shareholders of family companies.
2. A small salary should always be paid to protect entitlement to contributions-related social security benefits, such as the State Pension.
3. The company must have sufficient distributable reserves to cover any proposed dividends.
4. If the director is employed under an "explicit" employment contract then the National Minimum Wage must be applied, increasing the profits which must be extracted as salary.

12.2.2 Benefits in kind

A limited company is a separate legal entity from its directors. This means that where a director meets personal expenditure with company funds, there will be a benefit in kind that will be charged to tax and NICs on the director as employment income. The taxation of benefits in kind is studied at CAP 1; however, there are certain items that tend to apply more specifically to company directors.

Unlike other employees, directors are subject to the benefit in kind provisions even where their earnings are less than £8,500 per annum (unless they, together with their associates, own 5% or less of the ordinary share capital of the company and either work full-time or work for a charitable or non-profit-making body).

Where a company meets the personal expenses of a director, these are taxable expense payments. The payments should be included on the director's Form P11D and subject to income tax. Class 1 NICs will also be payable and should be collected through the payroll. The taxable amount may be reduced where there is legitimate business use.

Example 12.6
Cora is a director of Firefly Ltd and the company pays her home telephone bills. Cora is the subscriber. The total amount paid in 2014/15 was £800, including line rental of £100. Cora has determined that about 10% of the calls made from her home telephone were business calls relating to Firefly Ltd's trade (and has evidence for this). What is the PAYE/NICs treatment?

PAYE Income Tax
The full amount of line rental plus 90% of the cost of calls (i.e. the private portion) should be declared on form P11D. Income tax will therefore be charged on an amount of £730.

NICs
No Class 1A NICs are due as the company is meeting Cora's personal expenditure rather than providing a benefit. Class 1 NICs are however due and will be collected by putting an amount equal to the full line rental, plus 90% of the cost of calls through the payroll. The total amount on which Class 1 NICs are therefore due is £730.

Care should be taken to ensure that any company credit cards used by a director are not used for personal expenditure, as this would give rise to a taxable expense charge.

Assets transferred by the company to the director will give rise to a taxable benefit in kind which should be reported on Form P11D. Such a transfer will be subject to income tax and Class 1A NICs.

Certain payments or transfers made by a "close" company to a participator are treated as distributions in the hands of the participator for income tax purposes (see **Chapter 7**). When the participator is also a director, such payments/transfers will instead be taxed as employment income.

Example 12.7
Serenity Ltd is a family-owned and managed company. The shareholders are Neil (who has a shareholding of 40%), his sister Carol (who has a shareholding of 40%) and his brother David (who has a shareholding of 20%). Both Neil and Carol are directors in the company. David is not a director or employee of the company.

Serenity Ltd pays the rent on each of the shareholders' houses. As Neil and Carol are directors of the company, they will be subject to an income tax charge based on the benefit in kind rules for the provision of living accommodation.

As David is not an employee of the company, the rent paid on his house will be grossed up and taxed as a distribution in his hands under the rules relating to participators.

12.2.3 Loans to Participators

Loans by a close company to a participator (including directors) can give rise to a potential charge on the company under section 455 CTA 2010 (see **Chapter 7**). The recipient, if he/she is a director, will be treated as having received a beneficial loan under the benefit in kind rules, rather than a distribution, and taxed accordingly. It should be noted that such a loan can arise where a director's current account in the company becomes overdrawn. Even where no charge arises under section 455 CTA 2010 (e.g. where the overdraft is repaid within nine months of the accounting year-end), there may still be a taxable benefit in kind.

Example 12.8
Peter is a full-time working director of Bap Ltd, in which he has a shareholding of 60%. Bap Ltd prepares its accounts to 31 December. On 6 May 2014, Peter purchased a painting for £10,000. As he had insufficient funds, he borrowed this amount from the company. On 5 March 2015, he repaid the £10,000 to the company.

As the amount borrowed is repaid within nine months of the year end, there is no charge under section 455 CTA 2010.

However, the loan is subject to the benefit in kind rules and Peter will be charged income tax on the cash equivalent on the loan. Bap Ltd will also have a Class 1A NICs liability in respect of the loan.

FA 2013 introduced anti-avoidance provisions whereby the loan repayment rules were reinforced. It is intended that relief is only given for genuine repayments as opposed to instances where the loan is repaid and shortly there after drawn down again.

12.3 Pensions

Pension contributions can be a very tax-efficient form of remuneration for directors. They qualify for tax relief on personal contributions in the same way as other employees but may also have the option of more significant employer contributions.

The tax relief available on pension contributions is covered at CAP 1, but it is worth mentioning here that a company contribution into a director's pension scheme is a deductible expense for corporation tax provided it is wholly and exclusively for the purposes of the trade. When determining whether a company contribution is excessive (thereby failing the wholly and exclusively test), the complete remuneration package and pattern of profit extraction by the director will be taken into account.

As pension funds benefit from tax-free growth, extracting profits in this way can be a more tax-efficient method than taking a salary or dividend. However, it is only really useful for those who can afford to lock the profits into their pension pot until they retire. Also, it must be remembered that the funds eventually available to draw down from the pension will depend on the performance of the fund investments and may also be affected by changing legislation.

The annual allowance for pension contributions for an individual for the 2014/15 tax year is £40,000. This is the maximum level at which an individual can benefit from tax relief; however, there is no limit on the amount an individual can save in a pension scheme. The contributions can be made by either the individual or their employer. Any contributions in excess of this amount will be subject to income tax on the individual. Where an individual has not fully utilised the annual £40,000, the unused surplus of the previous three years can be carried forward to the current tax year, providing a pension payment has been made in those years. Tax relief is available for gross personal contributions up to the higher of £3,600 or 100% of relevant earnings.

12.4   Other Issues

12.4.1   Timing

It may be the case that the total remuneration payable to a director in respect of an accounting period will not be finally determined until the accounts have been prepared and the profits have been assessed. Also, remuneration may be credited to a director's loan account rather than being paid in cash.

The date of payment of remuneration for the purposes of PAYE/NICs will be the **earlier** of:

- the date the payment is made;
- the date the director becomes entitled to be paid;
- the date the payment is credited in the company accounts or records, even if:
  - the director cannot draw the money immediately because there is a block on the right to payment; or
  - the credit is not specifically in an account in the director's name; or
- the date the remuneration is fixed or determined:
  - if the amount for a particular accounting period is determined before the end of that period, take the date as being when the period ends; and
  - if the amount is determined after the period ends, take the date as being when the amount is determined.

In the case of profits extracted by way of dividend, the date of payment for the purposes of calculating the income tax charge is the date of the dividend as stated in the board minute declaring the dividend and the supporting documentation (i.e. tax voucher). It is important that this documentation is properly maintained, especially where a dividend is being credited to a director's current account rather than being paid out.

12.4.2 Limits on Remuneration

It should be remembered that remuneration, like any other trading expense, must be incurred wholly and exclusively for the purposes of the trade. HMRC may disallow a deduction for corporation tax purposes where they regard the remuneration as excessive.

12.4.3 "Income Shifting"

Over the past few years there have been several cases relating to the settlements rules contained in sections 624–627 ITTOIA 2005. The detailed provisions are outside the scope of this course but, briefly, they aim to prevent someone gaining a tax advantage by allocating their income to someone else (generally their spouse/civil partner) who pays tax at a lower rate. The rules may apply where a director takes a small salary from their company to enable higher dividends to be paid to a non-working shareholder spouse paying income tax at lower rates. There is much confusion as to the proper application of the rules and it is likely that the legislation in this area will be reformed in the near future.

12.4.4 Personal Liability

If PAYE/NICs are not properly deducted in respect of remuneration paid to a director, then the director may be personally liable to pay the tax if he knew of the failure to deduct or account for the tax.

Questions

Review Questions
(See Suggested Solutions to Review Questions at the end of this textbook.)

Question 12.1

To recognise the increased contribution by one of its directors, Annette, over the past year, a company has decided to reward her with an additional gross payment of £100,000 to be paid before the end of the current tax year 2014/15. Annette's gross salary for the year was £120,000.

Requirement
Outline the tax implications to the company and Annette of making this payment either as a bonus or as a dividend. Assume that the company pays corporation tax at the marginal rate. Conclude which is more tax efficient overall.

Question 12.2

It is March 2015 and you have just had a meeting with your clients, Mr and Mrs Andrews, who are both in their early fifties. At the meeting you discuss a number of issues. However, it is apparent that they would like some immediate advice in respect of the strategy for their remuneration by their company.

They each hold 50% of the shares in Andrews Transport Ltd (ATL) being 50 shares each and have done so since the company was incorporated in 1988.

The current total value of the company is £3 million. Annual pre-tax profits are in the region of £250,000. Most of the value of the company is in goodwill, current assets and motor vehicles, although there is also spare cash of £750,000. The cash has built up as no dividends have been paid by ATL over the years. Distributable reserves in ATL currently amount to over £1 million.

Currently, Mr Andrews is paid £100,000 per annum by the company, and Mrs Andrews is not paid anything in respect of the secretarial services she provides to the company. Mr Andrews has been a full-time director of the company since 1988, while Mrs Andrews has never been an employee or director of ATL.

They have two children who are currently at university and who also work part time for the company. The children are not paid by the company, but are rewarded by Mr Andrews himself, who also pays their college expenses. Several years ago the company set up a Revenue-approved pension scheme to provide Mr Andrews with a pension. However, the actual contributions made to the scheme have been relatively low and the projected pension on his retirement is quite small.

Mrs Andrews has no company pension and Mr Andrews is concerned that his expected pension will not be sufficient to meet their needs.

Requirement

Draft a letter to Mr and Mrs Andrews dealing with the current remuneration structure, the various options for remunerating them from the company and make suggestions for potential savings. There is no requirement for detailed calculations at this stage.

Part Two
Capital Gains Tax

Introduction, General Principles and Administration

The Chartered Accountants Ireland *Code of Ethics* applies to all aspects of a Chartered Accountant's professional life, including dealing with CGT issues. As outlined at the beginning of this book, further information regarding the principles in the *Code of Ethics* is set out in **Appendix 2**.

13.1 Introduction

Legislation introduced taxation on capital gains arising from the disposal of chargeable assets on or after 6 April 1965. The legislation has been modified by amendments contained in subsequent Finance Acts and was consolidated in 1979 and 1992. The Taxation of Chargeable Gains Act (TCGA) 1992, as amended by subsequent Finance Acts, contains the main provisions for the taxation of chargeable gains.

13.2 The Basic Charge to CGT

There are three basic elements which must exist before the provisions relating to the taxation of capital gains come into operation:

1. there must be a **chargeable disposal**,
2. of a **chargeable asset**,
3. by a **chargeable person**.

13.3   Disposal

In order for a liability to CGT to arise, a disposal of an asset must take place or must be deemed to take place. A disposal for these purposes will occur in each of the following situations:

- on the sale of an asset;
- on the sale of part of an asset (part disposal);
- on the gift of the whole or part of an asset;
- on the receipt of a capital sum resulting from the ownership of an asset, e.g. receipt of compensation for damage to, or total destruction of, assets or the receipt of a capital sum in return for forfeiture or surrender of rights;
- on the receipt of a capital sum as consideration for use or exploitation of assets;
- on the transfer of an asset to a trust or a corporate body;
- on an exchange of assets in a barter transaction.

However, the sale of an asset in the course of a trade (for example, the sale of trading stock) is **not** a chargeable disposal since any gain arising is taxed as a trading profit.

In respect of **gifts**, the asset is treated as if it were sold for CGT purposes and the consideration is deemed to be its market value even though the transferor receives no consideration. Certain disposals are **exempt** from CGT including gifts to charities and gifts of national heritage property (subject to certain conditions). A list of exempt assets is included below.

As a general rule, CGT is not triggered on **death**. There is, therefore, no chargeable disposal on death. Chargeable assets held on death are, however, revalued to their market value as at the date of death. The market value at the date of death becomes the base cost for the person inheriting the asset (probate value).

It is **important** to note that, although transfers of assets between **husbands and wives** are chargeable disposals for CGT purposes, they are specifically deemed to occur at a value such that neither a chargeable gain nor allowable loss occurs on the transfer (disposal). A similar rule was enacted with effect from 5 December 2005 to apply to same sex civil partners who enter into a legally recognised civil partnership.

A chargeable disposal occurs at the date of the unconditional contract or the date that the condition is satisfied on a conditional contract. A contract can be written or verbal. See **Section 13.9** for further details.

13.4   Chargeable Assets

Chargeable assets for CGT purposes include all forms of property, whether situated in the UK or not, including options, debts and foreign currency. The basic rule is that any capital asset of an individual or company is a chargeable asset unless it is specifically exempt from CGT or corporation tax on chargeable gains. Specifically included is an interest in property, e.g. a lease. As seen in the previous chapters, a company generally calculates its chargeable gains on the same basis as individuals (apart from indexation, which has been abolished for individuals and trustees on disposals post-6 April 2008, and there is no annual exemption for companies). Special rules within the following regimes treat certain gains as income for corporation tax purposes rather than as capital gains:

- Intangible Fixed Assets Regime
- Loan Relationships
- Derivative Contracts

The main **exempt assets** for CGT purposes include:

- motor cars;
- chattels (items of tangible movable property) which are disposed of for gross proceeds of £6,000 or less;
- wasting chattels, which are chattels with a predictable useful life of 50 years or less (unless used in the taxpayer's business and eligible for capital allowances);
- a taxpayer's principal private residence (subject to conditions);
- winnings from betting, lotteries and the Pools;
- decorations for valour (unless purchased), life insurance policies (unless purchased from a third party);
- National Savings & Investment Certificates, Premium Bonds and ISAs;
- shares in an Enterprise Investment Scheme and shares in a venture capital trust (provided certain conditions are met);
- gilt-edged securities (e.g. Treasury stock) and qualifying corporate bonds (QCBs);
- foreign currency for private use abroad; and
- damages for personal or professional injury.

13.5 Chargeable Persons

CGT is charged on gains accruing (realised or deemed to be realised) by individuals, business partners, trustees and personal representatives of a deceased person. Companies are also chargeable persons but are assessed to corporation tax and not to CGT. A UK domiciled person is chargeable to CGT in respect of worldwide chargeable gains accruing to them in the year of assessment if during any part of the tax year they are "resident" in the UK.

Residence and the previous concept of ordinary residence (for periods prior to 6 April 2013) are defined in **Chapter 14**. Prior to 6 April 2013, a UK domiciled individual could also have been liable to CGT if they were 'ordinarily resident' in the UK. However the concept of ordinary residence has been abolished from this date by FA 2013 with the introduction of a new statutory residence test.

Persons who are not resident in the UK for a tax year are not subject to UK CGT unless they fall into one of the exceptions below:

1. A non-resident person carrying on a business in the UK through a branch or agency (or, if a company, through a permanent establishment (PE)) will fall to be charged to CGT (or corporation tax in the case of a company) on those gains arising from assets in the UK that are used for the purposes of the business. Gains will be triggered on the disposal or the removal of an asset from the UK. A charge will also arise if the UK business/trade ceases, in which case there will be a deemed disposal of the assets at their market value.
2. A person who is a "temporary non-resident" may also be chargeable to CGT (see **Chapter 14**).

CGT is **not** limited to gains on the disposal of UK assets.

From 6 April 2008, a non-UK domiciled individual who is resident in the UK is subject to CGT on gains arising on non-UK assets unless a claim is made for the remittance basis of taxation to apply, or unless they fall within certain exceptions (see **Chapter 14**). The broad effect of the remittance basis of taxation is to only tax non-UK gains if and when they are remitted to the UK. Prior to 6 April 2008, this treatment applied automatically but the rules were very different. The remittance basis of taxation is explained further in **Chapter 14**.

13.6 Rate of Tax, Date of Payment and Returns

13.6.1 Rates of CGT

CGT is charged by reference to fiscal years of assessment for individuals, i. e. year ending 5 April.

Prior to 6 April 2008, CGT was charged at rates of up to 40%. Gains arising between 6 April 2008 and 22 June 2010 are charged at a flat rate of 18%, irrespective of income levels.

For gains made on or after 23 June 2010, individuals need to work out their total taxable income before working out which CGT rate to use, as follows:

1. First, calculate taxable income by deducting any tax-free allowances and reliefs that are due.
2. Next, see how much of the basic rate band is already being used against taxable income. The maximum basic rate band for 2014/15 is £31,865.
3. Allocate any remaining basic rate band first against gains that qualify for entrepreneurs' relief; these are charged at 10%.
4. Next, allocate any remaining basic rate band against other gains; these are charged at 18%.
5. Any remaining gains above the basic rate band are charged at 28%.

Trustees and personal representatives pay CGT at 28% on all gains, regardless of the level of income.

Example 13.1

Julie's total taxable income in 2014/15, after deducting allowances and reliefs, is £26,000 and her capital gains, after tax-free allowance and reliefs, are £17,000. £5,000 of the gains qualify for entrepreneurs' relief.

The maximum basic rate band for 2014/15 is £31,865. Julie has used £26,000 of this amount against her income, so she has £5,865 remaining.

Julie then allocates £5,000 against the gains that qualify for entrepreneurs' relief, so these are taxed at 10%.

She allocates the remaining £865 against her other gains, so these are taxed at 18%. The remaining £11,135 gains (£17,000 less £5,865) are taxed at 28%.

Companies pay corporation tax on their chargeable gains at the company's effective tax rate.

13.6.2 Date of Payment

Self-assessment applies to CGT.

CGT due must be paid on or before 31 January following the end of the relevant tax year. For example, the CGT due on a chargeable gain arising during 2014/15 falls due for payment on or before 31 January 2016. The payment of CGT does **not** impact on the following tax year's payments on account.

Example 13.2
An individual disposes of an asset in July 2014 giving rise to a chargeable gain of £10,000 and disposes of a second asset in November 2014 giving rise to a chargeable gain of £6,000. The individual had a loss forward of £3,000 from the disposal of shares in 2013/14. The total taxable income for the year (after tax free allowance and reliefs) was £15,000. CGT is payable by the individual as follows:

CGT rate computation

	£
Basic rate band 2014/15	31,865
Less total taxable income	(15,000)
Remaining basic rate band	16,865

Total chargeable gains are less than £16,865 so the CGT rate of 18% will be applied to all taxable gains.

CGT computation

	£
Chargeable gains	16,000
Less losses from 2013/14 (see later)	(3,000)
Less annual exemption (see later)	(11,000)
Taxable gain	2,000
CGT @ 18%	360

CGT for 2014/15, payable on or before 31 January 2016, is £360.

13.6.3 Payment by Instalments

In the situation where the taxpayer receives the disposal proceeds in instalments over a period of 18 months or more, then they may choose to make a claim to pay the CGT liability by way of interest-free instalments. The size and frequency of the instalments are at the discretion of HMRC, but the period over which they are paid must not exceed:

1. an eight-year period; **or**
2. the date on which the last instalment of the consideration is payable.

It is also possible for the taxpayer to elect to pay by instalments where gift relief is not available (see later). This election for payment by instalment is not interest-free and interest will accrue on outstanding balances.

13.6.4 Returns

An individual who has not received a notice to file a tax return, or who has a new source of income or gains in the tax year, is required to give notice of chargeability to HMRC within six months from the end of the tax year, i.e. by 5 October 2015 for 2014/15. The maximum penalty for not notifying HMRC is 100% of the tax assessed which is not paid on the due date, i.e. 31 January 2016 for tax year 2014/15.

A return of chargeable gains must be made within the self-assessment income tax return filing deadline for individuals.

General rules: the latest filing date for a personal tax return is:

- 31 October following the end of the tax year for paper returns; and
- 31 January following the end of the tax year for online returns.

There are **two exceptions to the general rules:**

1. If the notice to file a tax return is issued by HMRC to the taxpayer after 31 July following the end of the tax year, but on or before 31 October following the end of the tax year, then the latest filing date is:

    (a) the end of three months following the notice for a paper return; or
    (b) 31 January for an online return.

2. If the notice to file the tax return is issued to the taxpayer after 31 October following the end of the tax year, then the latest filing date is the end of three months following the notice.

However, taxpayers are normally **not** required to complete the CGT pages of their tax return if **both** the following conditions are satisfied:

1. the total disposals proceeds from the tax year do not exceed four times the amount of the annual exemption (£44,000 for 2014/15); **and**
2. the total chargeable gains for the tax year do not exceed the annual exemption (£11,000 for 2014/15).

In this case, a statement to this effect in lieu of the CGT pages will suffice. For the purposes of these conditions, the total chargeable gains are before deduction of either current year capital losses or capital losses brought forward from previous years.

It should be noted that relief for capital losses cannot be claimed unless they are notified to HMRC within four years from the end of the tax year in which the losses were incurred. So if a loss is made in 2014/15, the deadline for claiming the loss (although not for claiming relief for the loss) is 5 April 2019.

13.6.5 Interest on Tax Paid Late and Repayment Supplement

HMRC will charge interest, calculated on a daily basis, on any tax which remains unpaid after the due date of payment. The actual interest rate will be set by HMRC and will vary from time to time. Interest runs from the due date until the day before the actual date of payment.

The taxpayer will be entitled to receive repayment supplement on overpaid income tax, CGT and Class 4 NICs. The repayment supplement is calculated from the original date of payment until the day before the date the repayment is made. Repayment supplement is not charged to tax.

13.6.6 Penalties: Late Payment of Tax

In addition to any interest that may fall due as a result of income tax or CGT being paid late, HMRC may also impose a "surcharge".

The surcharge scheme applies only to the balancing payment and does not affect the payments on account (POA) that a taxpayer has to make. A surcharge arises if any part of the balancing payment (which will include any CGT due) remains unpaid more than 28 days after its due date. The level of surcharge is 5% of the unpaid amount. If any amount remains unpaid more than six months after the due date, the taxpayer will be levied with a further surcharge of 5% of the outstanding liability. If any amount remains unpaid more than 12 months after the due date, the taxpayer will be levied with a further surcharge of 5% of the tax unpaid at the due date. Surcharges fall due for payment within 30 days of the date that they are imposed and interest charges will also accrue on late payments.

No surcharge will be applied where the late paid tax has attracted a tax-geared penalty.

13.6.7   Penalties: Late Filing of Tax Return

A taxpayer who fails to comply with the statutory requirements may fall foul of HMRC's penalty regime. The level of penalty may be a fixed amount or it may be tax-geared, i.e. a percentage of the tax foregone. HMRC officials have the discretion to mitigate the amount of any penalty where the taxpayer has a reasonable excuse.

The maximum penalties for late filing of a self-assessment tax return from 6 April 2011 (introduced by FA 2009) are:

1.	Not filed by the due date	£100
2.	More than three months late – daily penalty (maximum of 90 days)	£10 per day
3.	More than six months late but not more than 12 months late	Greater of 5% of tax due or £300
4.	More than 12 months late	Greater of 5% of tax due or £300

Higher penalties of up to 100% of the tax due may be imposed where there is deliberate behaviour by the taxpayer to withhold or conceal the return.

Prior to 6 April 2009, the penalties were as follows:

1.	Up to six months late	£100
2.	More than six months late but no more than 12 months late	£200
3.	More than 12 months late	£200 + 100% of tax due

Also, the Tax Tribunal had the power to impose a maximum penalty of £60 per day if the failure to file the return continued after a notice of direction had been given to the taxpayer. In this case, the additional £100 penalty under 2. above is not imposed.

Prior to 6 April 2011, where the overall tax liability was less than the fixed penalty, then the fixed penalty was capped at the tax liability due. From 6 April 2011, this is no longer the case.

"Reasonable excuse" is a factor outside the taxpayer's control, e.g. industrial action by the Post Office meaning the return was not received, serious illness of a family member (in certain cases), destruction of records through fire and flood, etc.

As discussed in **Part One** of this textbook, a new common penalty regime came into force on 1 April 2009 and applies if an incorrect return or document leads to an understatement of the amount of tax due and the inaccuracy was either careless or deliberate. As already stated, this regime will apply to all taxes, levies and duties administered by HMRC, including inheritance tax. HMRC has also clarified that there will be no penalty for failure to notify chargeability, unless tax and NICs are unpaid as a result, or where the taxpayer has a "reasonable excuse" for the failure to notify.

The actual mechanics of the regime have already been set out in **Part One** of this textbook and, thus, are not repeated in this chapter.

13.6.8   Record-keeping

Taxpayers are required to keep proper records so that they can make a correct tax return and (if necessary) substantiate the figures entered on their return. In general, a taxpayer who is in business, or who rents property, must normally preserve these records for five years after the 31 January following the end of the tax year. Otherwise, records must be preserved for one year after the 31

January following the tax year if the return is filed on time, or 15 months from the date of filing if the return is filed late.

13.6.9 Amending a Return

A taxpayer may amend his or her tax return within 12 months of the filing date for that return.

13.6.10 Claim for Overpayment Relief (formerly Error or Mistake Relief)

A claim for overpayment relief may be made for errors in a return where tax would otherwise be overcharged. A claim may not be made where the tax liability was computed in accordance with prevailing practice at the time the return was made. A taxpayer who believes that there has been an error or mistake made in their tax return can make a claim no later than four years following the end of the tax year to which the return relates. The deadline for a claim in respect of the return for 2014/15 would, therefore, be 5 April 2019.

13.6.11 Enquiries

HMRC has the power to enquire into any individual's tax return or amendment.

From the tax year 2007/08, an officer of HMRC must give written notice of his/her intention of enquiry within 12 months of the actual filing date. Where the return is filed late or is amended after the date on which the return was due to be filed, then the "enquiry window" is extended until the quarter day which follows the first anniversary of the date on which the return or amendment was submitted. For these purposes, the quarter dates are 31 January, 30 April, 31 July and 31 October.

HMRC does not have to give the taxpayer a reason for enquiry selection and enquiries can take the form of aspect or full enquiries.

On completion of the enquiry, a closure notice will be issued by HMRC and the taxpayer will have 30 days to lodge any appeal.

13.6.12 Discovery Assessments

Where it is believed that full disclosure has not been made in a tax return and this has resulted in a loss of tax, HMRC may raise a "discovery assessment".

A discovery assessment may be made to recover tax that has been under-assessed or over-declared, or over-repaid or paid or credited.

The time limits are:

1. In the case of deliberate behaviour by the taxpayer or his/her agent, 20 years from the end of the year of assessment.
2. In the case of careless behaviour by the taxpayer or his/her agent, six years from the end of the year of assessment.
3. Where loss of tax is **not** due to careless or deliberate behaviour by the taxpayer or his/her agent, four years from the end of the year of assessment.

These time limits apply from 1 April 2010. Certain transitional provisions apply where a person has overpaid income tax or CGT and is outside the self-assessment regime.

13.6.13   Determinations

If an individual has received notice to file a tax return and fails to submit a tax return by the required filing date, then an Officer of HMRC may make a determination of the tax due calculated according to the best of his/her available information and belief. Such an assessment allows the Officer to collect tax, penalties and interest charges.

There is no right of appeal against a determination and the tax cannot be postponed. A determination can only be displaced if the individual files the required return.

13.6.14   Appeals

Under the self-assessment regime, taxpayers have a right of appeal against a variety of HMRC decisions, e.g. discovery assessment, amendment to a self-assessment, etc. (but not a determination as seen above). An appeal must be lodged within 30 days of the assessment. In some instances, it may be possible to agree the point at issue with the HMRC, in which case the appeal may be settled by agreement/negotiation. If the appeal cannot be agreed, then it will be heard by the Tax Tribunal.

An appeal does not relieve the taxpayer of liability to pay tax on the normal due date unless he obtains a "determination" of the Tax Tribunal or agreement from the Inspector that payment of all or some of the tax may be postponed pending determination of the appeal.

13.7   Computation of Gain or Loss

13.7.1   General

In summary, taxable gains are the net chargeable gains (after current year capital losses) of the tax year reduced by unrelieved losses brought forward from previous years and the annual exemption.

The capital gain is the difference between:

1. the consideration for the disposal of the asset, or the deemed consideration (e.g. market value in the case of a gift or disposal between connected persons); and
2. the cost of acquisition of the asset or its market value if not acquired at arm's length (e.g. property acquired by way of inheritance or gift).

If any part of the sales consideration is taken into account in computing income tax profits or losses, it is excluded from the amount under 1 above. Any expenditure which is allowable as a deduction from income tax profits, or which would be so allowable if the asset had been employed as a fixed asset of a trade, is excluded from 2 above.

Allowable expenditure for CGT purposes includes the following:

1. The cost of acquiring (or providing) the asset and certain incidental costs of acquisition or disposal, e.g. agent's commission, stamp duty, valuation costs, cost of transfer or conveyance, auctioneers', accountants' or solicitors' fees, and advertising costs.
2. Expenditure incurred for the purposes of enhancing the value of the asset which is reflected in the state of the asset at the time of disposal, e.g. **improvements to property**. To be allowable, the expenditure must not have been abortive nor must its value have wasted away before the disposal of the asset. Expenditure incurred in establishing, preserving or defending an owner's title or interest in an asset is allowable within this definition. Enhancement expenditure does not include costs of repairs and maintenance, costs of insurance, and capital grants expended out of public funds.

A typical CGT computation for an asset sold during 2014/15 might be as follows:

J. Jones – Capital Gains Tax Computation for 2014/15

	£	£
Sales proceeds (or market value)	X	
Less incidental costs of sale	(X)	
		X
Deduct allowable costs:		
Original cost of asset	X	
Incidental costs of acquisition	X	
Enhancement expenditure	X	
		(X)
Gain		X
Deduct: Loss relief (if any)		(X)
Deduct: Annual exemption (see later)		(X)
Taxable chargeable gain		X
CGT payable: Taxable gain at 10/18/28% (for individuals)		X

13.7.2   Indexation Allowance

As seen in earlier chapters, indexation allowance is available to increase acquisition and enhancement costs in line with inflation for companies. This allowance was abolished for individuals by FA 2008. There is, however, protection of indexation allowance where a no gain/no loss transfer between spouses took place pre-6 April 2008. The acquiring spouse is deemed to have a base cost equal to the cost to the transferor plus an amount equal to the indexation allowance available.

13.7.3   Annual Exemption

Every individual is entitled to an annual exemption, which is available for offset against the "taxable" gains of the particular tax year. The annual exemption cannot be carried forward and thus any excess over the taxable gains is lost. Furthermore, the annual exemption cannot be transferred, say between spouses or civil partners.

The annual exemption for 2014/15 is £11,000 (for 2013/14 it is £10,900).

The "taxable" gains are usually the chargeable gains accruing to the taxpayer for a year of assessment after deduction of allowable losses. Thus, allowable losses of the current year must be utilised against the chargeable gains arising in that year, even if this means that part or all of the annual exemption will be wasted. However, one can preserve the full annual exemption where capital losses are being carried forward or carried back (applicable only on death), i.e. one can restrict the amount being carried forward or back so as not to waste any of the annual exemption. Current year losses must be claimed in priority to losses brought forward.

For the 2010/11 tax year, FA (No. 2) 2010 confirmed that both the annual exemption and losses could be used in the most beneficial way possible, i.e. they could be set against gains taxed at the higher CGT rate of 28% in preference to gains charged at 10% (i.e. gains qualifying for entrepreneurs' relief) or 18%. Since 2012/13 this is no longer relevant, as the same rates of tax apply throughout the year.

Individuals who claim the remittance basis of tax from 6 April 2008 are no longer able to claim the annual exemption. Only those individuals who are exempt from making a claim for the remittance basis of tax may continue to claim the annual exemption. See **Chapter 14** for further information on the remittance basis.

Companies are not entitled to an annual exemption.

Example 13.3

Four taxpayers, John, Paul, George and Matthew, each make chargeable disposals during 2014/15. None of them have any capital losses brought forward from previous years, and it is to be assumed that they will have none to carry back (allowed only on death). All of them have used up their total basic rate band against income. You are required to set out their CGT assessable chargeable gains for 2014/15.

(a) John had gains of £2,800 (30 June), £3,600 (15 September) and £5,150 (10 January) and a capital loss of £2,450 (5 May).

(b) Paul had gains of £10,300 (18 May), £3,600 (5 December) and capital losses of £1,000 (30 April) and £800 (1 February). He has £5,000 of his basic rate band remaining.

(c) George had a gain of £9,600 (5 August) and capital losses of £3,500 (30 November), £2,900 (12 December) and £8,200 (4 March).

(d) Matthew had gains of £5,800 (15 May), £8,600 (10 October) and £9,100 (8 February). He has £10,000 of his basic rate band remaining.

Solution

(a) John's "net" position is a net gain of £9,100. This is less than the annual exemption and thus he will have a CGT assessment of nil and the unused part of his annual allowance £1,900 (£11,000 − £9,100) is lost.

(b) Paul's "net" position is a net gain of £12,100. Deducting his annual exemption leaves a taxable gain of £1,100, which is within his surplus basic rate band. Therefore, tax is payable @ 18% × £1,100 = £198.

(c) George's "net" position is a net loss of £5,000 and his CGT assessment for 2014/15 will be nil and all of his annual exemption will be lost.

(d) Matthew's "net" position is a gain of £12,500 (£23,500 − £11,000) after deducting the annual exemption. £10,000 of this will be taxed @ 18% and £2,500 @ 28%, resulting in a CGT liability of £2,500.

Example 13.4

Three taxpayers, George, Robert and Denis, have capital losses carried forward from previous years of £3,000, £4,000 and £5,000 respectively. All three had made chargeable gains of £14,600 and a capital loss of £1,400 during 2014/15. Calculate each of their CGT assessments for 2014/15. You can assume that each has used up their basic rate band in full before the gains are taken into account.

Solution

Each has a "net" position for 2014/15 (prior to utilisation of their annual exemption and their individual capital losses brought forward) of £13,200. Each taxpayer needs only to utilise sufficient of his carried forward losses to reduce (where possible) the "net" gain to the level of the annual exemption.

In order to arrive at how much, if any, of the capital losses each taxpayer must use, one has to consider the position after deducting the annual allowance, **before** looking at losses forward. In each case, this would be a figure of £2,200 (£13,200 − £11,000).

continued overleaf

Thus, George would use £2,200 of his carried forward capital losses of £3,000 and leave no taxable gain (after deduction of his annual exemption). He would carry forward the remaining £800 of his losses. His CGT assessment for 2014/15 is nil.

Robert would only utilise £2,200 of his capital losses brought forward (i.e. he leaves sufficient "net" gain to be covered by his annual exemption). He would then have capital losses to carry forward of £1,800 (£4,000 less £2,200 used in 2014/15). His CGT assessment for 2014/15 is nil.

Similarly, Denis would only utilise £2,200 of his brought forward losses and his carried forward capital losses would thus be £2,800 (£5,000 less £2,200 used in 2014/15). His CGT assessment for 2014/15 is nil.

Denis – CGT computation

	£
Chargeable gain	14,600
Less current year capital losses	(1,400)
	13,200
Less losses brought forward	(2,200)
	11,000
Less annual exemption	(11,000)
Net chargeable gain	0
CGT @ 28%	0
Memo of losses carried forward	5,000
Utilised 2014/15	(2,200)
Losses available for carry forward	2,800

Note differences in claiming relief for current year losses and losses carried forward.

13.7.4   Special Rules Relating to Allowable Deductions

As outlined above, the expenditure which is allowable as a deduction in computing the quantum of the chargeable gain is:

1. The costs of acquiring (or providing) the asset, which includes certain incidental costs of acquisition wholly and exclusively incurred for the purposes of the acquisition (such as stamp duty land tax, fees, commission, valuation fees and professional services of estate agents, solicitors, surveyors, etc.) and advertising costs.
2. Enhancement costs for the asset and any costs of establishing, preserving or defending title to an asset.
3. Certain incidental costs of disposals. While the allowable incidental costs of disposal are generally similar to those for incidental costs of acquisition, specifically excluded are the costs associated with resolving valuation disputes with HMRC. As stated above, no deduction is allowable for expenditure which is allowable as a deduction in computing the profits or losses of a trade for income tax purposes.
4. Foreign gains – double taxation relief. Where a UK resident, or ordinarily resident (prior to 5 April 2013), individual makes a capital gain on the disposal of a foreign asset and foreign tax is paid, relief can be claimed against the UK CGT liability.

There are general provisions relating to the making of arrangements with governments of territories outside the UK for avoiding double taxation. The purpose of a double taxation agreement is primarily to avoid the incidence of double taxation by limiting the taxing rights of each contracting state.

Relief for foreign tax suffered on gains that are chargeable to CGT (or corporation tax) in the UK may be obtained under the terms of a double taxation agreement between the UK and the relevant overseas territory. Under the terms of an agreement, it may be the case that the gain is only taxable in one of the contracting states (i.e. the state of residence or the state in which the gain arose). Where double taxation remains, i.e. where both states retain the right to tax the gain under the agreement, it is generally the case that the agreement will provide relief which, in the case of UK residents, invariably takes the form of a credit for the foreign tax against the UK tax liability on the profits or gains concerned.

If the overseas territory does not have a double taxation agreement with the UK, the taxpayer can avail of "unilateral relief". **Unilateral relief** will be the lower of:

(a) the UK tax on the foreign gain; or
(b) the foreign tax suffered.

Unilateral relief reduces the UK CGT charge.

If there is no double taxation agreement and unilateral relief is not claimed then the foreign gain, net of foreign tax, is charged to UK CGT, i.e. the foreign tax is treated as an additional cost in CGT computation. This treatment may be appropriate where there is no UK tax to shelter, perhaps due to the utilisation of losses or other deferral reliefs.

When calculating the CGT liability for a taxpayer where there are foreign gains, the annual exemption is allocated first against UK and foreign gains on which no double taxation or unilateral relief is being claimed, and then against gains on which relief is being claimed, beginning with the gain that has been subjected to the lowest effective rate of foreign tax.

5. Grants – No deduction is allowed in computing chargeable gains for any expenditure which has been met by the provision of Government, public or local authority grants.

13.7.5   Part Disposal

As we have seen above, the partial disposal of an asset is a chargeable event for CGT purposes. Where a portion of an asset is sold, the sale proceeds are easily quantified but it is necessary to calculate **how much of the original cost of the asset is allowable as a deduction in computing the chargeable gain or allowable loss arising on the part disposal**.

The legislation provides that this is calculated as being the proportion of the original cost of the asset which the value of the part being disposed of bears, at the time of disposal, to the market value of the whole asset. The formula is, therefore:

$$\text{Original Cost} \ \times \ \frac{A}{A + B}$$

where A is the amount of the "gross" proceeds/market value of the part disposal (i.e. before deducting incidental costs of disposal) and B is the market value of the portion of the asset which is retained.

Example 13.5
Assume an asset cost £1,000 on 1 September 2004 and part of the asset was sold for £600 on 6 June 2014. The market value of the remainder of the asset was £700. The chargeable gain in respect of the disposal would be computed as follows (assuming that the annual allowance has been used elsewhere):

	£
Sales proceeds	600
Less: allowable cost: $£1,000 \times \dfrac{600}{600+700}$	(462)
Chargeable gain	138

The base costs for onward disposal of the remaining part of the asset is:

	£
Original cost of asset	1,000
Less: Cost of part disposal	(462)
Cost of remaining part	538

Example 13.6
Asset cost £10,000 on 10 April 1982. Part of the asset was sold on 10 November 2014 for £27,000. The market value of the remainder asset at that date was £50,000. The individual has other income in 2014/15 of £78,000.
Calculate the CGT liability.

	£
Proceeds	27,000
COST $\quad 10,000 \times \dfrac{27,000}{27,000 + 50,000}$	(3,507)
	23,493
Annual exemption	(11,000)
	12,493

CGT payable is £12,493 × 28% = £3,498 (due by 31/01/2016)
Base cost of the remaining part for onward disposal is

	£
Original cost	10,000
Less: Cost of part disposal	(3,507)
Cost of remaining part	6,493

Note: any expenditure incurred wholly in respect of a particular part of an asset should be treated as an allowable deduction in full for that part and not apportioned, e.g. selling costs which are wholly attributable to the part disposed of.

"Small Disposal" Proceeds of Land

Where the proceeds for a part disposal of land are small compared with the value of the land held, then the taxpayer may claim not to be treated as having made a capital disposal, but instead deduct the proceeds from allowable expenditure on a subsequent disposal. This claim can only be made if the proceeds for the part disposal of land are:

1. not more than 20% of the entire holding of the land's market value **and** not more than £20,000, **and** the aggregate proceeds from the part disposal and any other disposals of land (including buildings) in the same tax year do not exceed £20,000; **or**

2. the land is subject to a compulsory purchase order and the proceeds received are deemed to be small, i.e. 5% or less of the market value of the entire holding, or £3,000 or less (irrespective of whether the 5% test is met).

The claim cannot be made if the allowable expenditure is less than the part disposal proceeds.

Example 13.7

An individual bought five acres of land in October 2005 for £10,000 and sold one acre for £5,000 in November 2014. The market value of the land prior to sale is £40,000. The disposal costs were £500. What is the CGT position?

Can the taxpayer claim to be treated as if no disposal has been made? As the consideration is £5,000, which is less than 20% of the market value (20% of £40,000 = £8,000), a claim can be made.

Claim small disposal relief:	£
Base cost: Cost of five acres	10,000
Deduct net proceeds of part disposal (£5,000–£500)	(4,500)
Allowable base cost of land retained	5,500

As a claim has been made, no disposal takes place at this time; therefore there is no taxable capital gain. Instead the base cost of the land is reduced by the proceeds received and the reduced base cost is carried forward to be used in the CGT computation on any future sale of the land.

13.7.6 Application of Market Value

Normally, where a disposal is at arm's length and the consideration is known in money terms, the consideration paid is accepted for CGT purposes. However, in certain circumstances, the market value of an asset is substituted for the actual consideration paid for the disposal:

1. where there is a transaction between connected persons, i.e. between an individual and:

    (a) the individual's spouse or civil partner,
    (b) a relative of the individual – brother, sister, lineal descendant (e.g. child, grandchild) or ancestor (e.g. parent, grandparent),
    (c) spouse or civil partner of a relative of the individual,
    (d) a relative of an individual's spouse or civil partner,
    (e) the spouse or civil partner of a relative of the individual's spouse or civil partner,
    (f) business partners – see **Section 13.13.1**,
    (g) a person, in their capacity as trustee of a settlement – see **Section 13.13.1**, or
    (h) a company controlled by a person, whether alone or together with connected persons – see **Section 13.13.1**;

2. where a disposal is not made at arm's length (e.g. a gift);
3. where the consideration is not valued in money terms or is a barter transaction;
4. where the asset is acquired or disposed wholly or partly for a consideration that cannot be valued; or
5. where the asset is acquired by way of a distribution from a company in respect of shares in the company.

In 1–5 above, the market value is deemed to be the consideration for the purpose of determining the chargeable gain or allowable loss.

However, as was seen earlier, the market value rule is overridden when the asset is transferred between husband and wife and between civil partners. In such situations, the transfers are deemed to occur at a value such that there is neither a chargeable gain nor allowable loss (i.e. no gain/no loss).

13.8 Specific Computational Rules

13.8.1 Enhancement Expenditure

Where enhancement expenditure has been incurred on an asset, the cost, and each subsequent item of enhancement expenditure, is treated as a separate asset for the purposes of CGT. The chargeable gain is calculated as the difference between the various items of expenditure, i.e. both original cost and enhancement expenditure, as adjusted, and the sale proceeds.

13.9 Time of Disposal

The time of disposal for the purposes of CGT is generally determined by reference to the time a contract is made. Briefly, the rules for the following situations are:

1. In the case of an **unconditional contract**, the date of the contract is the relevant date, irrespective of the date of the conveyance or transfer of the asset (i.e. "the closing date" is not relevant).
2. In the case of a **conditional contract**, the time of the disposal for the purposes of CGT is the date on which the condition is satisfied.
3. In the case of **gifts**, the date of disposal is the date on which the property effectively passes. This rule also applies to gifts into settlements, e.g. in the case of the gift of a chattel, the date that the chattel is delivered is the date of disposal for CGT purposes.
4. In the case of **compulsory purchases**, the date of disposal is the time at which the compensation for the acquisition is agreed or otherwise determined (e.g. by arbitration). Variations in the compensation on appeal are disregarded in determining the date of disposal and acquisition.
5. In **compensation cases**, the effective date is the time of the deemed disposal which is when the loss or destruction occurs. The position is unclear where the owner of the asset receives compensation for the loss, since the date of receipt is then the time of disposal.

13.10 Assets Situated Abroad

13.10.1 Location of Assets

The legislation contains rules for determining the location of assets. These rules are particularly relevant to an individual who is not UK domiciled but who is UK resident (or ordinarily resident in the UK prior to 5 April 2013). Such an individual is chargeable to CGT on chargeable gains accruing on the disposal of assets situated outside the UK (foreign assets) only to the extent that he remits the gains to this country. **Note: from 6 April 2008, the remittance basis of tax does not apply to every non-domiciled individual**. See **Chapter 14** in relation to when the remittance basis of tax applies. Accordingly, it will be important for such an individual to establish that the gains were realised from the disposal of assets which were in fact situated outside the UK. The following particular rules apply:

1. Rights or interests in **immovable** or **tangible movable property** or **chattels** are situated where the property is situated.
2. In general, **debts** (secured or unsecured) are situated in the UK if the creditor is resident in the UK.
3. **Shares or securities** issued by a Government, governmental authority or municipal authority are situated in the country where that authority is established.
4. **Other registered shares and securities** are situated where they are registered and, if registered in more than one register, where the principal register is situated.
5. **A ship** or **aircraft** is situated in the UK if, and only if, the owner is resident in the UK.
6. **Goodwill** of a business is situated at the place where the trade, business or profession is carried on.
7. **Patents, trademarks** and **registered designs** are situated in the country where they are registered.
8. **Copyrights** and **licences** to use any copyrights, patents, trademarks or designs are situated in the UK if the rights derived from them are exercisable in the UK.

13.11 Married Couples and Civil Partners

13.11.1 General

A husband and wife, or each member of a civil partnership, are separate "persons" for CGT purposes and their gains or losses should be computed separately. (For the rest of this section references to couples and spouses should be treated as referring also to civil partnerships and civil partners). Losses made by one spouse cannot be transferred to the other spouse. Each spouse is responsible for making returns of his or her own gains, and for paying the CGT due on those gains. The residence status of each spouse must be considered individually to decide whether or not that person is chargeable to CGT.

13.11.2 Annual Exemption

Each person is entitled to their own annual exemption. For 2014/15, the annual exemption is £11,000 for individuals.

13.11.3 Disposal by One Spouse to the Other

A disposal of an asset from one spouse to the other does not give rise to a CGT liability where the spouses are living together. The asset is deemed to have passed from one to the other at a value which gives rise to a no gain/no loss position. On a subsequent disposal of the asset to a third party, there is a chargeable gain or allowable loss by reference to the whole period of ownership by both spouses. With the abolition of the indexation allowance and taper relief from 6 April 2008 for individuals, this aspect has become less relevant. As noted above, there is protection of indexation allowance where a no gain/no loss transfer between spouses took place pre-6 April 2008. The acquiring spouse is deemed to have a base cost equal to the cost to the transferor plus an amount equal to the indexation allowance available. There is no requirement that the spouses should be living together throughout the tax year, as it is sufficient for them to have lived together at some time in the year. In addition, it does not matter that one spouse is UK-resident and the other is not.

There is **one exception** to this important **no gain/no loss rule**, which is where the asset concerned forms part of the stock-in-trade of either spouse. In that case, there is a disposal and the consideration is always deemed to be the market value, regardless of the value agreed between the spouses.

13.11.4 Principal Private Residence Relief

Only one residence per couple can qualify for this relief (this is dealt with in **Chapter 16**). Where a couple has two residences, they must jointly nominate one as their principal private residence. If a principal private residence passes from one spouse to another (by sale, gift or on death), the period of ownership should be treated for the purposes of the principal private residence relief as going back to the date of acquisition by the spouse who first acquired the house.

13.11.5 Jointly-held Assets

Where a couple disposes of an asset which has been held in their joint names, any chargeable gain arising is apportioned between them in accordance with their respective beneficial interests in the asset at the time of the disposal. If the split of ownership between the spouses is clear, the respective gains should be reported to HMRC on the basis of that split. If the split of ownership is not clear, HMRC normally accepts that the spouses hold the asset in equal proportions.

13.12 Partnerships

An asset owned by all the partners is a "partnership asset". If not all the partners own an asset, then HMRC treat this as simply "other assets". Rollover relief will be available where a partner disposes of a qualifying asset (this is dealt with in **Chapter 19**). Where partners own assets personally, HMRC may allow rollover relief where the owner lets the assets to the partnership in which they are a partner, provided such assets are used for the partnership's business.

Dealings in partnership assets are treated as dealings by the individual partners and not by the firm. Each partner has to be considered to own a fractional share of each partnership asset, rather than an interest in the partnership as a whole. Chargeable gains or allowable losses accruing on the disposal of partnership assets are therefore apportioned among the partners in accordance with their capital profit-sharing ratio. An individual's share of a partnership's allowable loss may, therefore, be set-off against personal (non-partnership) gains and vice versa. If a partnership makes a part disposal, then the part disposal rules are applied before the gain is divided among the partners.

Example 13.8

A and B are in partnership sharing profits and losses at 60% and 40% respectively. During 2014/15, the partnership disposed of a building which it had originally acquired for £30,000 in June 1983. It realised £100,000 on disposal.

Computation of gain	£
Sale proceeds	100,000
Deduct: cost	(30,000)
	70,000

continued overleaf

Apportioned to A 60% × 70,000	42,000
Apportioned to B 40% × 70,000	28,000
	70,000

Each partner would be entitled to claim any personal capital losses against the above gains and, of course, each would be entitled to claim his/her annual exemption.

Partnership goodwill is a chargeable asset, and consequently a gain on the disposal by a partner of their share of a firm's goodwill is chargeable.

Partners may decide to change their profit shares in the firm, e.g. when a new partner joins the firm or a partner retires. Each partner is treated as acquiring or disposing of an appropriate share in the partnership assets.

A reduction in an individual partner's share of a partnership asset is a disposal for CGT purposes. The actual CGT treatment will depend on whether the consideration is dealt with in the accounts or outside them, and whether the assets have been revalued.

If there is no direct payment outside the partnership, then the consideration for the disposal will be the fraction of the asset's current balance sheet value that corresponds to the fractional share passing between the partners. Where no revaluation of the asset has taken place on the balance sheet, the disposal is treated as one on which there is no gain/ no loss.

Example 13.9

James and John are in partnership and share profits and losses in the ratio 70:30. The only chargeable asset on the balance sheet is a property, which has not been revalued. They change their profit share to 50:50. In this situation, James has disposed of 20% of his share and John has acquired 20%. If the current balance sheet value of the property is £100,000, then James's disposal proceeds and John's acquisition cost would both be £20,000.

Since the asset has not been revalued, James's disposal will be on a no gain/no loss basis. However, if there had been a revaluation (upward) in the past, then the two partners would have had the proportional fraction of the increase credited to their respective capital accounts. While there would have been no capital gain at the time of revaluation, the change in the profit sharing will mean that John has now effectively realised a proportion of the unrealised gain. A chargeable gain for each partner is now crystallised.

Where a payment is made outside of the partnership accounts on a change of profit-sharing arrangements, a chargeable gain will crystallise on the partner whose profit share has been reduced. The partner who has acquired the additional profit share will treat his payment as an acquisition cost for onward disposal.

The special rules relating to disposals between connected persons (i.e. market value rules) will **not** apply on disposals and acquisitions between partners where an interest in a partnership asset is transferred between partners on commercial terms and provided that the individuals are not otherwise connected, e.g. father and son.

13.13 Connected Persons

13.13.1 *Meaning of Connected Person*

Where there is a transaction between "connected persons", the consideration is **deemed to be the open market value** (unless specifically overwritten, as in the case of husband and wife transfers, etc.). Any consideration agreed between the connected persons is ignored for the purposes of computing chargeable gains or allowable losses. The following are connected persons:

1. **Relatives** Relatives include husband, wife, brother, sister, ancestor and lineal descendants but **excludes** uncle, aunt, niece and nephew.
2. **Trustees** A trustee of a settlement is connected with:
   (a) the settlor;
   (b) any person connected with the settlor; and
   (c) any company connected with the trust.
   A company will be deemed to be connected with the trust if, at any time during the year of assessment, it is a close company and the shareholders include the trustees of, or a beneficiary under, the settlement.
3. **Partners** A person is connected with any person with whom he is in partnership, and with the spouse or civil partner or a relative of any individual with whom he is in partnership. In this case, there is an exception to the market value rule in relation to the acquisition and disposal of partnership assets pursuant to bona fide commercial arrangements.
4. **Company** A company is connected with another person if that person has control of the company or if that person and the persons connected with him together have control of the company. Companies under common control are also connected persons.

13.13.2 Losses

Where a disposal to a connected person results in an allowable loss, that loss may only be set-off against chargeable gains on disposals to the same connected person.

13.13.3 Treatment of a Series of Transactions between Connected Persons

Where a person disposes of assets by means of a series of transactions to one or more connected person(s) (as defined) through a series of linked transactions (rather than in one transaction), and:

- the aggregate market value of the asset acquired as a whole is greater than the combined total of their separate values when acquired singly; then
- all of the acquisitions are treated as if they were acquired in one single transaction for a consideration equal to their aggregate market value (when acquired in a single transaction); and
- that revised aggregate market value is then apportioned rateably to each transaction for the purposes of determining the consideration for which each disposal is deemed to have taken place.

Transactions are linked if they occur within six years of each other.

Example 13.10

George and Jimmy are brothers. George has three sets of rare Cuban stamps. He gifts them to Jimmy in three separate transactions as follows:

Date of gift		£
1/5/2012	Set 1 Market Value (on individual basis)	5,000
1/6/2013	Set 2 Market Value (on individual basis)	10,000
1/7/2014	Set 3 Market Value (on individual basis)	15,000
		30,000

continued overleaf

The market value of the three sets, if disposed of together, is £40,000.

For the purpose of computing George's CGT liability (if any) on the disposals, the aggregate £40,000 market value will be apportioned rateably to the three transactions as follows:

Revised consideration

				£
Set 1:	$\frac{5,000}{30,000}$	×	40,000	6,667
Set 2:	$\frac{10,000}{30,000}$	×	40,000	13,333
Set 3:	$\frac{15,000}{30,000}$	×	40,000	20,000
				40,000

George's liability to CGT would then be computed by reference to the increased consideration for each of the three disposals separately.

13.14 Losses

13.14.1 General

Losses are computed in the same manner as gains. An allowable loss may arise in certain circumstances even where the asset is not disposed of, e.g. a loss arising from the value of an asset becoming negligible (see **Section 19.7**). Note that, when computing a company's chargeable gain, **indexation allowance cannot create or increase a loss**, i.e. the indexation allowance is limited to the amount required to reduce the gain to nil.

Subject to certain specific exemptions, **allowable losses may not be carried back** prior to the year of assessment in which they are incurred. They may **not be set-off against other income**, except in certain situations (see later).

In general, a loss is an allowable loss if, had there been a gain on the disposal of the assets, the gain would have been a chargeable gain.

Current year capital losses

Allowable losses arising must be set-off against chargeable gains accruing in the same year of assessment insofar as this is possible, even if this wastes all or part of the annual exemption. Current year capital losses may be set against gains subject to the higher rate of CGT in order to maximise tax relief. To the extent that there is an unutilised balance, the capital losses unutilised must be carried forward and set-off against chargeable gains arising in subsequent years.

Capital losses carried forward

As seen at **Section 13.7.3**, the taxpayer does not have to use all of the losses brought forward. The taxpayer may "restrict" the quantum of the brought forward loss (or not use it at all) in order to ensure that the full benefit of that year's annual exemption is preserved.

Note: good tax planning would be to reduce the chargeable gain with enough losses brought forward to bring the chargeable gain down to the level of the annual exemption, and then carry forward any excess capital losses.

Example 13.11
An individual has the following gains/losses for 2014/15:

		£
Asset 1	Gain	6,000
Asset 2	Gain	2,000
Asset 3	Loss	(4,000)
Asset 4	Gain	1,000

The individual also has allowable losses forward of £2,000 from 2013/14. Loss relief will be claimed as follows:

	£
Chargeable gains	9,000
Deduct: 2014/15 current year capital losses	(4,000)
Brought forward losses not utilised (gain already covered by annual exemption)	5,000
Deduct: annual exemption	(5,000)
Net taxable gains after loss/annual exemption	nil
£6,000 of annual exemption would be lost	

Carry forward capital losses of £2,000 remain.

13.14.2   Carry-back of Losses

The general rule is that capital losses cannot be carried back to earlier years. An exception to this rule is made in the case of losses which accrue to an individual in the year in which they die. These losses may be carried back and set against gains of the three years of assessment preceding the year of assessment in which the individual died, with these losses set-off against the later years first.

As with capital losses carried forward, capital losses carried back are set against the net gains only to the extent that those net gains exceed the annual exemption for the year in which they arise.

Example 13.12
Mr X dies on 31 August 2014. In the period 6 April to 31 August 2014, Mr X made disposals of assets and realised allowable losses of £15,000.

The losses of £15,000 will first be available for set-off against any chargeable gains assessed on Mr X in 2013/14, with any residue against any chargeable gains in 2012/13 and, finally, against any chargeable gains in the tax year 2011/12. Any overpaid tax will be repaid to his estate by HMRC.

Example 13.13
Patricia died on 30 December 2014. She had made a capital loss of £8,500 in 2014/15 prior to her death. Patricia had net gains in the previous three years of £12,900 (2013/14), £8,600 (2012/13) and £10,200 (2011/12).

Given that the annual exemption for each year was £10,900 (2013/14), £10,600 (2012/13) and £10,600 (2011/12), show the amount assessable to CGT for each tax year.

Solution

2014/15: Losses in this tax year, so nil assessable and £11,000 of annual exemption is wasted.

continued overleaf

> 2013/14: Net gains exceed the annual exemption of £10,900 by £2,000. Hence, only £2,000 of carried back losses will be utilised, leaving the excess of £6,500 available to carry-back to earlier years.
>
> 2012/13: Gain of £8,600 can be covered by the annual exemption (£2,000 of which is wasted). No utilisation of carried back losses required.
>
> 2011/12: Net gain exceeds the then annual exemption of £10,600 by £100, so taxpayer can utilise loss of £100. The remainder of the carried back losses of £6,400 (£6,500 – £100) **cannot be relieved.**
>
> The assessable amounts for each of the years are thus NIL and the taxpayer's estate or personal representatives will be entitled to a repayment of the CGT already paid in the tax years 2011/12 and 2013/14.

13.14.3 Losses on Chattels

We will see below that, where a chargeable chattel is disposed of for gross proceeds of £6,000 or less, it is **exempt** from CGT.

13.14.4 Losses between Connected Persons

Losses realised by a person on the disposal of an asset to another person with whom they are connected may **only** be set-off against any chargeable gains realised by them on the disposal of an asset to the **same connected person**.

13.14.5 General Restriction on Loss Relief

The following general rules apply in relation to relief for capital losses:

1. Losses may not be set-off against gains of an earlier year of assessment except in the case of losses accruing to an individual in the year of death.
2. Relief may not be given more than once in respect of any loss.
3. A loss accruing to a person who is neither resident nor ordinarily resident in the year of assessment is not an allowable loss for CGT purposes unless, if a gain had accrued instead of a loss on the disposal, the person would have been chargeable on the gain. Thus, in general, relief for capital losses arising to non-resident persons is limited to losses incurred on the disposal of assets of a business carried on in the UK through a branch or agency (or PE in the case of a company).

13.14.6 Personal Representatives

Personal representatives are treated as having the deceased's residence, ordinary residence and domicile at the date of death. They are liable to CGT on any disposal made by them during the administration period of the estate. They are entitled to the annual exemption for the year of death and the following two years.

However, UK representatives of a non-resident deceased person are **not** chargeable to CGT. This exception does not apply to trustees.

13.14.7 Losses on Assets Qualifying for Capital Allowances

In general, expenditure allowable as a deduction in computing trading profits is not deductible in computing chargeable gains. There is no general exclusion of expenditure for which a "capital allowance" is made. However, if a capital loss accrues on the disposal of such an asset (e.g. machinery used in a business), it may be restricted with reference to any capital allowances claimed. This would have the effect of reducing the capital loss to nil, but it can never turn a loss into a gain. Where a gain arises on the disposal of such an asset, no account is taken of capital allowances claimed and the normal rules apply.

Example 13.14

Patricia purchased a machine used in her business for £115,000 on 6 April 2011. The machine was eligible for capital allowances (no first year allowances (FYAs) were claimed). She sold the machine in May 2014 for £65,000. Compute her chargeable gain/loss on this sale. The accounting date of the business is 31 March.

Solution

As capital allowances have been claimed on the cost of the asset, the loss arising is restricted by the capital allowances claimed. This is necessary as otherwise double tax relief would be obtained on the asset. Therefore, any loss arising on the sale of the asset will not be allowable for CGT purposes as it will have been effectively relieved already for income tax purposes.

Capital allowances after any balancing adjustment is £50,000 (£115,000 – £65,000).

To confirm:

	£	£
Cost	115,000	
Capital allowances claimed to date: 3 yrs (W1)	(53,139)	53,139
TWDV	61,861	
Entry in pool (lower of cost and proceeds)	(65,000)	
Balancing adjustment to pool in yr of sale	(3,139)	(3,139)
Total allowances claimed:		50,000

CGT Computation

	£
Gross proceeds	65,000
Cost	(115,000)
Gain/(Loss)	(50,000)
Reduced by relief obtained for capital allowances against income tax	50,000
Capital loss	0

	Allowances
	£
W1: Purchase price	115,000	
Less 20% WDA 11/12	(23,000)	23,000
TWDV c/f to 12/13	92,000	
Less 18% WDA 12/13	(16,560)	16,560
TWDV c/f to 13/14	75,440	
Less 18% WDA 13/14	(13,579)	13,579
TWDV c/f to 14/15	61,861	
Total capital allowances claimed		53,139

13.15 Other Issues

FA 2008 introduced a number of fundamental reforms to the CGT regime. One of the main changes was the introduction of a single rate of tax to be applied to the chargeable gains of an individual, namely 18% (a higher rate of 28% was introduced with effect from 23 June 2010 by FA (No. 2) 2010). Other major changes were the abolition of the indexation allowance, the simplification of the rules relating to the disposal of shares or securities and the abolition of taper relief. Furthermore, there was the abolition of the "kink test".

CGT was introduced in 1965 and originally applied to assets disposed of after that date. FA 1988 changed the CGT base date to 31 March 1982, with only the part of any gain accruing after 31 March 1982 being taxable (obviously this only affected assets acquired prior to 31 March 1982). This was achieved by allowing the taxpayer to substitute the asset's market value at 31 March 1982 for its acquisition cost. The taxpayer had the option to still use the acquisition cost if greater, and this comparison became known as the "kink test". FA 2008 abolished this rule. Thus for disposals after 6 April 2008 of assets acquired before 31 March 1982, the gain or loss arising is **always** calculated with reference to the market value as at 31 March 1982 (rebasing) and no other calculations are necessary.

Thus, all acquisition and enhancement costs incurred on or before 31 March 1982 are irrelevant for CGT purposes for individuals as they will be replaced by the asset's market value as at 31 March 1982.

It is important to note that the CGT reforms introduced by FA 2008 do **not apply** to companies, which still have the "kink test" and indexation allowance (a company cannot avail of the annual exemption or taper relief).

FA 2008 also clarifies that, on spousal no gain/no loss transfers which took place pre-6 April 2008, the transferee's base cost will be the sum of the transferor's 31 March 1982 value and the accrued indexation allowance.

Questions

Review Questions
(See Suggested Solutions to Review Questions at the end of this textbook.)

Question 13.1

1. Maurice purchased a holiday home for £20,000 on 2 February 1987 and subsequently sold it on 30 November 2014 for £80,000. Incidental legal costs on purchase amounted to £600 and £750 on sale. Maurice's taxable income for the year, after all deductions and allowances, was £30,400.

2. Vincent bought shares in a plc in December 1971 for £800. He sold the shares for £9,300 on 30 April 2014. The market value of the shares on 31 March 1982 was £1,200. Vincent's taxable income for the year, after all deductions and allowances, was £19,750.

Requirement
Compute the CGT due or allowable losses in each case.

Note: assume that the individuals had no other realised gains or losses during the year or brought forward from previous years and ignore indexation.

Question 13.2

1. James acquired an asset in July 1967 for £160,000. Additional capital expenditure was incurred as follows:

	£
July 1971	8,000
July 1993	10,000

James sold the asset on 31 May 2014 for £650,000. The market value of the asset at 31 March 1982 was £230,000.

James had no other capital gains during 2014/15 and no capital losses brought forward. He had other taxable income in the year (after personal allowance and other reliefs) of £58,000.

Requirement

Compute the CGT payable by James (ignoring indexation).

2. Declan purchased a property on 6 April 1971 for £15,000. Additional expenditure was incurred as follows:

	£
Additional 5 June 1973	5,000
Additional 6 August 1984	20,000
Additional 1 February 2003	39,250

The market value of the property at 31 March 1982 was £55,000.

Declan sold the property for £400,000 on 1 July 2014.

Declan had no other capital gains during 2014/15 and no capital losses brought forward. He had other taxable income in the year (after personal allowance and other reliefs) of £26,865

Requirement

Compute the CGT payable by Declan on the sale (ignoring indexation).

Question 13.3

Paulette owned a five-acre plot of land, which she had acquired as an investment in August 1995 for £18,000. On 25 March 2015, she sold two acres of it for £80,000, from which selling costs totalling £3,500 were deducted. The remaining three acres were valued at £145,000 on 25 February 2015.

Paulette had taxable income for 2014/15 of £25,000 and made no other disposals during the year.

Requirement

Calculate Paulette's capital gains tax liability for 2014/15 and state when the capital gains tax liability falls due for payment.

Territoriality Rules

14.1 Territoriality Rules

An individual's exposure to UK Capital Gains Tax (CGT) generally depends on residence and domicile status. The UK comprises Great Britain and Northern Ireland and includes its territorial waters. The Channel Isles and the Isle of Man are **not** part of the UK. Finance Act 2013 saw the introduction of a new statutory residence test effective from 6 April 2013. With that came the abolishment of the concept of "ordinary residence". Prior to 6 April 2013, a UK domiciled individual was chargeable to CGT in respect of worldwide gains if they were resident or ordinarily resident in the UK.

The terms "residence", "ordinarily resident" (prior to 6 April 2013) and "domicile" have the same meaning for CGT as they have for income tax.

From 6 April 2008, a "day" in the UK is a day the individual is present at the end of the day, i.e. at midnight. Prior to 6 April 2008, the day of arrival and the day of departure were not counted as a "day" in the UK.

With effect from 6 April 2013, HMRC's guidance in HMRC6 *Residence, Domicile and the Remittance Basis* has been replaced with the statutory residence test introduced in FA 2013.

14.2 Statutory Residence Test

14.2.1 Background

After an extensive consultation process, which began in June 2011, a new statutory residence test came into force on 6 April 2013. Prior to its introduction, there was no statutory definition of "residence" in UK tax law. Instead, a combination of case law, statutory provisions and non-binding guidance from HMRC prevailed. This had resulted in uncertainty for taxpayers, given that recent decided cases had demonstrated that reliance could not necessarily be placed on published HMRC guidance.

The new rules seek to produce a test that taxpayers can use to produce a conclusive answer as to whether they are UK resident or not in any given tax year.

14.2.2 New Rules

The new test took effect from 6 April 2013 and determines an individual's liability to UK income tax, capital gains tax and (in some cases) inheritance tax. There are three levels to the test:

1. an automatic overseas test;
2. an automatic residence test; and
3. a sufficient ties test.

Each test should be reviewed in turn and, if this does not conclude an individual's status, then it is necessary to review the next test. As soon as a conclusion is reached as to an individual's status, then there is no need to consider the remaining elements of the test.

For example, if the automatic overseas test is fulfilled, the individual will be classed as a non-UK resident. Otherwise it is necessary to progress through the two remaining tests and, if either one is satisfied, then the individual will be regarded as resident in the UK for tax purposes.

The test also distinguishes between "arrivers" and "leavers".

- Arrivers are individuals who have *not* been resident in the UK in any of the past three years.
- Leavers are individuals who have been resident in the UK for any of the past three years.

14.2.3 Automatic Overseas Tests

If any of the automatic overseas tests are met for a tax year, the individual is automatically non-resident for that year. These three tests should therefore be considered first, because if any one of them is met, it is not necessary to consider any of the remaining parts. The three tests are:

1. Resident in the UK for one or more of the three tax years preceding the tax year, and visits the UK for fewer than 16 days in the UK in the tax year.
2. Resident in the UK for none of the three tax years preceding the tax year, and visits the UK for fewer than 46 days in the UK in the tax year.
3. Work full-time overseas over the tax year, spends less than 91 days in the UK in the tax year with no more than 31 days spent working in the UK.

Example 14.1: Automatic Overseas Tests

1st automatic overseas test
Eamonn left the UK (where he had always lived and worked) on 6 April 2014 to live with his Italian girlfriend in Florence. He returned later that year on 23 December 2014 for two weeks to attend his eldest brother's wedding as he was best man.

He is non-UK resident in 2014/15 under the first automatic overseas test as he was UK resident for one or more of the three tax years preceding 2014/15 (he was UK resident for all of the previous three) and he visited the UK for fewer than 16 days in the tax year (his visit constituted 14 days only).

2nd automatic overseas test
Philip has been Swiss resident in previous tax years. He comes to the UK in 2014/15 on several occasions. First, he visits Belfast for a week to attend several unsuccessful job interviews. He meets a girl at one of the interviews and returns two months later to see her, spending two weeks travelling around Northern Ireland. He then returns for another round of interviews (again unsuccessful) for two weeks in March 2015.

continued overleaf

He is non-UK resident in 2014/15 under the second automatic overseas test as he was non-UK resident for the three tax years preceding 2014/15 and he visited the UK for fewer than 46 days in the tax year (his visits totalled 35 days, only being five weeks).

3rd automatic overseas test
James left the UK on 1 June 2014 after taking up a two-year secondment with the German company of the multinational group he works for. He works a standard 37.5-hour week from that date. As part of his contract he returns to the UK on a regular basis for meetings and work purposes, spending two days each month in the UK. He also returns to the UK for the month of February 2015 to be with his mother, who is terminally ill.

James is non-UK resident in 2014/15 under the second automatic overseas test. This is because:

- he works full time overseas over the tax year; and
- he spent less than 91 days in the UK (James spent 46 days in the UK); and
- no more than 31 days were spent working in the UK (James worked 18 days in the UK (being two days per month for nine months)).

14.2.4 Automatic Residence Tests

Subject to not meeting any of the automatic overseas tests, the individual will be classed as resident in the UK for a tax year if they meet any of the four automatic UK tests:

Test 1. Present in the UK for 183 or more days.

Test 2. Have a home available in the UK for more than 90 days and visits that home for 30 days in the tax year and either:

    (a) this is the individual's only home, or

    (b) the individual has an overseas home but does not use it for at least 30 days in the tax year.

Test 3. Works full time in the UK for 365 days or more without a significant break and more than 75% of these days are in the UK.

Test 4. Where the individual dies and was UK resident for each of the three preceding years and has a home in the UK when they died.

Example 14.2: 1st, 3rd and 4th automatic UK tests
1st automatic UK test
James came to the UK to stay with his girlfriend's family on 25 May 2014. He is resident under the first automatic UK test in 2014/15 as he was present in the UK for more than 183 days.

3rd automatic UK test
Sonya comes to the UK on 1 September 2014 after taking up a secondment with the UK company of the multinational group she works for in France. She works a standard 37.5-hour week from that date until 31 August 2015, when she returns to France for work. During that time she has holidays of 20 days.

Sonya is resident in 2014/15 as she does not meet an automatic overseas test but does meet an automatic UK test. This is because:

- she carries out full-time work in the UK for a period of 365 days, with no significant break (at least 31 days) and all or part of that 365-day period falls within the tax year; and
- more than 75% of the total number of days in the 365-day period when more than three hours work per day are worked in the UK; and

continued overleaf

▨ at least one day in the tax year is a day on which she does more than three hours of work in the UK.

However, Sonya may attract split-year basis in 2014/15 when she arrives in the UK and in 2015/16 when she leaves the UK to return to work in France.

4th automatic UK test
David died on 5 December 2014 and has lived and worked in the UK all his life. He died at home in the house he owned with his wife surrounded by his family. David is resident in the UK in 2014/15 as he was UK resident for each of the three preceding years and had a home in the UK when he died.

Example 14.3: 2nd automatic UK test
The following examples are adapted from HMRC's *Guidance Note: Statutory Residence Test (SRT)*, available on www.hmrc.gov.uk.

▨ Stan has lived in Australia all his life. In June 2014 he takes a holiday in London and likes it so much he decides to emigrate to the UK. He spends the next few months preparing for the move. He sells his Australian house (his only home) on 10 January 2015 and arrives in the UK on 25 January 2015. He finds a flat in London and moves in on 1 February 2015. The London flat is now his only home and he lives there for a year. During the tax year 2014/15 Stan is present in his Australian home on 250 days, and he is present in his London flat on 55 days.

In 2014/15 Stan has a home in the UK from 1 February 2015 and is present in it on at least 30 days. Also from 1 February 2015, there is a period of 91 consecutive days, at least 30 of which fell in 2014/15 (the tax year under consideration), when Stan has a UK home and no overseas home.

As Stan does not meet any of the automatic overseas tests, he is resident under the second automatic UK test for tax year 2014/15.

▨ Jane has a home in the UK throughout tax year 2014/15 and tax year 2015/16. She is present in that home on more than 30 days during tax year 2014/15.

Jane acquires an overseas home on 1 March 2015 and is present there on 30 days in tax year 2014/15.

Although there is a period of 91 consecutive days, 30 of which fall in 2014/15 (the tax year under consideration), when Jane had both a UK home and an overseas home, there is also a period of at least 91 consecutive days (6 April 2014 to 28 February 2015) when she had a UK home (in which she spent sufficient time in 2014/15) but no overseas home.

Jane is therefore resident in the UK for 2014/15 under the second automatic UK test.

▨ Edith has had a home in Cheshire for many years. It is her only home. Edith retires towards the end of tax year 2014/15 and decides to use her retirement lump sum to see the world.

During tax year 2015/16 she takes three long holidays, visiting 22 different countries. She moves around and does not establish a home overseas. She keeps her Cheshire home throughout, returning to it briefly between trips, and is present there on 41 days in tax year 2015/16.

In 2015/16 Edith has a home in the UK in which she is present on at least 30 days in the tax year. During the year Edith has no overseas home.

Edith does not meet any of the automatic overseas tests and therefore she is resident under the second automatic UK test for tax year 2015/16.

continued overleaf

> At 6 April 2015 Berni considers whether she meets the second automatic UK test for 2014/15:
>
> - She bought a home in the UK on 1 January 2014. It was her home throughout 2014/15.
> - She was present in that home on at least 30 days in the tax year 2014/15.
> - She came to the UK on 10 April 2014 and rented out her overseas home (which she had owned for many years) from 11 April 2014 to 10 March 2015.
>
> Therefore, during 2014/15 there was a period of 91 days, 30 of which fell in the tax year during which Berni had a UK home in which she was present for a sufficient amount of time, and had no overseas home. As Berni did not meet any of the automatic overseas tests, she is resident under the second automatic UK test.

14.2.5 Sufficient Ties Tests

This test is to be applied if the individual does not meet any of either the automatic overseas tests or the automatic residence tests.

The sufficient ties test sets out five further factors which must be considered together with the number of days spent in the UK in order to determine an individual's residence. The five connecting ties are:

1. *Family*: this test of connection concerns the individual's 'relevant relationships' with people who are resident in the UK. This is taken to include spouses, civil and common law partners and minor children.
2. *Accommodation*: this tie exists if the individual has accommodation in the UK which is available for a continuous period of at least 90 days in that year and at least one night is spent there. The threshold is reduced to 16 days where the accommodation belongs to a close relative.
3. *Work*: if the individual performs more than three hours work a day in UK for at least 40 days then a work tie is established.
4. *90 days*: this test is satisfied if the individual spends more than 90 days in the UK in either the preceding tax year or the year immediately previous to that.
5. *Country*: this test only applies to leavers and is fulfilled if the UK is the country in which the individual was present at midnight for the greatest number of days in that tax year. It is designed to catch leavers who do not take up residence in any other country following a period of UK residence.

Since 6 April 2008, a "day" of residence in the UK has been counted where the individual is present in the country at the end of the day i.e. at midnight. This day counting methodology is retained within the statutory residence test. However, a deeming rule has been added which overrides the conventional day counting mechanism and is to be applied in instances where individuals regularly spend time in the UK but leave before midnight.

Whether the individual is considered to be UK resident is a factor of the number of ties established taken together with the number of days the individual has spent in the UK with reference to the following table:

Days spent in the UK	Ties needed for a Leaver	Ties needed for an Arriver
16–45	At least 4	N/A - Always non-resident
46–90	At least 3	All 4
91–120	At least 2	At least 3
120+	At least 1	At least 2

Example 14.4

Stefan arrives in the UK on 1 February 2015 and leaves on 1 April 2015, staying with a close friend during that time. Stefan was UK resident in 2010/11. His daughter Arya (who is 12) attends a boarding school in London. Two days after Stefan arrives he succeeds in getting temporary full-time work until he leaves on 1 April to return to Switzerland.

Stefan does not meet any of the automatic UK or overseas tests. The sufficient ties test dictates that as an arriver in the UK and spending between 46 and 90 days (Stefan spends 60 days) in the UK, Stefan must have all four ties – family, accommodation, work and 90 days – to be UK resident in 2014/15.

Stefan only has two ties (family tie by virtue of his minor daughter attending a UK boarding school and a work tie by virtue of working full time for at least 40 days). Stefan does not have an accommodation tie as he does not have UK accommodation for a continuous period of at least 90 days. Nor does he have a 90 days tie as he did not spend 90 days in the UK in either 2013/14 or 2012/13. Therefore Stefan is non-resident in 2014/15.

14.3 Domicile

Domicile is a difficult concept as it has evolved through case law and is not legislatively defined. In broad terms, unlike residence, an individual can only ever have one domicile at any one time. An existing domicile is presumed to continue until it has been proved that a new domicile has been acquired.

1. *Domicile of Origin*   An individual acquires a domicile of origin at birth. This is usually the domicile of their father (or that of their mother if the father predeceased the child's birth, or the parents were unmarried). This is not necessarily the country where they were born.
2. *Domicile of Dependency*   If, before the age of 16, the parent from whom they have taken their domicile should change, then the child's domicile will follow that of this parent.
3. *Domicile of Choice*   At aged 16, an individual can acquire a different domicile by a combination of residence and intention. The individual must sever all ties with the country of their former domicile and settle in the new country with the clear intention of making their permanent home there indefinitely.

14.4 Foreign Tax

If a gain made on the disposal of a foreign asset suffers foreign tax, then relief will be available in the UK against any CGT on the same disposal. As discussed earlier, there are two forms of relief: reducing the net gain charged to UK CGT by the foreign tax paid and (the more widely used) credit relief. The form of relief available depends on whether a double taxation treaty exists and, if so, what provisions are included therein.

14.5 Residence Condition is Met

14.5.1 UK Assets

A person is chargeable to UK CGT on gains arising on the disposal of UK assets if the residence condition is met in the year of assessment. The residence condition is, in the case of an individual, that the individual be resident in the UK for the year in question. Losses arising on the disposal of such assets are allowable losses available for set-off (see **Chapters 13** and **19**).

14.5.2 Foreign Assets

A UK domiciled individual who is resident in the UK for 2013/14 is chargeable to UK CGT on an arising basis on **worldwide** chargeable gains arising on the disposal of assets.

Therefore, an individual who is resident in the UK and is UK domiciled is taxable in the UK on gains arising anywhere in the world, regardless of whether or not the proceeds are remitted to the UK.

Please note below the special rules introduced from 6 April 2008 in relation to individuals with a foreign domicile. In essence, a foreign domiciled individual who is resident in the UK for 2013/14 may, in certain instances, only be liable to UK CGT on foreign gains to the extent that the proceeds are remitted to the UK, i.e. be able to apply the remittance basis of tax. Such individuals will always be liable to UK CGT on gains arising in the UK. Where the remittance basis does not apply, the individual will be assessable on foreign gains on an arising basis. See below for rules applying to overseas losses for individuals taxed under the remittance basis.

It is important to determine if a gain is a UK gain or a foreign gain. **Chapter 13** sets out the CGT rules on location of assets. For example, shares of a UK incorporated company are treated as UK located assets regardless of where the share certificate is kept.

14.5.3 Split-year Residence

Prior to the introduction of the statutory residence test, the above rules were applied so that, if for any part of the tax year in which the disposal occurred, an individual was resident or ordinarily resident in the UK, then any gain arising on that disposal was charged to UK CGT. However, by concession, if during a tax year an individual arrived or left the UK, then the split-year residence rules may have applied and they may only have been assessed on gains arising after they arrived in the UK or before they left the UK, as applicable. Certain conditions must, however, have been met.

The concept of a split year between a resident and non-resident period within a single tax year is put into statutory form for the first time with effect from 6 April 2013.

14.6 Residence Condition is not Met

The general rule is that an individual who is non-resident (and not ordinarily resident prior to 6 April 2013) in the UK is not subject to UK CGT. There are, however, two exceptions to this rule:

1. A non-resident person carrying on a business in the UK through a branch or agency (or PE in the company case) is chargeable to UK CGT (or corporation tax) on gains arising from assets in the UK that are used for the purposes of the UK business.
    Note: rollover relief will be available where the replacement asset is situated in the UK. (See **Chapter 19**.)
    There is also anti-avoidance legislation to deal with the situation where assets are transferred abroad before a disposal or where the branch or agency trade has ceased. In such situations, HMRC imputes a deemed disposal at market value at the relevant date.
2. Gains arising under anti-avoidance provisions for temporary non-residents (see below).

14.7 Temporary Non-residents

A person who is a "temporary non-resident" may be chargeable to CGT on gains accruing during their period of absence from the UK. This is anti-avoidance legislation designed to cover the situation where the individual crystallises their unrealised gains whilst temporarily abroad (i.e. temporarily residing outside the UK). In the absence of the following rule, the taxpayer could escape UK CGT by simply leaving the UK for a relatively short time and realising any gains on their chargeable assets during their period of non-UK residence. The statutory residence test builds upon the existing legislation to make the test of temporary non-residence more comprehensive.

In essence, where an individual has left the UK and subsequently returns, they are chargeable to CGT on gains arising during their absence on the disposal of assets they **owned prior to their departure** if:

- following a residence period (i.e. a full tax year or the overseas/UK split part of a year) where the individual has a sole UK residence, one or more residence periods occur for which they do not have sole UK residence;
- in four or more of the seven tax years immediately preceding the year of departure the individual had either:
  - sole UK residence for the tax year; or
  - the year was a split year that included a residence period for which the individual had sole UK residence, and
- the period of non-residence is five years or less.

Note that, for the above rules to not apply, the period of temporary non-residence has to be for more than five years. It does not have to be for five complete tax years as was previously the case prior to the introduction of the statutory residence test.

The gains arising in their year of departure are taxable in that year, while the gains arising during their absence from the UK under the temporary non-resident rules are deemed to arise and be taxed in the tax year of their return to the UK.

The individual will be able to claim the annual exemption for the year of departure and the year of return but will not be able to avail of annual exemptions during the period of non-residence.

If losses are made during the period of non-residence, then these losses are allowable and will be set-off against the gains arising in the year of return.

Note: these anti-avoidance rules do not apply to assets acquired while non-UK resident.

Example 14.5

Richie Rich owns 40% of the shares in TeleUK Ltd. The shares cost him £200,000 in 2000/01. He lived in the UK from birth until he emigrated in October 2013. He sold the shares for £500,000 in December 2014 and realised a gain of £300,000.

During February 2016 he sold other shares making a loss of £10,000. He had also acquired these shares during 2000/01.

On 20 April 2016 he sold a UK property, which he had acquired in December 2013, realising a gain of £100,000.

He returned to live in the UK in August 2018.

Solution

Date of departure: October 2013
Date of return: August 2018

As Richie Rich returned to the UK within five years the gains arising in the non-resident period which were owned at the time of departure are taxable in the year of return.

	£
2014/15	300,000
2015/16	(10,000)
Total chargeable gains 2018/19	290,000

Note: the gain on the UK property in 2013/14 does not come into charge as it was acquired after Richie had left the UK and was disposed of during a tax year in which he was non-resident.

Therefore, if a person who has always lived in the UK wishes to become non-resident to avoid paying UK CGT on assets which he owns, he must remain resident outside the UK for at least five years. Prior to the introduction of the statutory residence test, the period of non-residence was at least five full tax years.

14.8 Apportionment of Non-resident Company's Gains

If a foreign company would be a "close company" if it were UK resident, then certain chargeable gains accruing to such a company may be treated as accruing to any UK resident and domiciled individual shareholders who are participators in the foreign company.

For such attribution of gains to UK shareholders under these rules to apply, the shareholders must hold more than 10% of the company.

There is no charge accruing on the disposal of an asset used only for the purposes of a trade carried on outside the UK.

Capital losses arising to the foreign company may be attributed back up to the UK shareholders for offset against any attributed gains arising in the same tax year.

Finance Act 2008 widened the scope of this legislation to include non-domiciled individuals. The application of these provisions is beyond the scope of this course.

14.9 Days Spent in the UK

From 6 April 2008, for a "day" to count for residence test purposes an individual must be in the UK at midnight. Whilst this day count test is retained within the statutory residence test, it is subject to three exceptions:

1. a day does not count if the individual is in transit through the UK and does not engage in activities that are to a substantial extent unrelated to their passage through the UK;
2. time spent in the UK due to exceptional circumstances (i.e. beyond the individual's control). Those days may not count towards the total day count for certain parts of the statutory residence test; and
3. a new 'deeming rule' has been introduced to take account of individuals who spend considerable numbers of days in the UK but without ever being present in the UK at midnight. The deeming rule applies to for a tax year if the individual has:
   (a) been UK resident in one or more of the preceding three tax years;
   (b) at least three UK ties for the tax year; and
   (c) been present in the UK on more than 30 days without being present at the end of each such day (called "qualifying days") in the tax year.

If the individual meet all these conditions the deeming rule means that, after the first 30 qualifying days, all subsequent qualifying days within the tax year are treated as days spent in the UK.

14.10 Non-UK Domiciles – post-6 April 2008

Prior to FA 2008, a resident or ordinarily resident but non-domiciled individual was taxable on foreign gains only to the extent that the proceeds were remitted (i.e. taken back) to the UK. Therefore, if the proceeds remained outside the UK, no UK CGT would arise on the foreign gain. This was the remittance basis of taxation and it was applied automatically (UK CGT was still chargeable on gains on UK assets on an arising basis).

However, the rules were changed with effect from 6 April 2008 and only certain individuals are now permitted to avail of the generous remittance basis of taxation.

Under the current rules, there is a **basic assumption** that a resident (or ordinarily resident prior to 6 April 2013) but non-UK domiciled individual will be taxed on foreign chargeable gains on the arising basis of taxation **unless** they make a claim for the remittance basis of taxation to apply.

Up until 5 April 2012, special rules applied where the individual was regarded as a long-term resident of the UK. Such individuals are required to pay a "remittance basis charge" of £30,000 in addition to any tax on sums remitted into the UK if they wish to claim the remittance basis of taxation in relation to their income and/or gains.

FA 2012 announced that the annual remittance charge would increase to £50,000 from non-UK domiciled individuals who have been UK resident for 12 or more of the 14 tax years preceding the year of claim. The £30,000 charge will be retained for those who have been resident for at least seven of the preceding nine years.

14.10.1   Remittance Basis of Taxation with No Claim Required

No formal claim is required for the remittance basis of taxation to be applied in the following two instances:

1. Where the unremitted income or gains arising overseas is less than £2,000. The £2,000 is the net unremitted income or gains for the year.

    For example, Pierre is UK resident but French domiciled. He has lived in the UK for the past 10 years and makes a capital gain in France of £120,000 (€145,000) in the tax year 2014/15. He has no other income or gains outside the UK and he remits all except £1,000 of the proceeds on the sale to the UK. Pierre will be taxed automatically on the remittance basis of taxation.

2. Where there is no UK income or gains, and no remittances are made, and provided the individual has been here for fewer than seven out of the preceding nine years or 12 of the last 14 tax years or is under 18 years old. In determining if relevant income and gains have been remitted, account must be taken of pre-6 April 2008 remittances.

    For example, Pierre's sister Marie is a student living in the UK since mid-2006. She is aged 21. She has no UK income or gains but has small French savings. She has not made any remittances to the UK. She can have the benefit of the remittance basis of tax without having to make a formal claim.

If either of these cases applies, the individual will not lose their entitlement to UK personal allowances, income tax reliefs or the annual exemption for CGT.

14.10.2   Remittance Basis of Taxation with a Formal Claim Required

Where a formal claim is made, certain allowances are withdrawn including the CGT annual exemption of £11,000.

An individual who is not a long-term resident will be required to make a formal claim for the remittance basis of taxation to apply; however, they will not have to pay the remittance basis charge noted below. Such individuals could not avail of the annual exemption.

14.11   Remittance Basis Charge

An individual who is over 18 years of age during the tax year and has been **resident in the UK for seven out of nine years (or 12 of the last 14 years) immediately preceding the year of assessment** will only be able to use the remittance basis if they pay the "remittance basis charge" (RBC) for the year. These are long-term residents. The charge will not apply in situations where the remittance basis is available without a formal claim.

A non-domiciled individual who arrived in the UK in 2004/05 (or earlier) will need to pay the RBC of £30,000 if they wish to have the benefit of the remittance basis of taxation. Such an individual now has a choice as to whether they wish to be assessed on their foreign income and gains on the remittance basis of taxation or on the arising basis of taxation. If they do not claim and so do not pay the RBC, they will be assessed to UK tax on their worldwide income and gains on the arising basis.

If the non-domiciled individual arrived in the UK in 1998/99, the increased RBC of £50,000 would become payable assuming the remittance basis of taxation is selected. The £30,000 or £50,000 charge is in addition to any tax due on the foreign income and gains remitted to the UK.

An individual with a foreign domicile who pays the £30,000 or £50,000 is known as a "remittance basis user" (RBU).

The RBC is a charge on *nominated unremitted income and gains* rather than a standalone charge and the foreign domiciled individual can nominate any amount of income or gains. The nominated amounts are then charged to tax as if they were taxed on an arising basis. They cannot be charged to tax again if they are remitted to the UK. However, HMRC states that any other unremitted income and gains that the individual may have are deemed to be "remitted" **before** the nominated income and gains. The nominated tax within the RBC will usually be eligible for relief for the purposes of the double taxation treaties (i.e. against foreign tax in the country in which foreign income/gains arise).

HMRC has confirmed that, if the RBC payment is paid directly to HMRC from an overseas account, this will not be treated as a remittance of tax and there will be no liability on it. If the individual were to remit £30,000 or £50,000 to the UK **and** then use that money to pay the additional charge, this latter remittance would be taxable.

14.11.1   Summary: Claims for Remittance Basis

An individual who is UK resident and non-domiciled and who wishes to pay tax on the remittance basis, must, as from 6 April 2008, pay the £30,000 additional charge (or £50,000 from 6 April 2012) **and**

1. make a claim to have access to the remittance basis;
2. have unremitted foreign income and gains of £2,000 or more arising in the year of the claim;
3. have been resident in the UK for that tax year;
4. have been resident in the UK for at least seven out of the preceding nine tax years (£30,000 charge); or,
5. have been resident in the UK for at least 12 out of the preceding 14 tax years (£50,000 charge).

The remittance basis can be applied to:

(a) chargeable overseas earnings;
(b) relevant foreign income; and
(c) foreign chargeable gains (i.e. gains accruing on the disposal of assets situated outside the UK).

It is important to note the loss of personal allowances and CGT annual exemption when the remittance basis of taxation is claimed.

The RBC will be administered and collected through the self-assessment system and normal filing and payment dates will apply. When considering whether the additional RBC charge is applicable, the individual will need to look back over the last 10 years, the 10th year being the year of the claim. If they have been resident for at least seven out of the nine tax years immediately preceding the year of the claim, then they will have to consider paying the RBC.

It should also be noted that the RBC applies irrespective of whether the individual is not present in the UK for the whole of the year; there is no *pro rata* reduction for those coming to or leaving the UK part way through a tax year.

14.12   Overseas Losses of Foreign Domiciles

Losses on foreign assets are allowable losses if the individual is taxed on their worldwide gains on an arising basis, e.g. the individual is UK domiciled.

Until April 2008, there was no relief for any overseas losses made by foreign domiciled individuals. However, from 6 April 2008, provisions have been made to introduce limited loss relief where a foreign domiciled individual is claiming the remittance basis of taxation and is paying the RBC.

In order to avail of this limited loss relief, **an election must be made in the first year when the remittance basis is claimed**, even if there are no foreign gains or losses realised in that year. If no election is made, foreign losses of that year and future tax years will **not be** allowable losses, even if the individual later opts to be taxed on an arising basis (unless they accept that they are domiciled in the UK).

An individual who is non-UK domiciled but has not claimed the remittance basis (e.g. because income and gains are less than £2,000 and no claim is required) may claim relief for losses on foreign assets as well as availing of the annual exemption.

Foreign chargeable gains remitted to the UK in a tax year later than that in which the foreign asset was disposed of **cannot** be reduced by losses of a later year or any year later than that in which the gains arose.

14.13   Meaning of Remittances

HMRC guidance on what constitutes a remittance is very widely drawn and it would be very easy to inadvertently remit monies to the UK for these purposes. These provisions are beyond the scope of this course.

Questions

Review Questions
(See Suggested Solutions to Review Questions at the end of this textbook.)

Question 14.1

Apply the statutory resident test to determine whether the following persons are or are not UK resident in the tax year 2014/15:

(a) Janet spends 10 days in the UK in 2014/15. She was previously resident in the UK in 2011/12.

(b) Paul comes to the UK in July 2014 and stays until March 2015, renting an apartment in Belfast. Paul was not resident in the UK in a previous tax year.

(c) In the tax year 2014/15, Victor works full time in Paris. He spends his summer holidays (three weeks of July 2014) in the UK, working five hours per day. He was resident in the UK in 2012/13.

(d) Christine comes to the UK in mid-November 2014. She buys a house in the UK on 1 February 2015, which she lives in as her home. This house is her only home and she stays in the UK for a number of years. Christine has never had an overseas home. She was not resident in the UK in a previous tax year.

(e) Terry spends 35 days in the UK in 2014/15. He was previously resident in the UK in 2010/11.

(f) Margaret comes to the UK on 22 November 2014 and begins full-time employment (eight hours per day) from 1 December 2014 to 30 November 2015. During that time she obtains holidays of 25 days.

(g) Ned loses his full-time job in the UK in March 2014. He remains unemployed in the UK and moves to Italy on 1 September 2014, and starts to work there full time the next day. He was resident in the UK in all previous tax years. He purchases an apartment in Italy shortly after he arrives, which he lives in as his home. Ned does not return to the UK during the remainder of 2014/15 and returns back to the UK permanently on 10 April 2015, when he starts a new full-time job. Ned does not have a home in the UK.

Question 14.2

You arrive into work on a Monday morning in mid-January to find the following email from a client, Jessica Arnold:

To:	An Accountant
From:	Jessica Arnold
Date:	10 January 2017 at 19.58pm
Subject:	Help!

Dear An Accountant,

I'm hoping you remember me; I was a client of your practice some years ago before I emigrated to Brisbane, Australia, and I need help with some tax issues.

I'm back in Northern Ireland briefly for a month-long visit from Oz, where I moved to from Armagh in June 2013. I only went on a yearlong secondment originally, but a week after arriving I met my husband, who was born here, and extended my stay indefinitely after getting married. We have just had our second child.

I'm here in Belfast for two weeks and we are hoping to move back permanently in early December of this year. We are hoping to have sold our flat in Australia by then.

The plan is that the proceeds of that sale will help towards a down payment on a wee house in Holywood. Our estate agent is very positive and expects me to make a profit on the flat of around £80,000.

Another useful source of funds to help us start a life in Northern Ireland will be the proceeds from the sale of a painting I inherited from my favourite Aunt Delilah in January 2010. I got £750,000 for the painting at an auction last October. I couldn't believe it as the probate value had only been £520,000. Apparently the artist has a huge following in Oz!

I'm a bit worried, though, if that creates any UK tax issues for me?

Best wishes,
Jessica

Requirement
Assess whether the temporary non-residence rules for capital gains tax apply to the above transactions. What practical advice would you give Jessica?

Question 14.3

Sophia has been UK resident since 6 April 2001 but is Belgian domiciled. She sold a foreign asset during 2014/15, resulting in a chargeable gain of £220,000 and remitted £25,000 of this to the UK during the year. Sophia is employed in the UK and pays the higher rate of tax on her employment income. She had no other sources of income during the tax year.

Requirement
Assess, with comparative calculations, if Sophia should make a claim to use the remittance basis in 2014/15 in respect of the above chargeable gain. Include calculations of the capital gains tax under each scenario and address any other relevant considerations.

Chattels and Wasting Assets

15.1 Chattels

A chattel is an item of "tangible movable property". Movable is not defined in the legislation. If an asset is attached to land or any building, it is usually regarded as part of that land or building and, therefore, is not movable, so the chattel rules will not apply. As you will see below, a wasting chattel is an asset with a remaining life of less than 50 years and such assets are generally exempt from CGT.

15.1.1 Chattels Rules

There are three special rules to be aware of for non-wasting chattels:

1. **Exemption relief**   If a chattel is sold for gross proceeds of £6,000 or less, then **any gain** will be exempt from CGT (even if capital allowances have been claimed). This is a very practical relief and can prove to be very beneficial.

   The £6,000 limit relates to the gross proceeds, prior to the deduction of any incidental costs of sale such as commission costs, etc.

Example 15.1
A work of art is bought for £1,000 and later sold for £3,500. The chargeable gain on disposal of £2,500 is exempt from CGT. There is no chargeable gain as the asset is a non-wasting chattel sold for less than £6,000, therefore the exemption rule applies.

---

2. **Marginal relief**   Where the gross proceeds exceed £6,000, an individual is able to avail of "marginal relief" in that the chargeable gain is restricted to the **lower of**

   (a) the gain itself, and
   (b) 5/3 of the excess of gross disposal proceeds over £6,000 (5/3 × (gross proceeds − £6,000)).

Example 15.2
Angela purchased a watercolour painting in May 2006 for £5,250. She sold the painting in June 2014 for £5,940, having incurred commission costs of 10% of the selling price. Calculate her chargeable gain.

Solution

	£
Gross sale proceeds (£5,940 × 100/90)	6,600
Incidental costs of sale (commission at 10%)	(660)
	5,940
Cost	(5,250)
Chargeable gain	690

Gain is the lower of:

(i) actual gain, £690 and

(ii) 5/3 × (£6,600 − £6,000) = £1,000

So the taxable gain is £690.

What would her gain have been if the cost in 2006 had been £4,600?

	£
Gross sale proceeds	6,600
Incidental costs of sale (commission at 10%)	(660)
	5,940
Cost	(4,600)
Chargeable gain	1,340

Gain is the lower of:

(i) actual gain of £1,340; and

(ii) 5/3 × (£6,600 − £6,000) = £1,000.

So the gain is restricted to £1,000.

---

3. **Restricted loss relief**   If the disposal consideration is less than £6,000 there is no tax charge on the chargeable gain arising. However, if a loss arises instead, any loss relief claim is restricted. So where a chattel is sold for less than £6,000, then any capital loss arising is restricted. In preparing the CGT computation, the actual proceeds are replaced by deemed proceeds of £6,000, which has the effect of reducing the allowable capital loss. This rule cannot turn a loss into a gain, instead the loss would be reduced to nil and there is neither a gain nor a loss.

Example 15.3
Geraldine purchased an antique table in January 2006 for £9,700. She sells this table for £6,400 in August 2014 (selling costs £200). Compute the allowable loss.

Solution
Since the gross proceeds exceed £6,000, the disposal of the chattel is not exempt.

	£
Gross proceeds	6,400
Less: disposal costs	(200)
Net proceeds	6,200

continued overleaf

Cost	(9,700)
Allowable loss	(3,500)

The special rules at 1, 2 and 3 above do not apply.

What would Angela's loss be if the gross sales proceeds had instead been £5,100?

In this instance, the gross proceeds are less than £6,000 (namely £5,100) and the cost is in excess of £6,000, so rule 3 above applies, and the loss is restricted by deeming the gross proceeds to be £6,000.

	£
Gross proceeds	5,100
Notional gross proceeds	6,000
Less: disposal costs	(200)
Net proceeds	5,800
Cost	(9,700)
Allowable loss (restricted)	(3,900)

Without this rule, the loss would have been £4,800.

15.2 Disposal as Part of a Set and Part Disposals

Since the chattel exemption can be quite beneficial, taxpayers may try to abuse this relief by selling off parts of a set of chattels individually, with each sale being less than £6,000, thereby qualifying for the chattels exemption. A set of chattels would be chattels which are essentially similar and complementary, where their value taken together would be greater than their total individual value, e.g. a set of four antique chairs, a set of two candlesticks, etc.

There is anti-avoidance legislation to counter this. Where a series of disposals of chattels forming part of a set are made **to the same person** (or persons acting in concert or persons connected with each other), HMRC will treat the series of disposals as one single transaction. The special rules at 1, 2 and 3 above apply to the set as a whole, so the gain will only be exempt if the total gross proceeds of the **set** are less than £6,000; otherwise, the marginal relief at rule 2 above applies.

Example 15.4

Sarah purchased a set of six chairs in May 2005 for £2,500. In April 2014, she sold two of the chairs to her sister for £3,000 and, in December 2014, she sold the remaining four chairs to this sister's husband for £4,600.

Solution

Without the anti-avoidance legislation, the taxpayer's disposals would each be exempt (being less than £6,000). However, one must look at the entirety of the transaction as the set was sold to persons connected to each other.

	£
Gross proceeds (total of £3,000 + £4,600)	7,600
Cost	(2,500)
Gain	5,100

continued overleaf

But the gain qualifies for marginal relief and is restricted to 5/3 × (£7,600 − £6,000), i.e. £2,667.

The overall taxable capital gain is, therefore, £2,667, which must be apportioned between the disposals as follows:

First disposal: 3,000/7,600 × £2,667 = £1,053

Second disposal: 4,600/7,600 × £2,667 = £1,614

15.2.1 Part Disposals of Chattels

Where the taxpayer disposes of a part interest in a chattel, the allowable expenditure is apportioned in the same way as for other part disposals (see **Chapter 13**). Where the part disposal is affected by any of the rules at 1, 2 and 3 above, i.e. the £6,000 exemption relief, marginal relief and restricted allowable losses rules, then it is the total gross proceeds value and not just the consideration received for the specific part disposal that must be considered when calculating any chargeable gain. The total gross proceeds value is the consideration received for (or market value where applicable) the part disposal **plus** the value of the interest remaining.

1. **Exemption relief**   If the total value (value of the part disposal plus the value of the remaining interest) is less than £6,000, the chattel exemption applies.

2. **Marginal relief**   If the total gross proceeds value exceeds £6,000, a part disposal calculation is carried out, bearing in mind that any gain is limited to 5/3rds of the excess (proportionately reduced). In this instance a special formula is applied in determining the marginal relief. The formula is as follows:

$$5/3 \times (\text{total proceeds} - £6,000) \times \text{part disposal fraction, i.e.:}$$

$$5/3 \times (A+B - £6,000) \times A/(A+B)$$

where, A = consideration received, and
      B = the market value of the asset remaining.

3. **Restricted loss relief**   If the total gross proceeds value is less than £6,000, then a part disposal calculation is carried out, bearing in mind that any loss is restricted. In this instance, a special formula is applied to the proceeds figure. The normal part disposal calculation is then prepared. The formula is as follows:

Notional proceeds = consideration received + ((£6,000 − total proceeds) × part disposal fraction/proceeds), i.e.:

$$NP = A + (6,000 - (A+B) \times A/(A+B))$$

where, A = consideration received, and
      B = the market value of the asset remaining.

These rules are best illustrated by way of an example.

Example 15.5
Carmel acquired a painting for £2,600 in June 2005. In October 2014 she sells a one-quarter interest in the painting for £1,500, when the value of the remaining three-quarter interest is a figure of £5,000. Compute her chargeable gain.

Solution
The total value of the whole chattel as at October 2014 is £6,500 and, hence, the part disposal is not exempt.

	£
Gross proceeds	1,500
Cost 1,500/(1,500+5,000) × £2,600	(600)
Gain	900
The gain is restricted to 5/3 × (£6,500 − £6,000) × 1,500/6,500	192

Example 15.6
Rhonda acquired a painting for £10,600 in June 2004. In October 2014, she sells a one-quarter interest in the painting for £1,500, when the value of the remaining three-quarter interest is £4,000. Compute her chargeable gain.

Solution
As the total value of the whole chattel at October 2014 is £5,500 and the cost exceeds £6,000, we have to consider restricting the allowable loss.

	£
Deemed proceeds (Note)	1,636
Cost 1,636/(1,636 + 4,000) × £10,600	(3,077)
Restricted loss	(1,441)

Note: Deemed proceeds:
  A + [(6,000 − (A+B)) × A/(A+B)]
  £1,500 + [(£6,000 − £5,500)] × 1,500/5,500] = £1,636

Allowable loss = £1,441

15.2.2 Wasting Chattels

Chattels which have an effective useful life of 50 years or less are referred to as "wasting chattels" and are generally exempt from CGT, with the disposal normally giving rise to neither a chargeable gain nor an allowable loss. Wasting chattels include, for example, racehorses, leases with a useful life of less than 50 years and movable plant and machinery (however, see below). Plant and machinery will always have a useful life of less than 50 years and so are wasting chattels (unless fixed to premises and immovable, in which case they are not chattels). Machinery includes motor vehicles (except cars, which are exempt under general rules), railway and traction engines, engine-powered boats and clocks.

Wasting chattels and capital allowances
There is an exception to the general rule that wasting chattels are exempt from CGT. Movable plant and machinery used in a business and eligible for capital allowances **is not exempt**. In this case, the wasting chattels are treated as chattels and the normal chattel rules above apply. Therefore, the gain will only be exempt if the gross proceeds are less than £6,000.

Thus a calculation of the potential chargeable gain must be carried out under the normal chattel rules. One slight nuance is where a capital loss arises and the sales proceeds are actually less than the original cost. In this case, the allowable loss will be reduced by any capital allowances (including balancing adjustments) claimed. This effectively reduces the capital loss to nil and the result is a no gain/no loss disposal.

If the gross proceeds are less than £6,000, any gain arising will be exempt under the exemption relief explained above. However, if the gross proceeds exceed the original cost (and £6,000), the subsequent chargeable gain will, as for chattels, qualify for marginal relief and be restricted to the lower of the gain and 5/3rds of the excess over £6,000.

Example 15.7

Andrew purchased a machine used in his business for £5,200 in May 2007. The machine was eligible for capital allowances. He sold the machine in July 2014 for £7,900. Compute his chargeable gain on this sale.

Solution

The machine is a wasting asset; however capital allowances have been claimed. Therefore, we apply the normal chattel rules.

	£
Gross proceeds	7,900
Cost	(5,200)
Gain	2,700

The gain is not restricted to 5/3 × (£7,900 − £6,000), i.e £3,167 as this is higher.

Example 15.8

Louise purchased a machine used in her business for £125,000 in April 2010. The machine was eligible for capital allowances (no FYAs were claimed). She sold the machine in May 2014 for £80,000. Compute her chargeable gain/loss on this sale. The accounting date of the business is 31 March.

Solution

Though the machine is a wasting asset, capital allowances have been claimed, so we must apply the normal chattel rules. As capital allowances have been claimed on the cost of the asset, the loss arising is restricted by the capital allowances claimed. This is necessary as otherwise double tax relief would be obtained on the same asset. As such, any loss arising on the sale of the asset will not be allowable for CGT purposes, as it will have been effectively relieved for income tax purposes already.

Capital allowances after any balancing adjustment are £45,000 (£125,000 − £80,000).

To confirm:

	£	£
Cost	125,000	
Capital allowances claimed to date (W1)	(71,208)	71,208
TWDV	53,792	
Entry in pool (lower of cost and proceeds)	(80,000)	
Balancing adjustment in pool in yr of sale	(26,208)	(26,208)
		45,000

continued overleaf

CGT Computation:			
Gross proceeds			80,000
Cost			(125,000)
Loss			(45,000)
Reduced by income tax relief claimed as capital allowances			45,000
Capital loss			0
Working 1 – Purchase price:	125,000	Allowances	
Less WDA @ 20% 10/11	(25,000)	25,000	
TWDV c/f to 11/12	100,000		
Less WDA @ 20% 11/12	(20,000)	20,000	
TWDV c/f to 12/13	80,000		
Less WDA @ 18% 12/13	(14,400)	14,400	
TWDV c/f to 13/14	65,600		
Less WDA @ 18% 13/14	(11,808)	11,808	
TWDV c/f to 14/15	53,792		
Total capital allowances claimed		71,208	

15.2.3 Wasting Assets (Not Chattels)

If a wasting asset is not a chattel, then it **is not** exempt from CGT. The main types of non-chattel wasting assets are intangible assets (as they are neither tangible nor movable), fixed plant and machinery (as it is not movable) and leases (as they are neither tangible nor movable).

As its name implies, the original cost of the asset "wastes away" over time. Generally, the allowable cost is reduced on a straight line basis in proportion to the total length of ownership. The chargeable gain is calculated by comparing the disposal proceeds with the unexpired part of the asset's cost at the disposal date. Note that assets eligible for capital allowances and used throughout the period of ownership in a business do not have their allowable expenditure wasted away.

Example 15.9
Deborah acquired a 30-year patent for £24,000 in December 2006. In December 2014 she sold the patent for £41,000. Compute her chargeable gain.

Solution
The patent had 22 years unexpired life when Deborah sold it, having had a 30-year life when she acquired it.

	£
Sale proceeds	41,000
Allowable cost = 22/30 × £24,000	(17,600)
Gain	23,400

Note: the treatment of leases and options under the wasting assets rules is beyond the scope of this textbook.

Questions

Review Questions
(See Suggested Solutions to Review Questions at the end of this textbook.)

Question 15.1

Shauna Quinn made the following disposals in 2014/15:

1. A painting at auction for gross proceeds of £50,000 on 12 January 2015. The auctioneer's costs of sale were 1% of the gross proceeds. Shauna had inherited the painting from her great aunt Margaret on 31 March 1982. Its value at this time was £2,500.
2. An antique vase on 2 March 2015 for £4,000. This vase was purchased for £14,000 in May 2000.
3. A commercial unit on 2 March 2015 for £185,000. The unit was purchased by Shauna's husband on 1 August 2004 for £55,000. Darren transferred the unit to Shauna on 30 June 2014 when it was worth £75,000. The unit was let out to a local engineering trading company throughout the period that it was owned by Shauna and Darren. On sale the legal fees were £2,250 and the estate agent's fee was £1,850.
4. Sale of four acres of land on 30 November 2014 for proceeds of £80,000. This was part of a 10-acre plot of land acquired as an investment by Shauna on 1 May 2002 for £40,000. The remaining six acres were valued at £48,000 on 30 November 2007.
5. Sale of her cherished vintage 1963 MGB Roadster car for £13,250 on 5 November 2014. Shauna bought the car in January 2003 for £11,250.

Requirement
Calculate Shauna's capital gains tax liability for the financial year 2014/15. Shauna's only other source of income for this tax year was employment income of £27,000. She has capital losses carried forward at the start of the year of £210,000.

Question 15.2

John Smith is a new client of your office, and at a recent meeting in July 2014 he was interested in a number of capital gains issues, as he owns several capital gains assets. However, he has never taken capital gains tax advice and therefore would like some general UK capital gains tax advice on what would happen if he sold a number of his assets. John is a wealthy man who earns in excess of £100,000 of income each year.

Requirement
Write a memo to John dealing with the following issues, with reference to the 2014/15 tax year:

(a) Rate of capital gains tax payable.
(b) Date that any capital gains tax will be due.
(c) How any significant capital gains are declared to HMRC.
(d) Amount of gains that can be realised in a tax year without a cash tax charge arising.
(e) John has heard that some countries give an "inflationary allowance" to deductible costs when a capital gains asset is sold. Clarify the position in the UK.

(f) What types of expenditure qualify as deductible from the sales proceeds received when he sells a capital asset?

(g) John thinks that he might have capital losses of about £15,000 carried forward from a sale of a painting many years ago. How can these capital losses be used?

(h) How is the answer to requirement (g) different if the asset had been sold to his brother?

(i) John inherited a rental property from his grandmother on her death in February 2008, and wants to know what capital gains base cost will be on a future sale.

(j) What would the capital gains base cost of the property have been in his hands if his grandmother had gifted it to him the day before she died?

Principal Private Residence and Lettings Relief

16.1 Principal Private Residence Relief

16.1.1 The Relief

This is one of the major CGT reliefs that can potentially have an impact on the majority of individuals.

Provided certain conditions are met any gain on the disposal by an individual of their principal private residence (PPR) is exempt. Note, this is an exemption relief and not a deferral relief. PPR relief is deducted from the chargeable gain arising on the disposal.

	£
Gain on property	X
Less: PPR relief	(X)
Chargeable gain	X

What is a PPR?
A PPR is an individual's only or main principal private residence. It includes:

1. a **dwelling house** or part of a dwelling house which is, or has been at any time during the period of ownership, an individual's only or main residence; and
2. **surrounding land**, which the individual has for their own occupation and enjoyment with that residence as its garden or grounds up to an area (inclusive of the site of the dwelling house) of half a hectare (approx 1.24 acres) or such larger area as, having regard to the size and character of the dwelling house, is required for the reasonable enjoyment of the property as a residence. If the house does not warrant grounds in excess of half a hectare, PPR relief will not apply to the excess grounds.

A dwelling house includes relevant buildings within the curtilage of the main house, e.g. garage, outhouses, etc. There is extensive case law on this area, some of which is summarised towards the end of this chapter.

It is important to note that:

1. A taxpayer may have only one PPR at any given time.
2. It is not sufficient to simply own the property as the taxpayer must have occupied the property as a residence (i.e. not merely as temporary accommodation). Therefore, there must be a degree of permanency in the individual's occupation of the property.
3. As the relief prevents qualifying gains from becoming chargeable, it also prevents losses from being allowable. However, HMRC states that losses are not disallowed where a dwelling house is let as residential accommodation.
4. A married couple or civil partners who live together may only have one PPR between them.
5. If a taxpayer owns and actually resides in two (or more) properties, they must elect which of the properties is to be treated as their PPR (see **Section 16.3**).
6. The actual residence requirement can be set aside if the taxpayer is required to live elsewhere in job-related accommodation (see **Section 16.5**).
7. There is no PPR relief available where a property (or interest therein) was purchased with a view to resale to make a gain. This restriction also extends to expenditure subsequently incurred wholly or partly for the purposes of realising a gain on the disposal.
8. PPR relief is denied where there is a related claim to gift relief under section 260 TCGA 1992 (see the gift relief section in **Chapter 19**).

16.1.2 Full Exemption

A chargeable gain arising on the disposal of a PPR will be wholly exempt if the owner has occupied the whole of the residence throughout the entire period of ownership as his only or main residence.

Where the residence has been occupied for only part of the period, or only part of the property has been occupied as a residence, then the relief available is diluted.

16.1.3 Partial Exemption

If occupation of the PPR has been for only part of the period of ownership, the proportion of the gain which is exempt from CGT is given by the formula:

$$\frac{\text{Period of Occupation post-31 March 1982}}{\text{Total Period of Ownership post-31 March 1982}} \times \text{Total Gain}$$

Note: it is only the period of occupation and period of ownership since 31 March 1982 which is taken into account.

The above formula is further adjusted if only part of the property has been occupied as the owner's PPR (see below). For ease of calculation, the periods are normally calculated to the nearest month.

16.2 Deemed Periods of Occupation

For the purposes of determining the availability of the relief there are two types of periods of occupation:

(i) actual occupation where the individual resides in the property as their only or main residence, and
(ii) deemed occupation where the legislation treats periods of absence as periods of occupation for the purposes of the formula above.

Deemed periods of occupation include the following:

1. If an individual has resided in a property as their only or main residence at some point in time during the ownership period, then the **last 18 months will always be treated as a period of occupation**. Prior to 6 April 2014, the final period exemption was 36 months.

    This is the case even if, during those last 18 months, the taxpayer has another property which he has elected to be his new PPR.

Example 16.1

Jane bought a house in April 1979 for £25,000. She lived in this property until she purchased a new home on 1 April 2011. She immediately moved into this new property and elected for it to be her PPR. Jane sold her former home on 31 December 2014 for £310,000. The 31 March 1982 value of the property was £70,000.

Solution

The total period of ownership (ignoring the period prior to 31 March 1982) is 32 years 9 months (393 months). Jane actually resided in the property for 29 years. The last 18 months are also deemed to be a period of residence (since she lived in the property as her PPR at some point). Thus her period of residence is 30 years and 6 months (366 months).

	£
Proceeds	310,000
MV 1982	(70,000)
Gain	240,000
PPR exemption (366/393 × £240,000)	(223,511)
Chargeable gain (after PPR) (before AE)	16,489

Jane is effectively taxed on that proportion of the gain (27 months) when she was not residing in her former home and which did not relate to the last 18 months of deemed occupation. If Jane's annual exemption has not already been utilised in tax year 2014/15, then this will reduce the above chargeable gain to £5,489.

---

2. Certain other periods of absence are regarded as deemed periods of occupation provided that:

    (a) the taxpayer had no other exempt PPR at the time; and

    (b) there is a period of actual physical occupation both at some time before and after the period of absence. For these purposes, **deemed** occupation of the last 18 months **does not** count as actual occupation. It is not necessary for the periods of occupation to immediately precede and follow the periods of absence. It is enough that there was occupation at some time before and after periods of absence.

    Hence, subject to (a) and (b) above, the **"deemed periods of occupation"** are:

    (i) any period (or periods taken together) of absence, for **any reason,** up to a total of **36 months**;

    (ii) **any periods of absence** during which the taxpayer is **working abroad**;* and

    (iii) a total of up to **four years** of absence during which the taxpayer is **working elsewhere in the UK** (either employed or self-employed) such that they could not occupy their PPR.*

    Note: these three periods of absence can apply cumulatively. In addition, it does not matter if the PPR was let during the period of absence.

        * An extra-statutory concession waives the requirement that the taxpayer must reside in the property at some time after the period of absence where their absence is work-related (i.e. (ii) and (iii) above) and they are unable to resume residence in their home because the terms of their employment require them to work elsewhere.

Example 16.2

John purchased a house in Omagh on 31 March 1990 for £45,000. He lived in this house as his PPR until 30 September 1997 when he went abroad to work for three years, returning to live in the house again on 1 October 2000. John's job meant that he had to move to Belfast on 1 April 2009 and he lived in rented accommodation until he purchased a new house on 1 July 2010 and elected for this to be his PPR. John sold his former home in Omagh for £275,000 on 30 June 2014.

Compute the chargeable gain.

Solution

	£
Sale proceeds	275,000
Cost	(45,000)
Chargeable gain (before PPR)	230,000

John's period of ownership of the house in Omagh is a total of 24 years 9 months (297 months) and can be broken down as follows:

Dates	Period	Residence	Absence	Actual Occupation	Deemed Occupation
01/04/1990 – 30/09/1997	90 mths	Actual		90	
01/10/1997 – 30/09/2000	36 mths	Working abroad			36
01/10/2000 – 31/03/2009	102 mths	Actual		102	
01/04/2009 – 30/06/2014	63 mths	Up to 48 mths working elsewhere in UK (by concession) plus the last 18 mths			63
Total	291 mths		0	92	99

Hence all of the gain is exempt.

	£
Gain as above	230,000
Less: PPR 291/291 × £230,000	(230,000)
Chargeable gain	0

Example 16.3

Celine bought a semi-detached house in Portrush on 1 March 1993 and lived in it from purchase. In March 1994, she relocated to Milton Keynes for employment, where she lived in an apartment which she leased until February 2003. She returned to Portrush and lived in her house until the end of February 2007, at which point she moved to Belfast to reside with her mother. Celine never returned to the house after this date. She sold the house in Portrush on 28 February 2015, making a gain of £200,000.

continued overleaf

What is the chargeable gain on the sale of the house?

Solution

Dates	Period	Residence	Absence	Actual Occupation	Deemed Occupation
Mar 1993 – Feb 1994	12 mths	Actual		12	
Mar 1994 – Feb 2003	108 mths	Working elsewhere in UK (36 deemed "any" reason and 48 deemed "employment elsewhere")	24		84
Mar 2003 – Feb 2007	48 mths	Actual		48	
Mar 2007 – Feb 2015	96 mths	Elsewhere in UK (last 18 deemed)	78		18
TOTAL	264 mths		102	60	102

	£
Gain	200,000
Less: PPR 162/264 × £200,000	(122,727)
Chargeable gain (before AE)	77,273

16.2.1 Delay in Moving In

There is a further relief where a taxpayer purchases land and builds a house on it but is unable to take up residence immediately (because he has still to sell his old home or is doing work on the new property). Provided the period from purchase to actually moving in does not exceed one year and is **immediately** followed by actual residence then, by concession, this period will count as a period of residence. This period of one year may be extended by another year at HMRC's discretion.

16.3 More than One Residence

16.3.1 Election

Where a person has more than one residence (owned or rented), they may elect for one of the properties to be regarded as their main or sole residence by giving notice to HMRC within two years of commencing occupation of the second residence. It should be noted that, for the election to be valid, the individual must actually reside in both properties.

An election is not required if the second residence is being treated as a residence by means of the "delay in moving in rule" discussed above.

In the absence of an election, HMRC will impose a ruling as to which house is to be treated as the PPR of an individual with more than one residence.

Example 16.4

Applying the facts of *Example 2* above, if John had purchased another property on 1 April 2009 when his job located him in Belfast and elected this new property to be his PPR from that date, would the CGT position differ?

Solution
If he had elected for his second new home to be his PPR then the 45 months from 1 April 2009 up to 31 December 2012 (the commencement of the last 18 months), **would not have been a deemed period of occupation**, as John was claiming another property as his PPR during that time. The last 18 months would still have qualified as deemed occupation as John lived in the house at some point as his PPR.

The chargeable gain would be as follows:

	£
Gain as above	230,000
Less: PPR 246/291 × £230,000	(194,433)
Chargeable gain (before AE)	35,567

16.4 Married Couples/Civil Partnerships

Where a husband and wife or civil partners live together, only one residence may qualify as the main residence for PPR. Where they each owned one property before the marriage/registration of the civil partnership, a new two-year period for electing which property is to be treated as their main residence commences on their marriage/registration.

On a marriage breakdown, provided one spouse disposes of their interest to the other spouse, the departing spouse will, by concession, be treated as continuing to be resident for CGT purposes provided that they have not claimed another house as their PPR and the remaining spouse has continued to reside in the former matrimonial home.

Where a PPR passed from one spouse/civil partner to the other (e.g. on death) the recipient also inherits the previous spouse/civil partner's periods of ownership and occupation for PPR purposes.

16.5 Job-related Accommodation

The general rule above where an individual can only have one PPR is relaxed where an individual lives in job-related accommodation.

Where an individual lives in job-related accommodation, they will be treated as occupying any second dwelling which they own if it is their intention, in due course, to occupy the dwelling house as their only or main residence. It is not therefore necessary to establish actual occupation. This rule also extends to self-employed individuals who are required to live in job-related accommodation (e.g. tenants of public houses).

A person is treated as living in "job-related accommodation" where:

1. it is necessary for the proper performance of their duties (e.g. minister/clergy);
2. it is provided for the better performance of their duties and their employment is one of the kinds of employment in which it is customary for employers to provide accommodation (e.g. publican); or
3. there is a special threat to the employee's security, and the use of the accommodation is part of the security arrangements (e.g. army officer, policeman).

Note: accommodation cannot be regarded as job-related, except in case 3 above, where it is provided by a company and the employee is a director of that company or an associated company, unless they have no material interest in the company (direct or indirect, alone or together with other associates, in more than 5% of the company), and they are either a full-time working director or the company is non-profit-making, or a charity.

16.6 Business Use

As stated above, where part of a residence is used **exclusively** for business purposes throughout the period of ownership, PPR relief will not be available on the portion of the gain relating to this part of the property. Note that it is the use throughout that period of ownership which is considered and not just the use at the date of disposal. In addition, the last 36 months of deemed occupation will not apply to this portion.

Example 16.5

Denise acquired a property in June 2006 and sold it in May 2014 making a gain of £350,000. The house contains seven rooms. From the date of purchase, four of the seven rooms in the property were used exclusively as Denise's main residence, one room was used partly for her hairdressing business and partly as her residence. The remaining two rooms were used wholly for her business. It is assumed that all the rooms are of equal size.

		Proportion used exclusively for business (2/7)	Remaining proportion (5/7)
	£	£	£
Chargeable gain	350,000	100,000	250,000
Deduct: PPR		(0)	(250,000)
Chargeable gain (annual exemption)		100,000	Nil

The total gain before annual exemption is £100,000. If a room is not used exclusively for business, then PPR should be available.

The part used for trade purposes may qualify for relief as the replacement of a business asset (see rollover relief in **Chapter 19**) or entrepreneurs' relief (see **Chapter 18**) if the conditions in each instance are met.

An apportionment between business and residential use must be undertaken on a just and reasonable basis, e.g. number of rooms in use, floor area, etc. Each case would be judged on its own merits.

16.7 Case Law

This section is included for general awareness purposes only.

Goodwin v. Curtis (1998)	The Court held that a considerable degree of permanence and continuity is required in order to turn a simple occupation into a residence. This meant that the taxpayer was not entitled to exemption in respect of one of three properties which he had consecutively acquired and disposed of between April 1985 and December 1985 because he had only occupied each property for a short time during which the property was up for sale.

Varty v. Lynes (1976)	A dwelling house and part of a garden were sold leaving the rest of the garden to be sold separately for development purposes in the future. While PPR was obtained on the original sale of the house and gardens, it was denied on the later sale of the garden because, at this time, the garden no longer formed part of the individual's PPR, as the PPR had been sold some time earlier.
Batey v. Wakefield (1981)	The taxpayer built a bungalow for the use of a caretaker who occupied it rent-free. Since the bungalow was within the grounds of the main dwelling house, it formed part of the taxpayer's PPR.
Lewis v. Rook (1992)	A gardener's cottage, 175m from the main house, was held not to be part of the same residence.
Honour v. Norris (1992)	Several flats close together in different buildings in a single London square and used by members of one family for various domestic purposes were held not to be a single private residence.
Makins v. Elson (1977)	A caravan connected to mains water and electricity was held to be a qualifying dwelling for the purposes of PPR.
Morgan v. HMRC (2013)	A taxpayer purchased a residential property in the expectation that it would become the matrimonial home pending marriage to his fiancée. The relationship broke up prior to completion. The taxpayer moved into the property initially hoping his fiancée would return, but she didn't. After a period of two months, he decided to move out and rent the property instead. The First Tier Tribunal found that the property was the taxpayer's PPR as it was his intention to make the property his permanent residence on the day he moved in.

16.8   Lettings Relief

PPR relief is extended to a gain accruing, up to a certain limit, while the property is let to tenants as residential accommodation. This extended relief is known as "lettings relief". Please note that PPR takes priority over lettings relief.

There are two main circumstances in which the letting exemption will apply, namely:

1. the property has been used entirely as a PPR during periods of occupation and is let out to tenants during periods of absence (where the absence is not a deemed period of occupation); and

2. part of the property has been used as a residence, whilst the other part has been let to tenants as residential accommodation (e.g. there are three floors of a property, with two floors used as the owner's residence and the top floor is let out to tenants). The absence from the let part cannot be deemed a period of occupation as the owner has another PPR at the same time (namely the rest of the property). However, the let part will qualify for the last three years of deemed occupation (i.e. the last 36 months) if the let part formed part of the only or main residence at some point in time.

In relation to 1 and 2 above, the letting must have been for residential purposes only.

Lettings relief may be available to cover some or all of the gain which is not covered by PPR. Relief will normally be given where the let accommodation forms part of the owner's dwelling and the owner previously resided in the whole premises. It will not be available if the let accommodation is a dwelling which is entirely separate from the owner's residence.

Lettings relief is restricted to the **lower** of:

1. the gain accruing during the letting period (the letting part of the gain);
2. the part of the gain which is exempt under the PPR provisions (including deemed periods of occupation); or
3. £40,000.

Example 16.6

Christopher purchased a house on 1 June 1994 for £100,000 and occupied the entire house up to 1 July 2004 when he rented part of the top floor (comprising one-quarter of the house) to residential tenants. Christopher continued to reside in the remainder of the house. On 1 January 2015, he sold the house for £585,000. Compute the chargeable gain.

Dates	Period	Residence	Let	Actual	Deemed
01/06/1994 – 30/06/2004	121 mths	Actual		121	
01/07/2004 – 31/12/2014	126 mths	3/4 Actual		67.5	
		1/4 Let	22.5		
		Last 3 years			36
Total	247 mths		22.5	188.5	36

Solution

	£
Sales proceeds	585,000
Cost	(100,000)
Chargeable gain (prior to PPR exemption and letting relief)	485,000

The total period of ownership was 20 years 7 months (247 months). He resided in the whole property for 10 years 1 month (121 months) and the last 36 months, a total of 157 months. Christopher resided in three-quarters of the property for the remaining 90 months, so three-quarters of the gain arising in this period will also be exempt.

Lettings relief will be available on any residue.

	£
Gain (as above)	485,000
Less: PPR exemption (188.5 + 36 = 224.5)	
224.5/247 × £485,000 (Note 2)	(440,820)
	44,180
Less: Letting exemption – restricted (Note 1)	(40,000)
Net chargeable gain (before AE)	4,180

continued overleaf

Note 1: Letting relief, being the lowest of:

    (i)   Gain during letting period:
        22.5/247 × £485,000 = £44,180*

    (ii) PPR relief £440,820

    (iii) £40,000

    *Gain during letting period could, alternatively, have been calculated as follows:

     90/247 × £485,000 × 1/4 = £44,180

Note 2: PPR – could alternatively have been calculated as follows:

	£
157/247 × 485,000	308,279
90/247 × 485,000 × ¾	132,541
Total	440,820

Where the letting consists of taking in a lodger who shares the taxpayer's living accommodation and has their meals with the family, HMRC does not consider that the taxpayer has ceased to occupy any part of the property as their only or main residence and there is no restriction on the exemption. HMRC takes this view only where a taxpayer takes a single lodger into their home, not where a taxpayer runs a lodging house as a business. Where an individual lets a room under the "rent a room" scheme, PPR should still be available in full on the subsequent sale of the property.

Questions

Review Questions
(See Suggested Solutions to Review Questions at the end of this textbook.)

Question 16.1

James sold a house in the 2014/15 tax year and realised a gain, before any available reliefs, as follows:

Proceeds	£2,000,000
Original cost	(£1,200,000)
Gain arising	£800,000

James owned the house for a total of ten years. He lived in it for the first three years, and then let it for five years when he cycled across America. He returned to Northern Ireland to live in the house for the last year of ownership.

Requirement
Calculate, with appropriate explanations, the capital gains tax, if any, that is due for 2014/15. James has not made any other asset disposals in 2014/15, he is an additional rate taxpayer and it was the only house he owned in that ten years.

Question 16.2

Jack Bates, a widower with no children, is currently living in retirement in a rented apartment in Spain. His only investment in property to date is his residence in Belfast.

Jack has recently been offered a sum of £1.3 million for his Belfast property by developers, who wish to incorporate the property into a large commercial development.

After acquiring the property on 1 September 1990 for its residential value of £65,000, Jack resided there until 1 January 1998, when he was transferred by his employer to their London office. During his period in London, Jack let his residence at a rental of £400 per month.

On 30 April 2006, Jack was transferred back to his employer's head office in Belfast, where he remained until his retirement on 31 January 2012. On 1 February 2012, Jack immediately moved away to live in Spain. While in Belfast between 2006 and 2012, Jack again lived in his residence there. However, since retiring to Spain in 2012, Jack has again been letting the Belfast residence.

Requirement

Write a letter to Jack outlining the following:

(a) How principal private residence relief operates and the consequences of absences from the property.
(b) The capital gains tax implications for Jack if he sells the Belfast property to the developer for £1.3 million on 1 July 2014, supported with a computation of the capital gains tax payable (if any). Jack is an additional rate taxpayer.

Shares

17.1   Introduction

Shares present special problems when attempting to compute gains or losses on disposal.

Example 17.1

Joe bought the following shares in X Ltd:

1,000 in January 1994 for £2,000

1,000 in January 2005 for £8,000

If he sells, say, 1,200 shares today, how would his base cost be determined? To determine the chargeable gain, Joe needs to work out which shares out of the two original holdings were actually sold.

Where a taxpayer disposes of shares or securities in a company (hereafter referred to as "shares") which they have built up over a period of time, the calculation of the gain or loss arising on a disposal of some of the shares cannot be undertaken until one establishes the base cost of the shares being sold. The shares were purchased at different times at different costs. Thus, a set of share identification *(share matching)* rules are used to *match disposals with acquisitions.*

The share matching rules are only applied when there is a pot of shares of the same class in the same company. If Joe above purchased 1,000 ordinary shares and 1,000 preference shares in X Ltd, then each would be dealt with separately and the share matching rules do not apply as each class of share is distinguishable.

17.1.1   The General Rule

The general rule is that disposals of shares that occur on or after 6 April 2008 are matched against acquisitions of the **same class** of shares in the **same company** in the following strict order:

1. Acquisitions made on the **same day** as the day of disposal.
2. Acquisitions made during the **following 30 days.** If there is more than one acquisition, then on a 'first in first out' (FIFO) basis – also known as the 'bed and breakfast' rule.

3. Shares forming the **share pool** "section 104 holding" – this holding will contain all the shares of the class in the same company that were acquired before the date of disposal and which have not been matched at either 1. or 2. above.

FA 2008 greatly simplified the share matching rules for individuals, but the old rules remain where a company makes a disposal of shares.

Example 17.2

Jeremy had the following disposals and acquisitions of ordinary shares in Razor Plc:

Number of shares	Date	Acquisition/Sale
1,900	06/04/2013	Bought
800	09/09/2014	Bought
1,100	09/09/2014	Sold
180	30/09/2014	Bought
1,200	01/03/2015	Sold
950	23/03/2015	Bought

Set out how the disposals will be matched against the various acquisitions.

Solution

The disposal of 1,100 shares on 9 September 2014 is first matched with the 800 shares bought on the same day (point (1) above), leaving 300 shares to be matched. Then the residue is matched against the shares purchased within 30 days (180 shares) on 30 September 2014 (point (2) above), leaving 120 shares still to be matched. These 120 shares are finally matched against the section 104 holding (point (3) above), leaving a balance of 1,780 shares in this holding as at 9 September 2014.

Sold:	9 September 2014	1,100
Bought:	9 September 2014 – same day rule	(800)
Bought:	30 September 2014 – 30 day rule	(180)
Bought	Share pool	(120) Leaves 1,780 in share pool

The disposal of the 1,200 shares on 1 March 2015 are first matched against the shares purchased within 30 days (point (2) above, as there were no shares bought on the same day), leaving a balance of 250 shares. Finally, these shares are matched against the section 104 holding (point (3) above), leaving a balance of 1,530 shares in this holding going forward.

Sold:	1 March 2015	1,200
Bought:	23 March 2015 – 30 day rule	(950)
Bought:	Share pool	(250) Leaves 1,530 in share pool

17.1.2   Section 104 Holding (TCGA 1992)

As seen in the previous paragraphs, the "section 104 holding" pooling arrangements eliminate the need to keep detailed records of the date and costs of each individual share acquisition. All that is required is to have a record of both the **number of shares** in the "section 104" holding and the **total allowable expenditure,** i.e. the cost of the shares in the holding. As stated previously, the rebasing "kink test" has been abolished for individuals and hence the only modification required to the section 104 holding will be to replace the acquisition cost of shares purchased before 31 March 1982 with the market value of those shares as at that date.

Example 17.3

Brian had made the following acquisitions over the past 36 years in Arnold Plc.

Number of shares	Cost £	Date
1,000	1,000	01/01/1978
3,200	5,600	01/01/1988
3,000	6,000	01/01/2004
2,400	7,200	01/01/2015
9,600	19,800	

The shares had a market value of £1.36 per share as at 31 March 1982 and Brian had made no disposals throughout the period.

Solution

The section 104 holding as at 1 January 2015 will be built up as follows:

Acquired	Number	Allowable Expenditure
01/01/1978	1,000	1,360 (MV)
01/01/1988	3,200	5,600
01/01/2004	3,000	6,000
01/01/2015	2,400	7,200
S104 holding as at 01/01/2015	9,600	20,160

Average price per share as at 1 January 2015 is £2.10.

Thus, with the removal of indexation and the kink test with effect from 6 April 2008, the previously complex rules have been greatly simplified. All that is required to be carried forward is the holding of 9,600 and its associated costs of £20,160. This principle can be demonstrated by the following worked example.

Example 17.4

Following on from the last example, Brian sold 4,000 shares in Arnold Plc on 27 March 2015 for £11,000. He made no further acquisitions within the next 30 days. Calculate Brian's CGT liability for 2014/15. He has already fully utilised his basic rate band but has made no other chargeable disposals in the year.

Solution

Since there were no acquisitions on the same day or within 30 days of the sale on 27 March 2015, the sale is matched with the section 104 holding as follows:

		Allowable Expenditure £
Section 104 holding cost b/fwd	9,600 shares	20,160
Allowable expenditure: $£20,160 \times \frac{4,000}{9,600}$		(8,400)
Section 104 holding cost c/fwd	5,600 shares	11,760
Calculation of chargeable gain:		£
Proceeds		11,000
Allowable cost		(8,400)
Gain		2,600
Less: annual exemption		(2,600)
Assessable		nil

17.2 Bonus Issues and Rights Issues

17.2.1 Bonus Issues (Scrip Issues)

For CGT purposes, a bonus issue is treated as a reorganisation of share capital. With the abolition of indexation allowance and the other reforms of FA 2008, the CGT treatment for bonus issues (and similarly rights issues) has been greatly simplified.

As its name implies, a bonus issue occurs when a company issues "free" shares to its existing shareholders, in direct proportion to their existing holding. So a "1 for 10" bonus issue would give each shareholder (of that class of share) one additional share for every 10 that they previously held **at no extra cost**; hence it is a reorganisation of the share capital.

All previous acquisitions are held within the section 104 holding, thus all that is required is to add the number of bonus issue shares to the carried forward share column and no cost to the carried forward allowable cost column – in essence, reducing the average value per share.

Example 17.5

In the earlier example, Brian had a carried forward section 104 holding of 5,600 shares in Arnold Plc with an allowable cost of £11,760 as at 27 March 2015. If the company had made a "1 for 8" bonus issue on 6 June 2015, then the resultant section 104 holding would become:

	Number of shares	Allowable Expenditure
		£
Section 104 holding b/fwd	5,600	11,760
Bonus issue (06/06/2015)	700	nil
Section 104 holding c/fwd	6,300	11,760

Example 17.6

Rianna had made the following acquisitions in Games Plc over the last 34 years.

Date	Number of shares	Cost £
01/01/1980	2,600	2,600
04/10/1986	1,000	2,000
11/09/2000	600	1,800
02/03/2004	1,800	4,200

The market value of the company's shares as at 31 March 1982 was £1.50 per share. On 1 July 2008, the company made a "1 for 6" bonus issue. Rianna sold 2,100 of her shares for £2.00 per share on 1 November 2014. She had no further acquisitions in the following 30 days. Calculate the chargeable gain arising on this latter sale, assuming that she has already utilised her annual exemption for 2014/15.

Solution

As the disposal on 1 November 2014 cannot be matched with any acquisition on the same day or the following 30 days, it must be matched with the section 104 holding.

continued overleaf

Date	Number of shares	Cost £
01/01/1980	2,600	3,900 (MV)
04/10/1986	1,000	2,000
11/09/2000	600	1,800
02/03/2004	1,800	4,200
Section 104 holding b/fwd	6,000	11,900
01/07/2008 Bonus issue (1 for 6)	1,000	0
Section 104 holding as at 01/07/2008	7,000	11,900
01/11/2014 − sold 2,100 shares	(2,100)	
Allowable expenditure = 2,100/7,000 × 11,900		(3,570)
Section 104 holding as at 01/11/2014	4,900	8,330
Chargeable gain:		
Proceeds (2,100 shares at £2 per share)		4,200
Allowable cost		(3,570)
Chargeable gain		630

Note: the average price of the section 104 holding after bonus issue on 1 July 2008 was £1.70 per share, being £11,900 divided by 7,000 shares.

17.2.2 Rights Issue

A rights issue occurs where a company offers its existing shareholders a right to buy extra shares at a price. Generally, the shares are offered in proportion to the existing shareholding and the price is usually set at a competitive rate compared to the open market value at that time. The company is offering shares at competitive rates to existing shareholders instead of going to the market for fresh capital investment.

A shareholder, having been offered the rights issue, will have effectively three options, namely:

1. to buy the shares being offered;
2. to not buy the shares, but instead sell the "rights" to buy the shares; or
3. do nothing and ignore the rights issue.

Depending on the route they choose, the CGT treatment will be different.

Option 1 – Buy the Shares
In this situation, the CGT treatment is similar to that for bonus issue shares except that the allowable cost column will have to incorporate the price paid for the shares.

Example 17.7
Continuing with the last example, let us assume that Games Plc had made a rights issue of "1 for 6" at a price of £1.40 on 1 July 2008 (instead of the bonus issue). If Rianna had purchased her entitlement to her shares, she would have purchased 1,000 shares at a cost of £1,400. In this situation, her section 104 holding would have become:

continued overleaf

Date	Number of shares	Cost £
01/01/1980	2,600	3,900 (MV)
04/10/1986	1,000	2,000
11/09/2000	600	1,800
02/03/2004	1,800	4,200
Section 104 holding b/fwd	6,000	11,900
01/07/2008 rights issue (1 for 6) @£1.40/share	1,000	1,400
Section 104 holding as at 01/07/2008	7,000	13,300

Note: the average allowable cost per share is now £1.90 (13,300/7,000).

Example 17.8

David had the following acquisitions of shares in Newbury Plc:

Date	Number of shares	Cost £
01/01/1977	2,000	2,000
04/01/1989	1,000	2,500
11/09/2000	600	1,800

The market value of the company's shares as at 31 March 1982 was £1.60 per share. On 1 September 2014, the company made a "1 for 9" rights issue at a price of £1.50 per share. David took up his shares. David sold 1,000 of his shares for £2.20 per share on 1 December 2014. He had no further acquisitions in the following 30 days. Calculate the chargeable gain arising on this latter sale, assuming that David had already utilised his annual exemption for 2014/15.

Solution

Once again, the disposal cannot be matched with same day or next 30-day acquisitions. Hence, the disposal must come from the section 104 holding.

Date	Number of shares	Cost £
01/01/1977	2,000	3,200 (MV)
04/10/1989	1,000	2,500
11/09/2000	600	1,800
Section 104 holding b/fwd	3,600	7,500
01/09/2014 Rights issue (1 for 9) @ £1.50/share	400	600
Section 104 holding as at 01/09/2014	4,000	8,100
01/11/2014 − sold 1,000 shares	(1,000)	
Allowable expenditure = 1,000/4,000 × 8,100		(2,025)
Section 104 holding c/fwd at 01/11/2014	3,000	6,075
Chargeable gain:		
Proceeds (1,000 shares at £2.20 per share)		2,200
Allowable cost		(2,025)
Chargeable gain		175

Option 2 – Sell the Rights to Buy the Shares

In this scenario, the taxpayer does not buy the shares but rather is selling the "right" or "option" to buy the shares. This process is known as "sale of rights nil paid". The proceeds of such a sale are treated either as a capital distribution, dealt with at **Section 17.3** below, or as a part disposal (see **Chapter 13**).

Option 3 – Ignore the Rights Issue

In this scenario, there will be no CGT implications.

17.3 Capital Distribution

If a company were to go into liquidation, the shareholders may not receive any payment from the company. However, when the shareholders are repaid part of their share capital, a capital distribution is said to occur. This will generally result in a CGT part disposal calculation, unless the amount of the distribution is "small" (which unfortunately can happen only too often in such circumstances). (**Note:** this is not an income distribution subject to income tax rules.)

The CGT calculations for such capital distributions adopt similar methodologies as in the part disposal and the "small part disposal of land" rules which were outlined earlier in **Chapter 13**. In summary, if the distribution is "**small**", then any gain can be deferred by treating the distribution as a deduction **from the base cost of the shares**. This is a form of rollover relief. It is this reduced base cost which is used for calculating gains or losses on future disposals of the shares.

A capital distribution is deemed to be "small" if it consists of no more than the higher of:

1. 5% of the value of the company's shares just prior to the distribution; and
2. £3,000.

If the individual would prefer to apply the part disposal rules instead of the "small" disposal rules, e.g. to use up their annual exemption, then HMRC will allow this.

Example 17.9

Jane acquired 15,000 shares in Blue Plc on 29 February 2004 for £20,000. Unfortunately, the company went into liquidation on 2 May 2014 and Jane received an initial distribution of £0.40 per share at that time. The market value of an ordinary share of Blue Plc just after this distribution was £0.60. Compute Jane's chargeable gain/loss.

Solution

On 2 May 2014 Jane received an initial distribution of £6,000 (£15,000 × 0.40). The value of the part disposed of exceeds £3,000 and the 5% test.

The value of the part remaining is £9,000 (£15,000 × 0.60).

Thus the distribution cannot rank as a "small" capital distribution and a part disposal calculation must be carried out.

continued overleaf

The part disposal fraction is applied in the normal way, i.e. A/A+B, and the section 104 holding will thus be:

CGT computation

	£
Disposal proceeds	6,000
Allowable expenditure:	
6,000/(6,000 + 9,000) × 20,000	(8,000)
Allowable loss	(2,000)
Section 104 holding	

	Number of shares	Allowable cost £
29/02/2004	15,000	20,000
Capital distribution (02/05/2014)	–	(8,000)
Section 104 holding	15,000	12,000

Example 17.10

Assuming the same facts as in the last example, except that Jane only received an initial distribution of £0.03 per share on 2 May 2014 (i.e. she received £450 in proceeds from the liquidator). This would thus meet the "small" criteria and, in this situation, the distribution is not treated as a part disposal, but rather the proceeds are deducted from the cumulative allowable cost, effectively reducing the allowable cost for future disposals.

	Number of shares	Allowable cost £
29/2/2004	15,000	20,000
Capital distribution (02/05/2014)	–	(450)
Section 104 holding c/fwd	15,000	19,550

Of course, the taxpayer is allowed to override the "small capital distribution" rule if it is more beneficial to them. Since the proceeds in such cases are generally going to be relatively minor, the taxpayer may choose to realise the chargeable gain in the knowledge that it will be covered by their annual exemption (if not otherwise utilised).

17.3.1 Sale of Rights Nil Paid

When a company declares a rights issue, it will usually send its shareholders a provisional letter of allotment for the new shares. This means the new shares have been allocated to the shareholders. If the shareholders want to take up all or part of the rights issue, they will accept the allotment by paying for the shares. As rights issues are often made at a discount to the prevailing market price, the provisional letter of allotment is valuable. The shareholders can renounce or sell the letter of allotment to another person who wants to subscribe for the shares. This is a sale of rights nil paid and is treated as a capital distribution.

> **Example 17.11**
> In June 2009, Bernard bought 10,000 shares in Marathon Plc at a price of £0.50 per share. In May 2014, Marathon Plc declared a 1 for 2 rights issue at £2.00 per share. Bernard sold all his rights for £0.50 per entitlement to each new share: 5,000 × £0.50 = £2,500.
> The market value of Marathon Plc shares at the date of the capital distribution was £2.50 per share.
>
> $$\frac{\text{Value of the capital distribution}}{\text{Market value of the shareholding}} = \frac{2,500}{25,000} \times 100 = 10\%$$
>
> The capital distribution is not small (i.e. it is greater than 5% of the company's value just before the distribution) so the sale of rights is treated as a disposal:
>
> | | £ |
> | --- | --- |
> | Disposal proceeds | 2,500 |
> | Allowable expenditure: | |
> | 2,500/(2,500 + 25,000) × 5,000 | (455) |
> | Chargeable gain | 2,045 |

17.4   Company Takeovers

Students are only expected to be aware of the general tax implications of company takeovers. Detailed calculations are beyond the scope of this textbook.

Company takeovers will occur when one company (the purchaser) acquires the shares of another company (the target). The purchaser can achieve the takeover by:

1. paying the shareholders of the target company cash for their shares;
2. paying the shareholders of the target company a combination of cash and shares in the purchaser company; or
3. paying the shareholders of the target company entirely with shares in the purchaser company.

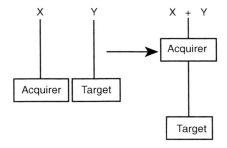

The takeover rules apply where the acquirer company, i.e. the company issuing the shares, ends up with more than a 25% interest of the ordinary share capital or the majority of the voting power of the target company, or it makes a general offer to the target company shareholders which is subject to a condition which, if satisfied, would give the acquirer company control of the target company.

Note: the takeover offer can take many forms including cash, ordinary share capital, preference share capital, loan stock, gilts, qualifying corporate bonds, etc. **Gilts and qualifying corporate bonds are beyond the scope of this textbook.**

17.4.1   Tax Treatment

The takeover must take place for bona fide commercial reasons and must not have as its main purpose, or one of its main purposes, the avoidance of CGT or corporation tax.

The CGT treatment in each of the three scenarios is as follows:

1. Consideration is wholly in cash: The shareholders of the target company have sold all their shares for cash and their chargeable gain or allowable loss is calculated in the normal way.
2. Consideration is a mixture of cash and shares in the acquiring company: There will be a part disposal for CGT purposes, following the procedures set out in **Chapter 13**. The amount of cash received is the value of the part disposed of, while the value of the part remaining is the value of the shares received. Where the quantum of cash received fulfils either of the "small" criteria above (i.e. not more than 5% of the total value of the takeover and £3,000) **and** is less than the cost of the original shares, then the cash received may instead be deducted from the allowable expenditure to be set-off on any subsequent disposal of the new acquired shares. Remember, even on a "small" disposal the individual still has the option to apply part disposal rules if preferred. In essence, the cash received will then be treated as if it were a "small" capital distribution (see **Section 17.3**). The tax treatment of the issue of new shares is as set out in 3 below.
3. Consideration is wholly shares in the acquiring company: The shareholders of the target company have received no cash but rather they have replaced their original shares with shares in the purchaser company. There has been an effective "paper for paper" exchange of shares and thus no chargeable disposal has taken place for CGT purposes. The base cost of the shareholders' newly-acquired shares in the purchaser company is the cost they originally paid for their shares in the target company (or the 31 March 1982 valuation if the original shares were purchased before this date). Thus, for CGT purposes, the new shares are deemed to have been acquired on the same date and at the same cost as the original holding. Effectively, the new shares step into the shoes of the old shares.

Example 17.12

Isabel purchased 6,000 shares in Saigon Plc on 2 January 2003 at a cost of £4 per share. In December 2014, Sea Plc offered the shareholders of Saigon Plc four Sea Plc shares plus £2 in cash for every three Saigon Plc shares. On 24 December 2014, the offer was accepted when the market value of shares of Sea Plc were £5.50 per share. Compute Isabel's chargeable gain.

Solution
Shares received = 6,000 × 4/3 = 8,000 shares valued at £5.50/share = £44,000
Cash received = £2 × 6,000/3 = £4,000

$$\frac{\text{Cash received}}{\text{Total value of cash and shares received}} = \frac{4,000}{48,000} \times 100 = 8.33\%$$

The cash proportion of this total is greater than £3,000 and 5% of the total value and so cannot be treated as a "small" capital distribution. Therefore, the part disposal rules apply to the cash consideration received.

The new shares in Sea Plc step into the shoes of the old shares under the "paper for paper" provisions. As noted above, this means that the new shares have the same base cost and date of acquisition as the original shares.

continued overleaf

Chargeable gain/loss:

	£
Disposal proceeds (cash received)	4,000
Allowable cost (£24,000 × 4,000/48,000)	(2,000)
Chargeable gain	2,000

Section 104 holding:

	Number of shares	Cost £
02/01/2006	6,000	24,000
Cost allocated against part disposal		(2,000)
24/12/2014	8,000	22,000

Example 17.13

Sarah holds 10,000 £1 shares in Poppers Ltd which she purchased in January 2003 for £2.00 each. The total issued share capital of Poppers Ltd is 100,000 shares.

On 1 July 2014, there is a successful takeover of the company by Party King Plc. Shareholders in Poppers Ltd receive three ordinary shares and two 10% preference shares in Party King Plc for every two shares held in Poppers Ltd, plus cash of £1.00 for every five shares held in Poppers Ltd.

Immediately following the takeover, the market value of the ordinary shares in Party King Plc is £3.00 per share and the preference shares have a market value of £1.10 per share.

How is the base cost of the old shareholding in Poppers Ltd attributed to the new takeover deal? Advise if the "small" distribution rules apply.

Ordinary shares received = 10,000 × 3/2 = 15,000 shares valued at £3.00/share = £45,000
10% preference shares received = 10,000 × 2/2 = 10,000 valued at £1.10/share = £11,000
Cash received = £1 × 10,000/5 = £2,000

$$\frac{\text{Cash received}}{\text{Total value of cash and shares received}} = \frac{2,000}{58,000} \times 100 = 3.45\%$$

The cash proportion is less than £3,000 and 5% of the total value (and the acquisition cost of the original shares) and so can be treated as a "small" capital distribution.

As we now have two different classes of shares, the base cost of the original shares is allocated by reference to their value:

Section104 holding:

		Cost £
January 2003	10,000 ordinary shares	20,000
Reduced by cash received July 2014		(2,000)
Base cost post-takeover		18,000
Allocated:		
15,000 ordinary shares	(18,000 × 45,000/56,000)	14,464
10,000 preference shares	(18,000 × 11,000/56,000)	3,536

17.5 "Bed & Breakfast" Rules

This is an anti-avoidance provision designed to prevent taxpayers benefiting from the creation of artificial losses. The transactions involved are commonly referred to as 'bed & breakfast' transactions. Typically, an individual would dispose of shares to trigger either a capital loss or a capital gain but would acquire the shares back within a short timeframe, as their long-term intention is to retain the shares. Any gain was typically calculated so as to be sheltered by the annual exemption and the new shares would have a higher base cost for a future sale. Clearly such a transaction was purely for tax reasons and not commercial reasons. The 30-day rule was introduced to remove the tax benefits of such transactions.

Example 17.14: Acquisition within 30 days of disposal

Harry owns 1,000 shares in X Ltd, which he originally purchased in 2005 at £5 each. On 30 December 2014, the shares are quoted at £1 each. Harry does not wish to sell his 1,000 shares as he believes they will rise in price in the future but, at the same time, he wishes to claim loss relief for the paper loss which he has suffered. He cannot do this unless he has a realisation, i.e. a disposal.

Accordingly, he arranges to sell his 1,000 shares at £1 each on 30 December 2014 on the understanding that his stockbroker will re-purchase 1,000 shares two or three days later. Harry will thereby realise a capital loss of £4,000 on the disposal which, in the absence of the anti-avoidance provisions, would be available to set-off against any gains in 2014/15. He will also still own 1,000 shares in X Ltd.

The legislation prevents this arrangement by providing that, as the disposal and re-acquisition of the same class of shares takes place within 30 days, then the disposal is not matched with the acquisition in 2005 but is instead matched with the acquisition which takes place within 30 days of sale, i.e. £1 per share. This greatly restricts, and may even eliminate, the capital losses arising. If the share price has not really altered in the short period between the sale and purchase, these rules mean that no gain or loss will be triggered.

17.6 Interaction with Entrepreneurs' Relief

There may be a problem where, after a reorganisation or takeover, the newly issued shares do not qualify for entrepreneurs' relief (ER) when they are eventually disposed of. This could be because the shareholder is no longer an employee/director or the shareholding requirements for ER are no longer met. Without legislative change, any ER accrued on old shares will be lost. The legislation, therefore, provides that the shareholder can elect to disapply the usual reorganisation or takeover treatment and so claim ER in the year of the reorganisation or takeover. The shareholder then applies the normal CGT rules, and the proceeds are the amounts received.

The election for this treatment must be made by the same date as the claim for ER. So, if the takeover occurs in tax year 2014/15, then the claim must be made by 31 January 2017.

17.7 CGT Treatment of Employee Share Options

Share options are a common feature in the remuneration packages of company executives. They usually consist of the right to subscribe at a specified price for a specified number of shares in the employer company during a specified period of time. The income tax treatment of share options has been covered in the CAP 1 course. Students will recall that a different tax treatment applies depending on whether the share option scheme is approved or unapproved.

17.7.1 Approved Share Option Schemes

There are a number of employee approved share option schemes, namely, the SAYE scheme, the Company Share Option Plan (CSOP) and Enterprise Management Incentives (EMI).

Broadly, the position can be summarised as follows:

- There is no income tax charge on the grant of the option.
- There is no income tax charge on the exercise of the option.
- The shares obtained on foot of the option are instead within the CGT regime and not the income tax regime, and have a base cost equal to the sum paid for them.

For each of the specific schemes, there are conditions to be met in order for the above tax treatments to be applied. The specifics of each scheme are outside the scope of this course.

Example 17.15

John works for ABC Plc. On 1 January 2007, he received options under the company's share option plan over 1,000 shares in the company exercisable at any time within the following five years at the market price of the shares at 1 January 2007. The option scheme was approved by HMRC. The market value of the shares as at 1 January 2007 was £10 per share. On 31 March 2008, John exercised his option and acquired the 1,000 shares for the sum of £10,000 (the shares having been worth £10 each on 1 January 2007).

On 1 January 2015, John sold the shares for £30,000.

Because the share option scheme was approved by HMRC, and because there was no discount at the time of grant of the option, neither income tax nor CGT was chargeable at the time of grant or exercise of the option.

Accordingly, on 1 January 2015, John is treated as having a CGT disposal in respect of his shares. His base cost in that computation is £10,000. The sale proceeds are £30,000, so John has made a chargeable gain of £20,000.

17.7.2 Unapproved Share Option Schemes

Broadly, an employee is subject to income tax on the exercise of an unapproved share option and this is based upon the market value of the shares obtained, less the amount paid for the shares and less the amount (if any) which has been paid at the time of the granting of the option.

For CGT purposes, any amount which has been assessed to income tax must be taken into account in determining the CGT liability. An individual cannot be subject to tax twice on the same gain. Therefore, the base cost for CGT purposes will take into account the amount paid by the individual plus the amount which has been subject to income tax at the time of exercise/grant of the option.

A taxpayer acquired shares after exercising an option. The shares are later sold. The pro forma computation is:

Proceeds	X
Less: Cost of shares on exercise	(X)
Less: Charge to income tax on exercise and grant	(X)
Chargeable gain/loss	X

Example 17.16

Patrick is granted an option in 2005 by his employer, XYZ Plc, to subscribe for 1,000 £1 ordinary shares at a price of £1 each at any time in the following eight years. He is granted this right by reason of his employment at a time when the shares are valued at £3 each. Patrick exercised the option during December 2014 when the shares were worth £10 each.

As the shares were granted after September 2003, there is no income tax suffered at the time of the granting of the option.

At the date of exercise Patrick is subject to income tax through the PAYE system on the uplift in the value of the shares, i.e. £10 less price paid of £1 = £9 per share. Specific employment income is £9 × 1,000 = £9,000.

CGT: Patrick's base cost of the shares is £10,000 (i.e. £1,000 actual cost + £9,000 subject to income tax). If Patrick sold the shares immediately for £10,000 on exercising his option, then he would have a no gain/no loss situation for CGT.

Questions

Review Questions

(See Suggested Solutions to Review Questions at the end of this textbook.)

Question 17.1

Mark had the following transactions in Magnet plc:

Purchase date		No. of shares acquired	Cost
			£
05/10/2001	Purchase	1,500	8,000
10/04/2004	Purchase	2,800	10,000
18/03/2006	Rights issue, 1 for 2 held at £1.50 per share	2,150	3,225

Disposal date	No. of shares	Proceeds
		£
29/07/2014	2,500	30,000

Requirement

Assuming Mark is an additional rate tax payer, calculate his capital gains tax (CGT) liability in respect of the above disposal and state the due date for payment of the CGT.

Entrepreneurs' Relief

18.1 Introduction

FA 2008 abolished, for individuals, indexation allowance and simplified the rules relating to the disposal of shares and securities. After 10 years of being in operation, taper relief was also abolished. These were significant changes to the UK CGT system.

18.1.1 Outline of Taper Relief

From 1998, taper relief was introduced to replace retirement relief and, through various changes, had become a very useful and somewhat generous relief, particularly for business assets. There were two sets of taper rules, one for business assets, and one for non-business assets:

1. Taper relief on the disposal of a business asset owned for at least two years attracted a maximum effective CGT rate of 10% where the taxpayer was a higher rate taxpayer.
2. Taper relief on the disposal of non-business assets owned for at least 10 years attracted a maximum effective CGT rate of 24% for a higher rate taxpayer.

Without these reliefs, the CGT rate applicable for a higher rate taxpayer was 40%.

As one might imagine, the abolition of such a generous relief was met with much consternation and, after due consideration, the Government introduced a relief, known as entrepreneurs' relief (ER), which offered some limited solace to the taxpayer.

ER is available in respect of gains on qualifying business disposals by individuals. From 6 April 2008 to 22 June 2010, the relief reduced the effective rate of CGT on such disposals to 10% (rather than the standard CGT rate of 18%) up to a lifetime limit of £2 million (increased from £1 million with effect from 6 April 2010). The way in which ER is calculated was changed with effect from 23 June 2010 and the lifetime limit was increased to £5 million. On 6 April 2011, the lifetime limit was increased further to £10 million.

Note: business asset taper relief was applied to the sale of business assets. You should note that, on the whole, ER applies on the disposal of a business and not on the disposal of business assets (except in very limited circumstances).

18.2 What is a Qualifying Business Disposal?

For ER, any kind of disposal which gives rise to a gain will qualify for relief if the relevant conditions are met. A disposal therefore includes a sale, a gift, a transfer (e.g. at undervalue) and a capital sum derived from an asset.

A "qualifying business disposal" includes:

1. a "material" disposal of business assets; and
2. a disposal "associated" with a relevant "material" disposal.

Each of these two conditions are discussed in detail at **Section 8.5**. First, we will consider how ER works in principle.

18.3 How does ER Work?

Up until 22 June 2010, ER relief worked by reducing the chargeable gain arising on a qualifying business disposal. Relief was given by reducing the gains (up to the maximum threshold of £1 million; or £2 million from April 2010) by a factor of 4/9. This meant that qualifying gains (ignoring annual exemption) were taxed at an effective rate of 10%. Reducing the gain by a factor of 4/9 left 5/9 of the gain taxable at the then standard CGT rate of 18%. This gave an effective rate of 10% (5/9 × 18% = 10%). All other gains not qualifying for ER were chargeable at the standard CGT tax rate of 18%.

Example 18.1
During May 2010, Margaret sells her retail shop business for £650,000. The chargeable gains arising were £250,000, all of which qualifies for ER.

Solution	£
Gains	250,000
Less: ER reduction in gain 4/9 × £250,000	(111,111)
Chargeable gain	138,889
Less: annual exemption	(10,100)
Taxable gain	128,789
CGT @ 18%	23,182
Check:	
£250,000 @10%	25,000
£10,100 @ 18%	(1,818)
Total	23,182

With effect from 23 June 2010, when the new higher CGT rate of 28% was introduced, ER is applied so that any gain qualifying for the relief is simply charged to tax at 10%.

Example 18.2
Taking the above example, if Margaret sells her retail shop business in August 2010 the CGT computation would be as follows:

	£
Gains	250,000
Less annual exemption	(10,100)
Taxable gain	239,900
CGT @ 10%	23,990

As noted above, there is a threshold limit for each individual on chargeable gains on which ER may be claimed. This limit is a lifetime limit. From 6 April 2008 to 5 April 2010, the lifetime limit was £1 million. This was increased to £2 million with effect from 6 April 2010, increased to £5 million with effect from 23 June 2010 and increased to £10 million with effect from 6 April 2011. An individual can claim ER on more than one occasion provided the overall limit is not exceeded.

Where an individual makes qualifying gains above the previous £5 million limit before 6 April 2011 (£2 million limit before 23 June 2010), no additional relief will be allowed for the excess above the old limit. However, if they make further qualifying gains on or after 6 April 2011, they will be able to claim relief on up to a further £5 million of those additional gains, giving relief on accumulated qualifying gains up to the new lifetime limit of £10 million.

In determining the rate of CGT charged on any other gains, those qualifying for ER are set against any unused basic rate band before non-qualifying gains.

Example 18.3
Siobhan has previously used £5 million of her lifetime ER limit. In 2014/15, her taxable income, after all allowable deductions and the personal allowance, is £17,400. In May 2014, Siobhan realises a chargeable gain of £3 million on the disposal of a business. In December 2014, she sells another business, realising further chargeable gains of £7 million. Both disposals qualify for ER (subject to the lifetime limits). Siobhan has no allowable losses to set against these gains.

The £3 million gain realised in May 2014 is subject to the £10 million lifetime limit for ER, of which Siobhan has previously used £5 million. Consequently all of the gain will qualify for ER. The annual exemption will be used against the later gain as it is exposed to a higher rate of CGT.

Solution – May 2014 Disposal

	£
Gains	3,000,000
Less: annual exemption	–
Chargeable gain	3,000,000
CGT payable: £3 million (qualifying for ER) @ 10%	300,000

The increase in the lifetime limit from 6 April 2011 means that £2 million of the £7 million gain realised by Siobhan on the disposal of a further business in December is chargeable at the 10% rate of CGT. While Siobhan's taxable income is £14,465 below the basic rate band (£31,865 − £17,400), the £5 million of the gain charged at 10% is taken into account in priority to other gains in determining whether total income and gains exceed the basic rate band. So the remaining £5 million gain, less the annual exemption, is charged at the higher rate of 28%.

continued overleaf

Solution – December 2014 Disposal

	£
Gains	7,000,000
Less: annual exemption	(11,000)
Chargeable gain	6,989,000
CGT payable:	
£2m (qualifying for ER) @ 10%	200,000
£4,989,000 @ 28%	1,396,920
Total	1,596,920

18.4   Losses and ER

If a qualifying business disposal would be such that both chargeable gains and allowable losses are created, it is the "net qualifying gains" on which ER is calculated.

For disposals before 23 June 2010, the annual exemption and losses arising on assets not qualifying for ER are deducted after the application of ER.

Example 18.4
Martina makes a chargeable gain of £700,000 in May 2010 which qualifies for ER. She makes no other chargeable gains in the 2010/11 tax year. Martina also has a current year loss of £200,000 on the disposal of various stock market shares. The stock market shares do not qualify for ER. Martina claims ER where possible.

	£
Gains	700,000
Less: ER reduction in gain 4/9 × £700,000	(311,111)
Chargeable gain	388,889
Less: capital losses	(200,000)
	188,889
Less: annual exemption	(10,100)
Taxable gain	178,789
CGT @ 18%	32,182
Check:	
£700,000 @ 10%	70,000
£200,000 + £10,100 = £210,100 @ 18%	(37,818)
Total	32,182

With effect from 23 June 2010, ER does not apply by reducing the taxable gain, but is rather a rate of tax applied to a gain qualifying for the relief. The annual exemption and losses on gains not qualifying for ER may be deducted from gains in whatever way is most beneficial, i.e. set against gains taxed at 28% in the first instance.

Gains qualifying for ER are taken into account in priority to other gains when determining whether total income and gains exceed the basic rate band.

Example 18.5

Niall makes a chargeable gain of £900,000 in October 2014 which qualifies for ER. He makes further chargeable gains on the disposal of various quoted shares during 2014/15 of £260,000. Niall also has a current year loss of £200,000 on the disposal of various quoted shares. The quoted shares do not qualify for ER. His taxable income for 2014/15, after all deductible tax reliefs and the personal allowance, is £21,865. Niall claims ER where possible.

	ER	Non-ER	Total
	£	£	£
Gains qualifying for ER	900,000		900,000
Other gains		260,000	260,000
Less: capital losses		(200,000)	(200,000)
Less: annual exemption		(11,000)	(11,000)
Taxable gains	900,000	49,000	949,000
CGT:			
Gain qualifying for ER @ 10%	90,000	–	90,000
£49,000 @ 28%	–	13,720	13,720
Total	90,000	13,720	103,720

Note that the gain qualifying for ER has used up the remaining £10,000 of the basic rate band when determining the CGT rate to be applied to other gains. Note also, that the capital losses and annual exemption are set against the gains not qualifying for ER, as this is the most tax-efficient utilisation.

18.5 Categories of Qualifying Business Disposals

18.5.1 Material Disposal of Business Assets

There are certain conditions which must be met for a gain to qualify for ER. The disposal must be "material", and be one of the following:

1. A disposal of the **whole or part of a business** (or a share in a partnership), as a going concern, which has been owned by the individual throughout the period of one year ending on the date of the disposal. The assets within this business must be used in the business, e.g. goodwill. This will not include investment assets.

OR

2. A disposal of **one or more assets after the business has ceased** provided that:
   - the assets had been in use for the purposes of the business at the date of cessation;
   - the business was **owned** by the individual throughout the period of one year ending on the date of cessation; **and**
   - the **date of cessation** is within **three years** prior to the date of the disposal.

OR

3. A disposal of shares or securities in a company which has been the individual's **personal trading company** and of which the individual has been an employee or officer, and these conditions are met either:
   - throughout the period of one year ending on the date of the disposal, **or**
   - throughout the period of one year ending with the date on which the company ceases to be a trading company and that date is within the period of three years ending with the date of the disposal.

Under 1. and 2. above, it should be noted that ER is only given in respect of "relevant business assets". These are assets used for the purpose of the business and, hence, investments or shares will not qualify. A business under 1. above will qualify for ER if it is a trade, profession or vocation conducted on a commercial basis with a view to making a profit. This does not include property letting businesses (taxable as property income) but does include the business of commercial letting of furnished holiday accommodation (taxable as trading income) in the UK or the European Economic Area (EEA).

Under 3. above, an individual's **personal trading company** is a trading company in which the individual holds at least 5% of the company's ordinary shares **and** that holding has an entitlement to at least 5% of the voting rights in the company.

18.5.2 A Disposal "Associated" with a Relevant "Material" Disposal

The disposal of an asset owned personally by an individual may qualify for ER if it can be "associated" with a relevant "material" disposal. Three conditions must be satisfied:

1. the individual makes a **"material"** disposal of either the whole or part of their interest in the assets of a **partnership** or the **shares** in a company; and
2. the associated disposal is made as part of the **withdrawal** of the individual from participation in the business of the partnership or the company; and
3. the assets are **in use** in the business throughout the period of one year ending with the earlier of the dates of "material" disposal of business assets or the cessation of the business of the partnership or company.

> **Example 18.6**
> A company director of X Ltd, who owns the factory premises from which the company operates its business, sells the premises at the same time as he sells his shares in the company; the sale of the premises may be treated as an associated disposal and so qualify for ER.

This "associated" disposal rule does not extend to disposals associated with a material disposal by a sole trader. It is also important to note that ER is restricted where the individual charges rent to the partnership or the company.

The general taxation of partnerships for CGT purposes is beyond the scope of this textbook.

18.6 How to Claim ER?

ER must be claimed by the individual on or before the first anniversary of 31 January following the end of the tax year in which the qualifying business disposal took place. For example, if the disposal took place during 2014/15, then the claim must be made by 31 January 2017.

18.7 Interaction with other CGT Reliefs

As discussed in **Chapter 19**, ER is applied after the following reliefs:

▓ Rollover relief – replacement of business assets relief (if claimed)
▓ Incorporation relief (if no election is made to disapply)
▓ Gift relief (if claimed)

Where both Enterprise Investment Scheme (EIS) deferral relief and ER relief are claimed, ER is applied first so that the gain to be deferred under EIS deferral relief is the reduced gain. With effect from 23 June 2010, it is not possible to claim ER and EIS deferral relief on the same gain as ER no longer reduces a gain. A gain qualifying for ER is instead subject to a lower rate of tax (10%).

Generally, where a gain is deferred as a result of a qualifying EIS investment, the rate of CGT applied when the gain comes into charge is the prevailing rate at that time (currently 18% or 28%). It is not possible to 'freeze' the application of the 10% ER rate and so ER can no longer be claimed in conjunction with EIS deferral relief.

In some instances, it may be preferable not to claim both ER and the reliefs above with a view to utilising the annual exemption and available losses.

Calculations of the interaction of ER with the above reliefs are beyond the scope of this textbook. The following example is included for illustrative purposes only.

Example 18.7

On 5 December 2014, Anita sold her pharmacy to her daughter Kerry. The chargeable assets on disposal were goodwill and the freehold shop. Details are as follows:

	Cost £	Market Value £
Goodwill	Nil (the goodwill was not purchased)	100,000
Shop	40,000 (purchased January 2000)	150,000

Kerry paid Anita £40,000 for the goodwill and £60,000 for the shop.

Anita made a claim for ER, and Anita and Kerry made a joint election for gift relief. Anita made no other gains or losses in 2014/15 and has already fully utilised her basic rate band. This is Anita's first lifetime claim for ER.

Anita's CGT position:	£	£
Goodwill:		
Market value	100,000	
Less: cost	(0)	
Gain	100,000	
Less: gift relief	(60,000)	
Chargeable gain (excess proceeds rule)	40,000	40,000
Shop:		
Market value	150,000	
Less: cost	(40,000)	
Gain	110,000	
Less: gift relief	(90,000)	
Chargeable gain (excess proceeds rule)	20,000	20,000
Chargeable gains after gift relief		60,000
Less: annual exemption		(11,000)
Taxable gain		49,000
CGT @ 10%		4,900

continued overleaf

Kerry's base cost position:	£
Goodwill:	
Market value	100,000
Less gift relief (joint election)	(60,000)
Revised base cost	40,000
Shop:	
Market value	150,000
Less gift relief (joint election)	(90,000)
Revised base cost	60,000

Note: stamp duty, stamp duty land tax and inheritance tax should also be considered in such a transaction.

Questions

Review Questions
(See Suggested Solutions to Review Questions at the end of this textbook.)

Calculate the effect of ER on each of the following circumstances, assuming that no earlier ER claim has ever been made and assuming that the annual exemption and basic rate band are otherwise utilised.

Question 18.1

Anthony disposed of his trading business, which he had owned for five years, in May 2014, crystallising a gain of £900,000.

Question 18.2

Geraldine sold her trading business for £1.2 million in December 2014, having commenced to trade on 2 February 2014.

Question 18.3

Denis disposed of his trading business on September 2014, having owned it for 10 years. He received £11.5 million and made a gain of £10.3 million. He has made no previous claims for ER.

Question 18.4

Donald sold a property in January 2015 which he has let unfurnished to the same tenant since April 2004, crystallising a gain of £240,000.

Question 18.5

Brian ceased his trading business, which he had owned for 20 years, on 20 June 2014. Over the last five years Brian operated the business from three separate premises. He realised a gain of £360,000 on the sale of one property during August 2014 but made a loss of £90,000 on the sale of another business property during December 2014. In June 2015, he disposed of the remaining business property making a gain of £72,000. Assume the rules and the rates in 2015/16 are the same as the rules in 2014/15. He has made no previous claims for ER.

Question 18.6

Thomas owns 4% of a UK trading company and has owned these shares throughout the past year. He sells the shares in March 2015, crystallising a gain of exactly £3 million. Thomas is an employee in the company throughout this time.

Question 18.7

Terry sold his trading business in May 2014, realising gains of £630,000, having owned and operated this business for many years. In June 2014, Terry purchases a 10% share in a trading company and becomes a working director. He accepts an offer for sale in July 2015 for his shares, realising a gain of £10 million. Assume the rules and the rates in 2015/16 are the same as the rules in 2014/15.

Question 18.8

Patricia ran a shoe shop for a number of years until she decided to cease trading on 30 April 2014. She did not sell the business but sold the premises in April 2015.

Question 18.9

Marie retires as a partner from her accountancy partnership on 30 June 2014. She realises capital gains on the disposal of her share of the trading premises of £150,000 and gains of £40,000 for the disposal of goodwill.

Question 18.10

You have attended a meeting with your client, James Devlin, in April 2015. James has recently retired and on 15 March 2015 he sold his 40% shareholding in the company, Devlin Communications Ltd, an independent mobile phone shop, for £851,000. James held these shares since the company was incorporated, when he subscribed for 1,000 £1 ordinary shares which he paid for in full. James was appointed as a full-time director of the company on 5 April 2006.

James also owned the Dungannon shop from which the company had always traded, having originally bought it as an investment on 1 April 2003 for £125,000. Devlin Communications Ltd started trading when it was incorporated on 1 April 2006 and from that date onward traded solely from the shop. James charged rent of £1,575 per month for the use of the shop from that date. A full commercial rent would have been £2,250 per month.

The shop was subsequently sold by James for £475,000 on 31 March 2015, as Devlin Communications Ltd was moving to larger premises and they no longer needed to rent the property.

Note: James is an additional rate taxpayer and the company is a trading company. The shares and Armagh property are the only assets he has ever owned.

Requirement

Prepare a report to James dealing with the sale of the shares and the building that considers the following:

(a) The capital gains tax payable by James as a result of the above transactions. You should identify any potential claims/relief(s) James could avail of to reduce his chargeable gains on the disposals, state why the disposals qualify for any claims/reliefs you are proposing and outline the saving to be achieved.

(b) The due date for payment of the capital gains tax arising, together with the time limit(s) which apply to any claims/reliefs you consider available to mitigate the gain.

Capital Gains Tax Reliefs

Learning Objectives

After studying this chapter you will have developed competency in the following:

- Determine and apply appropriate CGT reliefs including:
  - relief for the transfer of a business to a company;
  - rollover relief for business assets; and
  - holdover/gift relief.

- Demonstrate an awareness of:
  - relief for loans to traders which become irrecoverable;
  - relief for payments made under guarantee;
  - losses on shares in qualifying companies.

- Determine the appropriate reliefs available in relation to Enterprise Investment Scheme (EIS) shares.

19.1 Rollover Relief and Depreciating Assets

19.1.1 Rollover Relief

If an individual disposes of a business asset, a chargeable gain will crystallise. Where the individual reinvests the **proceeds** into a replacement asset within a fixed timeframe, they may make a claim to defer the CGT charge on the gain until a future date.

Rollover relief is relief for **the replacement of business assets** used in a trade. It is available for individuals as well as companies, but it cannot be claimed by an investment business.

Provided certain conditions are met, an individual may claim that a chargeable gain arising on the disposal of a business asset (the "old asset") may be "rolled over" against the cost of acquiring a replacement business asset (the "new asset").

In this scenario, the disposal of the old asset is deemed to give rise to neither a gain nor a loss and the cost of the new asset is reduced by the gain that would have arisen but for the "rollover" relief. In essence, the chargeable gain is "deferred" until such time as the new asset is disposed of (subject to the possibility of a further rollover claim being available).

The Relief

On a claim, full or partial relief is available depending on the circumstances. This relief is a deferral relief. The gain will, therefore, become taxable at some time in the future. In line with general CGT principles, as death does not trigger a CGT charge, a gain rolled over is not triggered on death.

Full rollover relief is only available provided all of the disposal **proceeds** (not just the chargeable gain) are applied in acquiring the new asset.

Partial relief is where any proceeds not reinvested fall to be taxed immediately. In this instance, the cost of the new asset is reduced by the amount of the gain which was not immediately chargeable.

No rollover relief is available where the amount retained (i.e. proceeds not reinvested) exceeds the chargeable gain.

The relief may be claimed by a person who carries on more than one trade, either consecutively or concurrently, on the basis that they are treated as a single trade. The relief is only available where the new assets are acquired by the taxpayer who made the gain on the old assets.

The **conditions** which must be met before a rollover claim can be made are:

1. Both the old and the new asset must be within one of the specified classes of assets (see below). However, it is not necessary that they should both be within the same class.
2. The old asset must have been used only for trade purposes throughout the period of ownership and the new asset must be taken into and used immediately in the trade.
3. The new asset must be acquired during the specified period beginning 12 months before and ending 36 months after the date of disposal of the old asset.

The **class of assets** referred to above include:

- land, buildings and fixed plant and machinery;
- ships, hovercraft, aircraft, satellites, space stations and spacecraft;
- milk, potato and fish quotas and certain other EU quotas;
- goodwill (from 19 March 2014 rollover relief is no longer available to companies making a disposal of tangible assets and using the proceeds to acquire intangible fixed assets);
- Lloyd's syndicate rights;
- EU Basic Payment Scheme (effective from 20 December 2013).

Note: shares are not a qualifying asset for rollover relief as they cannot be used for the purposes of the trade. FA 2012 brought in provisions to enable farmers to continue to obtain rollover relief in respect of the disposal and acquisition of entitlements under the EU Single Payment Scheme. These provisions have retrospective effect from 1 January 2009.

It is generally accepted that it is the disposal consideration net of incidental costs of disposal that should be compared with the total costs of acquisition including incidental costs of acquisition.

Example 19.1
On 1 January 2015, a farmer sells land for £40,000. The expenses of sale are £3,000. On 1 October 2014, the farmer buys land for use in the trade at a cost of £35,000 plus expenses of £4,000. For the purposes of a claim, the disposal consideration is £37,000 and the amount applied in acquiring new assets is £39,000. Full relief is therefore due.

Claims for Rollover Relief

Claims for the relief must be made within four years after the end of the tax year (or accounting year for companies) in which the later of the disposal of the old asset or the acquisition of the new asset took place. Where the disposal of the old asset takes place in 2012/13 and the acquisition of the new asset is made in 2014/15, the claim must be made on or before 5 April 2019. *(Previously, the rule was five years and 10 months after the end of the tax year, e.g. 2014/15 claim on or before 31 January 2021.)*

It is possible to make provisional claims for rollover relief if it is intended that a purchase of a qualifying asset will take place within the specified period.

It may be preferred not to claim rollover relief on business assets where sufficient capital losses and annual exemption are available for claim.

Note: it is not possible to specify the amount of rollover relief to be claimed. It is an all or nothing relief.

Example 19.2

On 1 July 2004, John Smith acquired freehold trade premises for £100,000. The business expanded and, during December 2014, new premises were acquired for £200,000 and the old premises were sold on 1 November 2014 for £160,000. His full basic rate band is utilised against other income.

In the absence of a claim for rollover relief, there would be chargeable gains as follows:

Sale of old premises – without rollover relief	£
Disposal proceeds	160,000
Deduct:	
Allowable cost	(100,000)
Chargeable gain	60,000
Less: annual exemption	(11,000)
Taxable chargeable gain	49,000
CGT @ 28%	13,720

Note: John Smith cannot claim ER on the disposal of the trade premises, as he is not disposing of the trade itself.

Where rollover relief is claimed, the position is as follows:

Sale of old premises – with rollover relief	£
Disposal proceeds	160,000
Deduct:	
Allowable cost	(100,000)
Chargeable gain	60,000
Less: rollover relief	(60,000)
Taxable chargeable gain	0
Base cost of new asset:	
Purchase of new asset	
Cost	200,000
Deduct rollover relief	(60,000)
Revised base cost	140,000

Where rollover relief is claimed, John's annual exemption is wasted as rollover relief is an "all or nothing" claim.

Example 19.3

Beth purchased a property for £80,000 in July 2002 for use in her business. In June 2014, she purchased another property for use in her business and two months later sold the original property for £175,000. Beth wishes to claim rollover relief on the sale of the original property. Compute her chargeable gain if the cost of the replacement property was respectively (assuming both the old and new asset are within the relevant class of assets):

(i) £190,000   (ii) £150,000 and   (iii) £70,000

Solution

The chargeable gain on the disposal of the original property is:

	£
	£
Proceeds	175,000
Cost	(80,000)
Gain	95,000

The quantum of the gain which can be rolled over will depend on the amount reinvested:

1. If the new property was purchased for £190,000, all of the sale proceeds have been reinvested and, thus, all of the gain of £95,000 can be rolled over into the cost of the new asset. The base cost for CGT purposes of the new asset is £95,000 (being £190,000 − £95,000 (rolled over)). In essence, the gain of £95,000 is deferred until the new asset is sold (subject to any potential further rollover claim).

2. In this situation, £25,000 of the disposal proceeds have not been reinvested and thus become **immediately** chargeable. The residue of the gain, namely £70,000 (£95,000 − £25,000) can be rolled over into the cost of the new property and the CGT base cost of the new asset will be £80,000 (being £150,000 − £70,000 (rolled over)).

3. In this situation, the amount of the proceeds **not** reinvested is £105,000, which exceeds the actual chargeable gain of £95,000. Thus, all of the gain of £95,000 is immediately chargeable and rollover relief does not apply.

19.1.2　Companies and Rollover Relief

For companies (unlike individuals), the list of assets on which rollover relief can be claimed does **not** include **goodwill** or **quotas** as these assets are within the Intangible Fixed Assets regime (IFAs).

Rollover relief is available within a CGTG of companies. If a group member disposes of an asset which is eligible for rollover relief, it can treat all the group members as a single entity for claiming such relief (provided, of course, that all relevant conditions are met). Thus, if another group member acquires a relevant asset within the qualifying period (12 months before the disposal or 36 months afterwards), the company making the disposal may match the acquisition for rollover relief purposes. The acquiring company must be a member of the group at the time of acquisition and the disposing company must be a member of the group at the time of sale. However, there is no requirement for them both to be a member of the group at the same time.

For it to be effective, both the acquiring company and the disposing company must make a joint claim for the relief to apply.

It should be noted that assets transferred intragroup on a no gain/no loss basis *cannot* **be matched for rollover relief purposes.**

19.1.3　Mixed Use (Business and Non-business Use)

In order to qualify for full relief, the old asset must have been used only for the purposes of the business throughout the whole period of ownership and the new asset must, on acquisition, be taken into use and used only for business purposes. However, where this is not the case, then the business portion and non-business portion must be treated as separate assets. There are two situations in which partial relief may be given when these conditions are not met.

1. This applies, if appropriate, to both the old and the new assets. If the old asset was used only partly for the purposes of the business and partly for non-business purposes, it is treated as two separate assets in calculating the rollover relief.

    The expenditure on acquisition and the disposal proceeds are apportioned between the business use and the non-business use, and only the part of the overall gain applicable to the business use qualifies for rollover relief. A similar apportionment is made where the new asset is used on acquisition, in part for the purposes of the business and in part for other purposes. Any gain can only be rolled over into the expenditure apportioned to the business use of the new asset.

2. The second situation arises only in relation to the old asset. If the claimant did not use that asset for the purposes of the business during part of the period of ownership, the asset is treated as two separate assets in calculating the rollover relief. In this case the expenditure on acquisition and disposal are apportioned by reference to the period and extent of business and non-business use. Only the part of the overall gain applicable to the business use qualifies for rollover relief. For these purposes, the period of ownership excludes any period before 31 March 1982.

The apportionment is to be made on a just and reasonable basis.

Example 19.4

Richard Moss, trading in fireplace manufacturing, acquired a building on 1 November 1999 for £110,000. 40% of the building was used as business offices and the remainder was let on leases to unconnected parties. On 1 November 2014, the building was sold for £400,000 and a new building acquired for £500,000, of which 25% was used for business.

The calculation of the gain on the old building before rollover relief is:

	Total	40% Business asset	60% Non-business asset
	£	£	£
Disposal proceeds	400,000	160,000	240,000
Deduct: Cost	(110,000)	(44,000)	(66,000)
Net gain	290,000	116,000	174,000

The business element in the new building is £125,000 (25% of £500,000); therefore, £35,000 of the proceeds of the £160,000 business disposal has not been reinvested. The amount not reinvested is less than the gain of £116,000; therefore, rollover relief is permitted for £81,000 of the gain. £35,000 is assessed to CGT immediately. The gain on the disposal chargeable to tax is:

	£
Gain on non-business asset	174,000
Gain on business asset: proceeds not reinvested	35,000
Chargeable gain	209,000

The deemed cost of the business element in the new building is £44,000 (£125,000 less gain rolled over of £81,000).

19.1.4 Interaction with Entrepreneurs' Relief

It should be considered whether it would be more beneficial for an individual to claim ER or rollover relief or both. Note: ER is only available on the disposal of the whole or part of a business and not on individual assets. Rollover relief is typically relevant where there is a sale of an individual business asset and the individual continues to carry on the business. If it is possible to claim both reliefs, an individual may wish to claim ER instead of rollover relief in order to crystallise a gain at 10%.

If both reliefs are claimed, rollover relief will apply before ER. This would apply, for example, where some proceeds have not been reinvested so that rollover relief does not cover the whole of the gain. In this case, ER will apply to the gain left after rollover relief has been applied.

19.1.5 Depreciating Assets

For the purpose of these provisions, a depreciating asset is fixed plant and machinery not forming part of a building, or an asset that has a predictable useful life not exceeding 60 years from the time it is acquired.

Where the new asset is a "depreciating asset", the chargeable gain arising on the disposal of the old asset **cannot** be rolled over and is **not** deducted from the base cost of the new asset. Instead, the chargeable gain is "frozen" or "temporarily parked" until it becomes chargeable (crystallises) on the **earliest** of the following three dates:

1. the date on which the new depreciating asset is disposed of;
2. the date on which the new depreciating asset ceases to be used in the trade; or
3. the tenth anniversary of the acquisition of the new depreciating asset.

It should be noted that, if a taxpayer were to purchase a non-depreciating asset (within the relevant class – see above) prior to the expiration of the earliest of the above three dates, then it could "convert" the temporary "frozen" gain into a "rolled over" gain. This effectively widens the window of opportunity for the taxpayer to reinvest the original proceeds into the relevant class of assets.

In effect, the taxpayer can "park" the gain against the purchase of a depreciating asset until such time as a qualifying asset for rollover relief is purchased and a claim for the relief can be made.

An example of a depreciating asset is a short-term lease.

Example 19.5

Michelle bought business premises in September 2007 for £115,000. She sold the premises for £150,000 on 1 October 2014. On 15 September 2011, she bought some fixed plant and machinery to use in her business costing £140,000. These were sold for £155,000 on 30 June 2015. What is Michelle's CGT liability?

The gain on the premises may be deferred by parking the gain against the purchase of the depreciating asset. Note that the gain on the premises is frozen; it is not rolled over into the cost of the depreciating asset. When the depreciating asset is sold, then as well as the gain on this sale being taxable, the gain on the frozen sale of the premises also crystallises.

2014/15 Sale of premises:	£
Proceeds	150,000
Cost	(115,000)
Gain	35,000
Less: Gain frozen on purchase of fixed P&M	(25,000)
Chargeable gain*	10,000
*Proceeds not reinvested.	

2015/16 Sale of fixed P&M:	£
Proceeds	155,000
Cost	(140,000)
Gain	15,000

2015/16: Total gain chargeable on sale of fixed P&M:	£
Gain on sale of fixed P&M	15,000
Crystallised gain	25,000
Total chargeable gain	40,000

It would be possible to transfer the frozen gain to a non-depreciating asset provided the non-depreciating asset is bought before the deferred gain crystallises.

19.2 Gift Relief/Holdover Relief (Gift of Business Assets)

When an asset is gifted, the transferor receives no proceeds from the transaction. For CGT purposes, the disposal is treated as a disposal at market value as the transaction is not at arm's length. This is the case even if the parties are unconnected. A chargeable gain will therefore crystallise, which means that taxpayers, in the absence of any "gift relief", could find themselves in a difficult financial position, having to pay CGT in respect of the gift but not having received any proceeds with which to fund it.

Gift relief is a form of rollover relief. Where a gain arises on a gift or a sale at an undervalue of a **business asset**, the gain may be "held over" until such time as the transferee disposes of the asset(s) concerned. Both the transferor and transferee must jointly elect for the gain on the gift to be held over. (No joint election is required if the asset is gifted into a trust.) Where gift relief is claimed, the taxable capital gain is deferred by deducting the gain from the base cost of the asset in the hands of the transferee/recipient.

> **Example 19.6**
> A gifts an asset to B. The market value of the asset is £100,000 at the time of the gift. The chargeable gain on disposal of the asset is £40,000. A and B jointly elect to claim gift relief.
>
> A has no CGT liability as the capital gain of £40,000 is reduced by the claim for gift relief. The base cost of this asset for B going forward is £60,000 (£100,000 – £40,000). B sells the asset for £130,000. B makes a gain of £70,000 (£130,000 – £60,000).

Gift relief is also available on gifts which are immediately chargeable to Inheritance Tax (IHT) (section 260 TCGA 1992), e.g. most gifts into trusts. In this instance, the asset does not have to be a business asset. NB: the transfer will be regarded as chargeable to IHT even if it falls within the IHT nil rate band or is covered by the IHT annual exemption. Gifts to settlor interested trusts do not qualify for gift relief.

Claim for Gift Relief (section 165 TCGA 1992)
Claims must be made within four years from the end of the tax year of disposal, e.g. in respect of disposals made in 2014/15, claims must be made on or before 5 April 2019. (*Previously the rule was five years and 10 months after the end of the tax year, e.g. a 2014/15 claim must be made on or before 31 January 2021.*)

19.2.1 Business Assets for Gift Relief Purposes

With the exception of gifts immediately chargeable to IHT (section 260), gifts must be business assets. So what is a business asset for gift relief purposes? The gifted asset must be one of the following:

1. An asset used in the business carried on by the transferor or by the transferor's "**personal trading company**" (a trading company in which the transferor can exercise at least 5% of the voting rights). A holding company of a trading group also qualifies if the holding company is the transferor's personal company.
2. Shares or securities of trading companies or holding companies of trading groups where:
   (a) the shares are unlisted (i.e. not listed on a recognised stock exchange) (AIM listed shares are not listed shares for these purposes); or
   (b) the shares are in the transferor's "**personal trading company**" (provided the transferee is not a company).
3. Agricultural land and buildings used for a farming trade which would qualify for IHT agricultural property relief.

Note: the definition of "trading company" is the same for gift relief and ER. However, the definition of "personal trading company" is **not** the same for both reliefs.

There are two instances where gift relief will be restricted: sales at an undervalue, and gifts of shares in a personal trading company. We will deal with each of these in turn.

Sales at an Undervalue

As stated above, gift relief will also apply where assets are "sold" at an undervalue, i.e. for less than their market value. For example, transfers to a connected person may be at an undervalue. The rule in this instance is that the "excess proceeds", i.e. the amount of the proceeds exceeding the original cost of the asset, fall to be taxed immediately and only the residue is available to be "held over" and deferred.

Example 19.7

In December 2014, Gordon gifts a property (used in his business) to his son Tony when its market value is £210,000. The property was purchased in June 2000 by Gordon for £95,000. Gordon and Tony jointly elect for the chargeable gain to be "held over". Calculate the quantum of gain which may be "held over" and indicate what effect, if any, there would be if the son were to pay £100,000 for the property.

Solution

(a) Outright gift

Chargeable gain for Gordon	£
Proceeds	210,000
Cost	(95,000)
Gain (available to be held over)	115,000
Less: gift relief	(115,000)
Chargeable gain	0

Tony's CGT base cost would thus be £95,000 (being the market value of £210,000 less held over gain of £115,000).

(b) Sale at an undervalue

If Tony paid £100,000 for the property, then the "excess proceeds" of £5,000 (the excess of the amount paid over the original cost) would become immediately chargeable and the held over gain would be reduced to £110,000 (being £115,000 less the £5,000 which is immediately chargeable). Tony's CGT base cost in this situation would be £100,000 (being the market value of £210,000 less the held-over gain of £110,000).

Chargeable gain for Gordon	£
Proceeds	210,000
Cost	(95,000)
Gain (available to be held over)	115,000
Less: gift relief	(110,000)
Chargeable gain	5,000

Gifts of Shares in a Personal Trading Company

If shares in a **personal trading company** are the subject of a gift relief claim and the company has any non-business assets (such as investments) at that time, the gain eligible for gift relief will be restricted. Gift relief is only available on that part of the gain which is represented by the proportion chargeable business assets (CBA) bear to the total chargeable assets (CA).

$$\text{Qualifying gain} = \frac{\text{CBA}}{\text{CA}} \times \text{share gain}$$

where: CBA = Market value of chargeable business assets and
CA = Market value of chargeable assets

Market values of the assets from the balance sheet at the date of disposal are used for these purposes.

Chargeable business assets are assets which are typically used in the business, e.g. goodwill, factory premises, plant and machinery, etc.

Chargeable assets are CBAs plus investments, e.g. rental properties, quoted shares held as investments. Stock, debtors, and cash are not chargeable assets and are, therefore, outside the scope of CGT.

This restriction only applies on a section 165 gift relief claim and not on a section 260 claim, i.e. where there is an immediate IHT charge.

Example 19.8
In December 2014, Gemma gave her daughter Lily shares in her personal company. The shares cost Gemma £40,000 when acquired in March 2005 and their market value is £300,000 in December 2014. The gain on the shares is £260,000. The company owned assets with the following values at December 2014:

	£
Freehold business offices	100,000
Plant and machinery (cost £50,000)	30,000
Goodwill	80,000
Trade debtors	40,000
Cash	20,000
Shares held as investments	50,000
Sundry net assets (all non-chargeable)	30,000

Chargeable assets and chargeable business assets are as follows:

	Chargeable assets	Chargeable business assets
	£	£
Freehold business offices	100,000	100,000
Plant and machinery	30,000	30,000
Shares held as investments	50,000	
Goodwill	80,000	80,000
	260,000	210,000

Gift relief is, therefore, restricted to the fraction 210/260.

	£
Gain on shares	260,000
Deduct: Held over gain = £260,000 × 210/260	210,000
Chargeable gain	£50,000

Base cost of the shares held by the recipient is £90,000 (i.e. £300,000 less the £210,000 held over gain).

19.2.2   Mixed Use (Business and Non-business Use)

As for rollover relief, gains on assets (other than shares) with mixed use must be apportioned, i.e.:

▨ an asset used partly for business and partly for non-business use; or
▨ during the ownership period the use of an asset changed so that for only part of the ownership period it was used for business purposes.

Only the gain relating to the business portion may qualify for gift relief. It is therefore necessary to treat the business and non-business portions as separate assets.

The restrictions set out above for periods of non-trade use or partial trade use do not apply where the asset sold qualifies for agricultural property relief under IHT.

19.2.3   Anti-avoidance Rules

Gift relief is only available if the transferee is either resident or ordinarily resident in the UK at the time of the gift.

If the transferee is an individual who becomes either non-resident or not ordinarily resident in the UK in any of the **six tax years following the year of the gift**, and before disposing of the asset transferred, then the gain held over is chargeable on them as if it arose immediately before they became either not resident or not ordinarily resident in the UK.

19.2.4   Instalment Payments

On election, CGT may be payable in 10 equal annual instalments for certain assets gifted where gift relief is not available. The instalment option is available for land and buildings, shares in unquoted companies (e.g. investment companies) and shares in quoted companies where the donor has control before the gift. Note, such instalments are interest-bearing. In certain circumstances, any outstanding CGT liability becomes due for payment if the asset is sold.

19.2.5   Interaction with Entrepreneurs' Relief

It should be considered whether it would be more beneficial for an individual to claim ER or gift relief, or both. It should be noted that ER is only available on the disposal of the whole or part of a business and not on individual assets. If qualifying, an individual may wish to claim ER instead of gift relief if the application of ER will reduce the gain to an amount covered by the annual exemption or losses.

If both reliefs are claimed, gift relief will apply before ER. This would apply for example, where some proceeds have been received, i.e. a sale at an undervalue.

19.3   Transfer of a Business to a Limited Company

Many individuals commence self-employment as a sole trader as this has relatively lower costs and more beneficial loss reliefs than corporate entities. As things progress and the business grows and expands, it may well be that the decision is made to incorporate and form a limited company. This will create a separate legal entity. The cessation of the sole trade business will result in adjustments in respect of capital allowances and also potentially crystallise a CGT liability on the chargeable assets which are transferred to the limited company.

The implications of the incorporation of a sole trade business include the following:

▨ There is a cessation of the sole trade business.
▨ The former proprietor of the business becomes an employee of the new company.
▨ Class 1 NICs will be payable by the company whereas the sole trader will have been subject to Class 2 and Class 4 NICs.

▨ There is a disposal of the sole trade assets (including goodwill) for CGT purposes on their transfer to the new company.

▨ The new company will be subject to corporation tax whereas the sole trader will have been subject to income tax on the profits of the business.

As the business owner and their limited company (i.e. the company in which they are the majority shareholder) are separate legal entities, the transfer of business assets from a sole trade to a new company on incorporation is a chargeable event for CGT purposes. In the absence of any relief, the taxpayer would potentially incur a CGT liability without having received any monies for the transfer with which to fund the payment of the tax. This is obviously an undesirable situation and would perhaps discourage individuals from incorporating their businesses even where it makes very sound commercial sense. It is for this reason that "incorporation relief" is available where a sole trade business is transferred to a company in return for consideration either wholly or partly in the form of shares. Where all of the conditions for this relief are met it is applied **automatically**, without the need for the taxpayer to make a formal claim.

19.3.1   Incorporation Relief (section 162 TCGA 1992)

The **conditions** for incorporation relief are:

1. the sole trade business must be transferred as a going concern;
2. all of the assets (except cash) of the business must be transferred to the company;
3. the transferor must receive shares in the new company as consideration.

The transfer is deemed to take place at full market value as it is a transaction between connected parties.

Full incorporation relief will be available where the only consideration for the transfer is shares.

Partial relief, where only part of the consideration is in shares, then only part of the chargeable gain is held over. The held over gain is computed as a ratio that the value of the shares bears to the total consideration. Where cash or loan stock is provided as part consideration, then a percentage of the gain will be immediately taxable. The cash can be left on a director's loan account and the director/shareholder can withdraw it, tax-free, from the company at any time.

$$\text{Held over gain} = \frac{\text{Value of shares issued}}{\text{Total consideration}} \times \text{whole gain}$$

Incorporation relief is another form of rollover relief as the **held over gain is deducted from the base cost of the shares received**. **Note**, it is the base cost of the shares that are reduced, not the assets transferred.

Sometimes it is preferable for a taxpayer that incorporation relief does not apply. The taxpayer therefore has the choice of opting out of this automatic relief and may elect that incorporation relief should not apply. Alternatively, the taxpayer could ensure that the above conditions are not met, e.g. s/he does not transfer all the assets into the company, or does not receive consideration in shares, so that incorporation relief will not apply. A taxpayer may prefer for incorporation relief not to apply where they have sufficient annual exemption and capital losses to cover any gain, and/or the rate of tax payable now is potentially less than what it may be in future years.

19.3.2   Gift Relief or Incorporation Relief?

If incorporation relief does not apply, then the option of claiming gift relief on chargeable business assets such as goodwill, business premises, etc., is still available. Transferring all the assets of the business, including property, into the company could have high tax costs, e.g. stamp duty land tax and a potential double tax charge on the subsequent disposal of the property by the company (i.e. corporation tax on the chargeable gain within the company and then tax on the individual on the future extraction of the net proceeds). The use of gift relief under section 165 TCGA 1992 gives greater flexibility than incorporation relief under section 162 by allowing capital gains planning to be dealt with on an asset-by-asset basis. The main disadvantage of gift relief is that the base cost of the assets in the hands of the transferee company is the former sole trader's original base cost rather than their market value at the date of transfer (i.e. under gift relief the base cost = MV less held over gain). Where incorporation relief is claimed, the base cost of assets transferred to the company is their market value at the date of transfer. It is the base cost of the shares that is reduced in value by any held over gain.

Example 19.9

Michael commenced business on 1 July 2000. On 1 October 2014, he transferred the business, comprising the assets set out below, to Comptech Ltd in consideration for the issue of 10,000 shares of £1 each fully paid in that company and £20,000 in cash. The value of the 10,000 shares was £140,000. The value of the assets transferred was £160,000 at the time of the transfer.

At the date of transfer, the balance sheet of the business was as follows:

		£
Assets:	Premises	25,000
	Plant and machinery	10,000
	Stock	6,000
		41,000
Liabilities:	Capital and reserves	41,000

	Chargeable gains	Market value 1 Oct 2014
	£	£
Premises	80,000	105,000
Plant and machinery	–	7,000
Stock	–	8,000
Goodwill	40,000	40,000
	120,000	160,000

The market value of the assets is £160,000. The cash received is £20,000; therefore, the shares are worth £140,000.

		£
Total chargeable gains		120,000
Incorporation relief:	$\dfrac{140,000 \times 120,000}{160,000}$	(105,000)
Gain chargeable in 2014/15 before annual exemption		15,000

Note: The goodwill has no base cost as it was not acquired.

On 1 January 2015, Michael sold the whole of his shareholding in Comptech Ltd for £220,000. His chargeable gain is computed as follows:

		£
Proceeds		220,000
Deduct: Cost of acquisition	140,000	
Less: Incorporation relief claimed	(105,000)	
		(35,000)
Chargeable gain before annual exemption		185,000

19.3.3 Transfer of Liabilities

Where business liabilities (e.g. bank loan, trade creditors) are taken over by a company on the transfer of a business to that company, then ordinarily this is treated as a cash consideration to the former proprietor and the deferred gain is reduced accordingly.

Example 19.10

Market value of the assets was £1 million and incorporation included consideration in the form of shares and trade creditors taken over of £100,000. Total value of consideration is £1 million. Share value is £900,000 (£1 million – £100,000 = £900,000 of shares) as trade creditors are treated as consideration other than shares (same as cash consideration). Full incorporation relief would not be allowed as the deferral would be diluted by the formula:

900,000/1,000,000 (total value of shares/total value of the consideration).

However, by concession, HMRC do not treat such liabilities as part of the consideration for the transfer if the other conditions of section 162 TCGA 1992 are satisfied. This means that there is no restriction and full rollover relief is available even if the sole trade's trade creditors are taken over by the company. Relief is also not precluded by the fact that some or all of the liabilities of the business are not taken over by the company.

Example 19.11

Following on from the example above, assuming all other conditions are met, the concession says that full incorporation relief would be permitted as the total value of shares equals the total value of the consideration (900,000/900,000).

It should be noted that the concession only applies in establishing whether the relief is available. It has no bearing in determining the net cost of the shares.

If, by contrast, liabilities which are not business liabilities (e.g. a personal income tax bill) are taken over by the company, these are treated as consideration other than in the form of shares, so that an immediate CGT charge arises on part of the gain.

Example 19.12

Michael's brother Martin commenced business as a pipe laying civil engineer on 1 January 1997. On 31 December 2014, he transfers his business to MMH Pipes Ltd in consideration for the issue of 20,000 shares of £1 each fully paid in that company, and £65,000 in cash. The value of the 20,000 shares is £450,000.

At the date of transfer, the balance sheet of the business was as follows:

		£
Assets:	Premises	150,000
	Plant and machinery	12,000
	Stock	20,000
	Debtors	40,000
	Goodwill	200,000
		422,000
Liabilities:	Trade creditors	75,000
	Capital and reserves	347,000
		422,000

continued overleaf

On 31 December 2014, the assets and liabilities of the business are as follows:

	Chargeable gains	Market value 31 Dec 2014
	£	£
Premises	50,000	200,000
Plant and machinery	–	15,000
Stock	–	25,000
Debtors	–	50,000
Goodwill	100,000	300,000
	150,000	590,000
Less liabilities: trade creditors		(75,000)
	150,000	515,000

All assets and liabilities are taken over by the new company MMH Pipes Ltd.

The market value of the assets is £515,000. The cash received is £65,000. Therefore, applying the HMRC concession, the shares are worth £450,000.

The chargeable gains arising on the disposal of the business to MMH Pipes Ltd are as follows:

		£
Total chargeable gains		150,000
Incorporation relief:	$\dfrac{450,000 \times 150,000}{515,000}$	(131,068)
Gains chargeable in 2014/15 before annual exemption		18,932

The allowable base cost of the shares is £450,000 less £131,068 = £318,932.

19.3.4   *Interaction with Entrepreneurs' Relief*

Since incorporation usually involves the disposal of all or part of a business, ER can usually also be claimed on incorporation. Incorporation is an automatic relief and it will be in priority to claiming ER. As noted above, it is possible to elect out of incorporation relief (usually within 34 months after the end of tax year of disposal).

If both reliefs are claimed, ER will be applied to any gain remaining after incorporation relief, e.g. where consideration is not wholly in the form of shares.

19.4   Reinvestment into EIS Shares

As seen earlier, a chargeable gain is capable of being deferred in certain circumstances (transfers of business to a limited company, gifts of business assets, rollover/holdover relief, etc.). For the aforementioned reliefs to be available, the assets broadly had to qualify as business assets. However, reinvestment into EIS shares can give rise to a relief available for any capital gain and not just gains on the disposal of business assets.

A "deferral" of the gain is possible on **any** gain where an amount of money equal to the **gain** is used to subscribe for eligible shares under the rules of the Enterprise Investment Scheme (EIS). It should be noted that it is not necessary to reinvest the whole proceeds – all that is required is to **reinvest the gain**.

While it is possible for the taxpayer to obtain income tax relief on a subscription for EIS shares, this is not a pre-condition in order to obtain the CGT deferral. Also the taxpayer can choose to restrict the amount of relief being claimed where this is beneficial (say to leave sufficient gains to utilise their annual exemption, etc.). Importantly, unlike income tax EIS relief, CGT relief has no cap.

In summary, the amount deferred is the lower of:

- the gain;
- the amount invested in EIS shares; and
- the amount specified in the claim.

The subscription for EIS shares must take place in the period starting 12 months before, or finishing 36 months after, the date that the chargeable disposal has taken place. In addition, the taxpayer must be UK resident.

The effect of the relief is to 'freeze' the gain. **Note:** the base cost of the new shares is **not** reduced by the deferred gain.

The deferred gain will become chargeable on:

1. the disposal of the EIS shares (but the taxpayer would have the option to defer again by subscribing for further EIS shares);
2. the taxpayer becoming non-resident within three years of the issue of the shares; or
3. the shares ceasing to be eligible.

Claim for Deferral Relief
Claims must be made before the fifth anniversary of 31 January following the tax year in which the EIS shares were issued.

19.4.1 Taxation of EIS Shares

A gain on the sale of EIS shares is exempt from CGT if the following conditions are met:

1. the shares are held for three years from the date of issue, and
2. income tax relief was obtained on the subscription for the shares.

A loss on EIS shares is always allowable but is restricted by the amount of income tax relief given and not withdrawn.

19.4.2 Interaction with Entrepreneurs' Relief

If both ER and EIS reinvestment relief are claimed, ER is applied first so that the gain to be deferred under EIS deferral relief is the reduced gain. This will only be possible in respect of gains on a disposal before 23 June 2010. For gains arising on disposals on or after 23 June 2010, it will no longer be possible to claim ER on a gain on which EIS deferral relief is being claimed. The taxpayer must choose to either defer the gain and pay tax at 18/28% when it later comes into charge, or claim ER and pay tax at 10% on the gain with no deferral. However, where a gain exceeds the £10 million lifetime limit for ER, it will be possible to claim ER up to the limit and claim EIS deferral relief on the excess.

19.5 Seed Enterprise Investment Scheme

The Seed Enterprise Investment Scheme (SEIS) was introduced on 6 April 2012 with the aim of incentivising investments into "early stage" qualifying companies.

The SEIS operates in a similar manner to the EIS, providing income tax and CGT reliefs for individual investors who subscribe in cash for qualifying shares in qualifying companies. It makes available tax relief to investors who subscribe for shares and have a stake of less than 30% in the company. The relief applies to investments made on or after 6 April 2012.

For the first year of the scheme, the Government offered a CGT 'holiday' – gains realised on the disposal of assets in 2012/13 that were invested through SEIS in the same year were exempt from CGT.

The scheme:

- applies to smaller companies, those with 25 or fewer employees and assets of up to £200,000, which are carrying on or preparing to carry on a new business;
- gives income tax relief worth 50% of the amount invested to individual investors with a stake of less than 30% in such companies, including directors who invest in their companies;
- applies to subscriptions for shares, using the same definition of eligible shares as EIS;
- applies to an annual amount of investment of £100,000 per investor, with unused annual amounts able to be carried back to the previous year, as under EIS;
- provides for relief within an overall tax favoured investment limit of £150,000 for the company. To give the greatest degree of flexibility, this will be a cumulative limit not an annual limit;
- provides for an exemption from CGT on gains on shares within the scope of the SEIS; and
- provides for an exemption from CGT on gains realised from disposals of assets in 2012/13, where the gains are reinvested through the new SEIS in the same year.

The relief was extended in FA 2013 as gains realised in 2013/14 could be reinvested in SEIS companies in both 2013/14 and 2014/15. The relief from CGT was however restricted to 50% of the gains reinvested (as opposed to 100% for 2012/13).

This relief was due to expire by 31 March 2014. However, FA 2014 sees the removal of the "sunset clause" and the relief will continue to be available. The 50% restriction in terms of the qualifying reinvested amount will also continue.

Example 19.13

Catherine sells an asset in June 2014 for £200,000 and realises a chargeable gain (before exemption) of £80,000.

If Catherine makes qualifying investments of at least £80,000 in SEIS shares in 2014/15, and all other conditions are met, the £80,000 gain will be completely free from CGT. She does not need to invest the whole £200,000 sale proceeds in order to get full exemption.

If Catherine makes qualifying investments of only £20,000 in SEIS shares in 2014/15, £20,000 of her gain will be exempt from CGT (provided all conditions are met) and she will be liable to CGT on a chargeable gain of £60,000 on the disposal of the asset in June 2014.

The remaining £60,000 chargeable gain will still be eligible for any other CGT reliefs that are available, and allowable losses and the CGT annual exempt amount can be set-off against it in the normal way.

19.6 Loans to Traders/Guarantees

19.6.1 Loans to Traders

When one person incurs a debt to another person, no chargeable gain accrues to the original creditor on his disposal of the debt (except in the case of a debt on security or money in a foreign currency bank account). Thus, for individuals, a debt is not normally subject to CGT unless it is a "debt on security", which is, essentially, a marketable loan. Without these provisions, a loss on a loan investment (not a debt on security) suffered by an individual would ordinarily attract no tax relief.

The loans to trader provisions (section 253 TCGA 1992) entitle lenders and guarantors to claim a measure of loss relief in respect of certain loans to UK resident traders which become irrecoverable. Typically, this would apply where a person lends funds to a UK trading business, or personally guarantees a loan, and the business runs into financial difficulties and the loan becomes irrecoverable or the personal guarantee is called in. Without this express provision, there would be no tax relief available for this investment. Section 253 relief allows the lender to treat the irrecoverable loan/ guarantee as a capital loss.

Debts on security are chargeable assets for CGT purposes; therefore, relief for lenders under these provisions is not available where the borrower's debt is a debt on a security, as an allowable loss would, in any event, accrue to the lender if the loss became irrecoverable.

There are strict conditions as to what are "qualifying loans", and to when a taxpayer can treat a loan as an allowable loss. These conditions include:

- money loaned is used for trade purposes;
- borrower is UK resident;
- not a debt on security;
- loan is not a discounted security;
- loan has not been taken into account for income tax purposes;
- loan has not been assigned;
- loan has become irrecoverable otherwise than as a consequence of the terms of the loan, any act or omission of the lender, etc; and
- the claimant and the borrower are not spouses or civil partners living together or companies in the same group at the time of the loan or subsequently.

The amount of the allowable loss is the amount of the outstanding principal that has become irrecoverable. No relief is allowed for interest suffered. Relief is not available for amounts taken into account for income tax purposes.

Claim for Loan to Trader Relief

Where the qualifying loan has become irrecoverable, the loss may be treated as arising either at the time of the claim or at a specified earlier time. An earlier time may be specified if the loan was irrecoverable at that earlier time and the earlier time is not more than two years before the beginning of the year of assessment in which the claim is made. This is another exception to the general rule that capital losses generally are only carried forward. In this instance, the loss may be thrown back one or two tax years which may be useful if gains had been realised during this period. Ordinarily capital losses are only allowed to be carried back on death.

19.6.2 Guarantees

A person who has guaranteed the repayment of a loan by a trader can make a similar claim for an allowable loss for CGT purposes. This relief can be given for payments in respect either of the outstanding principal of the loan or of the interest in respect of it.

A claim may be made if the loan constitutes a qualifying loan, which for this purpose may include a debt on a security. Other conditions include:

1. all, or part, of the principal debt, or any interest thereon, is irrecoverable;
2. the guarantor has been obliged to pay, either to the lender or to a co-guarantor, a sum of money in respect of the shortfall at 1. above;

3.   the guarantor has not assigned to anyone else their right of recovery; and
4.   not only were the lender of the money and the borrower not spouses living together, nor companies in the same group, when the loan was made or at any subsequent time, but also the guarantor and the borrower were not spouses living together, and the guarantor and the lender were not companies in the same group, when the guarantee was given or at any subsequent time.

The allowable loss will be equivalent to the payment actually made by the guarantor less the amount of any contribution which is payable to him by any co-guarantor.

The provisions which allow a lender's loss to arise before the date of the claim do not apply to guarantee payments.

Claim for Relief by Guarantor of a Debt

Unlike loans to traders there is no facility for backdating relief. Instead, the claim for a payment made under a loan guarantee is given by deeming a capital loss to have arisen at the date of payment.

Claims must be made within four years of the end of the tax year in which the payment is made under guarantee.

19.7   Losses on Disposal of Shares

As students are aware, capital losses are restricted for set-off against capital gains only. The only exception to this is in relation to share loss relief where allowable capital losses on shares in unlisted trading companies are eligible for income tax relief as an alternative to CGT relief in certain circumstances. These provisions can be found in Chapter 6 ITA 2007, section 131 onwards.

19.7.1   The Relief

Where an individual incurs an allowable loss on the disposal of qualifying shares, they may claim to set that loss against their total income (Step 2 of the income tax computation) for:

▨   the year in which the loss was incurred, and/or
▨   the preceding year.

Relief is only allowed in respect of a disposal of shares where the shares were originally acquired by way of **subscription** for money or money's worth. This is distinct from shares purchased from others or acquired by gift or inheritance.

The taxpayer may therefore be able to reduce their income tax liability where they have allowable capital losses available following:

1.   a disposal of shares at arm's length;
2.   a distribution in a liquidation;
3.   on a claim that the shares have become of negligible value; or
4.   a deemed disposal under the lost or destroyed provisions.

The year the losses are available for tax relief will depend upon the date of disposal or, if the loss arises from a claim for negligible value, on the date the claim is made and the deemed disposal date chosen by the claimant.

Relief may only be claimed for the full amount of the loss (partial claims cannot be made). Hence it is not possible to restrict the loss relief claim for the year to the amount required to reduce the taxpayer's income to the level of personal allowances or reliefs.

Relief under these provisions is given in priority to relief for trading losses set against total income.

A capital loss for which relief is given against income is not also available for relief under the CGT provisions. The balance of the capital losses, if any, can be deducted from chargeable gains in the normal way.

Example 19.14

Mr Bloggs subscribed £20,000 in 1997 for shares in a company making seating. The business failed in July 2014, with the shares becoming worthless. Mr Bloggs made a negligible value claim in respect of the shares in August 2014 and claimed an allowable capital loss of £20,000 for 2014/15 from the deemed disposal of shares.

It should be noted that, if all conditions for the relief are met, Mr Bloggs may claim to set the allowable capital loss on the shares either against chargeable gains in the normal way, or against his total income for 2014/15 or 2013/14.

Claim for Section 131 ITA 2007 Relief

The relief has to be claimed within one year of 31 January following the end of the tax year in which the loss was made. Thus, an allowable loss in 2014/15 has to be claimed on or before 31 January 2017. The claim must specify the year for which relief is claimed. Where a claim is to be made for both years, then it is necessary to specify which year takes priority.

19.7.2   What are Qualifying Shares?

Qualifying shares must either be:

- shares which already qualify for EIS relief; or
- ordinary shares in a qualifying trading company.

There are strict conditions as to what a qualifying trading company is, e.g. a trading requirement, an asset test requirement, a requirement that it traded in the UK within a certain timeframe, etc. The conditions are similar to those of a qualifying company under the EIS. **The detailed provisions are outside the scope of this course.**

19.8   Negligible Value Claims

Where an asset becomes worthless, a negligible value claim can be made to crystallise a capital loss. Where a claim is made, a disposal is deemed to take place and the asset immediately reacquired for consideration equal to the value specified in the claim. The effect of a claim is to trigger a capital loss even though a disposal has not actually taken place.

Ordinarily, a loss cannot be carried back against gains in earlier periods. However, in this instance, the loss can be claimed in that year or in either of the two preceding tax years provided that the asset was of negligible value in those years as well. Once allocated to a year, it is treated as a capital loss for that year.

There is no requirement to make a claim within a specified time of the asset having become of negligible value.

If the value of the asset subsequently increases in value, the subsequent gain (as compared with the negligible value on the notional reacquisition) is not chargeable until the asset is actually disposed of.

Negligible value relief triggers a capital loss. However, please note the interaction with the provisions under section 574 loss relief (see **Section 19.7**) where it is possible (if the conditions are met) for negligible value losses on qualifying shares to be converted into income tax losses.

19.9 Compensation/Insurance Monies

Where compensation or insurance monies are received as a consequence of an asset being damaged, the amount is assessed using the part disposal rules set out above and in **Chapter 13.** For these purposes, the value of the part disposed of is represented by the monies received, while the value of the part remaining is the value of the asset on the date the money is received.

The part disposal calculation is:

$$\frac{A}{A + B} \times \text{original cost}$$

where A = compensation received and B = value of the asset.

However, the part disposal calculation may be set aside where:

1. all the money received is applied in restoring the asset;
2. only a "small" amount of the monies received is not applied in restoring the asset; or
3. the sum received is "small".

"Small", in this context, is taken to mean a sum which does not exceed the larger of either £3,000 or 5% of the amount with which it is being compared (i.e. under 2. above, 5% of the compensation, and under 3. above, 5% of the asset value before damage).

If it is not treated as a part disposal, then a form of rollover relief applies and the amount of money received is instead deducted from the allowable expenditure, thereby increasing the gain on a subsequent disposal. Note that, in this instance, the receipts are deducted from the allowable expenditure and not the gain.

Where only part of the money received is used in restoration and the monies not so used are **not** small, the part disposal CGT calculation must be carried out. The taxpayer can however elect that the part disposal calculation is made only on the amount retained, i.e. not used in restoring the asset and not on the whole compensation/insurance monies, using the formula above but where A = compensation retained and B = restored value of the asset.

Where the asset is restored, the amount spent is treated as enhancement expenditure on eventual disposal of the asset in the normal way.

Example 19.15
David bought jewellery for £110,000 in January 2005 and it was damaged in a fire in June 2014. The insurance company paid David £35,000 in October 2014. Calculate the chargeable gain if David does not spend any of the insurance money on restoration and the jewellery was valued at £160,000 in October 2014.

Solution

This is a part disposal, where A = £35,000 and B = £160,000

Disposal proceeds:

	£
	35,000
Cost (35,000/(35,000 + 160,000)) × £110,000	(19,744)
Chargeable gain	15,256

> The balance of the allowable expenditure to be carried forward is £90,256 (£110,000 − £19,744).
>
> Note that, if the entire proceeds were used to restore the asset, the part disposal calculation is avoided and the balance of the allowable expenditure to be carried forward is £110,000. See below.
>
> | | £ |
> |---|---|
> | Incurred on January 2005 | 110,000 |
> | Incurred in restoration | 35,000 |
> | | 145,000 |
> | Less: Received in October 2014 (and not taxed as a part disposal) | (35,000) |
> | Allowable expenditure carried forward | 110,000 |

19.9.1 Lost or Destroyed Assets

If instead of being damaged an asset is lost or destroyed, this will be a chargeable disposal for CGT purposes. It is the receipt of the proceeds which triggers the disposal and not the disappearance or destruction of the asset for CGT purposes. This will normally result in a CGT calculation where the disposal proceeds will be the compensation/insurance monies received plus any scrap value of the asset.

However, there is a type of "rollover" relief available. This applies where a replacement asset is purchased within 12 months of the receipt of the funds. In this instance, the taxpayer can claim for the gain to be rolled over against the cost of the replacement asset. Any cash retained is immediately taxable under normal rules.

A claim for this relief must be made within four years of the end of the tax year in which the disposal is triggered.

Questions

Review Questions
(See Suggested Solutions to Review Questions at the end of this textbook.)

Question 19.1

In August 2014 Shane received an insurance payment of £43,000 in respect of jewellery he bought for his wife for their wedding in December 2002 at a cost of £5,000. The jewellery had been stolen in March 2014 but was never recovered. In December 2014 Shane spent £25,000 replacing the jewellery even though he knew it would never be the same.

Requirement
Calculate Shane's chargeable gain in 2014/15, assuming that all possible reliefs are claimed. Shane has employment income of £25,000 after his personal allowance is deducted. Calculate his capital gains tax liability as a result of the above transaction, assuming he fully used his CGT annual exemption on other disposals.

Question 19.2

Sarah owns 10% of the shares in Rathdiner Limited, which she purchased in December 1996 for £50,000. Sarah has worked in this company since its commencement. She gave the shares to her 22-year-old daughter Emily as a gift on 1 February 2015, when they had a market value of £105,000.
The market value of Rathdiner Limited as at 1 February 2015 is £1,050,000, as below:

	Market values
	£
Goodwill	410,000
Land and buildings	470,000
Plant and machinery *	2,500
Motor vehicle	4,000
Debtors	40,000
Stock	3,000
Cash	500
Rental property	120,000
Total	1,050,000

* The cost of each individual item of plant and machinery is less than £6,000 and no individual item has a market value in excess of this amount.

Requirement

(a) Calculate the capital gain arising to Sarah if she jointly claims gift/holdover relief under section 165 TCGA 1992 with her daughter.
(b) What is the base cost for Emily once a claim is made under (a)?
(c) Calculate the capital gain arising to Sarah if she and her daughter do not claim gift/holdover relief.
(d) Under (c), what would be the base cost for Emily?

Question 19.3

It is mid-November 2014 and you are working on the file of your client, Aine Taylor, who runs a manufacturing business as a sole trader. The factory used in the business was acquired in November 1998 for £500,000, but due to recent growth in orders is now too small to cope with demand, even though the business has been working night shifts as well as day shifts.

Aine has therefore been considering her options and has decided to sell the factory and move to new premises. An offer of £1,500,000 was accepted from a local property developer for the existing factory on 8 November 2014.

She has recently been to see you to discuss her options. She is open to whether the business will lease new factory premises or purchase new factory premises. Furthermore, she has recently been approached by a friend to invest in her company, Shoe Manufacturer Ltd, which needs some additional cash to fund expansion into a new market. Aine is very keen to ensure that she takes advantage of any available reliefs to reduce/defer any tax liability arising on sale of the factory.

Aine has not made any other capital disposals in the 2014/15 tax year and is an additional rate taxpayer. For the purposes of the question, assume that entrepreneur's relief is **not** available.

Requirement

Write a letter to Aine that covers the following topics:

(a) Calculate the tax payable on sale of the factory, state the date that the tax is due and the type of tax that is payable.

(b) Explain rollover relief and how it could be used to defer any tax payable on the sale of the factory.

(c) Explain how an investment in Shoe Manufacturer Ltd could be used to defer any tax payable on the sale of the factory. Assume that Shoe Manufacturer Ltd is a "qualifying company" for the purposes of relevant relief and that it is not a new company.

Acquisition by a Company of its Own Shares

Learning Objectives

After studying this chapter you will have developed competency in the following:
- Apply CGT rules appropriately to a company purchase of its own shares including:
  - knowledge of the income tax treatment; and
  - the conditions for CGT treatment to apply.

20.1 Overview

A company is legally entitled to buy back its own shares. A company might do this if a shareholder wishes to dispose of shares and the other shareholder(s) do not want to buy the shares. The purchase of shares by a company is governed by the Companies Acts/Orders.

For tax purposes, a company purchase of own shares will be treated as either an income distribution or a capital disposal.

20.1.1 Income Distribution

In the absence of any relieving provisions, where a company buys its own shares for more than the original subscribed share capital, any excess is treated as an income distribution for tax purposes

If it is deemed to be an income distribution, the recipients will be treated in the same way as the recipients of ordinary dividends. The dividend (distributions) will be grossed up to account for the notional 10% tax credit and treated as income when calculating the shareholder's income tax liability. Basic rate taxpayers will have no further tax to pay, as the notional tax credit will cover the liability. Higher rate taxpayers with marginal tax rates of 40% or 45% will have additional tax to pay (effectively 25% of the net dividend received for those with a marginal rate of 40%, or 30.56% of the net dividend received for those with a marginal rate of 45%).

Example 20.1

Philip and his brother set up ABC Limited in April 2008 for £1 per share nominal value. The issued share capital was 1,000 shares. The shareholding was split 50:50.

In September 2014, Philip decided to sell his shares back to the company for £1.75 per share. A market valuation of the company was undertaken. What is the tax treatment of Philip's disposal?

CGT treatment:

	£
Proceeds	875.00
Less: cost	(500.00)
Capital gain	375.00
Less: amount subject to income tax as a distribution	(375.00)
Capital gain	0.00
Income tax computation: gross dividends	
£375.00 × 100/90	416.67

Dividends are not tax deductible for the company.

20.1.2　Capital Disposal

Where certain **conditions** are met, the excess distribution noted above will be treated as a capital disposal subject to CGT, instead of an income distribution subject to income tax.

The rules which govern a capital distribution are included within section 1033 CTA 2010 and apply on two occasions:

1. Payments made by an **unquoted trading company or an unquoted holding company of a trading group** on the purchase or redemption of its own shares, provided certain conditions are met. For these purposes, shares dealt in on the Unlisted Securities Market or the Alternative Investment Market (AIM) are treated as unquoted.
2. Where the payments from the company are used by the shareholder wholly or mainly to discharge an IHT liability arising as a result of a death. The company must, in this instance, also be an unquoted trading company or an unquoted holding company of a trading group (see below).

20.2　Unquoted Companies

Where an unquoted trading company or an unquoted holding company of a trading group buys back its own shares from a UK shareholder in order to benefit its trade, the payment made to the shareholder is, subject to certain conditions being met, not to be treated as an income distribution but instead will be a capital disposal falling under the CGT provisions. Therefore, the purchase of shares by the company will be treated as a disposal of shares by the shareholder and normal CGT rules will apply.

Conditions for CGT Treatment

The following conditions must **all** be met in order for CGT treatment to apply to the buy-back of shares by a company:

1. The trade must not consist of dealing in shares, securities, land or futures.
2. The main objective of the repurchase must **not** be one of avoidance of tax. It must be for bona fide commercial reasons.

3. The repurchase must be wholly or mainly for the benefit of the trade. The "benefit to the trade test" will be satisfied where any of the following apply:

   (a) a dissident or disruptive shareholder is bought out;
   (b) the proprietor wishes to retire to make way for new management;
   (c) an outside investor who provided equity wishes to withdraw his investment; or
   (d) a shareholder dies and his personal representatives do not wish to retain his shares.

   Note: this list is not exhaustive.

4. There are also various conditions that must be satisfied by the vendor:

   (a) They must be resident in the UK when the shares are bought back. This ensures that the vendor is within the charge to UK CGT.
   (b) The vendor (or their spouse) must have owned the shares throughout a **five-year period** ending with the date of the buy-back. The period of ownership of a spouse living with a vendor at the date of buy-back is aggregated with that of the vendor. (Five years is reduced to three years if acquired on death and the ownership of the deceased can also be taken into account.)
   (c) Where the vendor's shareholding (and that of their *associates*) in a company is not fully purchased, redeemed or repaid, then the vendor and his associates must as a result of the purchase have their interest in the company's share capital substantially reduced, i.e. reduced to 75% or less of their interest before the disposal. This test is considered in two ways, first looking at the shareholding and secondly looking at their share in the profits of the company. Associates include spouses, minor children, controlled companies, trustees and beneficiaries and, if the company is a member of a group, then the whole group is treated as one for these purposes.
   (d) After the transaction, the vendor **must not** be connected with the company or any company in the same 51% group.

      For these purposes, a person is "connected" with a company if they directly or indirectly possess or are entitled to acquire more than 30% of the ordinary share capital, the issued share capital and loan capital, or the voting rights of the company or of the assets for distribution on a winding up.

Any shares repurchased by the company are usually cancelled and not re-issued.

Example 20.2

Karen owns 1,500 shares in Winddrops Ltd, a UK unquoted trading company which has issued share capital of 5,000 shares. If all other conditions are met, can the buy-back be treated as a capital disposal if the company buys back 400 shares from Karen?

Solution

	Winddrops Ltd Total Shareholding	**Karen's Shareholding**
Pre-repurchase	5,000	1,500
Repurchased and cancelled	(400)	(400)
Post-repurchase	4,600	1,100

continued overleaf

Karen originally held 1,500 shares (out of the issued share capital of 5,000 shares) which amounted to a 30% interest in Winddrops Ltd. After the repurchase, this dropped to 1,100 shares (out of the reduced issued share capital of 4,600 shares) which is a 23.9% shareholding. Karen's shareholding has dropped by 6.1%, which amounts to a decrease of 20.3% (6.1%/30%). This is not enough to meet the test at 4(c) above as the repurchase must reduce her shareholding by at least 25%. The transaction would therefore be treated as an income distribution.

Assuming all other conditions were met, if the company had repurchased 484 shares the repurchase would be a capital distribution and CGT rules would apply. Karen's interest has to reduce by at least 25%; therefore, her 1,500 shares must be reduced to 1,016 shares or less.

	Winddrops Ltd Total Shareholding	Karen's Shareholding
Pre-repurchase	5,000	1,500
Repurchased and cancelled	(484)	(484)
Post-repurchase	4,516	1,016

Karen's interest of 1,016 shares amounts to a shareholding of 22.5% in the company which means that Karen's interest has dropped by 25% (30% × 75% = 22.5%).

Example 20.3

Doyle Books Ltd has an issued share capital of 100,000 £1 ordinary shares, of which Emmett holds 20,000 shares (i.e. a 20% shareholding). If Emmett sells 5,000 shares to Doyle Books Ltd, the company's issued share capital is reduced for tax purposes to 95,000 shares, of which Emmett holds 15,000, a fraction of 15/95ths or 15.79% shareholding.

	Doyle Books Ltd Issued Share Capital	Emmett's Shareholding	%
Pre-repurchase	100,000	20,000	20%
Repurchased and cancelled	(5,000)	(5,000)	
Post-repurchase	95,000	15,000	15.79%

Thus, although Emmett has sold 25% of his original holding, Emmett's percentage holding has been reduced by only 21% ((20% − 15.79%)/20%), and the buy-back will not qualify for CGT treatment and it will be treated as an income distribution.

To achieve a reduction of 25%, Emmett would need to sell 5,890 shares.

	Doyle Books Ltd Issued Share Capital	Emmett's Shareholding	%
Pre-repurchase	100,000	20,000	20%
Repurchased and cancelled	(5,890)	(5,890)	
Post-repurchase	94,110	14,110	15%

Note: remember that the vendor must not be connected with the company or group company after the sale, i.e. the vendor and the vendor's associates must not, after the sale of the shares, be entitled to more than 30% of the capital, voting rights or assets on a winding-up of the company. Where the vendor maintains a shareholding in the company which is not small (i.e. more than 5%), it can be difficult to demonstrate that the "trade benefit" condition has been met.

20.3   Payments for Inheritance Tax

As noted above, where the whole of the payment (apart from any amount used to pay CGT arising) is applied by the recipient in discharging a liability for Inheritance Tax (IHT) charged on a death, and where it is so applied within a period of two years after the death, and the IHT so paid could not otherwise have been paid without undue hardship, then the payment may be treated as a capital disposal and CGT will apply. In this instance, there is no requirement to meet certain of the conditions as set out above, i.e. the benefit of trade test and the vendor conditions test; however, the company must be an unquoted trading company or an unquoted holding company of a trading group.

20.4   Other Aspects

20.4.1   Clearance Procedure

An advance clearance procedure is available under section 1044 CTA 2010, whereby the company will set out the precise reasons for the buy-back and provide HMRC with all relevant information to enable them to determine if all of the conditions for the CGT treatment are met.

It is recommended that this clearance procedure is used.

20.4.2   HMRC Notification

After the company makes the payment to the shareholder, it must file a return to HMRC within 60 days giving details of the payment and the circumstances surrounding it and, in particular, justifying the application of the CGT treatment to the transaction. The return must be made even if HMRC have confirmed that the capital treatment will apply to the payment under the advance clearance procedure.

Claiming CGT Treatment for Purchase of Own Shares
Once the conditions are met, the relief is an **automatic relief**.

20.4.3   Other Issues

There is no tax deduction for the company irrespective of whether the repurchase is treated as an income distribution or as a capital disposal.

Where a company acquires any of its shares (by purchase, bonus issue or otherwise), it is not treated for tax purposes as acquiring an asset. The company is not treated as a result of acquiring or holding the shares as being a member of itself.

Treasury shares are shares repurchased by the company but not cancelled. For tax purposes, the shares are treated as if they were cancelled and any subsequent cancellation is disregarded (and is, therefore, not a disposal of an asset and does not give rise to an allowable loss). If treasury shares are sold, the company is treated as having made a new issue of shares.

Up until 22 June 2010 the CGT treatment was generally more beneficial than the income tax treatment due to the comparatively low CGT rate of 18% (as compared to effective income tax rates of up to 36.11%).

However, with the introduction of the higher CGT rate of 28% with effect from 23 June 2010 more careful consideration will have to be given to determining the most tax-efficient treatment.

It is likely to be the case that the CGT treatment will only be preferred where ER can be claimed, or where the taxpayer has a marginal income tax rate of 45%.

Example 20.4

Harry and Peter, two UK resident individuals, set up Super Friends Ltd in 1992 to sell electronic equipment. Harry owns 80% of the shares, while Peter owns 20%. The company has been very profitable and now has revenue reserves of £2 million. Harry believes that the success of the company is due totally to his efforts. He believes that Peter does not really contribute to the success of the company and is more interested in his golf handicap. There have been a number of acrimonious board meetings and, as a result, Harry has decided to buy Peter out. Peter is happy to dispose of his shares provided that he receives £1 million and pays the least amount of tax on the disposal.

If Harry were to buy the shares, he would need £1 million of funds. As Harry does not have that amount of cash, he would have to either borrow the money (which would have to be repaid) or get money from the company (on which he would be liable to income tax, e.g. salary or dividend, etc.).

If Super Friends Ltd bought back the shares from Peter, then Harry would own all the shares, without having to find the cash to actually buy the shares. Peter will be liable to income tax on the cash received from Super Friends Ltd in excess of the amount he contributed for the shares. However, if he satisfies the conditions, he will be liable to CGT on the gain, and not income tax.

Checklist of conditions:

1	Trading company?	Yes
2	Will the acquisition benefit the trade?	Yes, there is disagreement between shareholders
3	Is the main purpose of the buy-back the avoidance of tax?	No, genuine exit of a shareholder from the business
4	Is Peter resident in the UK in 2014/15?	Yes
5	Has Peter owned the shares for five years?	Yes
6	Is Peter selling all his shares, or at least substantially reducing his shareholding?	Yes, he is selling all his shares
7	Confirm Peter is not connected with Super Friends Ltd after the disposal?	Yes, confirmed

As all the conditions have been satisfied, Peter will be liable to CGT on the disposal of the shares to Super Friends Ltd.

As Peter is disposing of shares in his personal trading company, he should be able to avail of ER and thus pay CGT at a maximum of £100,000 (assuming his annual exemption is otherwise utilised), i.e. at a rate of 10%. This compares with the figure of £305,600 (30.56%) that he would have had to pay if he had received the £1 million as an income distribution (assuming his marginal income tax rate is 45%).

Question

Review Question

(See Suggested Solutions to Review Questions at the end of this textbook.)

Question 20.1

Andrew Jameson is 63 years old and is a 75% shareholder in Andrewstones Limited, an unquoted trading company. He has lived and worked in the UK all his life. His 30-year-old son, John, holds the remaining 25% shareholding. Andrew is considering retiring from the business to make way for new blood and thus give his son control of the company. His son does not have the cash to buy his shareholding and does not wish to enter into a claim for gift relief. Therefore the most suitable option is for the company to buy back Andrew's shares as he does not want the shares to go outside the family. It is confirmed that the company has adequate distributable reserves and cash to do so.

Andrew's original investment in the company shares was £75,000 in £1 ordinary shares when the company was incorporated in 1991. There was no share premium account. Andrew has been an employee and director of the company throughout this period. The firm has recently valued Andrew's shares at £35 each.

Requirement

Write a letter to Andrew in December 2014 setting out the following:

(a) The conditions that must be met in order for the proceeds received from a company acquiring its own shares to be treated as a share disposal for capital gains tax purposes.
(b) Assess whether the conditions are met and, if so, calculate Andrew's capital gains tax liability claiming any available reliefs.
(c) The consequences for Andrew if the conditions for capital treatment are not met. Include a calculation of the tax due.
(d) Outline the stamp duty reserve tax consequences of the share buy-back, when any liability falls due for payment and who is responsible for payment of the liability.

Note: Andrew is UK resident for tax and has other income each year in the region of £200,000.

Question 20.2

It is early March 2015. Peter Maddley, a relatively new client of your practice, called you a few weeks back in early February with some bad news. One of his fellow directors in Maddon Engineering Limited ("Maddon"), Aaron Donaldson, was tragically killed in a car crash.

Peter and his two friends, Aaron and Jeremy, set up Maddon, a successful engineering company, when they left university in the late 1990s. At that time each of them subscribed for 10,000 £1 ordinary shares each, at a cost of £10,000.

Peter, Aaron and Jeremy were full-time directors of the company until Aaron's untimely death. As a result of his death, Aaron's shares will pass to his wife Sarah later this month. However, Sarah does not wish to keep the shares. Therefore, under the terms of the shareholder's agreement that was entered into when the company started, Maddon is going to buy back all the shares inherited by Sarah for £150 a share on 4 April 2015. This is also the value attributed to the shares on the date of Aaron's death in February.

Sarah is also a client of your practice. She has advised you that the transaction will only proceed if the "capital treatment" can be obtained. No one remembers what this actually means as the agreement was made so long ago. Sarah has also done some research and she would like to know what difference it would make if the 'income' treatment was adopted instead.

Sarah has also been in contact with you separately about her late husband's estate. She believes business property relief will be available on the Maddon shares.

She also mentioned to you that in December 2011 Aaron set up a discretionary trust using £500,000 in cash from the sale of a property in California, USA. All UK and US capital gains tax liabilities on the sale of the property have been paid. However, no inheritance tax was paid at the time as the solicitor involved stated that it was not an issue and Aaron had no other transactions in his lifetime.

Sarah has asked you whether this is now required to be included in Aaron's death estate because "it was set up using cash that the tax has been paid on". She also suggested that, if it is required to be included, she would like to think you would be willing to turn a blind eye and forget she ever told you about this as she thinks HMRC have no way of finding out about it.

Note: all parties are UK tax resident and additional rate taxpayers. Maddon should be treated as a trading company with no excepted assets on its statement of financial position.

Requirements

(a) Draft a letter to Peter, Jeremy and Sarah to include:
   (i) An explanation, together with calculations, of how Sarah will be taxed on the repurchase of the inherited shares. Include a comparison between the income and capital treatments and detail the conditions that must be met for capital treatment to be available for the share buy-back. Assess if the capital treatment will be available for this transaction and calculate the tax payable as a result of your assessment.
   (ii) A calculation of the stamp duty payable (if any) on the share buy-back and outline who is responsible for payment of the liability (if any).
(b) Write a briefing note for the partner to discuss with Sarah on the following matters:
   (i) Comment on the availability of business property relief (BPR) for the shares in Maddon held by Aaron at the date of his death. Calculate the value of the shares to be included in Aaron's death estate after any relief that may be available. If BPR is not available, what would the maximum inheritance tax liability be (if any)?
   (ii) Discuss the lifetime inheritance tax (IHT) implications of setting up the trust and support your analysis with calculations. Advise on the due date for payment of any lifetime IHT. Consider whether the transaction is required to be included in Aaron's death estate and calculate the amount of IHT payable (if any) on death.
   (iii) Outline what action you would take in relation to Sarah's suggestion that, if the lifetime gift is to be included in Aaron's estate, you should leave it out entirely.

Note: students should only attempt part (b) once they have completed the inheritance tax part of the CA Proficiency 2 course.

Part Three

Inheritance Tax

Introduction to Inheritance Tax

The Chartered Accountants Ireland *Code of Ethics* applies to all aspects of a Chartered Accountant's professional life, including dealing with inheritance tax issues. As outlined at the beginning of this book, further information regarding the principles in the *Code of Ethics* is set out in **Appendix 2**.

21.1 Introduction

Capital transfer tax became Inheritance Tax (IHT) as a result of Finance Act 1986, and the bulk of the legislation is contained in **Inheritance Tax Act (IHTA) 1984**. The legislation has been relatively unchanged since then, with the majority of changes coming in the form of anti-avoidance measures being introduced to tackle abuse and IHT avoidance.

IHT accounts for a very small proportion of the government's total annual tax revenue, mainly because there are a number of very valuable reliefs from IHT available and it is relatively easy to plan one's affairs to minimise any IHT exposure.

It is therefore important when advising clients to note that any IHT advice is given on the basis of the legislation currently in force and as applied in practice.

All legislative references in this section of the manual are to IHTA 1984 unless otherwise stated.

21.2 Meaning of Gift and Inheritance

21.2.1 Meaning of "Gift", "Inheritance", "Transfer of Value" and "Related Property"

Section 1 IHTA 1984 states that IHT is charged "on the value transferred by a chargeable transfer". The value transferred by an individual is measured using the loss to the donor principle. The amount that is subject to IHT is basically the value of the donor's estate before the gift, less the value of the donor's estate after the gift, i.e. transfer of value.

One important point to note, particularly in relation to gifts of shares, is that the value received by the donee may not necessarily equate to the value transferred from the donor.

When measuring the loss to the donor, it is necessary to include the value of any related property.

Related property includes that owned by an individual's spouse/civil partner plus any assets owned by a charity/trust that was transferred by the donor/spouse and which is either still held by the charity/trust or was held at any time in the last five years.

Example 21.1: Calculation of transfer of value including related property
Tinky owns 6,000 shares in Spartan Ltd. Tinky's husband and her brother each own 2,000 shares in Spartan Ltd. The company has 10,000 shares in issue.

Tinky wants to give 2,000 shares to her son Po, and would like to know what value would be relevant for IHT.

0–50%	£10 a share
51%–74%	£15 a share
75%–100%	£20 a share

Value transferred:

	£
Before (6,000/8,000*) £20 × 6,000	90,000
After (4,000/6,000*) £15 × 4,000	(40,000)
Value transferred	50,000

Note: Po has only received 2,000 × £10 = £20,000!

* The shares owned by the husband must be included to determine the relevant share price as these are related property. Tinky is then treated as owning a proportion of the enlarged shareholding.

A liability to IHT can arise in the following circumstances:

- making a chargeable lifetime gift,
- on a lifetime gift (both chargeable and potentially exempt transfers) following the death of the donor within seven years of the date of the gift, and
- on the value of the deceased's estate following death.

A gift, as defined in section 42, is:

"in relation to any transfer of value, means the benefit of any disposition or rule of law by which, on the making of the transfer, any property becomes (or would but for abatement become) the property of any person or applicable for any purpose".

What this legislation is effectively saying is that a gift is any instance where property has been transferred from one person to another and the value of the donor's estate has been reduced as a result.

The scope of IHT is further restricted by stating that a gift must include a "gratuitous intent" on the part of the donor for the transfer of value to potentially fall within the charge to IHT. This allows for some important exceptions from the scope of IHT as follows:

- **Genuine "arm's length" transactions between parties (section 10)** If market value has been received for the transfer of any property, then there will be no loss of value to the estate to the donor.

   A 'bad bargain' does not in itself mean that a transaction has been carried out on a non-arm's length basis. However, if the parties are connected then there would need to be clear commercial evidence to support the price agreed.

- **Maintenance of an individual's family (section 11)** In this case, the value of the donor's estate will be reduced but there is no associated "gratuitous intent". Examples would be the payment of school fees for a child, paying for medical or specialist care for a dependent relative or for the maintenance of an ex-spouse following divorce.

- **Waiver of remuneration (section 14)** If an employee gives up his right to remuneration or repays remuneration to an employer, this is not considered to be a transfer of value. The waiver must be by way of deed to be legally enforceable as there is no consideration paid for entering into the waiver.

- **Waiver of dividends (section 15)** If the right to the dividend is waived within 12 months before the right to the dividend accrues to the person. The waiver must be by way of deed legally enforceable as there is no consideration paid for entering into the waiver.

Inheritance is not defined in IHTA 1984 but its common law meaning is the passing on of property following the death of an individual. In modern legal use, inheritance generally refers to the succession of property from a person who has died intestate (i.e. the individual has not written a will). Where the deceased has written a will, the recipients of property are generally referred to as beneficiaries, legatees or devisees.

When an individual dies, whether it be intestate or having left a will, the person is treated as making a transfer of value equal to the value of their estate for IHT purposes on death but one must not forget that IHT can arise during lifetime.

21.3   Domicile Rules for IHT

IHT in the UK is subject to territorial limits. The UK does not seek to tax a transfer where neither the transferor nor the property transferred has a sufficient connection with the UK. Hence, it is important to consider both the domicile of the person and where the asset is located (situs).

Under UK law, every individual has a domicile, and an individual cannot have more than one domicile at a time.

Individuals who are domiciled in the UK are liable to IHT on their **worldwide estate**, wherever the assets are situated.

Individuals who are not domiciled in the UK are only liable to UK IHT to the extent that their assets are situated in the UK. To the extent that non-UK domiciled individuals hold non-UK property, this is **excluded property** for UK IHT purposes.

An individual's residence status is largely insignificant for the purposes of IHT (but see deemed UK domicile below).

An individual's domicile will depend on the specific circumstances but can generally be determined as follows:

Domicile of Origin

An individual will acquire their father's domicile at birth, unless they are illegitimate or the father is dead before their birth, in which case the child's domicile of origin will be that of the mother.

A domicile of origin is the most robust form of domicile and will be assumed to be the individual's domicile unless it can be otherwise proven. It may only be displaced by acquiring a domicile of choice or dependence.

Domicile of Dependence

This only relates to children under the age of 16 and persons of unsound mind. It also applies where a woman was married before 1 January 1974. In these circumstances, her domicile is dependent on the domicile of her husband.

Domicile of Choice

An individual can acquire a domicile of choice by both physical presence in another country **and** sufficiently evidencing the intention of staying there permanently. Thus it will not be possible to acquire a domicile of choice if the reason for staying there is conditional or if it is merely for the purposes of working there for a long period.

A domicile of choice may be lost by leaving a country without any definite intention of returning, in which case the domicile of origin is revived.

It should be noted that there is a heavy burden of proof on a taxpayer to show that a domicile of choice has displaced the domicile of origin. Supporting evidence can include purchasing a burial plot in the new country, selling up all property in the old country and retaining no business interests in the old country.

Deemed UK Domicile (section 267 IHTA 1984)

Where a non-UK domiciled individual has been resident in the UK for 17 out of the last 20 years they will be deemed to have a UK domicile for **UK IHT purposes only**. An individual will also be considered to be UK domiciled for IHT purposes for three years after they cease to be UK domiciled.

Example 21.2: Relationship between domicile and UK IHT
Ronaldo is Portuguese domiciled and owns a £7.5 million mansion in Cheshire. He also owns a £3 million apartment in Madrid. As he is non-UK domiciled, he will only be subject to IHT in respect of the Cheshire mansion. The apartment in Madrid is not subject to UK IHT. However, should Ronaldo become UK domiciled or acquire a deemed UK domicile through being resident in the UK, the worldwide estate of Ronaldo will fall within the UK IHT net.

Questions

Review Questions

(See Suggested Solution to Review Questions at the end of this textbook.)

Question 21.1

Grey Properties Ltd, an investment company, has 100,000 issued £1 ordinary shares. The shares are valued as follows:

76%–100% = £35 per share
51%–75% = £25 per share
26%–50% = £14 per share
25% or less = £8 per share

Mr Grey owns 50,000 shares and his wife owns 28,000. He makes a gift of 30,000 shares to his daughter Anne.

Requirement

(a) Calculate the transfer of value made by Mr Grey for inheritance tax purposes.
(b) What is the base cost of the shares for Anne for CGT purposes, assuming no reliefs are claimed?

Question 21.2

On the occasion of their wedding in 2001, Walter gave his daughter Stephanie and his new son-in-law Martin a unique set of six antique chairs as a wedding gift. Stephanie received four and Martin received two. Stephanie's son James is an avid antique fan, so in December 2014 she gave one of her chairs to him when he turned 21.

The value of the chairs at the date of the gift was as follows:

	£
1 chair	50,000
2 chairs	110,000
3 chairs	250,000
4 chairs	375,000
5 chairs	500,000
6 chairs	800,000

Requirement
Calculate Stephanie's transfer of value for IHT purposes.

Question 21.3

Requirement
Which of the following transactions are treated as a transfer of value for IHT purposes? Give explanations for your answers.

(a) Gift of shares in a family company to a daughter.
(b) Sale of a painting to a local art dealer.
(c) Waiver of dividend in a family company.
(d) Payment of a daughter's school fees.
(e) Purchase of a Lamborghini from a local car dealership.
(f) Gift of an investment property to a family trust.

Question 21.4

Three wealthy clients of your practice, Zelda, Willem and Cerys, have valuable assets located both in the UK and overseas. They are currently considering transferring these into a UK resident discretionary trust in March 2015. Details are as follows:

(a)   Zelda has been living and working in the UK since July 2000. Before that she lived in Hong Kong. Her parents are both non-UK domiciled. Zelda has not and does not intend to make the UK her domicile of choice.

(b)   Willem, who was German domiciled, settled in the UK many years ago and has taken all necessary steps to make the UK his domicile of choice.

(c)   Cerys was born in and brought up in the UK by her UK domiciled parents. In November 2013 she emigrated to Canada and, having broken all ties with the UK, has become non-UK domiciled.

Requirement

Briefly explain whether each of the above clients will be subject to inheritance tax on the transfers of their UK and overseas assets in March 2015.

Question 21.5

Pauline died aged 52 from cancer on 29 July 2014, leaving her whole estate (comprising her London home and a property in Italy) to her only daughter, Penny. Her mother and father never married. For several years while her mother had been ill, Penny lived and cared for her mother at the family home in London, which Pauline owned when she died.

Penny now plans to fulfil a lifetime ambition to emigrate to Australia and cut off all ties with the UK, as she has no living relatives left and all of her close friends have emigrated to Sydney over the last 10 years. She has no intention of ever returning to the UK and plans to leave before the end of 2015.

Her mother's death has got Penny thinking about her own mortality and she has recently spoken to a solicitor, who mentioned the concept of "domicile" and "deemed domicile" for inheritance tax.

Requirement

Explain the concept of "domicile" and "deemed domicile" in the context of Penny's circumstances and how these concepts affect her inheritance tax position both before and after her planned emigration.

Exemptions

There are a number of exemptions from the scope of IHT. The main conditions to be met in relation to each of these are considered in turn below.

22.1 Inter-spouse Transfers (to Include Non-UK Domiciled Spouses) (section 18)

The transfer to a UK domiciled spouse/civil partner either during lifetime or on death is completely exempt from IHT.

Where the donor is UK domiciled but the spouse/civil partner is non-UK domiciled, previously the first £55,000 of the transfer was exempt from IHT. The reason for this was to prevent a UK domiciled person transferring their assets to a non-UK domiciled spouse, effectively taking the assets outside of the UK IHT net.

With effect from 6 April 2013, the exemption was increased from £55,000 to £325,000 and any future increases are to be aligned to the prevailing nil rate band.

In addition, under a new election regime, from 6 April 2013 non-UK domiciled individuals who are married or in a civil partnership with a UK domiciled person will be able to elect to be treated as UK-domiciled solely for IHT purposes. This enables assets to be transferred between spouses or civil partners free of IHT, but would mean that the worldwide estate (i.e. irrespective of the location of the assets) of the spouse making the election would then come within the scope of IHT.

The election, in writing to HMRC, may be made at any time and it can be backdated for up to seven years (although not earlier than 6 April 2013). Elections that follow a death (again post 6 April 2013) can be made by the executors within two years of the death of a non-domiciled individual.

Elections will be irrevocable while the individual remains resident in the UK and will cease to have effect if the electing person is resident outside the UK for more than four full consecutive tax years.

22.2 Small Gifts (section 20)

Lifetime gifts of up to £250 per donee may be made in any one tax year and be completely exempt from IHT. If a gift exceeds £250, then the whole amount is treated as a transfer of value, and not merely the excess over £250.

22.3 Normal Expenditure out of Income (section 21)

A lifetime gift will not be treated as a transfer of value if the donor can evidence that it represents "normal expenditure out of income". This means that the expenditure must be of a habitual nature, year on year. The gift will be treated as being made out of income if the individual can show that they are left with sufficient income to maintain their normal standard of living. Examples would include the regular payment of life assurance premiums, school tuition fees or regular birthday/ Christmas presents.

22.4 Gifts in Consideration of Marriage/Civil Partnership (section 22)

Lifetime gifts on the occasion of a marriage/civil partnership are also exempt up to certain limits. The gift must be made, or promised, on or shortly before the date of the wedding or civil partnership ceremony. The limit depends on the relationship between the donor and donee. The limits are as follows:

£5,000 – From a parent
£2,500 – From a grandparent or remoter ancestor (or between the persons getting married)
£1,000 – From any other person

These exemptions apply per marriage/civil partnership and not per donee. Any excess over the exempt limit will be treated as a transfer of value.

22.5 Charities or Registered Clubs (section 23)

Gifts to charities or registered clubs (from 1 April 2010), whether during lifetime or on death, are wholly exempt if certain conditions are met. The charity must be a "qualifying" charity established in the EU or another specified country.

Where the loss in value to the donor exceeds the value received by the charity, HMRC takes the view that the charity exemption still applies to the whole of the value transferred by the donor.

22.6 Gifts to Political Parties (section 24)

Gifts to political parties, whether during lifetime or on death, are wholly exempt if the conditions are met. To qualify for exemption, the party must have obtained at the last general election either two members elected to the House of Commons or one member and not less than 150,000 votes were given to candidates who were members of that party.

22.7 Maintenance Funds and Gifts to Housing Associations (sections 24A, 27)

Gifts to maintenance funds, whether during lifetime or on death, are wholly exempt if the funds are to be used for the maintenance, repair or preservation of historic buildings.

Gifts of UK land to housing associations are similarly exempt, whether during lifetime or on death. The gift must be made to a registered housing association.

22.8 Gifts for National Purposes (section 25)

Gifts to some national institutions such as museums, universities and the National Trust are wholly exempt, whether made during lifetime or on death.

22.9 Annual Exemption (section 19)

The annual exemption (AE) reduces the value of lifetime transfers of value. The AE is £3,000 per tax year. The AE must be used against gifts in the chronological order in which they are made in the tax year.

Any unused AE for a tax year may be carried forward for **one year only**. It is necessary to use the current period AE first before taking relief for any unused brought forward AE from the prior year.

Where two or more transfers of value are made on the same day, the AE should be apportioned between the transfers in proportion to the value transferred.

Questions

Review Questions
(See Suggested Solution to Review Questions at the end of this textbook.)

Question 22.1

Sean, who is domiciled in the UK, transfers property worth £1.5 million in July 2014 to his spouse, Gita, who is not domiciled in the UK. Gita has never been UK resident or domiciled. In January 2016, Gita transfers some German shares valued at £200,000 to the trustees of a trust. Sean dies in June 2017.

Requirement
What are the IHT consequences of the gift in July 2014? Would you advise Gita to elect to be treated as UK domiciled for IHT at the time of her husband's death in 2017? Assume the nil rate band remains at £325,000 at all times.

Question 22.2

Annette, who is UK domiciled and has made no previous transfers, made the following gifts in 2014-15:

- 20 September 2014 – a plot of land, with a market value of £80,000, to her daughter Ana as a present for her forthcoming wedding.
- 20 December 2014 – cash gifts totalling £5,000 to her five grandchildren. Annette saved this cash from her surplus income over the year. She always gives her grandchildren cash as Christmas presents.
- 20 January 2015 – shares in an investment company, worth £380,000, to her husband Stefan, who is non-UK domiciled.

Requirement

Briefly explain the availability and amount of any immediate inheritance tax exemptions (ignoring potential exemption) in relation to each of the above gifts.

Calculation of IHT Liabilities for Dispositions in Lifetime and on Death

Learning Objectives

After studying this chapter you will have developed competency in the following:

- Compute IHT liabilities and demonstrate the scope of the charge, including, *inter alia*:
  - excluded property rules; and
  - valuation rules.

23.1 Potentially Exempt Transfers (PET)

A PET is a lifetime transfer that will become fully exempt from IHT if the donor survives seven years from the date of the gift. Therefore, a PET will only become a chargeable transfer (i.e. potentially subject to IHT) if the donor dies within seven years of making the gift. If the donor dies between three and seven years after the date of the gift, then taper relief may be applied to reduce any IHT charge.

All gifts between individuals are PETs for IHT purposes (as are gifts into interest in possession or accumulation and maintenance trusts that took place before 22 March 2006). However, if the donor gives an asset away at any time but keeps an interest in it, e.g. a property in which they continue to reside rent-free, then the gift will not be a PET (see **Chapter 25**).

23.2 Chargeable Lifetime Transfers (CLT)

Any transfer of value that is neither exempt nor a PET is a chargeable lifetime transfer (CLT). This includes gifts to discretionary trusts (and to all trusts after 22 March 2006) and gifts to companies.

The only occasion which can give rise to an IHT charge during the lifetime of a donor are CLTs. IHT is effectively a cumulative tax and has a nil rate band (£325,000 in 2014/15) applicable for cumulative transfers up to this limit. Therefore, IHT only becomes payable once chargeable transfers over a seven-year period exceed this threshold. The relevant nil rate band to consider is that applicable to the tax year in which the CLT is made.

As part of the 2013 budget, the Government updated its previous announcements that the current IHT nil rate band of £325,000 is frozen at that level until 2017/18. This has since been confirmed in FA 2014. From 2015/16, the Consumer Price Index (CPI) will be used as the default indexation assumption.

Note that PETs do not affect the lifetime tax payable save to the extent that they use up annual exemptions that could otherwise be set against CLTs. This is because annual exemptions are used in the chronological order in which lifetime gifts are made.

The rate of IHT on any CLT in excess of the nil rate band is 20%, i.e. half the 40% rate applied to transfers on death.

If the donor agrees to pay any IHT due on a CLT, then this must be "grossed up" by 20/80 as the tax paid will also represent a loss in value to the donor's estate.

In order to gross up a lifetime gift, first deduct the annual exemption and any other exemptions from the value transferred. Any available nil rate band is then deducted to arrive at the net transfer. This is the amount that must be grossed up.

By law, the primary responsibility to pay IHT rests with the donor. Therefore, if the donor does not expressly delegate this responsibility, assume that the donor will pay the IHT. Where this is the case, the gross gift is the value transferred plus the IHT paid by the donor and this value is included in the seven-year cumulation period calculation.

Example 23.1: IHT treatment of lifetime gifts

Barry gave his daughter a house on the occasion of her marriage on 12 June 2014. The house was valued at £125,000. In the previous month he gave his son £2,000, and a Celtic artifact to the National Museum that was valued at £25,000. These are the first lifetime gifts Barry has ever made.

In August 2014, Barry settled £450,000 into a discretionary trust for the benefit of his grandchildren. Barry decided to pay any IHT that fell due personally.

Solution

The gift to his son is covered by the annual exemption for 2014/15 and the gift to the museum is exempt for IHT purposes.

The gift to his daughter is a PET and will be subject to IHT if Barry dies within seven years. The transfer of value is:

	£
Loss to donor's estate	125,000
Less marriage exemption	(5,000)
Less A/E 2014/15 (£2,000 used up)	(1,000)
Less A/E 2013/14	(3,000)
PET	116,000

The gift to the trust is a CLT and an IHT charge will arise, applied at the lifetime rate. There are no annual exemptions available but the full nil rate band is available as there have been no CLTs in the previous seven years.

	£
Transfer to trust	450,000
Less nil rate band	(325,000)
Chargeable transfer	125,000

The net transfer must be grossed up for the loss to Barry's estate caused by him paying the IHT himself.

	£
(£125,000 × 20/80) + £125,000	156,250
IHT due @ 20%	31,250
Gross transfer (£450,000 plus £31,250)	481,250

The gross gift is important for the purposes of the seven-year accumulation.

23.3   Implications for IHT on Death

When an individual dies, there are three types of transfer which are chargeable to IHT:

1. PETs made within the seven years prior to death.
2. CLTs made by the deceased in the seven years prior to death.
3. The transfer of the estate itself on death.

23.4   PETs Becoming Chargeable and Additional IHT on Lifetime CLTs

23.4.1   PETs Becoming Chargeable on Death

When calculating any IHT due on a PET made within the seven years prior to death, it is first necessary to consider all CLTs made in the **seven years before the date of the PET**. The cumulative total of all such CLTs are deducted from the relevant nil rate band (that is, using the nil rate band applicable to the tax year of death) to arrive at the residual amount which will be available to set against the PET that has now become a chargeable transfer.

There is a further measure of relief (known as taper relief) given on any IHT that crystallises on a death occurring within seven years of the date of the PET. The longer the period between the date of gift and the date of death, the greater the rate of relief:

Time between the date the gift was made and the date of death	Taper relief percentage applied to the IHT due
Less than 3 years	Nil
3–4 years	20%
4–5 years	40%
5–6 years	60%
6–7 years	80%

23.4.2   Additional IHT on CLTs at Death

Where a CLT is made within the seven years prior to the date of death, all or part of which has been charged at the 20% rate, additional tax may be payable. This is because the IHT charge on the CLT is recalculated at the full scale rate applicable at the date of death, i.e. 40%, taking into account other CLTs and PETs within **seven years before the date of the CLT** and using the nil rate band applicable at the date of death.

Taper relief is also available on any IHT that becomes payable on death in respect of a CLT made within the last seven years. The only difference is that credit is given for any lifetime IHT paid in respect of the CLT after taper relief has been deducted. Note that the credit for lifetime IHT paid may reduce the further IHT payable on death to £nil but **cannot** result in a refund becoming due.

Example 23.2: Taper relief for lifetime gift between three and seven years of death
Mark made the following lifetime gifts before his death on 25 April 2014:

		£
March 2002	Gift to discretionary trust	132,000
August 2007	Gift to his brother	280,000

Calculate the lifetime tax and any tax payable by Mark's brother as a consequence of his death.

(i) March 2002 – CLT

	£
Gift to discretionary trust	132,000
Less: A/E 01/02	(3,000)
Less: A/E 00/01	(3,000)
CLT	126,000

No lifetime IHT due as below £242,000 (the then nil rate band)

(ii) August 2007 – PET

	£
Gift to brother	280,000
Less: A/E 07/08	(3,000)
Less: A/E 06/07	(3,000)
PET	274,000

No lifetime tax due as a PET.

(iii) On death, any transfers occurring within the previous seven years become chargeable.

Only the PET to the brother was made within seven years prior to the date of death. However, when calculating the IHT now due on that PET, we need to take into account the effect of the CLT that was made within the seven years prior to the date of the PET.

	£	£
PET		274,000
Nil rate band at death	325,000	
Less: CLT within seven years	(126,000)	
Nil rate band available to set against PET		(199,000)
Taxable on death		75,000
IHT @ 40%		30,000
Less taper relief (six to seven years = 80%)		(24,000)
IHT due		6,000

23.5 IHT on Estate on Death

On death, the deceased is treated as having made a final transfer of the whole of their estate and the tax charged depends on the value of the estate (ignoring any "excluded property"), and the effect of any CLTs and PETs made within the seven years prior to the date of death. The nil rate band applying to the tax year in which the death occurs that is not used by PETs or CLTs in the seven years prior to death will be available to reduce the value of the estate chargeable to IHT.

Any gifts out of the death estate that are exempt transfers (e.g. gift to UK domiciled spouse) are also left out of account in determining the value of the estate chargeable on death to IHT.

Important points to note in valuing the death estate:

- Only assets to which the deceased was beneficially entitled are included in the estate. For example, if the deceased was a beneficiary of an interest in possession trust then the trust forms part of the estate and is included, whereas the proceeds of a life assurance policy where the deceased was not the beneficiary is left out of account. Note also in relation to life assurance policies, the value to be brought into account in the estate of the beneficiary if they pre-decease the life assured individual is the open market value of the policy and not the policy surrender value.

- Assets should be valued at open market value, i.e. the value between a willing buyer and a willing seller (subject to special valuation rules for certain assets, which are discussed at **Section 23.8**).

- Excluded assets are left out of account, e.g. overseas assets of a non-UK domiciled individual.

- Debts and liabilities are deductible from the estate if they are owed by the deceased at the date of death. Where a debt is secured on a particular asset, it is deducted from the value of that asset, whereas other debts are deducted from the estate generally. Deductible debts include debts for goods or services, income tax or CGT; gambling debts are left out of account.

- Reasonable funeral costs including the cost of a tombstone and mourning expenses are allowable.

- Executor costs of administering the estate are generally not deductible.

- The exception to the previous rule is that the costs of administering or realising overseas assets are allowable but are limited to 5% of the asset value.

Any IHT payable on the death estate is borne by the executors and paid out of the estate. The person(s) who ultimately bear the IHT on the death estate depends on whether bequests made are 'tax-bearing' or 'tax-free'. The phrase "tax-free" does not mean that the assets are not charged to IHT, but refers to the fact that the recipient is to receive the asset and someone else will effectively bear the IHT.

Unless otherwise stated, specific gifts of UK assets out of the estate are tax-free gifts and any IHT due is to be borne out of the residue of the estate. The residue of the estate is what is left over after all specific bequests have been taken into account. Conversely, recipients of specific gifts of non-UK assets are to bear the IHT unless an expression is made to the contrary. It is normal practice to have a residuary beneficiary who is entitled to the residue of the estate.

The residue of the estate is calculated after all tax-free bequests have been made. The tax on the residue of the estate is also effectively borne by the residuary legatee where the beneficiary is chargeable. This will not be the case, however, where the residuary beneficiary is non-chargeable, e.g. the residuary beneficiary is a trust or the spouse/civil partner.

There are **two scenarios** that require consideration in relation to the **residue of an estate:**

1. **Residue partly chargeable and partly exempt**   In this case the residue of the estate is divided into two parts, the part that is chargeable and the part that is exempt. The chargeable part of the residue will bear its own IHT and the exempt residue will suffer no IHT.

2. **Tax-free specific legacies and the residue of the estate are wholly exempt**   In this case the tax-free gift must be grossed up at the death rate of IHT, i.e. by 40/60 (note that, for lifetime grossing, this fraction is 20/80). The IHT is then computed on this gross gift and the IHT is borne out of the residue of the estate.

Note that no IHT is payable on the exempt residue; the residue available for the exempt residuary beneficiary is only being reduced by the tax payable on the tax-free specific legacy.

The total IHT borne by an estate over the total chargeable assets of the estate is a percentage, referred to as the "estate rate".

23.6   Gifts to Charities

With effect from 6 April 2012, a reduced rate of IHT was introduced for an estate where a minimum level of legacy has been left by the deceased to a qualifying charity (i.e. an organisation that's recognised as a charity for tax purposes by HMRC). The actual legacy to charity remains exempt from IHT and, subject to meeting the qualifying conditions, the rate of IHT payable in respect of the remainder of the estate is reduced from 40% to 36%.

In order to qualify for the reduced rate, at least 10 per cent of the net value of the estate must be left to the charity. The net value of the estate is the sum of all the assets after deducting any debts, liabilities, reliefs, exemptions and the nil-rate band.

Example 23.3
Hugo died on 30 April 2014 leaving an estate valued at £600,000 after the deduction of liabilities. He leaves £35,000 to the National Trust in his will.

	£
Estate (net of liabilities)	600,000
Less: Nil rate band	(325,000)
Baseline amount	275,000
Baseline amount @10%	27,500
Legacy qualifies as it exceeds 10% of baseline amount	
Inheritance tax payable:	
Baseline amount from above	275,000
Less: Gift to National Trust	(35,000)
Total	240,000
Inheritance tax @ 36%	86,400

23.7   Excluded Property

The term "excluded property" is a technical term used to refer to certain types of property that are subject to certain conditions outside the scope of IHT. The most common examples of excluded property are:

1. Property situated outside the UK, where the person beneficially entitled to the property is domiciled outside the UK.
2. Settled property, where the settlor was domiciled outside the UK when the settlement was made.

In certain limited circumstances excluded property may need to be taken into account in valuing lifetime transfers of other property. However, it is generally dealt with in the same way as property that is exempt.

Example 23.4

Claude, a UK resident but French-domiciled individual, made a gift of a property in Bordeaux to his daughter Elaine in July 2009. He made no use of the property after the date of the gift. Claude became UK domiciled in January 2010 and died in March 2015. As Claude was not UK domiciled at the date of the transfer, the property is excluded from IHT and consequently there is no PET in July 2009 and the property is not included in valuing Claude's death estate in March 2015.

23.8 Valuation of Certain Assets

23.8.1 Quoted Shares and Unit Trusts

The process for valuing quoted shares is relatively straightforward. The stock exchange official closing price for the shares on the date of transfer is used. If a range of closing prices is provided, then use the lower of two values. The first is calculated using the 'quarter up' rule. What this means is that you take the lowest closing price and add it to a quarter of the difference between the lowest and highest closing price. The second value is the average of the highest and lowest normal marked bargains recorded on that day. The price used for the valuation of the quoted shares is the lower of these two values.

The process for valuing unit trusts is to take the lower of the two prices provided by the fund managers for the relevant date, i.e. the date of transfer.

Example 23.5: Valuation of quoted shares and unit trusts

Blake has the following assets in his death estate:

    100,000 shares in Aviva Plc

    6,000 units in the Meridian Unit Trust

On the day Blake died, the *Financial Times* reported Aviva Plc's bid price as 23p, an offer price of 35p with marked bargains at 24p, 29p, and a special marked bargain at 33p.

The fund managers of Meridian Unit Trust provided the following information for the date of death:

Bid price 117p

Offer price 121p

The assets will be valued as follows in the death estate:

Aviva Plc shares at the lower of the quarter up rule and the average of highest and lowest marked bargains (ignoring any special bargains):

    Quarter up = $(23 + (35 - 23) \times \frac{1}{4}) = 26$

    Average of normal bargains = $(24 + 29)/2 = 26.50$

So value of Aviva shares = 100,000 × 26p = £26,000

Units in Meridian using the lower of the two prices: 6,000 × 117p = £7,020

23.8.2 Unquoted Shares

Unquoted shares by their very nature do not have a readily ascertainable market value. It is therefore necessary to agree a value for unquoted shares with the Share Valuation Division of HMRC. It is important to note that the value of unquoted shares usually increases disproportionately as the number of shares held increases. This is due to the fact that the ability to influence, and eventually control, decisions made by the company increases at certain percentage holdings in the company, e.g.:

- less than 20%
- more than 51%
- more than 75%
- more than 90%
- 100% total ownership.

The relevant price to be used is given in examples and questions in this textbook and it is necessary to consider how the value is affected by the percentage of the shareholding held by the donor's related property, as well as the loss in value to the donor as a result of reducing their shareholding.

23.8.3 Life Insurance Policies

Lifetime transfers of life insurance policies are valued at the greater of the surrender value and the premiums paid. If someone takes out a policy on their own life and has it written in trust for the benefit of someone else, then each premium payment is a transfer of value and will be a PET unless it falls within an exemption (e.g. small gifts or normal expenditure out of income).

The maturity value of a policy taken out by the deceased on his own life will be included in his estate. If a policy has been assigned to another person during the deceased's lifetime, this is treated as a lifetime transfer.

23.8.4 Jointly-owned Property

Where a property is owned jointly by a married couple/civil partnership, the value of the property is equivalent to the proportion of ownership to the total value of the asset. So, if two spouses each own 50% of a property worth £200,000, then that property would have a value of £100,000 for each of them.

Where the joint owners are not married or in a civil partnership, then it is possible to make a deduction from the proportionate value based on the ownership percentage of between 5–15%. For the purposes of this textbook, assume a deduction of 10%. Using the example above, the value for each of the owners if not married would be £90,000 (i.e. £100,000 less 10%). The reason for this deduction is that the property must be valued on a stand-alone basis and a purchaser is less likely to buy a share in an asset that is part-owned by a third party.

23.8.5 Joint Tenants versus Tenants in Common

It is important to appreciate the distinction in holding property as joint tenants or as tenants in common. Property held by joint tenants automatically reverts to the fellow joint tenant (under the law of survivorship) whereas tenants in common can each gift their part of the property as they see fit. Joint tenants are always treated as having a joint and equal share to the whole property, whereas ownership between tenants in common does not have to be split equally.

Example 23.6: IHT treatment of death estate with prior lifetime gifts

Greg died on 19 October 2014 and left his estate of £750,000 to be divided equally between his wife and two children.

His only lifetime gift had been when he settled £350,000 into a discretionary trust in May 2008. Greg paid the IHT due on the gift so that the full value of the gift was available for the purposes of the trust's objectives.

Calculate the IHT payable on the death of Greg.

(i) CLT (in lifetime)

	£
Gift to discretionary trust	350,000
Less: A/E 08/09	(3,000)
Less: A/E 07/08	(3,000)
CLT	344,000
Less: Nil rate band for 2008/09	(312,000)
Taxable transfer	32,000
IHT on grossed-up transfer £32,000 + (32,000 × (20/80))	40,000
IHT @ 20%	8,000
CLT for cumulation = £344,000 + £8,000 = £352,000	

(ii) Additional tax due on CLT at death

	£
CLT	352,000
Less: Nil rate band for 2014/15	(325,000)
Taxable transfer	27,000
IHT @ 40%	10,800
Less: taper relief at 80% (six to seven years)	(8,640)
IHT due	2,160
Less: tax paid on lifetime gift	(8,000)
IHT due on CLT at death	NIL

No refund can be obtained of lifetime tax paid on CLT.

(iii) Tax on death estate

		£
Death estate		750,000
Less: exempt transfer (one-third to spouse)		(250,000)
Chargeable estate		500,000
Nil rate band 2014/15	325,000	
Less: CLTs within seven years	(352,000)	
Remaining nil rate band		NIL
Taxable estate		500,000
IHT @ 40%		200,000

23.9   Pro Forma Computation to Calculate the Value of the Death Estate

Death estate of Mr X who died on …

	£	£	£
Stocks and shares			X
Insurance policy proceeds			X
Personal chattels			X
Cash (including accrued interest net of tax)			X
Accrued income from interest in possession trusts (net of tax), etc…			X
			X
			X
Less:			
Debts due from deceased estate		(X)	
Funeral expenses		(X)	(X)
			X
UK property	X		
Less: mortgage	(X)	X	
Foreign property	X		
Less: mortgage	(X)		
Less: expenses of realisation (max. 5%)	(X)	X	X
Net estate			X
Gifts with reservation			X
Chargeable estate			X

All workings for reliefs, valuation calculations, etc. (e.g. business property relief (BPR), agricultural property relief (APR), post-mortem relief, etc.) should be shown as separate workings and referenced to the pro forma computation with supporting explanations provided.

Questions

Review Questions
(See Suggested Solutions to Review Questions at the end of this textbook.)

Question 23.1

Fredrick gave £400,000 in cash to a discretionary trust on 6 April 2011. This was his first gift of any kind.

Requirement

What inheritance tax is due, and on whom does the liability fall? Would any additional inheritance tax be due on the gift if Fredrick died on 10 April 2014 without making any further gifts? If so, how much?

Question 23.2

Portia di Rossi died on 29 July 2014. She is survived by her four children and six grandchildren.

During her life, Portia was always very generous. She turned 80 in October 2008 and, every Christmas from then on, she gave £200 to each of her grandchildren. For Christmas 2008 only, she also gave £4,500 to each of her children. When her godson was married on 19 March 2010, Portia gave him £6,000. She made no gifts of any sort in any tax years prior to 2008/09.

A sum of £25,000 was donated by her in July 2009 to an American charity established in New York for fire-fighters injured in 9/11 as her brother was a long-time resident of New York and had been rescued from the street that day by a passing fire crew.

Keen to also provide for her children, five months before her death, in February 2014, Portia gifted £380,000 cash to create a discretionary trust which she established for her children. Portia made it clear at that time that any tax that arose on the gift was to be taken care of by the trustees.

At the time of her death, Portia owned the following assets:

1. Her home in Armagh, valued at £725,000 for probate purposes, but sold after her death in December 2014 for £645,000.
2. The contents of the Armagh house, valued at £48,500.
3. A villa in Portugal, valued at £225,000.
4. 18,000 shares in Belfast Ceramics Plc. The closing bid and offer prices quoted in the Stock Exchange Daily Official List for the company at the date of death were £2.72 and £2.76. The shares were sold six months later for £1.45 each.
5. 3,500 shares in British Meats Plc. The closing bid and offer prices quoted in the Stock Exchange Daily Official List for the company at the date of death were £12.35 and £12.95. The shares were sold three months later for £13.60 each.
6. 390 of the 1,000 issued shares in Italiana Wine SA, a successful Italian trading company established by Portia's son, Paolo, which produces wine in Sicily mainly for the export market. Paolo owns the remaining 610 shares. Portia acquired the shares in January 2009. The shareholding is estimated to have a value of £180,000.
7. £69,000 in bank and building society accounts in Belfast.
8. £228,000 in a Guernsey bank account.

For tax purposes, Portia was domiciled in the UK at the time of her death.

Requirement

Calculate the IHT payable as a result of Portia's death, split between amounts payable in respect of her estate on death, and the amount(s), if any, payable on death in respect of Portia's lifetime gifts. Explain your treatment of each item and claim any reliefs possible to minimise tax which may be due.

Reliefs

24

Learning Objectives

After studying this chapter you will have developed competency in the following:

■ Apply appropriate reliefs, including, *inter alia*, the following:
- business property relief;
- agricultural property relief;
- quick succession relief;
- post-mortem relief;
- transfer of unused nil rate band; and
- fall in value of gift before death.

24.1 Business Property Relief (sections 103–114)

Business property relief (BPR) is available to reduce the amount chargeable to IHT on certain business assets for both lifetime and death transfers. The relief is given before annual exemptions in the case of lifetime transfers so that these are not unnecessarily wasted.

There is no need to claim the relief if it is due, as it is given automatically. The assets transferred must be **relevant business property** for BPR to be available. It should be noted that the relief is generally available on the transfer of a business or an interest in a partnership and not on the transfer of a single business asset.

The following are considered relevant business property with their applicable rate of BPR:

1.	A business or an interest in a business.	100%
2.	Shares in a unquoted trading company (no minimum holding).	100%
3.	Securities (loan stock) in an unquoted company where the company is controlled by the donor (i.e. where the donor holds more than 50% of the voting shares).	100%
4.	Shares and securities in a quoted company where the donor controls the company (i.e. more than 50% of the voting rights). It is very unusual for an individual to hold more than 50% of the shares of a quoted company, so in the majority of cases quoted shares will not qualify for BPR.	50%

5.	Land, buildings, plant and machinery used wholly or mainly in the donor's business (company or partnership controlled by the tranferor or by a partnership of which the transferor was a member) during the last two years before the business was passed on (or since the business acquired them if more recent).	50%
6.	Land, buildings, plant and machinery used in the donor's business and held in a trust that the donor has a right to benefit from.	50%

AIM-listed shares are treated as unquoted for the purposes of BPR.

BPR will not be available if:

▪ The business or company is involved primarily in dealing in shares, land or buildings, or in making or holding investments.
▪ The business is not carried on with a view to making a profit.
▪ The business is the subject of a binding contract for sale, unless that sale is to a company that will continue the business, and the sale is made wholly or mainly in shares in the acquiring company (i.e. an incorporation or company reconstruction). **Note:** HMRC consider a binding contract of sale to exist where there is a "buy and sell" agreement made by partners or company shareholders to take effect on their death, unless the agreement only gives an **option** to buy **and** to sell.
▪ Shares in the company are subject to a binding contract for sale or the company is being wound up, unless the sale or winding up is part of a process to allow the business to continue.

24.1.1 Ownership

The general rule is that property is not relevant business property for the purposes of BPR unless it has been held for a minimum of two years. Generally, if the property has not been held for this minimum period, then no BPR is due.

However, if the transferor became entitled to the property on the death of a spouse or civil partner, then relief is available for any period during which the spouse or civil partner also owned it. This has the effect of aggregating the period of ownership between spouses/civil partners where there has been a transfer on death.

Also, if the transferred property was acquired by way of an earlier transfer within the two-year period, then relief will still be available if the following conditions are met:

▪ The earlier transfer qualified for BPR.
▪ The earlier transfer was made to the current transferor or spouse or civil partner.
▪ One of the transfers was made on a death.
▪ The property would, apart from the two-year rule, qualify for BPR.

Where "old" relevant business property is sold by the owner and replaced by "new" relevant business property **before** the transfer, then it will satisfy the two-year ownership period if, when taken together with the property it has replaced (and indeed the property it in turn replaced, and so on), it has been owned by the transferor for at least two years during the five years immediately before the transfer, provided each item in the chain would have been relevant business property (apart from the length of ownership) if the transfer had been made immediately before it was replaced. However, BPR on the replacement asset cannot exceed the BPR that would have been available on the original asset.

The BPR available on shares is restricted where the company holds "**excepted assets**" on its balance sheet.

An excepted asset is one not used for business purposes throughout the two-year period preceding a transfer, or is not intended to be used in the future for the purposes of the business (i.e. a trading business). Items that are held for investment purposes, e.g. investment properties and share investments, are excepted assets for BPR purposes, as are assets used wholly or mainly for the personal benefit of the transferor or a person connected with the transferor.

BPR is restricted to that proportion of the total assets of a company that the relevant business assets represent, i.e.:

$$\text{Transfer qualifying for BPR} = \text{Gift} \times \frac{\text{Total assets} - \text{Excepted assets}}{\text{Total assets}}$$

Example 24.1: BPR and shares

Jack owns all of the shares in Gravy Ltd, an unlisted company which is mainly engaged in a catering trade. He died on 4 August 2014 and left the shares, worth £620,000, to his nephew Willis. He has held the shares for a number of years and the balance sheet of the company is as follows:

	£
	£
Factory	350,000
Plant	75,000
Investments	45,000
Quoted shares	15,000
Net assets	485,000

As the investments are an excepted asset, BPR relief is calculated as follows, assuming that the balance of the value relates to the trading goodwill:

100% × £620,000 × (425,000/485,000) = £543,299 BPR available

It should be noted that if the excepted assets represent more than 50% of the total assets, HMRC may deny BPR on the grounds that the business is non-trading.

24.1.2 BPR on Lifetime Gifts Following Death

Chargeable Lifetime Transfers

Where BPR is given on a lifetime chargeable transfer of value, it is not always the case that the relief continues to be available where the donor dies within seven years of the gift. In certain circumstances, normally where the donee has either sold or given away the business property, the relief may be withdrawn. The relief will also be withdrawn if the property no longer qualifies as business property.

The relief will **not be** withdrawn if the business property has been sold but has been replaced by other qualifying business property. The replacement business property must be purchased within three years of the disposal of the old business property and the whole of the original proceeds of sale of the old property must be reinvested.

Where BPR is withdrawn, it increases the tax payable by the donee as a consequence of the donor's death within seven years of the gift. It does not alter the IHT position at the point of the actual lifetime transfer. Similarly, where BPR is withdrawn, it does not affect the calculation of the donor's cumulative lifetime transfers for the purposes of using up the nil rate band available at the date of death.

Potentially Exempt Transfers

There can be no withdrawal of BPR on a PET as there is no lifetime tax charge on a PET, hence BPR will not have been claimed.

If a PET becomes chargeable as a result of the death of the donor within seven years of the date of the PET, then BPR will be a consideration.

If the donee still owns the business property at the date of death, then BPR may be available if the other conditions were met at the date of the gift. If the donee has sold the business property before the death of the donor, then no BPR will be available to reduce the IHT charge, unless the proceeds of the sale have been reinvested into replacement business property. If the property no longer qualifies as relevant business property at the date of death, then BPR will not be available. An example would be on the transfer of unquoted shares in a company that become listed on the Stock Exchange before the date of death.

Example 24.2: BPR

Barney gave his shares in an unquoted trading company to his sister Eileen in July 2008 when they were worth £400,000. This was his only lifetime gift. Eileen sold the shares on 1 July 2009 and used the proceeds to buy a holiday home in Florida. Barney died in September 2014.

Calculate the IHT payable by Eileen in respect of the shares on the death of Barney.

	£
Gift in July 2008	400,000
Less: 2008/09 AE	(3,000)
Less: 2007/08 AE	(3,000)
	394,000
Less: Nil rate band applying at date of death	(325,000)
Chargeable to IHT	69,000
IHT @ 40%	27,600
Less taper relief (80% 6–7 years)	(22,080)
IHT payable	5,520

BPR cannot be claimed as the property no longer qualified at the date of Barney's death. As the original gift was a PET and no lifetime tax was due, the annual exemptions are not displaced by the BPR that would have been available.

24.2 Agricultural Property Relief (sections 115–124C)

Agricultural property relief (APR) works in a similar manner to BPR. It is available for gifts of farmland and farm buildings during lifetime or on death. The relief is given before the annual exemptions and before BPR is given.

Prior to FA 2009, the farm had to be situated in the UK, Channel Islands or the Isle of Man. Due to pressure from the European Commission, APR is now available where the farm is situated in the European Economic Area (i.e. all EU countries plus Norway, Iceland and Liechtenstein).

The relief is available to shelter the **agricultural** value of the property which is **normally less than its market value or development value**. The agricultural value is the value of the land on the basis that it can only be used for farming.

The relief is available to a farmer who owns farmland and uses it in a farming business, or to a landowner who lets the land to a farmer who uses it for farming purposes.

APR is given at the rate of 100% of the agricultural value of the land, except in one very precise circumstance. APR is given at the rate of 50% where the land is let to a farmer and the lease was signed before 1 September 1995 and there is still more than two years left to run on the lease. If any of these conditions are not met, then 100% APR is due.

24.2.1 Ownership

Generally the land must be owned for the two years immediately preceding the transfer for APR to be available. This is increased to seven years where the land is let to a farmer.

As with BPR, if the land is sold and replaced by other qualifying land, then the combined period of ownership must be at least two out of the last five years for APR to be available. Where the land is let, the relevant period is seven out of the last 10 years.

Where a farmer runs a farming business then BPR may be available to cover any market value not otherwise covered by APR. Given the recent fall in the market value of land and the resurgence in the value of farmland, there may not be a significant difference between the market value and the agricultural value. The exception would be where the farmland has clear development value.

In Northern Ireland, it has been common to argue that the letting of farmland on "conacre" terms is a business and that the additional value of the farmland over the agricultural value therefore qualifies for BPR. HMRC successfully defeated this argument in the Northern Ireland Court of Appeal in *McCall & Keenan v. Revenue & Customs* (2009). The Court held that the letting on conacre was an investment business, and therefore the development value of the land did not qualify for BPR. However, APR should still be available on the agricultural value of any farm land let on conacre.

APR is also available to the controlling shareholder in a company that owns agricultural land. The relief is calculated with reference to the percentage of the agricultural value of the land to the total value of the company.

APR is also available for farmhouses/farm cottages as long as they are of an appropriate character in relation to the property. The occupation of the property must be in connection with the farming business and it should be normal for the land to include a dwelling of the type concerned.

The rules on withdrawal of BPR following the death of the donor noted above are also applicable to APR.

Example 24.3: APR

The Viscount of Antrim owns a significant holding of farmland which he lets to a local farmer who uses it mainly for growing potatoes. The lease on the property was granted in 1985 for a term of 39 years.

In June 2011 he gave his daughter, Lady Penelope, 150 acres on the occasion of her marriage. The land had a market value of £2,400,000 and an agricultural value of £2,250,000.

The Viscount died in October 2014 and had made no other gifts in the seven years preceding his death. Calculate the IHT payable by Lady Penelope on the Viscount's death.

	£
Gift	2,400,000
Less: APR @ 50% (£2.25m × 50%)	(1,125,000)
	1,275,000
Less: marriage exemption	(5,000)
Less: A/E 2011/12	(3,000)
Less: A/E 2010/11	(3,000)
PET	1,264,000
Less: nil rate band at death	(325,000)
Taxable transfer	939,000
IHT @ 40%	375,600
Less: taper relief (3 to 4 years = 20%)	(75,120)
IHT payable	300,480

24.3 Quick Succession Relief (section 141)

Where a donee dies after their estate has been increased by a chargeable transfer, tax may be due on the increased estate and may have already been charged on the earlier transfer. Where the death of the donee occurs within five years of the earlier transfer, quick succession relief (QSR) may be claimed. QSR is available for a transfer on death or for a PET that becomes chargeable due to the death of the original donor within seven years of the earlier transfer. If the time period is less than one year, 100% QSR will be available and this reduces by 20% for each additional year that passes between the date of the first and second death.

Years between transfer and death	Percentage relief
Up to 1 year	100%
More than 1 but no more than 2	80%
More than 2 but not more than 3	60%
More than 3 but not more than 4	40%
More than 4 but not more than 5	20%

The formula for calculating the available QSR is as follows:

$$\frac{\text{Previous transfer net of tax}}{\text{Previous gross transfer}} \times \text{Tax paid on previous transfer} \times \text{QSR \%}$$

The reason for the "tax paid on previous transfer" part of the formula is to take account of whether the gift had to bear its own tax or whether it was "tax-free". Unless specified to the contrary, gifts of UK assets do not bear their own tax whilst gifts of non-UK assets do bear their own tax. Where gifts do not bear their own tax, any IHT due is paid out of the residue of the estate.

It is important to note that QSR is available even if the donee has sold or disposed of the asset prior to death.

Example 24.4: QSR
Frank died on 3 April 2012 and left his entire estate valued at £554,000 to his cousin Vinny. Frank had made a gift of £126,000 to his best friend in the month before he died.

Vinny died in July 2014 leaving an estate of £625,000.

Step 1: Calculate the IHT due on Frank's estate

	£
Death estate	554,000
Less: Nil rate band (Note)	(205,000)
Net taxable estate	349,000
IHT due @ 40%	139,600
Note: Nil rate band	
Lifetime gift	126,000
Less: AE 2011/12	(3,000)
AE 2010/11	(3,000)
	120,000
Nil rate band	325,000
Utilised	(120,000)
Available	205,000

continued overleaf

Step 2: Calculate the IHT due on Vinny's estate

	£
Death estate	625,000
Less: Nil rate band	(325,000)
Chargeable estate	300,000
IHT @ 40%	120,000
Less QSR:	
$\dfrac{£414,400*}{£414,400 + £139,600} \times 139,600 \times 60\%$	(62,654)
IHT due	57,346

*Being £554,000 − £139,600

24.4   Relief for Surviving Spouse of a Deceased Person

This relief was introduced by FA 2008. The relief works by allowing the surviving spouse/civil partner to claim any unused nil rate band (NRB) of their deceased spouse/civil partner. It is available to all survivors of a marriage or civil partnership who die on or after 9 October 2007, no matter when the first partner died.

The NRB that is available to the surviving spouse or civil partner on their death will be increased by the proportion of the NRB unused on the first death. The amount of the NRB that can be transferred is not reduced by the value of the first spouse's estate to the extent that exempt transfers are made.

Example 24.5: Transfer of nil rate band
Jackie died when her chargeable estate was £150,000 and the NRB was £300,000. She left her entire estate to her son.

Jackie's husband has just died and his chargeable estate is £560,000. His son wants to know what NRB will be available in respect of his father's estate as the father had not made any transfers in the last seven years.

The NRB for 2014/15 is £325,000 and this is uplifted by 50% (i.e. the proportion of the NRB not used by Jackie at her death) to £487,500. The husband's estate will potentially be liable to IHT on the excess over the extended NRB of £72,500 (£560,000–£487,500).

24.5   Fall in Value of Gift Before Death (section 131)

An IHT relief is available, known as a "section 131 claim", where the value of an asset has fallen between the date of the original gift and the date of death of the donor. The claim reduces the further tax payable by a donee on a lifetime gift that comes into charge on the death of the donor within seven years. It is possible to make this claim if the donee no longer owns the property. In this case, the fall in value relief is determined by reference to the proceeds received for the disposal rather than the current market value at death. Relief is given by reducing the lifetime transfer by an amount equal to the fall in value, and it should be noted that this relief is calculated by reference to the loss in value to the donee, not by reference to the loss in value to the donor (which is used to calculate the value transferred by the donor).

Example 24.6: Fall in value relief

Ryan gave a painting to Sandra in January 2009. It was part of a set of two paintings which together were worth £750,000. Each painting on its own was worth £200,000. Ryan made no other lifetime gifts.

Ryan died in November 2014. At that date, the painting given to Sandra was only worth £80,000 as it had been damaged.

The painting will be valued as follows in calculating any IHT due on death.

	£
Value of two paintings before transfer	750,000
Value of one painting after transfer	(200,000)
Value transferred by donor	550,000
Less: A/Es for 2008/09 and 2007/08	(6,000)
Less: fall in value relief (£200,000 − £80,000)	(120,000)
Chargeable on death	424,000
Less: NRB	(325,000)
Chargeable to IHT	99,000

24.6 Growing Timber Relief (sections 125–130)

An IHT relief is available for woodlands where trees and underwood are grown for the purpose of producing timber. Note that it has been held that growing Christmas trees does not qualify for this relief, as the trees do not have the maturity to be able to produce timber. The underlying land will not qualify for the relief, but may qualify for APR if occupied with, and ancillary to, agricultural land or pasture.

The relief is not available for lifetime transfers and only applies on death. IHT can be deferred on death on an inheritance of qualifying trees/underwood (but not on the land). It is possible to make an election where the woodland is not occupied as agricultural land within two years of death. Where the election is made, the timber is left out of account for IHT purposes.

For a valid election to be made, the deceased must have owned the land for the previous five years or must have received the land for no consideration (i.e. from a previous gift or inheritance). The timber is brought back into charge to IHT when the timber is later sold at the sales price (uplifted to market value if necessary) less disposal costs and any cost of replanting incurred within three years (or a longer period if HMRC allows it).

The IHT charge is calculated by reference to the estate of the deceased at the date of death and the value of the timber is brought back into account. The value brought back into account is treated as the "top slice" of the estate and is therefore charged at the highest rate of IHT. However, it should be noted that it is the IHT rates of tax applicable at the date of **disposal** that are used rather than at the date of death.

The IHT is due six months from the end of the month in which the disposal of the timber takes place.

If the woodlands are managed on a commercial basis, then 100% BPR may be available. However, the rate of relief is reduced to 50% if an election is made to leave timber out of account on a death estate.

If the person who has inherited the woodlands subsequently dies before the timber is disposed of, then there will be no IHT due in respect of the earlier transfer. It will be possible to make a further election on the second death in respect of the woodlands.

24.7 Post-mortem Relief

The general rule that IHT is calculated on the value of the death estate at the date of death is relaxed in certain circumstances. It may be possible to substitute a lower value for certain assets if they are sold after the date of death and realise a lower value than that which applied at the date of death. There are three common cases where this IHT relief can apply and the conditions and bases of valuation are considered below.

24.7.1 Sale of Quoted Shares/Securities within 12 Months of Death (section 179)

If the proceeds realised on the sale of quoted shares or securities within 12 months of the date of death of the donor are lower than the value included in their estate, it is possible to make a claim to substitute the lower value for the purposes of calculating the IHT due on the estate.

When calculating the claim that may be made, it is a requirement to determine the net effect of all disposals of such assets that take place within 12 months of the death. Thus any relevant assets sold for an amount higher than the value included in the estate valuation will reduce the benefit of making the post-mortem claim.

There is an important planning point here in that it may be possible to delay sales that would achieve a higher sales price until after 12 months from the date of death to maximise the value of any claim.

Obviously, if the relevant sales that took place within 12 months of death would produce a higher value than originally included in the death estate, then no claim should be made.

In evaluating the possible benefit of making a claim, it is the gross sales figures that are used as a comparison against the original probate value included in the death estate.

There is also an anti-avoidance measure that must be considered. This is designed to stop shares being sold to realise post-mortem relief and then immediately reinvesting the proceeds (whether into the same shares/securities or not). The anti-avoidance legislation restricts the loss in value that can be claimed where there are any investments purchased between the date of death and the end of two months from the last sale of relevant assets within 12 months from the date of death. Where this restriction applies, it is calculated as:

$$\text{Loss} \times \frac{\text{Amount invested}}{\text{Total gross proceeds}}$$

Example 24.7: Post-mortem relief – quoted shares
Darina died on 12 August 2014 and left her estate of £725,000 to her three children. The estate included shares in AIG plc, valued at £50,000.

The executors sold the shares in September 2014, realising proceeds of £12,250 after deducting sales costs of £250. In November 2014, the executors purchased £10,000 of shares in Centrica plc.

Calculate any post-mortem relief available.

	£
Probate value	50,000
Less: gross proceeds	(12,500)
Loss	37,500
Less: Restriction	
$\frac{10,000}{12,500} \times £37,500$	(30,000)
Section 179 claim	7,500

24.7.2 Sale of Land or Buildings within Three Years of Death (section 191)

This relief works in a similar fashion to that for sales of quoted shares, etc. but with a few significant differences. The time period is three years from the date of death rather than one. The aggregation of profits and losses rule still applies but is modified in that it also includes sales that take place at a loss in the **fourth** year after death (sales at a profit in the fourth year are completely ignored).

When calculating the relief, differences in value between the date of death and the date of sale are ignored if they are less than the lower of £1,000 or 5% of the probate value.

A similar anti-avoidance rule on reinvestment also applies and covers the period from death to four months after the last sale in the three-year period. The relevant formula is:

$$\text{Loss} \times \frac{\text{Amount invested}}{\text{Total gross proceeds}}$$

Example 24.8: Post-mortem relief – land and buildings
Justin's death estate included the following assets at the date of his death on 5 May 2014:

	£
House in Bristol	165,000
Cottage in Donegal	185,000
Apartment in Benidorm	95,000

In administering Justin's estate the following transactions took place:

- Sold house in Bristol on 12 August 2014 for £160,000
- Sold cottage in Donegal on 9 September 2014 for £164,500
- Sold apartment in Benidorm on 3 December 2014 for £94,500
- Bought farmland in Fermanagh for £35,000 on 2 February 2015

Calculate any post-mortem relief that may be due.

The losses on the Bristol and Donegal properties are relevant to the section 191 claim. The loss of £500 on disposal of Benidorm must be ignored as it is below the lower of £1,000 and 5% of probate value.

The effect of ignoring the Benidorm disposal is that the last relevant sale took place on 9 September 2014 and only purchases taking place between death and four months from 9 September 2014 are relevant for restricting the claim. Therefore, the purchase of farmland in Fermanagh will not restrict the post-mortem relief.

The section 191 loss claim is therefore:

[(£165,000 − £160,000) + (£185,000 − £164,500)] = £25,500

24.7.3 Sale of Related Property to an Unconnected Party within Three Years of Death (section 176)

A claim for this relief will be possible where the death estate included related property which is sold within three years of death to an unconnected party for a value which is less than that included in the death estate. This relief works differently from the other post-mortem reliefs referred to above in that the relief is obtained by substituting the stand-alone value applicable at the date of death (rather than by reference to the proceeds received at the date of disposal).

Example 24.9: Post-mortem relief – related property

Rosie died on 3 May 2014 and her death estate included 40% of the shares in Arkle Investments Ltd. Her husband owns a further 30% of the shares in the company. At the date of death, a 40% shareholding is worth £250,000, whilst a 70% holding is worth £525,000.

As no BPR is due, the shares were included in the death estate as $40/70 \times £525,000 = £300,000$.

The executors sold Rosie's shares for £280,000 six months after her death to a third party. Calculate any post-mortem relief due. All the conditions necessary to qualify for post-mortem relief have been satisfied as:

- the asset was related property in the death estate;
- it has been sold to an unconnected third party within three years of death; and
- the proceeds realised (£280,000) are less than the amount included in the death estate (£300,000).

The relief is claimed by substituting the stand-alone value of £250,000 (note that this is not the sale price of £280,000!) for the original related property value of £300,000. Relief of £50,000 is effectively obtained.

Questions

Review Questions

(See Suggested Solution to Review Questions at the end of this textbook.)

Question 24.1

Relief from inheritance tax is available on relevant business property.

Requirement
(a) What is relevant business property?
(b) What types of business do not qualify for this relief?
(c) What is the nature of the relief and at what rates is it given?

Question 24.2

Relief from inheritance tax is also available for agricultural property.

Requirement

(a) Under what circumstances is a transferor entitled to inheritance tax relief when transferring agricultural property and what is the nature of the relief?
(b) Is the relief available to a transferor of shares or debentures in a farming company?

Question 24.3

Chris Adams is a wealthy individual whose grandmother died on 13 November 2014. Chris is an executor of her estate, and of the discretionary trust noted below, and is keen to finalise the inheritance tax issues associated with her death as soon as possible.

Chris realises that he does not have the necessary knowledge to calculate the inheritance tax that is due and does not want to miss out on any relief which could be claimed to reduce the IHT liability and so increase the funds available to the beneficiaries of his grandmother's will.

Chris has given you the following information:

1. His grandmother gave £500,000 to a discretionary trust in June 2011, and paid any IHT due. He can't find the papers showing how much inheritance tax was paid.
2. His grandmother owned three rental properties on the Lisburn Road, Belfast. He has obtained an independent valuation of the three properties which indicates that the value at the date of death was £560,000. However, as his grandmother's will states that the properties are to be sold and the proceeds divided between her four grandchildren, he placed them on the market in February 2015. At this point the estate agent recommended an asking price of £550,000, but due to the state of the property market, the highest offer received to date (which Chris is about to accept) is £525,000.
3. His grandmother had credit card debt of £15,000 at the date of her death.
4. She owed £50,000 to Bank of Ireland, secured on her collection of art. The loan was used by her to travel all around the country and display her art at various exhibitions and will be repaid from her estate. The art is worth £250,000.
5. His grandmother owned a holiday home in Iceland worth £78,000.
6. At the date of death she had cash of £250,000 in a UK bank account and cash of £40,000 in an account in the Isle of Man.
7. Chris had been given the family home by his grandmother in May 2013, when it was worth £600,000.
8. Chris has incurred the following costs in his role as executor, which have been paid for out of his grandmother's estate: solicitor's fees of £5,000 in administering the estate, £2,000 on a headstone, £550 on mourning clothes for his family for the funeral and £14,500 in obtaining probate on the holiday home his grandmother owed in Iceland.

Requirement

(a) Calculate the inheritance tax due as a result of the death of Chris's grandmother.
(b) State who has to pay any additional inheritance tax due on the lifetime gifts.

Question 24.4

You work in the trusts and estates division of a local mid-sized practice. Your client, Fionn O'Shea, died on 31 March 2015. During your review of Fionn's tax file, you note that, during his lifetime, he had made the following gifts:

1. £9,000 to his son Shay on the occasion of his marriage on 10 March 2009.
2. £300,000 to a discretionary trust on 28 December 2009. You note that the trustees agreed to pay any tax due.
3. 100,000 Angel Bank plc £1 ordinary shares valued at £175,000 to the same discretionary trust on 25 November 2010. Again, the trustees agreed to pay any tax due. The shares had fallen in value to £75,000 at the date of Fionn's death.

Fionn also owned the following assets when he died: his home valued at £225,000, cash and investments valued totalling £85,000 and chattels valued at £15,000.

Fionn was also the life tenant of a qualifying interest in possession trust created by his brother's will following his death in 1986. The value of the trust fund at Fionn's death was £276,000.

Fionn was married to Alanna, who died in 2010 with no assets. He never remarried.

Requirement

Prepare a memo to the partner in your practice dealing with the following matters:

(a) Calculate the lifetime inheritance tax payable, if any, in respect of the lifetime gifts.
(b) Calculate the inheritance tax due on Fionn's death estate, making any appropriate claims or reliefs available to reduce the liability arising (if any).

Question 24.5

James Quinn died on 20 November 2014. His brother Andrew predeceased him on 31 March 2011, leaving his entire estate, valued at £575,000, to James. The month before Andrew died, Andrew made a gift of £156,000 to their only sister Laura.

At the time of his death, James had amassed a significant estate, the value of which was £1.5 million including the assets left to him by Andrew in 2011.

Requirement

Calculate the inheritance tax payable due to James's death, making any appropriate claims or reliefs available to reduce the liability arising (if any). Outline the rational for any claims or reliefs.

Interaction between IHT and CGT

25.1 Explanation of the Interaction of IHT and CGT

The base cost for CGT purposes of a lifetime gift in the hands of the donee (for both PETs and CLTs) is the market value at the date of transfer. The donor will be subject to CGT if the gift is a chargeable asset for CGT purposes. Any tax charge will be based on the market value of the asset at the date of gift. This will be the case unless the asset is exempt from CGT or if it is possible to make a holdover election under section 165 or section 260 TCGA 1992. It may be possible to make a section 260 TCGA 1992 claim if the transfer is immediately chargeable to IHT, e.g. on a gift into a trust. The claim can be made even if the IHT charge is at 0%, i.e. within the nil rate band.

Where there is a gift of an asset and it is possible to make a CGT holdover election, the base cost for the recipient becomes the market value at the date of transfer less the amount held over. The effect of this is that the gain is effectively passed on to the donee.

When an asset has been acquired following the death of the donor, the probate value becomes the CGT base cost. This can be particularly valuable where 100% BPR or APR is available. There will be no IHT due on a transfer on death and the donee will receive the property at its current market value.

Where post-mortem relief is claimed, this lower value becomes the CGT base cost rather than the original probate value.

Example 25.1

Jonathan Williamson is 70-years-old and a widower. He has one child, his son Peter, to whom he intends to leave the whole of his estate on his death. Both Jonathan and Peter were born in the UK and have always lived and worked here.

Peter is currently planning to buy a house and so Jonathan would like to make a lifetime gift to him of one of his assets to fund the property purchase. Peter needs around £425,000. He will sell whatever gift he receives from his father immediately in order to buy the house

Jonathan owns two assets valued at £425,000 (see below) and would like advice on which he should gift (and why), factoring in all the relevant tax consequences. He would also like to know if he is better to gift the assets now or wait to pass them on to his son in his will.

1. 15,000 shares in Williamson Holidays Ltd

This is an unquoted trading company. Jonathan currently owns 30,000 shares in the company, representing a 75% holding. The 15,000 shares have an estimated market value of £425,000 and they cost him £325,000 in 2010.

The company owns a plot of land that it holds as an investment. The land comprises 6% of the value of its total assets and 10% of the value of its chargeable assets.

2. A sailing boat known as "William and Son"
The boat is also worth £425,000 but cost £200,000 in June 2006. Jonathan took it on as project and spent a further £125,000 the next year installing a more powerful engine and satellite navigation equipment.

The tax implications of the two proposed gifts are considered below.

Gift of shares
(a) CGT implications

Lifetime gift
Jonathan would make a capital gain by reference to the deemed sales proceeds equal to the market value of the shares – i.e. a gain of £100,000 (£425,000 – £325,000) as Peter is a connected party under Section 286 TCGA 1992.

Jonathan owns more than 5% of Williamson Holidays Ltd and has owned the shares for more than 12 months. In addition, Williamson Holidays Ltd is a trading company. However, entrepreneurs' relief will only be available if Jonathan is a director or employee of the company in the 12 months prior to the gift of the shares to his son.

Gift holdover relief would also be available as the shares are unquoted and Williamson Holidays Ltd is a trading company. However, the relief would be restricted to 90% only because the company owns non-business chargeable assets (the plot of land held as an investment comprises 10% of the company's chargeable assets).

If Jonathan is an employee of Williamson Holidays Ltd, gift holdover relief should not be claimed unless Peter has significant capital losses to use because gift holdover will create a sizeable gain for Peter when he sells the shares immediately after receiving them.

Entrepreneurs' relief is a better option. Jonathan's gain of £100,000 would be reduced by any available annual exempt amount; assuming he has none remaining, the maximum capital gains tax would be £10,000 (£100,000 × 10%). Peter's base cost in the shares would be their market value at the time of the gift being £425,000. Accordingly, there would be no gain on the immediate sale of the shares by Peter following the gift, as his sales proceeds would equal his base cost, assuming he can sell them immediately for the same price. This would mean that Peter would have a clear £425,000 of cash available for the property purchase.

If Jonathan is not an employee of Williamson Holidays Ltd, he and Peter can claim gift holdover relief as both could then benefit from their CGT annual exemption. Jonathan would make a gain of £10,000 (£100,000 × 10%) due to the non-business chargeable assets, which would then be reduced by any available annual exempt amount.

continued overleaf

The maximum CGT liability for Jonathan would be £2,800 (£10,000 × 28%) depending on the level of his income and the existence of any other capital gains. The remainder of the gain of £90,000 would be held over and would reduce Peter's base cost of the shares to £335,000 (£425,000 − £90,000).

Accordingly, Peter's gain on an onward immediate sale for £425,000 would be £90,000 (£425,000 − £335,000) as reduced by any available annual exempt amount. The maximum CGT liability would be £25,200 (£90,000 × 28%). The total CGT due would be a maximum of £28,000 between Jonathan and Peter (£2,800 + £25,200). Peter would only have £399,800 to fund the property purchase.

Gift via Jonathan's will
Gifts on death are exempt from CGT. Hence Peter's base cost would be the market value of the shares at the time of death. However he would not be able to fund the property purchase at the time he wants to and would be forced to wait, assuming he has no other way of funding the purchase.

(b) IHT implications

Lifetime gift
The gift would be a potentially exempt transfer that would only be subject to IHT if Jonathan were to die within seven years. If the gift became chargeable, business property relief would not be available as Peter would not own the shares at the time of Jonathan's death and he would not have replaced the shares with equivalent business property.

In addition, Jonathan will still hold 15,000 shares in Williamson Holidays Ltd. Accordingly, the value of the transfer for IHT would be calculated under the loss to the donor principle representing the fall in value of Jonathan's estate at the time of the gift. This is likely to differ from the market value of the shares gifted as Jonathan's holding would be reduced from 75% to 37.5%, such that he would no longer control the company.

The fall in value in Jonathan's estate would be reduced by any available annual exemptions. IHT would then be due on the excess of this amount over the nil rate band at the date of death as reduced by any chargeable transfers in the seven years prior to the gift of the shares. Taper relief would be available if Jonathan were to survive the gift by at least three years. The maximum IHT liability would be 40% of the fall in value.

Gift via Jonathan's will
100% business property relief would be available on the non-excepted assets. Accordingly, only 6% of the value of the shares as at the time of death would be subject to IHT (on the assumption that the proportion of the company's assets held in the form of investments has not changed).

The shares would be included in Jonathan's death estate. The excess of the death estate over the available nil rate band (as reduced by any chargeable transfers in the seven years prior to death) would be subject to IHT at 40%. The maximum liability would be 2.4% (6% × 40%) of the value of the shares.

Gift of yacht
(a) CGT implications

Lifetime gift or via Jonathan's will
The sailing boat is a wasting chattel (tangible, moveable property with a useful life of no more than 50 years) and, as such, is an exempt asset for the purposes of capital gains tax. So Peter would have £425,000 cash in hand from the sale.

(b) IHT implications

Lifetime gift
The gift would be a potentially exempt transfer and would only be subject to IHT if Jonathan were to die within seven years. IHT would be due on the excess of the value of the sailing boat at the time of the gift (as reduced by any available annual exemptions) over the available nil rate band (as reduced by any chargeable transfers in the seven years prior to the gift). Taper relief would be available if Jonathan were to survive the gift by at least three years.

continued overleaf

Gift via Jonathan's will

The sailing boat would be included in Jonathan's death estate at its value on death. The excess of the death estate over the available nil rate band (as reduced by any chargeable transfers in the seven years prior to death) would be subject to IHT at 40%.

Recommendation

It is clear that, purely from a tax point of view, Jonathan should give Peter the yacht rather than the shares.

There will be no tax at the time of the gift, either CGT or IHT. In addition, there will be no tax at the time of death, provided Jonathan survives the gift by seven years. Even if Jonathan were to die within seven years of the gift, the amount of IHT due on death is likely to be less than the amount due if the sailing boat were held by Jonathan until death due to the availability of taper relief. Before concluding on this, it would be necessary to consider the chargeable transfers made by Jonathan during the seven years prior to the proposed gift and the likelihood of the sailing boat increasing or falling in value.

The situation regarding a gift of the shares is not so straightforward. A lifetime gift will result in a CGT liability of up to £28,000. There is also the possibility of an IHT liability of 40% of the fall in value of Jonathan's estate if Jonathan were to die within three years of the gift. However, there would be no IHT liability if he were to survive the gift by at least seven years.

Retaining the shares until death would avoid the CGT liability, but would guarantee an IHT liability up to a maximum of 2.4% of the value of the shares. Accordingly, a lifetime gift of the shares would be a gamble by Jonathan. If he were to survive the gift by seven years, the total tax due would be CGT of either £10,000 or £28,000, depending on whether or not he is an employee of Williamson Holidays Ltd. If he were to die within three years of the gift, the total tax due is likely to be considerable due to the IHT payable. His alternative is to hold on to the shares and pay a relatively small amount of IHT out of his death estate. Finally, Jonathan could be advised that an insurance policy could be taken out on his life in order to satisfy any future IHT liability arising in respect of a lifetime gift.

The following general conclusions can be drawn from the above.

1. IHT – assets that are subject to IHT but not CGT (i.e. those that are exempt from CGT) can be planned for by reference to IHT only. From an IHT point of view, it is advantageous to give away assets as soon as possible as this opens up the possibility of surviving the gift by seven years or, failing that, the possibility of taper relief. It is particularly important to gift assets that are expected to increase in value as the value on which IHT is calculated is frozen at the time of the gift.

2. IHT – care must be taken when advising on assets that qualify for business property relief or agricultural property relief due to the need for the recipient to hold the assets until the death of the donor in order for the relief to be available on the donor's death. If it is clear from the facts that the recipient intends to sell the assets gifted, there is likely to be a significant difference between the IHT due on death within seven years of the lifetime gift and that due on the asset when comprised within the death estate.

3. CGT – it is not always advantageous to claim gifts holdover relief. Also, the relief is not always available; in particular, unless the gift is to a trust, the assets must qualify for the relief.

25.2 Consideration of the Impact of "Gifts with Reservation" and Pre-owned Assets Tax

25.2.1 *Gifts with Reservation*

The "gifts with reservation" (GWR) rules were introduced as an anti-avoidance measure to prevent individuals gifting assets but continuing to derive some benefit from those assets after the gift had been made. Without the rules, the assets could fall outside the taxable estate if the donor survived seven years from the date of making the PET, even where they continue to derive a benefit from the assets.

The rules operate by treating the asset as continuing to form part of the donor's estate for IHT purposes, i.e. the gift is ignored. The most common asset to be affected by this legislation is the main residence of the donor, where it is gifted to someone (e.g. the donor's son or daughter) but the donor continues to derive a benefit from the property by continuing to live there.

The anti-avoidance legislation does not apply where the donor pays full market value for the use of the property gifted or if the donor is virtually excluded from benefiting from the property. There is useful commentary in HMRC's November 1993 Tax Bulletin on insignificant benefits that are ignored and it is recommended that students review these comments which are available to view on the HMRC website.

If a donor makes a GWR and dies within seven years, there is a potential double charge, with tax becoming due both on the original lifetime gift of the property and on the property being included in the death estate as a consequence of the reservation of benefit. HMRC acknowledges that there could be a double charge and deals with the matter by requiring two IHT computations – one showing the tax charge on the original PET and one showing the tax charge if the asset is included in the death estate. Rather than imposing a double IHT charge, HMRC accepts the computation that produces the higher IHT charge.

Example 25.1: Gift with reservation (GWR)
Luke gave his daughter his holiday cottage in Portrush in January 2001. Luke continued to spend three months of each year in the cottage between the date of the gift and his death in July 2014. This is a GWR and the value of the property will be included in Luke's death estate for IHT purposes.

NB: The value of the property in January 2001 is the daughter's base cost for CGT purposes.

It is possible to release a GWR before death by relinquishing any benefit retained. However, this is treated as a deemed PET at the date of the release of the benefit (and at the value at the date of release). As this is a deemed PET it is not possible to claim the annual exemption(s) against it. To avoid the double IHT charge on the original gift and the subsequent release of the benefit, HMRC again accepts the IHT computation that produces the higher IHT liability.

The well-known case of *Ingram v. IRC* (1997) found in favour of the taxpayer, Lady Ingram, in avoiding the GWR anti-avoidance rules. This case involved gifting the freehold of a property which was the defendant's main residence and carving out a 20-year lease for herself. It was held in the House of Lords that the freehold and the leasehold interests were different assets so it was not possible to apply the GWR rules to the leasehold interest. The legislation was later amended to remove this tax planning opportunity.

25.2.2 Pre-owned Assets Tax

The IHT regime was being continually abused by taxpayers seeking to avoid the GWR rules and it proved difficult to satisfactorily prevent loopholes in the legislation. HMRC reacted by taking the unprecedented step of using new income tax rules – the pre-owned assets tax rules – to prevent abuse of the IHT rules. These are contained in Schedule 15 FA 2004.

The rules operate by imposing an income tax charge on benefits received by a former owner of a property. The income tax charge is calculated on notional income from the property based on the annual rental value of the property. The pre-owned assets tax (POAT) rules only apply to property gifted after 16 March 1986 which is not already subject to the IHT GWR rules.

For land, the income tax charge is based on the commercial rent that would be payable on the property, less any rent that the donor pays to the new owner of the property under a legal obligation (i.e. a lease or licence).

For chattels, the income tax charge is calculated by way of a notional interest charge using the HMRC official interest rate applied to the value of the chattel at the start of the tax year in which the gift was made. The asset must be revalued every five years and the POAT charge based on the new value. Again, it will be possible to deduct any rent paid by the donor to the new owner under a legal obligation.

It is not possible to retain a benefit if cash is given away as there are no tracing rules for cash gifts under the IHT rules. There are tracing provisions within the POAT charge where the donor directly or indirectly provides any of the consideration for the acquisition of an asset by a donee from which the donor will derive a benefit. An apportionment is required for POAT purposes where a part of the consideration has been provided by the donor. No income tax charge will arise if the aggregate POAT charges before offset of rents paid by the donor do not exceed £5,000. The only exception to this is if the annual rental value exceeds £6,000. If the POAT value exceeds £5,000, the full amount is taxable regardless of the annual value.

Gifts to spouses or disposals on arm's length terms are excluded transactions for the purposes of POAT.

If a donor does not wish to be caught by the POAT rules, they may elect out of them by agreeing to treat the gift as falling within the GWR rules. The election should be made by 31 January following the end of the tax year in which the POAT first arises. The election is irrevocable after the income tax return filing date has passed and the election is made on an asset by asset basis.

It will be necessary to examine the taxpayer's specific circumstances to decide whether to opt out of the POAT income tax rules and apply the IHT GWR rules.

Example 25.2: POAT charge

David gave his son £125,000 in 2009 and he used the money to buy a Harley Davidson for £180,000 in 2014. David stores the bike in his garage and uses it on a regular basis. He does not make any payment to his son for the use of the asset and it has an annual rental value of £1,200.

The official rate of interest is 4%.

There is a charge under the POAT rules tracing the cash gift to the purchase of the motorcycle. As the asset is a chattel, the charge is calculated using HMRC's official interest rate.

£180,000 × 4%   £7,200

Apportioned £7,200 × $\dfrac{£125,000}{£180,000}$ £5,000

No POAT charge arises as the value does not exceed £5,000.

Example 25.3: POAT charge
P. Stamp wishes to reduce the potential liability to IHT on his estate.

He gives his cousin £400,000 in cash in May 2009. His cousin then purchases an apartment in Portrush in January 2010 for £650,000. P Stamp visits the property for a week in Easter 2010 and decides that he would like to spend each summer (for six months of the year) at the property from 1 April 2014. His cousin does not charge P Stamp for the use of the property. P. Stamp continues to maintain and live in his Bangor property for the remainder of the year.

The annual value of the Portrush property is £40,000 for 2014/15 and its open market value is £800,000. P. Stamp is a higher rate taxpayer.

Income tax:

P. Stamp has provided £400,000 which was used to buy the property that he occupies in the summer months.

£40,000 × £400,000/£800,000 × 6/12 months = £10,000 p.a. from 1 April 2014

Election to mitigate charge:

P. Stamp could elect by 31 January 2015 that the Portrush property is not to be subject to an income tax charge, but instead, for as long as the property is occupied by P. Stamp, that a proportion of the property value will be treated as part of his estate.

The percentage value is:

| £400,000 | (Consideration provided) |

| £800,000 | (Value at first occupation date) |

If P. Stamp ceases to occupy the property, then the proportion of the value of the property at that date will fall out of his estate after seven years.

Note that this would not have been an issue if the gift of cash had been given more than seven years before the donor first occupied the property.

If a property is only occupied incidentally, then no POAT charge arises. Examples of incidental occupation include the following:

- staying only two weeks in the property (one month if with the owner);
- social visits without overnight stays;
- domestic visits (e.g. babysitting); and
- temporary stays after medical treatment or whilst ill.

25.2.3 Territorial Scope

No charge to tax under the POAT rules can arise in relation to any person for any year of assessment during which they are not resident in the UK. If a person is non-UK resident but later becomes UK resident, the POAT charge will apply from the time they become UK resident.

If a person is resident in but domiciled outside the UK in any year of assessment, the POAT rules will only apply to land, chattels or intangible property situated in the UK. If the person subsequently becomes UK domiciled, the rules will operate by reference to the donor's worldwide assets.

In applying the POAT rules to a person who was at any time domiciled outside the UK, no regard should be had to any property which is, for the purposes of the Inheritance Tax Act (IHTA) 1984, excluded property in relation to them, i.e. the rules would not apply to non-UK assets in a trust that was set up whilst the donor was not UK domiciled.

A person is to be treated as domiciled in the UK at any time if they would be so treated for the purposes of IHTA 1984. Hence, the deemed domicile rules will apply for the purposes of this income tax charge.

Questions

Review Questions
(See Suggested Solution to Review Questions at the end of this textbook.)

Question 25.1

Sean has gathered substantial wealth in his lifetime and is considering disposing some of it to his son Shay. He is considering the following two options:

(a)   Giving his home to Shay, however he would continue to live in the house until his death. This is not expected to be any more than three years as Sean has just been diagnosed, sadly, with a terminal illness. Sean has lived in the house all his life. He does not intend to pay any rent to Shay.

(b)   Giving Shay £150,000 in May 2014, which he will use to buy a valuable painting Sean has had his eye on for a long time. Luckily the painting would still hang in Sean's house until his death, so he will have plenty of time to admire it.

Requirement
Briefly explain the capital gains tax and inheritance tax implications of these options.

Question 25.2

Diarmuid and Aisling, two unconnected persons, made the following cash gifts:

1.   Diarmuid gifted £185,000 to his daughter Seana, who used the money to purchase a flat for him to live in on his own. The annual rental value of the flat is £15,000 and Diarmuid paid £4,000 per annum to live in the property.

2.   Aisling gave £15,000 to her favourite niece Aine, who used the money to buy a state-of-the-art cinema and sound system, which was installed in the house where Aisling lived on her own.

Requirement
Briefly explain whether pre-owned asset tax charges arise as a result of these arrangements and, if so, calculate the amount(s) on which tax is charged annually.

Question 25.3

Sean generously gave £150,000 cash to his brother Steven in May 2014. Later that year Steven spotted a rare Andy Warhol print at an auction and he used all of the money his brother had given him to buy the print, which he hung in the hallway of his house.

Unfortunately his house was broken into on two occasions later that year – the print was recovered but Steven no longer considered his home to be safe. He then lent the print to Sean to hang in his house, as Sean had just installed a very sophisticated alarm system and it would be safer there. At that time, the print had increased in value to £190,000. Sean is an additional rate taxpayer.

Requirement

(a) Explain and calculate the tax charge arising in 2014/15 as a result of the above.

(b) Sean is unhappy when you advise him of this tax charge. Explain how the charge could be mitigated and the consequences of same.

Administration

Learning Objectives

After studying this chapter you will have developed competency in the following:

■ Demonstrate an awareness of the IHT administration system.
■ Advise on the payment of IHT, penalties and interest.
■ Advise on the filing of IHT returns.

26.1 Payment of IHT on Lifetime Gifts

Primary responsibility for the payment of any IHT due on lifetime gifts rests with the donor. The donor may delegate responsibility for payment of IHT to the donee. Where a donor makes a chargeable lifetime gift and does not delegate the responsibility for payment to the donee, the gift must be grossed up for the IHT that the donor has paid. The reason for this is that the donor's estate has also been reduced by the IHT due.

The actual gift is deemed to be net of any IHT due. As the lifetime rate of IHT is 20%, it is necessary to gross-up the chargeable element (after available deductions and utilisation of the nil rate band) by 20 (lifetime IHT)/80 (the post-IHT value of the gift).

The due date for payment of IHT on a chargeable lifetime transfer (CLT) is the later of:

1. six months from the end of the month in which the transfer takes place; and
2. 30 April in the following tax year.

26.2 Payment of IHT on Lifetime Gifts Following Death within Seven Years

The due date for IHT on a CLT is six months from the end of the month in which the death occurs.

26.3 Payment of IHT on Death Estate

The due date for IHT on the death estate is payable on the earlier of:

1. six months from the end of the month in which the transfer takes place, and
2. the date of delivery of the IHT400 return.

Interest will accrue for any IHT paid late (with the exception that no interest will accrue for the first six months if the IHT400 is filed before the six-month date).

26.4 Instalments

Any IHT payable on certain qualifying assets (referred to as qualifying property) may be paid in instalments if a claim is made to HMRC. If a claim is made, the IHT is payable in 10 equal instalments with the first instalment falling due on the normal due date.

It should be noted that no claim for the instalment option may be made if the donor agrees to pay any IHT due on the lifetime gift. Furthermore, if there is IHT due in respect of a lifetime gift that becomes payable following the death of the donor, the instalment option will only be available if the donee still owns the asset. The only exception to this rule is that, where the donee has sold business property that does not qualify for full business property relief (BPR) and reinvests the proceeds in acquiring replacement business property, then the right to pay IHT in instalments is preserved.

Depending on the type of property transferred, the instalments may be either 'interest-bearing' or 'interest-free'. As the name suggests, interest-free instalments are more attractive as interest only accrues from each instalment date, whereas interest accrues from the normal due date for interest-bearing instalments. For interest-bearing instalments an interest charge is added at each instalment date based on the balance of unpaid IHT at the time.

Generally, the interest-free instalment option is available for transfers of land qualifying for APR, shares in trading companies and for a business or partnership share.

Qualifying property for the purposes of paying IHT by instalments is restricted to land or buildings, certain shareholdings, and a business or partnership share.

The instalment option is available in respect of all land and buildings, wherever situated. Generally, if BPR is available the instalment option is not relevant to the transfer of a business or partnership share. It may be relevant where the minimum period of ownership test has not been satisfied for BPR.

The rules to determine whether shares are qualifying property are a little more complex, and these are now considered below. There are four cases in which the instalment option may be available:

1. Shareholdings which gave the owner control of a company (and, for this purpose, related property is also taken into account to determine whether the company is under control of the donor) are qualifying property. The shares may be either quoted or unquoted.
2. Unquoted shares where the IHT payable on their transfer represents more than 20% of the total IHT payable on the estate.
3. Unquoted shares with a value for IHT purposes of greater than £20,000 and which represent at least 10% of the voting rights of the company.

OR

4. Unquoted shares where the executors have insufficient funds with which to settle the IHT due (known as a hardship claim). This is a subjective test and is normally only considered as a last resort if cases 1. to 3. above are not viable.

Whether the instalments are interest-free or interest-bearing will depend on whether the shares are in a trading company as noted above.

26.5 Filing of Returns

An IHT100 should be filed by the donor for any CLT within 12 months from the end of the month in which the gift takes place.

An IHT400 should be filed by the executors of the estate for any CLT and failed PETs together with details of the death estate within 12 months from the end of the month in which the death occurs. The executors may also include details of any GWR but there is no statutory obligation to do so.

There are provisions which allow for small estates, referred to as "excepted estates", to be exempted from the obligation to file an IHT400.

26.6 Penalties

FA 2009 introduced new penalties for not filing IHT returns by the due date, as follows:

- £100 penalty if not filed by the due date;
- £10 per day, for up to 90 days (but only if HMRC decides that the penalty should be payable and issues a notice to that effect);
- 5% of the tax due (or £300 if greater) if filed later than six months from the due date;
- 5% of the tax due (or £300 if greater) if filed later than 12 months from the due date;
- 70% of tax due where a person fails to submit a return for over 12 months and has deliberately withheld information that HMRC requires to assess the tax due; and
- 100% where there has been concealment.

Example 26.1: Payments

Frank left his home in his will to his son Rick following his death on 2 February 2014. £25,000 of IHT was payable.

Explain the IHT payments to be made and advise what will happen if the house is sold in December 2014.

The IHT may be paid in 10 equal interest-bearing instalments commencing 31 August 2014. Ten instalments of £2,500 may be paid and interest will be due on the unpaid balance of IHT due at each instalment date.

If the house is sold in December 2014, the balance of IHT plus any accrued interest becomes immediately due.

Questions

Review Questions
(See Suggested Solution to Review Questions at the end of this textbook.)

Question 26.1

Please refer to question 24.4 (Fionn O'Shea) in Chapter 24.

Requirement
In relation to the gift made on 25 November 2010:

(a) What is the due date for payment of IHT on this lifetime CLT and filing of the relevant IHT 100?

(b) If there had been additional IHT payable on death in respect of that gift, what would the due date have been?

(c) Assuming the executors of the estate deliver the IHT 400 on 29 July 2015, on what date is payment of IHT on Fionn's death estate due? What is the due date for filing an IHT400?

Question 26.2

Trevor Smyth inherited Smyth Farm from his father in 1989. In 1988 Trevor's father granted a tenancy over the whole of the farm to the family-owned farming company, Smyth Farms Ltd, which has carried on a mixed farming business there ever since.

In 2005 Trevor gave cash of £226,000 to a discretionary trust for his children, David and Sarah, and he was totally excluded from any benefit. In 2008 Trevor bought Windy Farm and Primrose Farmhouse. At the same time, he retired from any active part in the farm business in order to live in Primrose Farmhouse with his long-term partner, Eileen, whom he married in 2010.

On 14 June 2010, as an engagement present for Eileen, Trevor transferred Primrose Farmhouse into his and Eileen's joint names. At that time Primrose Farmhouse was worth £900,000. A half share owned by either party should be discounted by 15%, valuers have advised.

Trevor died on 1 January 2015. At the time of his death his assets were:

1. His half share as beneficial joint tenant of Primrose Farmhouse – the whole was valued at £1,000,000.
2. Smyth Farm valued at £1,900,000, of which £700,000 is the value of the farmhouse and £300,000 is the value of Smyth Farm Stables (see below).
3. Windy Farm valued at £950,000.
4. 50% of the shares in Smyth Farms Ltd valued at £425,000.
5. Personal bank accounts and investments (net of funeral expenses and other debts owing at death) worth a total of £240,000.
6. A collection of shotguns and other shooting equipment with a value of £48,000.

Smyth Farm Stables, which comprises a riding school, stables, and some 30 acres used for horse grazing, was released from the agricultural tenancy some years ago. Sarah has since run Smyth Farm Stables as a riding school and horse livery business and paid her father rent.

The rest of Smyth Farm (comprising the farmhouse, farmland and a number of farm buildings used for storage and for shelter of farm animals) has remained within the tenancy granted in 1987 and has continued to be used for the Smyth Farms Ltd farming business. Since his father's move to Primrose Farmhouse, David has lived at the farmhouse on Smyth Farm, from where he has run Smyth Farms Ltd.

The executors' valuer has advised that HMRC is likely to successfully argue that, although the market value of the farmhouse at Smyth Farm is £700,000, its agricultural value is £600,000, but that the agricultural value of the rest of Smyth Farm is equal to its market value.

Windy Farm, which comprises only agricultural land and does not include any buildings, has also been occupied and farmed by Smyth Farms Ltd since Trevor's purchase. In this case there is no formal tenancy agreement. The valuer has advised that its agricultural value is the same as its market value.

Requirement

Calculate the inheritance tax payable as a result of Trevor's death, with comments explaining reliefs or exemptions available, if any.

Other Sundry Matters

Learning Objectives

After studying this chapter you will have developed competency in the following:

- The treatment of gifts from companies.
- Variations/altering dispositions made on death.
- Overseas aspects of IHT.
- Associated operations.

27.1 IHT Treatment of Gifts from Companies

Students must be aware where a close company (as defined in **Part One**) makes a transfer of value, that value may be apportioned among the participators according to their interests in the company and treated as a transfer of value by them for the purposes of IHT.

There is no apportionment of any value that is treated as the participator's income for the purposes of corporation tax or income tax. There is also no charge in respect of excluded property, i.e. an amount that would be apportioned to a non-UK domiciled individual and which is attributable to property outside the UK.

Any deemed transfer is reduced by the amount by which the value of the estate of any participator is increased by the company's transfer (for this purpose, students must exclude any rights or interests in the company, for example, allotment of shares in the company).

Any transfers of value caught by this legislation are treated as an immediate chargeable lifetime transfer (CLT) and not as a potentially exempt transfer (PET). As they are "deemed" transfers, the lifetime exemptions are generally not available. However, the legislation specifically provides that the annual exemption is available against such transfers, as is the spousal exemption to the extent that the estate of the spouse/civil partner is increased.

A change in the rights or number of shares held by a participator in a close company will also be considered to be a transfer of value. This is a deemed disposition and will also be treated as an immediate CLT and not as a PET. As the transfer is a deemed disposition rather than a deemed transfer of value, all the exemptions are available against the resulting transfer of value.

> **Example 27.1**
> Delta Ltd has an issued share capital of 100 shares, Richard owns 60 shares and Sean owns 40.
>
> 60 shares are issued to Richard's daughter and 40 to Sean's son.
>
> Richard now has 60 shares out of 200 and has lost control of the company. Sean now has a "non-influential" 20% holding compared to his "influential" 40% holding. The values of both Richard and Sean's shareholding in the company have substantially diminished and each has made a transfer of value.

27.2 Double Tax Relief for Overseas Taxes Suffered

Relief for any overseas IHT is generally given under the provisions of a tax treaty, or more commonly by way of unilateral relief. Double tax relief is most commonly available where a UK domiciled individual dies whilst owning foreign property.

Unilateral relief is available in the UK for the overseas tax suffered and will be given as the lower of the overseas tax payable or the UK IHT due on the foreign asset. For this purpose, it will be necessary to calculate the "estate rate" to determine the UK IHT payable in respect of the foreign asset. Any unrelieved foreign tax is effectively wasted.

27.3 Deed of Disclaimer/Variation

If a beneficiary is entitled to receive assets on the death of the donor, the potential recipient is under no legal obligation to accept the gift. Instead, the beneficiary may disclaim the gift. If this is done by way of formal written deed, the asset passes to the residuary beneficiary of the estate.

The potential beneficiary must have received no benefit from the property before it is disclaimed. For example, if the potential recipient has received some dividend income from shares, then the gift cannot be disclaimed

If the potential recipient would prefer the gift to pass to a nominated person, then they may use a deed of variation to achieve this objective.

If a valid deed is made, the gift is treated as passing directly from the original donor to the revised beneficiary for IHT purposes. The original potential donor is not treated as having made a transfer of value.

In order to make a valid deed of disclaimer/variation, all of the following conditions must be made:

- it must be made in writing, normally in the form of a deed;
- it must be signed by the person making the variation/disclaimer;
- it should include a statement that section 142 IHTA 1984 and section 62 TCGA 1992 apply to the variation/disclaimer; and
- it must be made within two years from the date of death of the original donor.

Normally, no consent is required to enter into a disclaimer/variation; the only exception is where the amount of IHT payable by the estate is increased by the disclaimer/variation.

Where no section 142 IHTA 1984 statement is included, the act of variation or disclaimer is a PET/CLT depending on who the new recipient of the asset is. CGT may also fall due if there is a significant period between the date of death (where the property transfers and the CGT base cost is the probate value) and the later variation/disclaimer.

In order to ignore the CGT disposal, the statement that section 62 TCGA 1992 applies should be made.

Please note that the section 142 and section 62 statements are not mandatory and in certain cases they need not be made. An example would be where a small capital gain would arise which would be covered by the annual exemption.

Deeds of variation and disclaimer are very useful post-death planning tools. They can be used to derive the maximum benefit from any spouse NRB (e.g. where the entire estate is originally intended to pass to the surviving spouse and there is an unused NRB; this is less important nowadays, with the transfer of the unused NRB available to the surviving spouse) and for transferring bequests to the surviving spouse for later transfer as a PET (e.g. where the entire estate would be immediately chargeable and the surviving spouse may survive for more than seven years (or three to benefit from taper relief)).

27.4 Associated Operations (section 268)

All associated operations are considered as one disposition for IHT purposes. Associated operations are:

1. two or more operations which affect the property whilst other operations affect other property directly or indirectly representing the property; or
2. any two operations, one of which is affected, with reference to the other, or with a view to enable the other to be affected.

These rules are quite powerful anti-avoidance in that they prevent a donor from reducing the value of their estate by earlier action(s) which are designed to depress the value of their estate for IHT purposes.

Specific rules apply where a transfer of value is made by associated operations which are carried out at different times. These treat the transfer of value as being made at the time of the last associated operation.

Value

The transfer of value made through associated operations is usually the overall loss to the transferor's estate measured at the time of the last operation.

However, if any of the earlier operations also constitutes a transfer of value by the transferor, deduct the value transferred by the earlier operation(s) (so far as that value is not entitled to spouse or civil partner exemption from the overall amount). The case of *Macpherson and another v. CIR* (1988) involved associated operations. In this case it was decided that there must be a gratuitous intent on the part of the donor. For this purpose, it should be noted that if any associated transaction is entered into which confers a gratuitous benefit, then the anti-avoidance rules apply.

Example 27.2

Albert has a house with vacant possession worth £60,000.

Albert grants a controlled tenancy of it to Baxter at full rent. At this point the value is reduced to £42,000 but no liability to IHT then arises because there is no gratuitous intent. Albert has incurred a loss to his estate from £60,000 to £42,000, but he has not made a transfer of value. It is nevertheless a relevant operation for any later transfer.

Two years later, the house is worth £70,000 with vacant possession. Albert gives Baxter the freehold reversion which is a gratuitous gesture.

The two dispositions affect the same property and through the associated operations rule they are combined together. Consequently, tax can be charged on the full transfer of value of £70,000 at the time of the gift of the freehold reversion.

Questions

Review Questions
(See Suggested Solution to Review Questions at the end of this textbook.)

Question 27.1

You recently meet with the client of a new company you act for. Stewart Desmond is the sole shareholder of Desmond Engineering Limited and he wishes to discuss the tax implications of a transaction he is contemplating. He acquired his 100% shareholding in 1994 at a cost of £10,000. The company pays corporation tax at main rate and has a 31 March period end. The following is an extract of the discussion:

"As you know, the company has a plot of land which I would like to take out of the company in order to sell it on to an interested third party. The sale should be concluded by the end of April 2014. I recently obtained an independent valuation of the property in the amount of £625,000, but I would like to transfer the warehouse out of the company to myself for £350,000. The company only paid £100,000 for the plot in June 2000."

Requirement
Outline the corporation tax, inheritance tax and capital gains tax implications of the above proposed transaction.

Part Four
Stamp Duty

Introduction and General Principles

The Chartered Accountants Ireland *Code of Ethics* applies to all aspects of a Chartered Accountant's professional life, including dealing with stamp duty issues. As outlined at the beginning of this book, further information regarding the principles in the *Code of Ethics* is set out in **Appendix 2**.

28.1 Background

HMRC's Stamp Taxes Office is the oldest part of HMRC, having celebrated its 300th anniversary in 1994. The office is responsible for the assessment and collection of stamp duty, stamp duty land tax (SDLT) and stamp duty reserve tax (SDRT).

28.2 Charges to Stamp Duty

Up until 1 December 2003, stamp duty was a tax payable on documents which transfer certain kinds of property, and on some other legal documents. "Property" meant all items capable of being owned (i.e. not just houses and land); thus all transfers of property were subject to duty. However, where property could be merely handed over (known legally as "passing by delivery"), there was no charge to stamp duty because there was no document executed on which to charge the duty. Thus stamp duty applied to a conveyance, transfer or a lease of land, where the instrument was executed prior to 1 December 2003.

From 1 December 2003, stamp duty only applies to the transfers of stock/shares and marketable securities which are transferred by a stock transfer form and to certain transfers of interest in partnerships. Stamp duty is charged on instruments (written documents). From that same date, land transactions are subject to stamp duty land tax (SDLT).

The transfer of shares is charged to stamp duty at 0.5% of the consideration unless they fall within one of the specific exemptions mentioned below. It should be noted that this duty is rounded to the nearest £5.

From 13 March 2008, instruments transferring stock or marketable securities that were previously chargeable with £5 stamp duty are exempt. Legislation was also introduced which brought in a consideration threshold of £1,000 beneath which instruments transferring stock or marketable securities on sale are no longer chargeable to stamp duty. Most will not need to be presented to HMRC for stamping and may be sent direct to Companies Registry.

28.3 Exemptions

The exemptions from stamp duty are primarily for transfers where there is no consideration and these include:

1. gifts;
2. divorce arrangements or dissolution of civil partnership;
3. property or shares acquired through a will or variation of a will;
4. changes in trustees;
5. property (or shares in property) acquired on entering into marriage or a civil partnership from a spouse or civil partner; and
6. transfers that a liquidator makes as settlement to shareholders when a business is wound up.

Sales of Government securities and most company loan stock are exempt from stamp duty.

28.4 Administration

Stamp duty is normally payable by the purchaser. Failure to present a document for stamping is not an offence. However, an unstamped document can neither be relied upon nor used for legal purposes, such as registering a transfer of ownership or production as evidence in Court, except in a criminal case. Previously, this has been used as a means of enforcing the payment of stamp duty.

If a document is not stamped within 30 days of its execution, or within 30 days of being brought into the UK if it was executed outside the UK (and does not relate to UK land), a penalty may be imposed. Prior to 1 April 2009, where a document was not stamped within one year of the end of the relevant 30-day period, the maximum penalty was the lower of £300 or the amount of the duty. Where the delay was longer, the penalty was the greater of £300 or the duty. However, as stated earlier in previous chapters, from 1 April 2009 a new civil penalty regime applies for incorrect returns and this has been extended to stamp duty, SDLT and SDRT.

The new penalty regime focuses on the behaviour of the taxpayer, e.g. a company acting through its directors and officers. Where a company has made a mistake in a SDLT or SDRT return submitted to HMRC, but has taken reasonable care in the preparation of that return, no penalty will be applied by HMRC.

In their *Compliance Handbook*, HMRC state that appointing a tax adviser does not automatically mean that the company has taken reasonable care in the preparation of a return. The tax advisor should be competent and qualified. The company still bears responsibility for the return and the director is expected, within his ability and competence, to make sure that the return which he is signing is correct. As stamp duty and SDLT are considered to be "duties", rather than "taxes", and much of the legislation requires a knowledge of UK law (e.g. land law for SDLT), it is advisable for a solicitor to be involved in preparing the necessary returns.

The categories of behaviour where penalties will be imposed are:

1. careless (failure to take reasonable care);
2. deliberate but not concealed (the inaccuracy is deliberate but there are no arrangements to conceal it); and
3. deliberate and concealed (the inaccuracy is deliberate and there are arrangements to conceal it).

Once HMRC has categorised the "behaviour" of the taxpayer, the potential lost revenue (PLR) will be computed. The penalty imposed is based on a percentage of PLR. The PLR is the additional amount of tax due or payable as a result of correcting the inaccuracy.

However, HMRC may apply reductions to the proposed penalty where the company has disclosed the inaccuracy. Disclosure is split into two types (unprompted and prompted), with greater reductions being given where the company makes a disclosure which has not been prompted by HMRC.

HMRC states in its *Compliance Handbook* that a disclosure is unprompted if it is made at a time when the person making it has no reason to believe that HMRC has discovered or is about to discover the inaccuracy.

The ranges of percentage penalties which will be applied by HMRC to the PLR are based on the behaviour of the taxpayer and the extent of the disclosure. These are detailed in **Chapter 1**.

If paid late, interest is chargeable from 30 days after the date of execution, whether the document was executed in the UK or not.

28.5   Consideration

The consideration subject to duty is any money or money's worth provided by the purchaser. Where the payment of the consideration is subject to a contingency, it is assumed that the contingency is satisfied. On the other hand, any contingency that would result in a reduction of the consideration is assumed not to occur. Where the consideration is unascertainable at the time of the transaction, it must be estimated. For example, the shares in a company may be sold for a fixed amount plus a contingent amount (typically based on the company reaching certain financial targets in the periods after the sale). At the time of the sale, the purchaser of the shares will be required to pay stamp duty at 0.5% on the fixed consideration plus the best estimate of the amount of the contingent consideration.

Any changes to the consideration caused by future events must be notified to HMRC, and duty will be paid or repaid as appropriate.

29

Stamp Duty Reserve Tax

Learning Objectives

After studying this chapter you will have developed competency in the following:

■ Advise on the impact of stamp duty reserve tax.

29.1 General Principles

Stamp duty reserve tax (SDRT) was introduced in 1986 to deal with transactions in shares where no instrument of transfer was executed and which were therefore outside the scope of stamp duty. It is a transaction tax, charged on "agreements to transfer chargeable securities", unlike stamp duty which is charged upon documents. This would generally be in situations where the shares are acquired through the stock market or a stockbroker.

SDRT thus applies to paperless share transactions (including electronic transactions) instead of stamp duty and applies to agreements to transfer chargeable securities for consideration in money or money's worth.

29.2 Items Liable to SDRT

SDRT is payable on paperless transactions when a person buys:

1. shares in a UK company;
2. shares in a foreign company with a share register in the UK;
3. an option to buy shares;
4. rights arising from shares already owned; and
5. an interest in shares, like an interest in the money made from selling them.

Finance Act 2014 sees the abolition of the SDRT charge on UK unit trust schemes and UK open-ended investment companies with effect from 30 March 2014. It also confirmed that SDRT and stamp duty on shares in companies admitted to trading on recognised growth markets (e.g. AIM) is abolished from 28 April 2014.

29.3   Rate Charged

SDRT is charged at 0.5% of the amount or value of the consideration for the sale. The tax charge arises on the date the agreement is made or becomes unconditional.

Once again, the sale of government securities and most company loan stock is exempt.

29.4   Payment of SDRT

Many paperless share transactions that SDRT arises on are carried out electronically through CREST, the electronic settlement and registration system administered by Euroclear. CREST automatically deducts the SDRT and sends it to HMRC. CREST is then paid by the stockbroker who will bill the individual for the SDRT and their own fees.

If the transaction occurs 'off-market' (e.g. shares transferred outside of CREST and held by a nominee like a bank), a stockbroker deals with this type of transaction and pays the SDRT direct to HMRC.

However, if the individual deals with it themselves, they must notify HMRC about the transaction and make the payment. This also applies where units in unit trusts are purchased from anyone other than a fund manager.

29.5   Deadline for Notifying and Paying HMRC

When shares are bought off-market, the purchaser must notify HMRC about the transaction and pay the SDRT by the "due date", which is the seventh day of the month after the month in which they are bought. For example, if shares or units are bought on 18 April, the purchaser must notify HMRC and pay the SDRT on or before 7 May.

If payment is not made by the due date, interest will arise from the date the SDRT was due until the date when it is paid. Penalties may also apply, as detailed in **Chapter 28**.

Stamp Duty Land Tax

Learning Objectives

After studying this chapter you will have developed competency in the following:

- Advise on the impact of stamp duty land tax (SDLT), including:
  - when SDLT is chargeable;
  - the treatment of lease premiums;
  - group relief;
  - reconstruction and acquisition relief.

30.1 General Principles and Background

Stamp duty land tax (SDLT) was introduced by FA 2003 and became effective from 1 December 2003. It was designed to replace the then current stamp duty on land and buildings.

SDLT is thus a modern transaction tax on land transactions involving any estate, interest, right or power in or over land in the UK. It should be noted that documents evidencing land transactions effected on or after 1 December 2003 and chargeable to SDLT will no longer be physically stamped.

30.2 What and Who is Chargeable

SDLT applies to land transactions. An acquisition can take the form of the creation, surrender, release or variation of a "chargeable interest".

A "chargeable interest" means:

1. an estate, interest, right or power in or over land in the UK; or
2. the benefit of an obligation, restriction or condition affecting the value of any such estate, interest, right or power, other than an "exempt interest".

The chargeable consideration for the purpose of SDLT comprises anything given for the transaction that is money or money's worth, of which cash is by far the most common form. However, chargeable consideration can also be non-monetary, such as:

1. the release or assumption of a debt;
2. works or services; and
3. the transfer of other property.

As a general rule, any non-monetary consideration should be valued at its market value, unless otherwise provided. **SDLT is payable by the purchaser**.

30.3   Exemptions

Certain interests in land are exempt interests and as a result are not chargeable to SDLT. The following land transactions are exempt:

1.   Transactions where there is no chargeable consideration (except where there is a gift to a connected company).
2.   Certain transactions following a person's death (variations of a will or intestacy within two years of death for no consideration).
3.   Certain transactions on the ending of a marriage or a civil partnership (divorce, annulment or judicial separation).
4.   Transfers to charities if the land is to be used for charitable purposes.
5.   The grant of a lease by a registered social landlord in certain specific situations.

30.4   When SDLT is Chargeable

The fact that a purchaser enters into a contract for a land transaction does not automatically crystallise a liability to SDLT.

Generally, a contract governing a land transaction, which is to be completed by a conveyance, will be chargeable on completion. However, where such a contract is "substantially performed" before it is formally completed, the contract is treated as if it were itself the transaction provided for in the contract. In this case, the date of substantial performance is the effective date.

Broadly, substantial performance is the point at which:

1.   any payment of rent is made;
2.   payment of most of the consideration other than rent is made; or
3.   the purchaser is entitled to possession of the subject matter of the transaction.

Where a purchaser, B, transfers his rights under a contract for a land transaction (the original contract) to a third party, C, the charge to B depends on whether completion or substantial performance of the original contract takes place before completion or substantial performance of the secondary contract.

If completion or substantial performance of the original contract takes place at the same time as, and in connection with, completion or substantial performance of the secondary contract, then it is disregarded.

This means that there is no charge on B, and no requirement for B to submit a land transaction return. This is often referred to as "sub-sale relief".

It is immaterial for SDLT purposes whether the transfer of the chargeable interest to C is effected by one document or two documents, provided that both documents take effect at the same time and there is no intervening event. Where both documents require a registration, a covering letter to the appropriate registry may be needed.

On the other hand, if the completion or substantial performance of the original contract takes place in advance of completion or substantial performance of the secondary contract, then there will be a charge on B.

30.5 Rates of SDLT

The rate of SDLT is a percentage of the chargeable consideration for the transaction, the amount being rounded down to the nearest pound.

The percentage is determined by whether the land in question is entirely residential or is wholly or partly non-residential, and by the amount of the consideration. It should be noted that, where the transaction is linked to another chargeable transaction, then the rate of tax is determined by the reference to the sum of all linked chargeable transactions. (This is an anti-avoidance measure to prevent purchasers splitting sales to keep each part below the relevant threshold.) Transactions which are linked can be reported on the same land transaction return and the purchasers will be treated as joint or common purchasers.

30.5.1 Rates Tables

The rates of SDLT for land transactions are:

Table A – Residential

Chargeable consideration	Percentage
Up to £125,000 (temporarily increased to £175,000 until 31 December 2009 – see below)	0%
Over £125,000 (£175,000 until 31 December 2009) to £250,000	1%
Over £250,000 to £500,000	3%
Over £500,000 to £1,000,000	4%
Over £1,000,000 (from 6 April 2011)	5%
Over £2,000,000 (from 21 March 2012)	7%*
Over £500,000 (from 20 March 2014)	15%**

Table B – Non-residential/Mixed Use

Chargeable consideration	Percentage
Up to £150,000 (and annual rent under £1,000)	0%
Up to £150,000 (and annual rent is £1,000 or more)	1%
Over £150,000 to £250,000	1%
Over £250,000 to £500,000	3%
Over £500,000	4%

*15% if purchase by a company (or by a partnership including a company) or collective investment scheme enveloping the property.

**The 15% SDLT rate applied to residential properties purchased by certain non-natural persons (e.g. a company, etc. as highlighted above) will be extended to properties purchased for over £500,000 with effect from 20 March 2014.

Once the rate of SDLT has been ascertained, it applies to the whole transaction and not just the amount above the band threshold.

Example 30.1

Yong Mei buys a house in Belfast for £275,000 in November 2014. What is the SDLT payable by Yong Mei?

SDLT = £275,000 @ 3% = £8,250

30.5.2 New Rate for Residential Properties

FA 2012 saw the introduction of a new rate of 7% for purchases of residential property where the consideration was more than £2 million, effective from 21 March 2012. A higher rate of 15% was also introduced from the same date applying to UK residential property where the consideration exceeds £2 million and the acquiring persons are certain types of non-natural persons, i.e. companies, partnerships (with one or more corporate members) and collective investment schemes (including unit trusts). The threshold at which the 15% rate applies is reduced from £2 million to £500,000 for transactions on or after 20 March 2014.

30.5.3 SDLT Reform of Rules for Bulk Purchases

Legislation was introduced in FA 2011 to provide relief for purchasers of residential property acquiring interests in more than one dwelling. Where the relief is claimed, the rate of SDLT is determined not by the aggregate consideration but instead by the mean consideration (i.e. by the aggregate consideration divided by the number of dwellings), subject to a minimum rate of 1%.

The relief is available for transactions the effective date of which is on or after 19 July 2011 and which is not linked to any transaction with an effective date before that date.

The relief may be claimed in respect of a transaction which is a "relevant transaction" defined as either of the following:

1. a transaction, the main subject matter of which includes interests in more than one dwelling; or
2. a transaction which is one of a number of linked transactions, the main subject matter of which includes interests in at least one dwelling and where one or more transactions linked to it includes interests in at least one other dwelling.

Example 30.2

Paula purchases the freehold of a new block of 20 flats for £2.5 million.

The transaction is a relevant transaction for the purposes of the new relief as it involves the acquisition of more than one dwelling – i.e. the 20 flats. Therefore, the freehold is treated as if it were interests in the individual dwellings and the chargeable consideration is divided by the number of dwellings to give a chargeable consideration of £125,000 per flat.

Whilst this is below the normal 0% SDLT threshold, the minimum rate of tax under the relief is 1%. SDLT due is, therefore, 1% of £2.5 million = £25,000.

30.6 Temporary Exemption on SDLT

From 3 September 2008 until 31 December 2009, there was also a temporary exemption (holiday) from SDLT for acquisitions of residential property worth not more than £175,000. From 1 January 2010, this reverted back to £125,000, as detailed in Table A at **Section 30.5.1**.

The exemption was available for the acquisition of major interests in land (other than grants of leases for less than 21 years, or the assignment of leases with less than 21 years to run).

The conditions to be met in order for the exemption to apply were that the acquisition must have:

1. consisted entirely of residential property; and
2. been for a chargeable consideration of not more than £175,000.

The exemption was available where the effective date of the land transaction (normally the date of completion, but see earlier) was on or after 3 September 2008 **and** before 31 December 2009. The exemption was claimed using a return form, SDLT1.

When answering questions, watch carefully for dates of acquisition to determine if any of the special reliefs detailed are available or for the 7% rate applying to residential properties costing over £2 million from 21 March 2012.

30.7 Lease Premiums

When someone buys a leasehold property, the SDLT they have to pay depends on whether it is an existing lease or a new one. If it is an existing lease (an "assigned lease"), they only have to pay SDLT on the purchase price as if they'd bought a freehold property. The same rates, thresholds and conditions for deciding whether to complete an SDLT return also apply.

How SDLT is calculated on the grant of a new lease depends on the "premium" (the lump sum paid to buy a new lease), the rent payable under the lease, and whether it is a residential or non-residential lease.

30.7.1 Residential Property

SDLT on the premium paid for a lease of residential property is charged at a fixed percentage rate using Table A in **Section 30.5.1**. The amount of any rental payments is not taken into account in determining the amount of tax payable on the premium. However, if the net present value of the rent is more than the residential property SDLT threshold of £125,000, the buyer, including first-time buyers, has to pay SDLT on the rent as well as on the premium. In this case, the tax is calculated at a flat rate of 1% on the amount of the net present value that exceeds the SDLT threshold.

For example, if the net present value of the rent under a lease is £180,000 then the amount of the net present value that is over the £125,000 threshold is £55,000. SDLT has to be paid on this £55,000 at the rate of 1%. This is added to the amount of SDLT that is due on the premium.

30.7.2 Non-residential Property

For non-residential properties, the amount of SDLT due when someone buys a new non-residential lease depends on the amounts of the premium and rent they pay under the lease.

If the annual rent for the lease (not the net present value) is less than £1,000, the buyer pays SDLT on the premium at the same rate as they would pay on the purchase price of a freehold non-residential property, which means they will only have to pay SDLT if the premium is more than the threshold.

If the annual rent exceeds £1,000, the buyer has to pay SDLT on the whole of the premium. The zero rate of SDLT doesn't apply, even if the premium is within the £150,000 non-residential threshold. Therefore, students should use the 1% rate to work out the tax on a premium up to £250,000 and the higher rates if it is more than this.

For example, if someone paid a premium of £130,000 and an annual rent of £1,500, they would have to pay SDLT at the rate of 1% on the whole of the premium. The tax due would be £1,300.

Also, in respect of non-residential property, the lease rental payable during the term of a lease will also be charged to SDLT to the extent that the net present value of the rental exceeds the thresholds above in Table B. The rate of charge is 1% of the excess above the threshold.

30.8 Notification Threshold

Budget 2008 announced changes in requirements for notification of land transactions to HMRC. These changes had effect for transactions with an effective date on or after 12 March 2008.

The changes raised the threshold for notification of non-leasehold transactions involving major interests in land from a chargeable consideration of £1,000 to £40,000. The changes also affect transactions involving leases for a term of seven years or more, which will now only have to be notified where any chargeable consideration other than rent is equal to or more than £40,000 or where the rent is equal to or more than £1,000.

As a result of these changes, if the transaction is below the threshold it is not necessary to complete either form SDLT1 Land Transaction Return or form SDLT 60 Self Certificate.

It also means that there are **no circumstances** in which an SDLT 60 (certificate stating that no SDLT is due) is required in order for documents to be registered.

It should be noted that the acquisition of a chargeable interest other than a major interest in land remains notifiable only where there is a chargeable consideration for which SDLT is due at a rate of at least 1%.

Hence, the new notification threshold differs from the previous version in two important respects, namely:

1. The threshold for notification in relation to major interests in residential property has risen from £1,000 to £40,000.
2. There is now a threshold for mixed and non-residential property, where none previously existed.

30.9 Group Relief

There is potential relief from SDLT where land and buildings are transferred within a group of companies (or bodies corporate), provided certain conditions are met. This relief allows groups to move property for commercial reasons without having to consider the SDLT implications. The two group companies do not necessarily have to be resident in the UK.

Thus, if the purchaser and vendor of a chargeable interest are companies and, at the effective date of the land transaction, they are both members of the same group, relief from SDLT may be claimed by the purchaser. This is so that SDLT is not paid on property transfers within groups. However, the purchasing company **may** choose to pay the tax **by not claiming** the relief.

In the situation where group relief from SDLT has been claimed on a land transaction (the relevant transaction), any subsequent withdrawal of the relief must be reported by the purchaser on a **new** land transaction return.

A new land transaction return should also be submitted if the purchaser ceases to be a member of the same group as the vendor:

1. before the end of a period of three years beginning with the effective date of the relevant land transaction; or
2. in pursuance of, or in connection with, arrangements made before the end of a period of three years beginning with the effective date of the relevant land transaction.

For the purposes of this relief, companies are members of the same group if one is the 75% subsidiary of the other or both are 75% subsidiaries of a third company. One company, B, is the 75% subsidiary of another company, A, if company A satisfies the following conditions:

1. it is the beneficial owner (either directly or through another company) of not less than 75% of the ordinary share capital of company B;
2. it is beneficially entitled to not less than 75% of the profits available for distribution to equity holders of company B; and
3. it would be beneficially entitled to not less than 75% of any assets of company B available for distribution to its equity holders on a winding up.

Also, the term "arrangements" includes any scheme, agreement or understanding, whether or not legally enforceable.

30.9.1 Restrictions on Availability of Group Relief

Where the purchasing company (purchaser) and selling company (vendor) are in the same group (as defined above), **no** group relief will be available to the purchaser in three situations, which are as follows:

1. Where arrangements are in existence which would mean that a person, or persons, could obtain control of the purchaser **but** not the vendor. This restriction operates where the arrangements are in existence at the effective date of the land transaction. The arrangements must be such that a person, or persons, could obtain control of the purchaser on or after the effective date of the transaction. It does not matter whether the arrangements are actually used to transfer control.
2. Where a non-group member, or person, is to provide or receive, directly or indirectly, all or part of the consideration for the transaction, and this is done in connection with, or in pursuance of, an arrangement.
3. Where, in connection with, or in pursuance of, an arrangement or arrangements, the purchaser ceases (or could cease) to be in the same group as the vendor.

30.9.2 Withdrawal of Group Relief

For the withdrawal of the relief to be considered at the time the purchaser ceases to be a member of the same group, the purchaser (or a relevant associated company) must hold either:

1. the chargeable interest that was acquired under the relevant transaction; **or**
2. a chargeable interest derived from the chargeable interest acquired under the relevant transaction; **and**
3. that the chargeable interest has not subsequently been acquired at market value by means of a chargeable transaction where group relief was available **but** not claimed.

For the purposes of the withdrawal of relief, a relevant associated company is a company that:

▪ is a member of the same group as the purchaser immediately before the purchaser leaves the same group as the vendor; or
▪ ceases to be a member of the same group as the vendor as a consequence of the purchaser ceasing to be a member.

30.9.3 Vendor Leaving Group

The above withdrawal of relief mainly concerned the situation where the purchaser left the group. HMRC has identified that there were avoidance schemes which circumvented the clawback provisions. This was achieved by structuring the transactions so that the vendor left the group first, thereby allowing the purchasing company to subsequently leave the group without there being any clawback of SDLT group relief.

The amendments brought in by FA 2008 will apply where the vendor leaves the group and there is a subsequent change in the control of the purchaser within a period of three years of the asset having been transferred. In these circumstances, HMRC has powers to link these two events and treat the purchaser as having left the group first (and thus the clawback provisions are applicable).

Group relief will not be clawed back where only the vendor leaves the group.

30.10 Reconstruction and Acquisition Relief

30.10.1 Reconstruction Relief

Reconstruction relief allows land and buildings to be transferred between two companies, as part of a transfer of an undertaking in exchange for shares, where there is no change of ownership, without any charge to SDLT, provided certain conditions are met.

This would apply, for example, in the situation where a company decided to split its existing business into two separate businesses.

The following conditions must be met:

1. The consideration for the acquisition consists wholly or partly of the issue of non-redeemable shares in the acquiring company.
2. The shares must be issued to all the shareholders of the company being taken over (the target company). If the consideration consists partly of the issue of non-redeemable shares, this condition is only fulfilled if all of the balance of the consideration consists of the assumption or discharge, by the acquiring company, of liabilities of the target company.
3. After the acquisition has been made:
    (a) The shareholders of the acquiring company are all shareholders of the target company and vice versa.
    (b) For each shareholder, the proportion of shares held in one company is the same (or as nearly as may be the same) as the proportion of shares held in the other company.
4. The acquisition is for bona fide commercial reasons and is not part of a scheme or arrangement where the main purpose, or one of the main purposes, is the avoidance of a liability to tax (to include all taxes and not just SDLT).

Thus relief is not available, for example, where the target company is a company limited by guarantee, not having a share capital, or an unincorporated association.

30.10.2 Acquisition Relief

On purchasing all or part of the undertaking of another company (the target company), the acquiring company (the company acquiring the target company) may enter into a land transaction as part of, or in connection with, the transfer of the purchased undertaking.

This relief reduces the rate of tax from the relevant SDLT rate to a rate of 0.5%. The relief applies where a property is transferred as part of the acquisition provided certain conditions are met.

The conditions, all of which must be met, are that:

1. the consideration for the acquisition consists wholly or partly of the issue of non-redeemable shares in the acquiring company; and
2. the shares must be issued to:
    (a) the target company; or
    (b) any or all of the shareholders of the target company.

    If the consideration consists partly of the issue of non-redeemable shares, this condition is only fulfilled if all of the balance of the consideration consists of:
    (i) cash which does not exceed 10% of the nominal value of the non-redeemable shares issued for the transaction; or
    (ii) the assumption or discharge, by the acquiring company, of liabilities of the target company; or
    (iii) both (i) and (ii).
3. The acquiring company is not associated with any other company that is a party to arrangements with the target company relating to the shares issued to the target company as a result of the undertaking.

30.10.3 Withdrawal of Reconstruction and Acquisition Relief

Reconstruction and acquisition relief is withdrawn:

1. if control of the acquiring company changes within three years of the transaction; or
2. if there are arrangements put in place within that period which result in a change of control after the period of three years.

Questions

Review Questions (Chapters 28–30)
(See Suggested Solutions to Review Questions at the end of this textbook.)

Question 30.1

A client, Mr Symon Cawell, has been involved in a number of transactions during the tax year ended 5 April 2015 and has approached you in February 2015 for advice. Details of the transactions are as follows:

Transaction 1 – 11 October 2014 – Symon took on a newly executed lease on commercial property in a prime area with a premium payable of £575,000, and a net present value of the rent payable of £185,000.

Transaction 2 – 31 October 2014 – Symon's oldest son married in December having purchased a property on 31 October costing £225,000 which he and his wife are living in as their first home. This is the only property either party owns.

Transaction 3 – 12 December 2014 – Symon purchased government securities valued at £325,000.

Transaction 4 – 1 January 2015 – Symon recently lent £1,750,000 interest-free to a friend's Internet advertising company. The company is now proceeding with a reorganisation and, in order to settle the debt, Symon agreed to receive, as consideration for the debt, 1,750,000 10p shares issued by the company in full satisfaction of the original loan.

Transaction 5 – 12 January 2015 – Symon gifted shares in his trading company worth £565,000 to his only daughter who works alongside him and has helped him grow the business.

Requirement
In letter format to Mr Cawell, calculate the amount of stamp duty arising on each transaction (if any) and include details of any reliefs available. Provide explanations for your analysis.

Question 30.2

Armour Ltd owns 77.5% of Brent Ltd, and 82% of Destiny Ltd. Brent Ltd owns 51% of Gaston Ltd.
   On 1 September 2014, Armour Ltd sold the freehold of two warehouses, one for £750,000 to Destiny Ltd, and one for £120,000 to Gaston Ltd.
   On 1 January 2015, Armour Ltd sold 8% of its shares in Destiny Ltd to an unconnected third party. As of that date, both Destiny Ltd and Gaston Ltd continued to own the freeholds and remained in occupation of the warehouses.

Requirement
Explain the SDLT implications of these transactions, together with supporting calculations where necessary.

Question 30.3

Owen owns a commercial property that has an open market value of £350,000. There is an outstanding mortgage on the property of £50,000.

Requirement
Calculate the stamp duty due if he sells it to his son for £200,000 (both with and without the outstanding mortgage) or sells it to his son for full market value and uses the proceeds to pay off the mortgage.

Question 30.4

Please refer to Chapter 10, question 10.2.

Requirement
What are the stamp duty land tax implications of transferring the freehold property from Solar to Neptune?

Question 30.5

Apple Ltd owns 77.5% of Banana Ltd, and 85% of Date Ltd. Banana Ltd owns 51% of Grape Ltd. On 1 July 2014, Apple Ltd sold the freehold of two warehouses, one for £750,000 to Date Ltd, and one for £120,000 to Grape Ltd. Both Date Ltd and Grape Ltd continue to own the freeholds and remain in occupation of the warehouses.

Requirement
Explain the SDLT implications of these transactions and calculate any SDLT payable.

Administration

31.1 Duty to Deliver Land Transaction Return Form

The relevant legislation requires that, for every notifiable transaction completed or effectively completed, a land transaction return form SDLT1 must be delivered to HMRC within 30 days of the effective date of the transaction.

The return must include a self-assessment of the liability and be accompanied by payment of the SDLT due. It **must** be signed by the purchaser. Supplementary land transaction return forms may have to be completed in certain circumstances, e.g. if there were more than two purchasers or vendors or more than one piece of land, etc.

The return must be:

▨ in a prescribed form;
▨ contain the prescribed information; and
▨ include a declaration by the purchaser that the return is, to the best of their knowledge, correct and complete.

Interest is chargeable on unpaid tax from the relevant date until the date of payment. Prior to 1 April 2009, failure to deliver a land transaction return by the filing date resulted in a fixed rate penalty and could also have resulted in a liability to taxed-geared penalties. However, as discussed in **Chapters 1** and **28**, the new civil penalty regime was extended to SDLT from 1 April 2009. This is discussed in more detail below.

A notifiable transaction can be notified in any of the following ways:

1. electronically, using either the HMRC system or a system provided by an approved software provider; or
2. using paper form SDLT1 and, if necessary, the supplementary forms SDLT2, SDLT3 and SDLT4 (new style returns were issued by HMRC and must be used from 4 July 2011).

A return is required for all notifiable transactions even where there is no SDLT to pay or where a relief is being claimed, e.g. group relief.

31.2 Who is Chargeable?

The purchaser is responsible for submission of the Land Transaction Return (LTR) and payment of the SDLT due.

If there are joint purchasers, only a single LTR is required and this can be completed by any one of them. However, **each** purchaser must sign the declaration. If the purchaser is a partnership, the declaration must be signed by all of the partners or by a representative of the partnership nominated to HMRC.

Where there are joint purchasers, they are jointly liable for payment of the tax although that obligation can be discharged by any one of them.

31.3 Penalties

Under the regime prior to 1 April 2009, the purchaser would be faced with both flat-rate and tax-geared penalties in respect of non-compliance as follows:

31.3.1 Flat-rate Penalties

A purchaser who failed to deliver the LTR by the filing date would be liable to:

1. a flat-rate penalty of £100 if the LTR is delivered within three months after the filing date, or
2. £200 in any other case.

31.3.2 Tax-geared Penalties

A purchaser who is required to deliver a LTR in respect of a chargeable transaction and fails to do so within 12 months of the filing date is liable to a tax-geared penalty.

The penalty is an amount not exceeding the amount of tax chargeable in respect of the transaction (and this is in addition to the above flat-rate penalty).

Often the most appropriate way of encouraging the submission of a late LTR is for HMRC to make a determination. HMRC may also choose this option where it considers that a purchaser, from other information that it holds, should have made a LTR and the filing date has passed. In this situation, if the purchaser does not comply with the notice of determination within the specified period, HMRC may ask the Tax Tribunal to impose a daily penalty.

As discussed earlier, the new civil penalty regime applies to SDLT and SDRT from 1 April 2009.

The SDLT regime gives purchasers new and more clearly defined obligations and, accordingly, gives HMRC more clearly defined powers to ensure compliance with these obligations. SDLT is a 'process now–check later' regime, similar to self-assessment. The 'check later' aspect is supported by new enquiry and information powers.

31.4 Compliance Checks – an Overview

From 1 April 2010 HMRC has changed the way it carries out compliance checks for SDLT, stamp duty and SDRT. This is due to new legislation and processes introduced to make the tax system simpler and more consistent.

The changes include:

1. one set of powers to visit businesses to inspect premises, assets and records and ask taxpayers and third parties for information and documents;
2. important safeguards for taxpayers;
3. greater flexibility in setting record-keeping requirements; and
4. new time limits for assessments and claims which came fully into force in April 2011.

Questions

Review Questions

(See Suggested Solution to Review Questions at the end of this textbook.)

Question 31.1

Adam purchased his first house on 31 October 2014 for £150,000, funded by a bank mortgage of £120,000 and a deposit of £30,000.

Requirement

(a) What stamp duty land tax (SDLT) was due and why?
(b) What is the threshold of chargeable consideration above which a SDLT return is required for a residential property transaction?
(c) On the basis that Adam's purchase completed on 31 October 2014, on what date is the associated SDLT return due for filing?

Question 31.2

Please refer to Chapter 18, question 18.10.

Requirement

Calculate the stamp duty land tax payable on the sale of the Dungannon building. State who is responsible for this liability, the due date for payment of any liability that may arise and the filing date of the relevant return.

Question 31.3

Shaun is UK resident and is due to undertake the following transactions on 30 April 2014:

▧ Purchase of shares in Apple plc, a British company, for £950.
▧ Purchase of shares in Peaches plc, a British company, for £6,725.
▧ Purchase of shares in Blackberry SA, an Italian company, for £1,600.

Shaun is old fashioned. He likes to complete as much as possible on paper, so he will not use the electronic share trading systems and will therefore use hard copy share transfer forms for his purchases.

Requirement

Calculate the stamp duty due on the above transactions, providing explanations for your calculations. State the due date for payment of any liability that may arise and the filing date of the relevant stamp duty return.

Question 31.4

Requirement

Outline the stamp duty payable (if any) on the following:

(a) A transfer of UK unlisted shares worth £90,000 on the divorce of husband to wife.
(b) A sale of shares in a UK unlisted company for £524,000 to a registered UK charity.
(c) A sale of shares in a UK unlisted company for £150,000 between unconnected individuals.
(d) A sale of UK shares worth £895 between unconnected parties.
(e) A sale of shares in a UK unlisted company for £60,000 in cash and an agreement to waive £20,000 debt owed by the seller to the purchaser.

Taxation Reference Material for Tax Year 2014/15

Income Tax Rates

Band		Rate
£		%
0 – 2,880	Savings Starting Rate	10*
0 – 31,865	Basic Rate	20**
31,866 – 150,000	Higher Rate	40***
Over 150,000	Additional Rate	45****

* Only applicable to dividends and savings income. Applicable to savings income only where an individual's taxable non-savings income is below the Savings Starting Rate.

**Except dividends – 10%

***Except dividends – 32.5%

****Except dividends – 37.5%

Income Tax Allowances

Income tax personal and age-related allowances – 2014/15		
		£
Personal allowance*	Born after 5 April 1948	10,000
	Born after 5 April 1938 but before 6 April 1948	10,500
	Born before 6 April 1938	10,660
Married couples allowance (relief at 10%)	Born before 6 April 1935	N/A
	– maximum	8,165
	– minimum	3,140
Income limit for personal allowances (born before 6 April 1948)		27,000
Blind person's allowance		2,230
Maintenance payment relief allowance		3,140

*The personal allowance reduces where income is above £100,000 – by £1 for every £2 above the £100,000 limit. This reduction applies irrespective of age.

Car Benefit Percentage

CO_2 emissions (g/km) (round down to nearest 5g/km)	% of car's list price taxed	CO_2 emissions (g/km) (round down to nearest 5g/km)	% of car's list price taxed	CO_2 emissions (g/km) (round down to nearest 5g/km)	% of car's list price taxed	CO_2 emissions (g/km) (round down to nearest 5g/km)	% of car's list price taxed
Up to 75	5	130	19	160	25	190	31
94	11	135	20	165	26	195	32
95	12	140	21	170	27	200	33
100	13	145	22	175	28	205	34
105	14	150	23	180	29	210	35
110	15	155	24	185	30		
115	16						
120	17						
125	18						

Maximum percentage rate	35%
Non-electric cars with emissions of 75g/km or less (up to 5 April 2015)	5%*

For cars registered before 1 January 1998 the charge is based on engine size.

* Subject to the diesel surcharge where appropriate.

Car Fuel Benefit

Base figure   £21,700

Van Benefit

Van benefit   £3,090
Fuel benefit   £581

The charges will not apply if a "restricted private use condition" is met throughout the year.

Corporation Tax

Level of Profit		Rate
£0 – £300,000	Small profits rate	20%
£300,001 – £1,500,000	Marginal rate	21.25%
£1,500,001 +	Main rate	21%
Marginal fraction		1/400th

Capital Allowances

Plant and Machinery

Main pool	Writing down allowance	18%
Special rate pool	Writing down allowance	8%
Annual investment allowance (from 1 April 2014 to 31 December 2015)		£500,000
Enhanced capital allowances on energy saving and water saving plant and machinery		100%

Research & Development

	Rates for deduction	Rates for surrender of losses	ATL credit
SMEs	225%	14.5%	–
Large companies	130%	10%	10%

Motor Cars

Acquired before 6 April 2009

Non-expensive cars costing less than £12,000	WDA 25%	
Expensive cars costing at least £12,000	WDA 25%	Maximum £3,000

Acquired from 6 April 2009

CO_2 emissions up to 95g/km	First year allowance	100%
CO_2 emissions between 96g/km and 130g/km*	WDA	18%
CO_2 emissions over 130g/km*	WDA	8%

* 160g/km prior to 2013/14

Authorised Mileage Allowance Rates

Use of own vehicle:

Vehicle	Flat rate per mile with simplified expenses
Cars and goods vehicles first 10,000 miles	45p
Cars and goods vehicles after 10,000 miles	25p
Motorcycles	24p

Use of company car (rates from 1 March 2014):

Engine size	Petrol	LPG
1400cc or less	14p	9p
1401cc to 2000cc	16p	11p
Over 2000cc	24p	17p

Engine size	Diesel
1600cc or less	12p
1601cc to 2000cc	14p
Over 2000cc	17p

Pension Scheme Contribution Limits

Annual allowance*	£40,000
Lifetime allowances	£1,250,000
Maximum gross contribution that can qualify for tax relief without any earnings	£3,600
Lifetime allowance charge – if excess drawn as cash lump sum Lifetime allowance charge – if excess drawn as income	55% 25%
Annual allowance charge on excess – linked to individual's marginal tax rate	20%/40%/45%

*Any unused allowances can be carried forward for three years.

Individual Savings Accounts (ISAs)

2013/14	1 July 2014	6 April 2014
Overall annual investment limit	15,000	11,880
Comprising cash up to	15,000	5,940
Comprising balance in stocks and shares	15,000	11,880 maximum

Value-Added Tax

Registration limit – 1 April 2014	£81,000
Deregistration limit – 1 April 2014	£79,000
Standard rate – 4 January 2012	20%
Reduced rate	5.0%

Capital Gains Tax

Annual exemption	£11,000
Rate of tax for individuals – up to basic rate income	18%
Rate of tax for individuals – higher/additional rate income	28%
Rate of tax for trustees and personal representatives	28%
Rate of tax on gains subject to Entrepreneurs' Relief	10%
Entrepreneurs' Relief lifetime limit of gains	£10,000,000

Statutory Residence Test

Sufficient Ties Test

Where an individual has been resident in the UK for at least one of the previous three tax years:

Number of ties to the UK	Number of days in the UK to be resident
Four or more	Between 16 and 45 days inclusive
Three	Between 46 and 90 days inclusive
Two	Between 91 and 120 days inclusive
One	More than 120 days

Where an individual has not been resident in the UK for in any of the previous three tax years:

Number of ties to the UK	Number of days in the UK to be resident
All four	Between 46 and 90 days inclusive
Three	Between 91 and 120 days inclusive
Two	More than 120 days

Tax Credits

£ per year (unless stated)	2014/15 £
Working Tax Credit	
Basic element	1,940
Couple and lone parent element	1,990
30-hour element	800
Disabled worker element	2,935
Severe disability element	1,255
Childcare element of the Working Tax Credit	
Maximum eligible cost for one child	£175 per week
Maximum eligible cost for two or more children	£300 per week
Percentage of eligible costs covered	70%
Child Tax Credit	
Family element	545
Child element	2,750
Disabled child element	3,100
Severely disabled child element	1,255

Income Thresholds and Withdrawal Rates	
First income threshold	6,420
First withdrawal rate	41%
First threshold for those entitled to Child Tax Credit only	16,010
Income rise disregard	5,000
Income fall disregard	2,500

National Insurance Contributions

	Weekly £	Monthly £	Yearly £	Employee Class 1 (Primary) %	Employer Class 1 (Secondary) %
Lower earnings limit	111	481	5,772	Nil	Nil
Earnings threshold – primary	153	663	7,956	Nil	Nil
– secondary	153	663	7,956	Nil	Nil
Upper accrual point	770	3,337	40,040	12	13.8
Upper earnings limit	805	3,489	41,865	12	13.8
Above upper earnings limit	Above 805	Above 3,489	Above 41,865	2	13.8

		%
Class 1 employee (primary)	£0–£7,956 per year	Nil
	£7,957–£41,865 per year	12
	£41,865 and above per year	2
Class 1 employer (secondary)	£0–£7,956 per year	Nil
	£7,957 and above per year	13.8
Class 1A	Expenses and benefits	13.8
Class 1B	PAYE settlements	13.8
Class 2	Small earnings exception limit £2.75 per week	£5,885
Class 3	£13.90 per week	
Class 4	£0–£7,956 per year	% Nil
	£7,957–£41,865 per year	9
	£41,865 and above per year	2

Inheritance Tax

Rate	40%
Lower rate (from 6 April 2012 where 10% or more of deceased's net estate left to charity)	36%
Nil rate band	£325,000

Stamp Duty Land Tax

Rate	Residential	Non-residential
0%	£0 – £125,000	£0 – £150,000
1%	£125,000 – £250,000	£150,001 – £250,000
3%	£250,001 – £500,000	£250,001 – £500,000
4%	£500,001 – £1,000,000	£500,000 +
5%	£1,000,001 – £2,000,000	N/A
7%	£2,000,001 +	N/A
15%	£500,000 + where property is acquired by non-natural persons (e.g. companies)	N/A

Other Reliefs

Rent-a-Room Limit		£4,250
Venture Capital Trust	Rate @ 30%	Max. £200,000
Enterprise Investment Scheme	Rate @ 30%	Max. £1,000,000
Seed Enterprise Investment Scheme	Rate @ 50%	Max. £100,000
Non-domiciled Remittance Charge	For adult non-UK domiciliary after UK residence in seven or more of the previous nine years	Annual limit £30,000
	For adult non-UK domiciliary after UK residence in 12 or more of the previous 15 years	Annual limit £50,000

Rates of Interest

Official rate of interest   3.25% (from 6 April 2014)

UK Retail Price Indices

	Jan	Feb	Mar	Apr	May	Jun	Jul	Aug	Sep	Oct	Nov	Dec
1987	100.0	100.4	100.6	101.8	101.9	101.9	101.8	102.1	102.4	102.9	103.4	103.3
1988	103.3	103.7	104.1	105.8	106.2	106.6	106.7	107.9	108.4	109.5	110.0	110.3
1989	111.0	111.8	112.3	114.3	115.0	115.4	115.5	115.8	116.6	117.5	118.5	118.8
1990	119.5	120.2	121.4	125.1	126.2	126.7	126.8	128.1	129.3	130.3	130.0	129.9
1991	130.2	130.9	131.4	133.1	133.5	134.1	133.8	134.1	134.6	135.1	135.6	135.7
1992	135.6	136.3	136.7	138.8	139.3	139.3	138.8	138.9	139.4	139.9	139.7	139.2
1993	137.9	138.8	139.3	140.6	141.1	141.0	140.7	141.3	141.9	141.8	141.6	141.9
1994	141.3	142.1	142.5	144.2	144.7	144.7	144.0	144.7	145.0	145.2	145.3	146.0
1995	146.0	146.9	147.5	149.0	149.6	149.8	149.1	149.9	150.6	149.8	149.8	150.7
1996	150.2	150.9	151.5	152.6	152.9	153.0	152.4	153.1	153.8	153.8	153.9	154.4
1997	154.4	155.0	155.4	156.3	156.9	157.5	157.5	158.5	159.3	159.5	159.6	160.0
1998	159.5	160.3	160.8	162.6	163.5	163.4	163.0	163.7	164.4	164.5	164.4	164.4
1999	163.4	163.7	164.1	165.2	165.6	165.6	165.1	165.5	166.2	166.5	166.7	167.3
2000	166.6	167.5	168.4	170.1	170.7	171.1	170.5	170.5	171.7	171.6	172.1	172.2
2001	171.1	172.0	172.2	173.1	174.2	174.4	173.3	174.0	174.6	174.3	173.6	173.4
2002	173.3	173.8	174.5	175.7	176.2	176.2	175.9	176.4	177.6	177.9	178.2	178.5
2003	178.4	179.3	179.9	181.2	181.5	181.3	181.3	181.6	182.5	182.6	182.7	183.5
2004	183.1	183.8	184.6	185.7	186.5	186.8	186.8	187.4	188.1	188.6	189.0	189.9
2005	188.9	189.6	190.5	191.6	192.0	192.2	192.2	192.6	193.1	193.3	193.6	194.1
2006	193.4	194.2	195.0	196.5	197.7	198.5	198.5	199.2	200.1	200.4	201.1	202.7
2007	201.6	203.1	204.4	205.4	206.2	207.3	206.1	207.3	208.0	208.9	209.7	210.9
2008	209.8	211.4	212.1	214.0	215.1	216.8	216.5	217.2	218.4	217.7	216.0	212.9
2009	210.1	211.4	211.3	211.5	212.8	213.4	213.4	214.4	215.3	216.0	216.6	218.0
2010	217.9	219.2	220.7	222.8	223.6	224.1	223.6	224.5	225.3	225.8	226.8	228.4
2011	229.0	231.3	232.5	234.4	235.2	235.2	234.7	236.1	237.9	238.0	238.5	239.4
2012	238.0	239.9	240.8	242.5	242.4	241.8	242.1	243.0	244.2	245.6	245.6	246.8
2013	245.8	247.6	248.7	249.5	250.0	249.7	249.7	251.0	251.9	251.9	252.1	253.4
2014	252.6	254.2	254.8									

Chartered Accountants Ireland *Code of Ethics*

Under the Chartered Accountants Ireland *Code of Ethics*, a Chartered Accountant shall comply with the following fundamental principles:

1. **Integrity** – to be straightforward and honest in all professional and business relationships.
2. **Objectivity** – to not allow bias, conflict of interest or undue influence of others to override professional or business judgements.
3. **Professional Competence and Due Care** – to maintain professional knowledge and skill at the level required to ensure that a client or employer receives competent professional services based on current developments in practice, legislation and techniques, and act diligently and in accordance with applicable technical and professional standards.
4. **Confidentiality** – to respect the confidentiality of information acquired as a result of professional and business relationships and, therefore, not disclose any such information to third parties without proper and specific authority, unless there is a legal or professional right or duty to disclose, nor use the information for the personal advantage of the Chartered Accountant or third parties.
5. **Professional Behaviour** – to comply with relevant laws and regulations and avoid any action that discredits the profession.

As a Chartered Accountant, you will have to ensure that your dealings with the tax aspects of your professional life are in compliance with these fundamental principles. You will not be asked to define or list the principles, but you must be able to identify where these ethical issues arise and how you would deal with them.

Examples of situations that could arise where these principles are challenged are outlined below:

Example 2.1

You are working in the Tax Department of ABC & Co and your manager is Jack Wilson. He comes over to your desk after his meeting with Peter Foley. He gives you all the papers that Peter has left with him. He asks you to draft Peter's tax return. You know who Peter is as you are now living in a house that your friend Ann leased from Peter. As you complete the return, you note that there is no information regarding property income. What should you do?

Action

As a person with integrity, you should explain to your manager that your friend Ann has leased a property from Peter and that he has forgotten to send details of his property income and expenses. As Peter sent the information to Jack, it is appropriate for Jack to contact Peter for details regarding property income and related expenses.

Example 2.2

You are working in the tax department of the Irish subsidiary of a US-owned multinational. You are preparing the corporation tax computation, including the R&D tax credit due. You have not received some information from your colleagues dealing with R&D and cannot finalise the claim for R&D tax credit until you receive this information. Your manager is under pressure and tells you to just file the claim on the basis that will maximise the claim. He says, "It is self-assessment, and the chance of this ever being audited is zero." What should you do?

Action

You should act in a professional and objective manner. This means that you cannot do as your manager wants. You should explain to him that you will contact the person in R&D again and finalise the claim as quickly as possible.

Example 2.3

Anna O'Shea, financial controller of Great Client Ltd, rings you regarding a VAT issue. You have great respect for Anna and are delighted that she is ringing you directly instead of your manager. She says that it is a very straightforward query. However, as you listen to her, you realise that you are pretty sure of the answer but would need to check a point before answering. What should you do?

Action

Where you do not know the answer, it is professionally competent to explain that you need to check a point before you give an answer. If you like, you can explain which aspect you need to check. Your client will appreciate you acting professionally rather than giving incorrect information or advice.

Example 2.4

The phone rings, and it is Darren O'Brien, your best friend, who works for Just-do-it Ltd. After discussing the match you both watched on the television last night, Darren explains why he is ringing you. He has heard that Success Ltd, a client of your tax department, has made R&D tax credit claims. Therefore, you must have details regarding its R&D. Darren's relationship with his boss is not great at present, and he knows that if he could get certain data about Success Ltd, his relationship with his boss would improve. He explains that he does not want any financial information, just some small details regarding R&D. What should you do?

Action

You should not give him the information. No matter how good a friend he is, it is unethical to give confidential information about your client to him.

Example 2.5

It is the Friday morning before a bank holiday weekend, and you are due to travel from Dublin to west Cork after work for the weekend. Your manager has been on annual leave for the last week. He left you work to do for the week, including researching a tax issue for a client. He had advised you that you were to have an answer to the issue by the time he returned, no matter how long it took. It actually took you a very short time and you have it all documented for him.

Your friend who is travelling with you asks if you could leave at 11am to beat the traffic and have a longer weekend. You have no annual leave left, so you cannot take leave. You know that if you leave, nobody will notice, but you have to complete a timesheet. Your friend reminds you that the research for the client could have taken a lot longer and that you could code the five hours to the client. What should you do?

Action

It would constitute unprofessional behaviour and would show a lack of integrity if you were to charge your client for those five hours.

Suggested Solutions to Review Questions

Chapter 2

Question 2.1

The corporation tax computation would be as follows:

Telestar Ltd Corporation Tax Computation for the 12-month Accounting Period Ended 31 March 2015

		£	£
			117,000
Add:	Depreciation	15,389	
	Motor expenses (Note 1)	–	
	Entertainment (Note 2)	1,050	
	Finance lease depreciation (Note 3)	–	
	Legal fees (Note 4)	2,400	18,839
			135,839
Less:	Grant for extension of premises (Note 5)	10,000	
	Employment grant (Note 6)	–	
	Patent royalty (Note 7)	1,600	
	Dividends from UK company (Note 8)	1,300	
	Profit on sale of van (Note 9)	1,000	
	Profit on sale of shares (Note 10)	3,000	
	Bank deposit interest (Note 11)	600	
	Capital allowances	7,272	(24,772)
	Trading income		111,067
	Loan relationships – bank interest (gross)		600
	Miscellaneous income		2,000

Patent royalty (gross) $= 1{,}600 \times \dfrac{100}{80}$

Total income			113,667

Chargeable gain (Note 12)	1,632
Taxable total profits (TTP)	**115,299**
Corporation tax payable:	
£115,299 @ 20%	23,059.80
Less: Income tax suffered on patent royalty £2,000 × 20%	(400.00)
Corporation tax payable	22,659.80

Corporation tax is due on or before 1 January 2016.

Notes

1. As motor expenses are wholly allowable, there is no add-back.
2. Entertainment costs are disallowed as follows:

	£
Christmas gifts for suppliers	150
Entertainment costs incurred by MD	350
General customer entertainment	550
	1,050

   Costs incurred for benefit of staff, i.e. Christmas party and prizes, are deductible.
3. As depreciation on finance lease assets is deductible, no adjustment is required.
4. Legal fees are of a capital nature and, therefore, are disallowed.
5. Grant for extension of premises is a capital receipt and is not liable to corporation tax.
6. Employment grant is taxable as a revenue receipt relating to the trade.
7. Patent royalty is not taxable as trading income. The gross amount is taxable as miscellaneous income. However, the income tax suffered can be set-off against the corporation tax chargeable. As **only** the net amount (i.e. the amount after deduction of standard rate income tax) has been credited in the profit and loss account, then this is the correct amount to deduct.
8. Dividends from UK company are exempt from tax under the exemption in section 931B CTA 2009 for "small" companies.
9. Profit on sale of van is a capital profit and not a trading receipt and, so, it is not taxable as trading income. (See Note 12)
10. Profit on sale of shares is a capital profit and not a trading receipt and, so, it is not taxable as trading income. (See Note 12)
11. Bank deposit interest is taxable as income from a non-trading loan relationship.
12. Chargeable gain:
    (a) Sale of van:
    Although a tax loss arose on the sale of the van (£12,000 − £40,000), this is not an allowable loss. This is exempt from CGT as it is a wasting chattel with proceeds less than £6,000.
    (b) Sale of shares:

	£	£
Proceeds		6,000
Cost	3,000	

		£	
Indexation		1,368	
Indexed cost			(4,368)
Chargeable gain			1,632

Note: SSE is not available as the company did not own at least 10% of the shares in Video Plc.

Question 2.2

Zaco Ltd Corporation Tax Computation Year Ended 30 September 2014

		£	£
Profit per Accounts			379,900
Add:	Disallowed repairs	5,200	
	Disallowed professional fees	300	
	Political donations	750	
	Entertainment	600	
	Depreciation	13,000	19,850
Less:	Dividends (Note 2)	3,600	399,750
	Profit on sale of fixed assets	15,200	
	Bank interest receivable	1,200	
	Property income	4,300	(24,300)
			375,450
Less:	Capital allowances		(9,846)
	Tax-adjusted trading profits		365,604
	Loan relationships		1,200
	Property income		4,300
	Total income		371,104
Add:	Chargeable gains (Note 1)		Nil
Taxable total profits (TTP)			**371,104**

Corporation tax payable:

FY 2013 (01/10/2013 − 31/3/2014)
FY 2014 (01/4/2014 − 30/9/2014)
Note that the year end straddles 31 March, so need to split into relevant financial years:
FY 2013 182/365 × £371,104 = £185,043
FY 2014 183/365 × £371,104 = £185,061

Lower and upper limits are reduced proportionately to £150,000 and £750,000 respectively again to reflect the proportion of the profits falling into each FY. Therefore, the profits of each FY as apportioned are taxed at the marginal rate as follows:

Financial year 2013

			£	£
Corporation tax @ 23%	£185,043 × 23%		42,559.89	
Less: Marginal relief				
$(750,000 - 185,043) \times \dfrac{185,043}{185,043} \times 3/400$			(4,237.18)	
				38,322.71
Financial year 2014				
Corporation tax @ 21%	£185,061 × 21%		38,862.81	
Less: Marginal relief				
$(750,000 - 185,061) \times \dfrac{185,061}{(P)189,061} \times 1/400$			(1,382.46)	
				37,480.35

P = £185,061 + (£3,600 x 10/9) = £189,061

Corporation tax liability (due on or before 1 July 2015)   **75,803.06**

Note that the simplified calculation of marginal relief is utilised as the company has no FII.

1. Chargeable gain on sale of building

		£	£
Proceeds			215,200
Cost		200,000	
Indexation (£200,000 × 0.035)		7,000	(207,000)
Gain			8,200
Less capital loss forward (restricted)			(8,200)
Chargeable gain			NIL
Capital loss carried forward			(1,800)

2. The foreign dividend is exempt from UK tax; therefore no credit is required for foreign tax suffered.

Question 2.3

Alpha Ltd Corporation Tax Computation Year Ended 31 March 2015

	£	£
Profit per accounts		424,605
Add:		
Repairs	15,000	
Insurance	350	
Loss on sale of investments	600	
Legal expenses	2,000	
Depreciation	13,260	
Subscriptions (Note 1)	1,815	

Motor expenses (Note 2)	3,169	
Sundry (Note 3)	2,201	
Entertainment	1,191	
		39,586
		464,191
Less:		
UK dividends	4,500	
Royalties received	2,500	
Gain on sale of fixed assets	1,000	
Amortisation of grant	240	
Interest on tax overpaid	475	
Rents received	6,000	
Deposit interest	1,500	
		(16,215)
		447,976
Capital allowance		(26,006)
Trading income for period		421,970
Less loss carried forward		(20,000)
		401,970
Net credit from loan relationships (£475 + £1,500)		1,975
Miscellaneous income: Patent royalties (tax of £625)		3,125
Property income:		
Gross rents	6,000	
Less:		
Insurance		(350)
Net property income		5,650
Chargeable gains (Note 4)		0
Taxable total profits (TTP)		412,720
Franked investment income (Note 5)		2,000
Profits		414,720

Corporation tax payable:
As the company has two associates, the upper and lower limits are divided by the number of associates plus one, i.e. three. This reduces the limits to £100,000 and £500,000 respectively.
As the company's profits are in the marginal band, P = 414,720, I = TTP = 412,720.
Thus, corporation tax payable is as follows:

	£
TTP £412,720 @ 21%	86,671.20
Less: Marginal relief	
1/400 × (500,000 − 414,720) × 412,720/ 414,720	(212.17)
	86,549.03
Less income tax deducted at source on royalties	(625.00)
Corporation tax payable	85,834.03

Due on or before 1 January 2016.

Notes

1.	Subscriptions	£
		—
	Political	1,815
		1,815
2.	Motor expenses	
	Leasing charges: Disallowable £21,126 × 15%	3,169
3.	Sundry	
	Interest on late payment of VAT	1,630
	Parking fines	30
	Gifts to customers	541
		2,201

4.   Profit on sale – excluded from calculation of taxable total profits.

5.   Only the dividend from Bank of Ireland is FII as FII does not include group dividends. It must be grossed up by 100/90 and added on to TTP to arrive at the profits figure.

6.   Property income of £1,000 received on sub-letting to a tenant on a short-term basis is treated as trading income by concession by HMRC – see **Section 1.7.4**.

Question 2.4

To:	Finance director
From:	Financial controller
Re:	Proposed claim for tax relief on qualifying Research & Development (R&D) expenditure

I refer to our recent meeting in relation to my review of the draft corporation tax computation which identified that no claim for R&D expenditure has been included therein.

By way of background and as requested, relief in the UK is available for capital R&D through the capital allowances regime (100% relief for capital expenditure related to R&D activities as defined under UK GAAP) and for revenue R&D through the various tax regimes available for qualifying R&D expenditure.

Revenue expenditure

The enhanced tax relief for revenue R&D can only be claimed on "relevant" R&D, i.e. R&D is related to the trade carried on by the company. As the work carried out by the R&D department directly relates to the trade of Comtech, this condition of the regime is not an issue.

Qualifying R&D expenditure

Whilst the definition of R&D follows that of SSAP 13 and IAS 38, HMRC recommends that DTI guidance tests must be applied. In essence, a project will qualify as an R&D project if it is carried on in the field of science or technology and is undertaken to extend knowledge and to address scientific or technology uncertainties. The projects of our R&D department clearly qualify in this regard.

There are two regimes in the UK – one for the SME sector (giving a further 125% tax deduction on qualifying revenue expenditure) and a deduction of 130% for qualifying expenditure by large companies.

Under both regimes, the expenditure must *inter alia* meet the following conditions:

1. must not be capital in nature;
2. must be attributable to relevant R&D that is either directly undertaken by the company or on its behalf; and
3. must be incurred on qualifying costs.

The qualifying expenditure must be such that it would have been allowable as a deduction in computing the taxable profits of a trade carried on by the company. The tax relief is claimed as an adjustment to the trading income computation. The expenditure on which I propose to submit a claim on behalf of Comtech Limited meets all of the above conditions.

Under the SME scheme, where the enhanced deduction creates a deemed trading loss, the company can choose to surrender the loss for a cash payment of 14.5% of the loss for the chargeable period.

An SME may also make a claim under the large companies rules if it fails to meet the specific criteria for that regime, but in so doing will be restricted to the limits for such companies.

Tax saving

See Appendix 1 for my calculations of the reliefs available to Comtech Limited for qualifying expenditure in the 2015 period. Overall, a corporation tax saving of £414,450.54 is available to the company.

I would be pleased to meet with you to discuss this claim in more detail and would also suggest we conduct a review to establish if Comtech Limited would still be within time to submit claims for any prior periods. Please also note that, since 1 April 2012, R&D relief for SMEs has increased to 225% with the payable tax credit of 14.5% available in respect of qualifying expenditure incurred from 1 April 2014. Also, since 1 April 2012, the £10,000 minimum expenditure conditions have been abolished for all companies and the rule limiting the payable R&D tax credit to the amount of PAYE and NICs paid has also been abolished. I suggest we implement procedures to easily capture R&D costs in future periods given the significant cash flow benefits and savings available.

Appendix 1 – Comtech Limited

Claim for R&D relief for the accounting period ended 31 March 2015

Qualifying revenue expenditure:

	£
Gross wages	212,567
Redundancy payments (Note 1)	0
Employer's NIC	27,209
Pension scheme contributions	15,000
Company car benefit in kind (Note 1)	0
Consumable items	22,425
Power, water and fuel	8,762
Software	4,933
Rates (Note 1)	0
Sub-contracted costs (Note 2)	7,963
	298,859
Enhanced R&D deduction (Note 3)	373,574

Capital allowances on qualifying R&D capital expenditure:

New building (Note 4)	1,075,000
Plant and equipment (Note 4)	525,000
	1,600,000

Amended corporation tax computation:

	£
Taxable total profits (TTP) before R&D claimed	3,428,925
Enhanced R&D deduction on revenue expenditure	(373,574)
Capital allowances on R&D expenditure	(1,600,000)
Amended taxable total profits	1,455,351
Tax payable:	
TTP × 21%	305,623.71
Tax saved as a result of the R&D claims above:	
Draft tax liability on TTP of £3,428,925 × 21%	720,074.25
Amended liability	305,623.71
Tax saving	414,450.54

Notes

1. Redundancy payments, non-cash benefits in kind (in this case, company car benefits) and rates do not qualify for the enhanced R&D deduction.
2. Sub-contracted costs payable to a non-connected third party are a qualifying cost. As the amount that qualifies must be restricted to 65%, the calculation is as follows:
£12,250 × 65% = £7,963.

3. The amount of relief the company is entitled to claim will depend on whether it is classed as a small company, which attracts 225%, or a large company, which attracts 130% relief under the R&D regime. Alternatively, as a large company, Comtech could elect into the new 'above the line' R&D tax credit regime for expenditure incured from April 2013.

   SME is defined in accordance with the EU guidelines as follows:

   A company meeting either the turnover requirement of €100 million or the balance sheet total of €86 million plus the headcount limit for employees of 500.

   As the company has a turnover of £34.6 million and 55 employees, it meets the EU definition of an SME and thus qualifies for the SME R&D regime, giving an additional 125% tax deduction on qualifying expenditure.

4. In respect of the capital expenditure on the new research facility and plant and equipment, the company can claim 100% capital allowances on the following items:

	£
Buildings (see sub-note 4(a))	1,075,000
Plant and equipment	525,000
	1,600,000

   (a) In order to establish if 100% relief is available on the building expenditure it is necessary to compare the qualifying cost of this building with the overall cost of land and buildings in the company. If this exceeds 25% of the overall cost, then the expenditure will not qualify. The total cost of land and buildings in the accounts is £10,200,000. As 25% thereof is £2,555,000, the expenditure on the new building qualifies for the 100% capital allowances deduction in the 2014 period.

Chapter 3

Question 3.1

	£
Profit	96,000
Add: Depreciation	5,000
Trade profit	101,000
UK property business	17,000
	118,000
Less: Qualifying charitable donation	(8,000)
Total taxable profits	110,000

Question 3.2

Credits	£
Interest received	15,000
Loan written off by bank	20,000
	35,000
Less:	
Debits	
Legal fees incurred re: loan write-off	(1,500)
Net loan relationship credit	33,500

Question 3.3

(a) Loan relationships cover all loans made both by and to the company. These will either be trading or non-trading.
(b) Examples include: bank overdrafts and loans, mortgages, employee loans, interest on underpaid and overpaid corporation tax, corporate bonds, interest on savings.
(c) All non-trading debits and credits, calculated in line with generally accepted accounting principles, are aggregated separately and the overall debit or credit is included in the corporation tax computation. Trading debits are deductible in calculating trading profits. Excess non-trading credits are taxable and included in the calculation of total taxable profits.

Question 3.4

	£
Non-trade interest received	
Bank deposit interest	6,233
Bond held with local council	775
	7,008
Less:	
Non-trade interest paid	
Mortgage on rental property	(3,178)
Bank loan for shares	(555)
	(3,733)
Net non-trade loan relationship credit	3,275

All of the remaining sources of interest received and paid are trade-related.

Chapter 4

Question 4.1

Enya Limited

31/03/2012	£
Trading income	600,000
Net credit from loan relationships	100,000
Property income	50,000
Total profits	750,000

31/03/2013	
Trading income	700,000
Net credit from loan relationships	50,000
Property loss	(40,000)
Total profits	710,000

Less: section 37(3)(b) claim	(710,000)
Taxable profits	Nil

31/03/2014

Trading income	–
Net credit from loan relationships	100,000
Property income	60,000
Total profits	160,000
Less: section 37(3)(a) claim	(160,000)
Taxable profits	Nil

31/03/2015

Trading income	100,000
Less: section 45 offset	(100,000)
Trading income	Nil
Net credit from loan relationships	35,000
Property income	80,000
Taxable profits	115,000

Loss Memo

	£
Relevant trading loss for y/e 31/03/2014	1,300,000
Utilised by way of section 37(3)(a) against y/e 31/03/2014	(160,000)
Utilised by way of section 37(3)(b) against y/e 31/03/2013	(710,000)
Utilised by way of section 45 against y/e 31/03/2015	(100,000)
Loss carried forward at 31/03/2015	330,000

Question 4.2

Hells Bells Ltd Year ended 31 March 2014

	£
Trading income	167,000
Property income	4,000
Net credit from loan relationships	10,000
Total profits	181,000
Less: section 37(3)(b)	(174,000)
Total profit	7,000
Tax payable £7,000 @ 20%	1,400

9 months ended 31 December 2014

Trading income	–
Property income (Note 1)	(4,000)
Net credit from loan relationships	20,000
Chargeable gains (Note 2)	–
Total profits	16,000
Less: section 37(3)(a) claim	(16,000)
Taxable profits	Nil

Notes

1. Property income – A property loss must be set against other profits in the current accounting period.

2. Chargeable gains

	£
Gain	10,000
Less: capital loss forward	(19,000)
Loss forward	(9,000)

Loss Memo

	£
Relevant trading loss for p/e 31/12/2014	190,000
Utilised by way of section 37(3)(a) p/e 31/12/2014	(16,000)
Utilised by way of section 37(3)(b) y/e 31/03/2014	(174,000)
Loss forward to 2015	Nil

Question 4.3

Monk Ltd Year ended 31 March 2015

	£
Trading income	–
Net credit from loan relationships	30,000
Property income	20,000
Chargeable gain	126,000
Taxable profits	176,000
Less: section 37(3)(a)	(176,000)
Taxable total profits (TTP)	Nil

Year ended 31 March 2014

	£	£
Trading income	360,000	
Less: Capital allowances	(20,000)	340,000
Less: section 45 − loss carried forward		(20,000)
Trading income		320,000
Net credit from loan relationships		5,000
Property income		15,000
Chargeable gain		12,000
Taxable profits		352,000
Less: section 37(3)(b)		(224,000)
Taxable total profits (TTP)		128,000
Tax:		
£128,000 @ 20%		25,600

Loss Memo

	£
Relevant trading loss for y/e 31/03/2015 (£310,000 + £90,000)	400,000
Utilised by way of section 37(3)(a) against y/e 31/03/2015	(176,000)
Utilised by way of section 37(3)(b) against y/e 31/03/2014	(224,000)
Loss forward to 2015	Nil

Chapter 5

Question 5.1

The dividend is exempt from corporation tax as Ice Sculptors Ireland Limited can be controlled by Ice Sculptors Limited and therefore (as we have no further information to the contrary) the dividend falls with section 931E CTA 09 as an exempt distribution from a controlled company. Therefore the dividend receipt is not taxable and thus no double taxation relief is available for the 10% withholding tax deducted at source.

Question 5.2

The general rule is that dividends paid by a UK company to another UK company out of post-tax profits are exempt from further taxation. The rule was extended to dividends paid on or after 1 July 2009 by a UK or overseas company to a company or branch within the charge to UK corporation tax, so that dividends received are exempt if the conditions for the exemption are met. In general, dividends that fall to be taxed as trading profits, profits of a UK property business or insurance company profits will always fall outside the dividend exemption.

The dividend exemption rules and how they work depend on whether the recipient company is a "small company" or a "large company", but companies can always elect for exempt dividends to be taxable on a receipt-by-receipt basis. This can sometimes reduce the rate of withholding tax under double taxation treaties and may be beneficial if the recipient company has tax losses.

Currently, the definition of a small company is as follows:

- has no more than 50 employees; and
- has an annual turnover of less than €10 million; or
- gross assets of less than €10 million.

All companies that are not "small companies" are "large companies" for the purposes of the dividend exemption.

The small company exemption applies to dividends received where:

- the payer is resident in the UK or a qualifying territory. HMRC produce a list of qualifying territories, but essentially they are countries with which the UK has a comprehensive double taxation treaty and contain a non-discrimination clause; and
- the dividend is not interest which has been re-categorised as a distribution, and
- the dividend has not been allowed as a deduction from taxable profits outside the UK; and
- the general anti-avoidance rule that the distribution is not part of a scheme of tax avoidance is met.

The large company exemption applies to dividends that fall in to one of five classes, is not re-categorised interest and where no deduction is allowed outside the UK.

The five classes of exempt dividend are:

1. Where the recipient controls the payer (subject to detailed rules).
2. Distributions in respect of non-redeemable ordinary shares.
3. Distributions in respect of portfolio holdings (broadly where the recipient controls less than 10% of the payer).
4. Distributions from transactions not designed to reduce tax.
5. Dividends from shares accounted for as liabilities.

Question 5.3

The following transactions are classed as distributions by a company:

- Dividends paid by a company.
- Any distribution of assets in respect of shares, except any part of which represents a repayment of capital.
- A bonus issue subsequent to a repayment of share capital.
- Interest payments in excess of a normal commercial rate of return.
- Redemption of bonus securities or redeemable shares.
- Certain expenses incurred by a close company.
- Sale of assets by a company at undervalue, or purchase of assets by a company at overvalue from a shareholder.

Chapter 6

Question 6.1

The trustees of A's settlement are associates of Mrs A by virtue of section 448(1) CTA2010 and their rights and powers may be attributed to Mrs A, who therefore controls the company. Company X is therefore a close company as it is under the control of Mrs A, being five or fewer participators.

Question 6.2

Control by voting rights is determined under section 450(3) CTA2010.
   The associates of A are:

- his wife and his brother; and
- the trustees of A's settlement (section 448(1) CTA2010).

The rights and powers attributable to A are:

- the rights and powers of his associates (section 451(4) CTA2010); and
- the rights and powers of Company X (section 451(4) CTA2010).

As a total of 510 votes are thus possessed by A or attributable to him, the company is a close company controlled by one person.

Question 6.3

Control – the rights in the shares held by Company Z in Company Y may be attributed to F, who controls that company (section 451(4) CTA2010).
   F is an associate of E but the rights attributed to F cannot be further attributed to E (section 451(4) CTA2010).
   No group of five participators or fewer can control Company Y, nor do the director/participators control it, and nor would the winding up test be of assistance here.
   Therefore company Y is not a close company.

Chapter 7

Question 7.1

(a) Tax law provides that the company must account for tax as if the loan were a net annual payment after deduction of tax. If the loan amounted to £8,000 in the accounts to 31 December 2014, the company must self-assess tax liabilities in respect of any loans and this can mean that it will have to pay tax to HMRC equal to 25% of the outstanding loan made during the accounting period, i.e. £2,000. This will be the case where the loan remains unpaid and has not been released or written off within nine months and one day following the end of the relevant accounting period (the effective due date for payment of corporation tax for all but large companies).
   If and when the loan is repaid, the company may claim a refund of £2,000. Exemption from this tax charge is, however, available:

- where the business of the company is or includes the lending of money and the loan is made in the ordinary course of that business, or

■ where a debt is incurred for the supply of goods or services in the ordinary course of the business of the close company, unless the credit given exceeds six months or is longer than the period normally given to the company's customers, or

■ the borrower satisfies the following conditions:

● total loans to borrower or spouse do not exceed £15,000, and

● the borrower works full-time for the close company or any of its associated companies, and

● the borrower and/or his associates is not the beneficial owner of or able to control more than 5% of the ordinary shares of the company or an associated company.

(b) Corporation tax liability – Year ended 31/12/2011

FY 2010   Small profits rate was 21%
FY 2011   Small profits rate was 20%

Period 1 January 2011–31 March 2011:

	£
£133,000 × 3/12 × 21%	6,982.50
Period 1 April 2011–31 December 2011:	
£133,000 × 9/12 × 20%	19,950.00
Total corporation tax payable	26,932.50

Corporation tax payable on or before 1 October 2012.
The company is not a close investment holding company as it is carrying on a trade.

Question 7.2

(a) Corporation Tax Computation for y/e 31/12/2014

	£	£
Net profit per accounts		32,900
Add: Depreciation	15,000	
Disallowed sundry (Note 1)	800	15,800
		48,700
Less: Interest	8,500	
Capital grants	1,500	(10,000)
		38,700
Less: Capital allowances		(4,000)
Trading income		34,700
Net credit from loan relationships		8,500
Total income		43,200
Corporation tax payable		
£43,200 × 20%		8,640
Total corporation tax payable		8,640

(b) Specific Items

Note 1. The expense payment is treated as a "distribution" in the hands of Y's brother and added back in the trading income computation.

Question 7.3

Corporation Tax Computation for y/e 31/03/2015

		£	£
Net profit per accounts			1,870,000
Add: Entertainment	W1	11,900	
Depreciation		100,000	
Loss on sale of plant		20,000	
			131,900
Less:			
Profit on sale of building		1,480,000	
Rents		200,000	(1,680,000)
			321,900
Capital allowances			(50,000)
Trading income			271,900
Trading losses forward			(210,000)
			61,900
Property income	W2		181,000
Income			242,900
Chargeable gain	W3		1,377,000
Taxable total profits (TTP)			1,619,900
Corporation tax			
£1,619,900 × 21%			340,179
Tax on loan £550,000 × 20/80*			137,500

*If the loan is not repaid within nine months and one day of the year end.

Workings

1. Entertainment disallowed	£
Entertaining customers	6,000
Entertaining suppliers	5,000
Christmas gifts for suppliers	900
	11,900

2. Property Income	£
Portion of premium subject to corporation tax: £50,000 × (50−19)/50	31,000
Property income (£200,000 − £50,000)	150,000
Property income	181,000

3. Chargeable gain

   Sale of building

		£
Proceeds from building		1,500,000
Legal fees		(18,000)
		1,482,000
MV at 31/3/1982	50,000	
Indexation: 1.10	55,000	(105,000)
Gain		1,377,000

Question 7.4

Servisco Ltd Corporation Tax Computation year ended 31 March 2015

	£
Trading income	430,000
Less loss forward	(9,000)
	421,000
Net credits from loan relationships	50,000
Property income	100,000
	571,000
Chargeable gains	86,400
Taxable total profits (TTP)	657,400
FII (£10,000 × 10/9) + £7,500	18,611
Profits	676,011
Corporation Tax	
£657,400 × 21%	138,054.00
Less: Marginal relief	
(£1,500,000 − £676,011) × £657,400/£676,011 × 1/400	(2,003.20)
Total	136,050.80

Question 7.5

Machinery Ltd Corporation Tax Computation year ended 31 March 2015

	£	£
Net profit from trading		626,700
Add: Depreciation	59,790	
Loan interest treated as a distribution (Note 1)	2,731	62,521
		689,221
Less: Capital allowances		(10,700)
Trading income		678,521
Net credits from loan relationships		10,000

Property income	50,000
Taxable total profits (TTP)	738,521
Corporation tax payable:	
Payable: £738,521 × 21%	155,089.41
Less: Marginal relief: (£1,500,000 − £738,521) × 1/400	(1,903.70)
Total due	153,185.71

Note 1:
Loans from directors (and/or associates) with material interest

	Loan £	Interest paid £	Interest at 6%	Deemed distribution
V. Duffy	4,000	600	240	360
Mrs J. Duffy	5,000	600	300	300
Trustees	5,000	750	300	450
Executors	5,000	750	300	450
D. O'Connell	5,000	750	300	450
L.T. Smith	10,000	1,321	600	721
	34,000	4,771	2,040	2,731

Question 7.6

Tax Advisors Ltd

Corporation Tax Computation for the year ended 31 December 2014

	£
Trading income	100,000
Net credits from loan relationships	100,000
Total profits	200,000
Qualifying charitable donations	(60,000)
Taxable total profits (TTP)	140,000

Total corporation tax payable is £140,000 @ 20% = £28,000.

Chapter 8

Question 8.1

Controlled Foreign Companies (CFC) Rules
The CFC rules apply to prevent international groups of companies from generating and retaining profits in low-tax jurisdictions. Where the rules come into play the profits of CFCs are apportioned back to the UK and charged to tax at a rate equal to the main rate of corporation tax.

The rules significantly changed from 1 January 2013, therefore as the joint venture commenced after that date the newly revamped legislation only is relevant here. The new rules apply to accounting periods commencing on or after 1 January 2013, so they will apply to the accounting period beginning 1 July 2014 and ending 30 June 2015, which is the period in which the joint venture was undertaken.

The purpose of the new rules is to better target the CFC charge so that it is not applied to profits arising from genuine foreign economic activities or where there has been no artificial diversion of UK profits.

The CFC regime applies to companies resident outside the UK that are controlled by UK residents. The rules define what is meant by UK control, including by reference to accounting standards.

Control for these purposes includes the scenario where a foreign company (MedAssist Ltd) is controlled by two persons together, one of whom is a UK resident company (Medtech Ltd) that holds at least 40% of the interests, rights and powers in the foreign company (MedAssist) and the other of whom is not UK resident (Medservices SA) and holds at least 40% but not more than 55% of the interest rights and powers in the foreign company (MedAssist). These conditions are both met as Medtech holds 48% of the shares and Medservices SA holds 52% of the shares in MedAssist Ltd.

Under section 371AA TIOPA 2010, **any** controlled foreign company is a CFC. Chapter 2 of Part 9A TIOPA 2010 sets out the steps for determining if a CFC charge arises now that it is established that MedAssist is a CFC.

There is a CFC charge only if the following apply:

- the CFC has "chargeable profits";
- none of the CFC exemptions apply; and
- there is a UK "interest holder" that is not exempt and that (together with connected companies) holds an interest of at least 25%.

As the investment in MedAssist meets the last of these (Medtech holds a 48% interest), it is therefore necessary to consider if it meets either one of the CFC exemptions or if it has "chargeable profits".

A CFC's chargeable profits are the part of its profits that pass through the "CFC charge gateway". The gateway is a series of definitions of profits that may fall within the CFC regime. So while MedAssist may be profitable, it may not have chargeable profits.

We do not have enough information regarding the profits of MedAssist to determine whether it has chargeable profits. To determine if it has chargeable profits, we would need sight of MedAssist's most recent accounts and tax computation to be able to conclude on this, and information on projected future activities and results.

However, even if MedAssist does have chargeable profits it may still meet one of the exemptions under the legislation removing the CFC charge completely.

There are a number of entity level exemptions which, if they apply, will exempt all the profits of MedAssist from the CFC charge. These are:

1. *Exempt period (for foreign companies becoming CFCs for the first time)*
   This applies for the first 12 months after MedAssist comes under UK control by Medtech, provided any necessary restructuring is undertaken to ensure no CFC charge arises in the subsequent accounting period. This would be available for the accounting period 30 June 2015 only. It is only a potential exemption and is dependent on there being no CFC charge or one of the other entity level exemptions being met in all subsequent accounting periods after 30 June 2015.

2. *Excluded territories (for CFCs resident in certain territories, subject to conditions)*
   MedAssist is resident in Cyprus – this is not on the list of excluded countries.

3. *Low profits (for CFCs with low levels of profit)*
   Applies if the total accounting or taxable profits of the CFC are < £50,000, or if total accounting or taxable profits are < £500,000 and non-trading income therein is < £50,000. We do not have the information to determine if this would be the case in relation to MedAssist.

4. *Low profit margin (for CFCs whose profit is no more than 10% of operating expenditure)*
   Again, we do not have the information to determine if this is the case.

5. *Tax exemption (for CFCs that pay at least 75% of the tax they would have paid in the UK)*
   The Cypriot corporate tax rate of 10% is well below 75% of the current main rate in the UK of 21% (i.e. 15.75%), so MedAssist will be subject to a lower level of taxation. Therefore this exemption would not be met.

The exemptions that may be met in relation to MedAssist are exemptions 1, 3 and 4. First we would recommend that exemptions 3 and 4 are considered to determine if these exemptions will be met in subsequent accounting periods. If it is the case that these are unlikely to be met, then consideration will need to be given to exemption 1 and to whether any action can be taken to remove the CFC charge. This action, however, would need to be taken before 12 months has expired (i.e. by 30 June 2015 at the latest), otherwise the exempt period exemption will not apply to the first period.

Even if one of these exemptions cannot be met, it may still be the case that MedAssist does not have chargeable profits and for this reason it will be important to provide the accounting information and projections requested to establish this as soon as possible.

With careful planning, before the 12-month period ended 30 June 2015 is up, it should be possible to ensure a CFC charge does not arise. It would therefore be reasonable at this stage to expect that the CFC rules will not therefore apply to MedAssist for the 12-month period from July 2014, but further analysis is required to confirm this point definitively.

Question 8.2

(a) Under section 371AA of the Taxation of International and Other Provisions Act 2010, **any** controlled foreign company is a CFC. The CFC regime applies to companies resident outside the UK that are controlled by UK residents. The rules define what is meant by UK control, including by reference to accounting standards.

A company will be a CFC if it meets all of the following conditions:

- it is resident outside the UK; and
- it is controlled by persons resident in the UK.

Control for these purposes includes the scenario where a foreign company (Black Widow Co.) is controlled by two persons together, one of whom is a UK resident company (Hulk Ltd) that holds at least 40% of the interests, rights and powers in the foreign company (Black Widow Co.) and the other of whom is not UK resident (Hawk Eye Srl) and holds at least 40% but not more than 55% of the interest rights and powers. This test is met.

Therefore Black Widow Co. is a CFC as it is resident outside the UK and is controlled by persons resident in the UK, under the 40% control test. It meets the 40% control test as Hulk Ltd holds more than 40% (46%) of its shares and Hawk Eye Srl holds more than 40% but less than 55% of the shares (54%). This particular test is designed to catch joint venture situations such as this.

(b) A CFC charge is levied because Black Widow Co. is a CFC, it does not meet any of the CFC exemptions and 75% of its profits pass through the trading profits gateway test as 75% of its profits have been artificially diverted from the UK. A CFC charge is therefore imposed on Hulk Ltd.

The CFC charge levied on Hulk Ltd is calculated as follows:

	£
Chargeable profits of Black Widow Co. (£1,500,000 × 75%)	1,125,000
Chargeable profits attributable to Hulk Ltd. (£1,125,000 × 46%)	517,500
UK corporation tax (£517,500 × 21%)	108,675
Less creditable tax (£150,000 × 75% × 46%)	(51,750)
CFC charge	56,925

The above CFC charge is required to be reported to HMRC by Hulk Ltd on its corporation tax return form CT600 for the accounting period ended 31 March 2015. In addition, the company must also complete and submit supplementary corporation tax return for CT600B – Controlled Foreign Companies.

Chapter 9

Question 9.1

Corporation Tax Computation Period Ended 31 March 2015 – Z Ltd

	£
Trading income	NIL
Net credit from loan relationships	20,000
Total profits	20,000
Loss (under section 37(3)(a))	(20,000)
TTP	NIL

Corporation Tax Computation Period Ended 31 March 2015 – B Ltd

	£
Trading income	170,000
Deduct: Losses forward	(16,000)
	154,000
Net credit from loan relationships	4,000
Property income	20,000
Profit liable to corporation tax:	178,000
Deduct: Group relief surrendered by Z Ltd	(76,000)
TTP	102,000
Corporation tax	
£102,000 @ 20%	20,400

Loss memo

	£
Loss	96,000
Used against other income of current year	(20,000)
Surrendered under section 99 CTA 2010	(76,000)
Loss available	Nil

Question 9.2

A Ltd – Corporation Tax Computation Period to 31 March 2015

	£
Net credit from loan relationships	1,000
Property income	20,000
	21,000
Loss set-off	(21,000)
TTP	NIL

B Ltd – Corporation Tax Computation Period to 31 March 2015

	£
Trading income	56,000
Net credit from loan relationships	2,000
Property income	25,000
	83,000
Less: Group loss surrendered by A Ltd	(69,000)
TTP	14,000
Corporation tax £14,000 × 20%	2,800

C Ltd – Corporation Tax Computation Period to 31 March 2015

	£
Trading income	48,000
Less: Losses forward	(26,000)
	22,000
Net credit from loan relationships	3,000
Property income	2,000
TTP	27,000
Corporation tax £27,000 × 20%	5,400

Loss memo of A Ltd

Trading losses brought forward	4,000
Loss – current year	90,000
Used against other income of current year	(21,000)
Claim section 99 balance of loss to B Ltd	(69,000)
Loss available to carry forward	4,000

The brought forward loss of £4,000 can only be carried forward to set against future profits of the same trade.

Alternatively, part of the loss could have been surrendered to C Ltd to reduce its trading income to nil, or all of the losses could have been surrendered without utilising £21,000 against current year first.

Note that, as no company is within the marginal relief band, alternative group relief solutions would yield similar results.

Question 9.3

Queen Group

	Note	Queen Ltd £	Rook Ltd £	Pawn Ltd £
Profit/Loss per accounts		199,313	(80,586)	(2,030)
Disallow:				
Depreciation		12,000	16,000	10,000
Entertainment		1,350	1,650	1,200
Interest	1	400	–	10,720
		213,063	(62,936)	19,890
Capital allowances		(7,375)	(5,627)	(3,000)
		205,688	(68,563)	16,890
Trading losses brought forward				(16,890)
		205,688	(68,563)	–
Net credit/(deficit) from loan relationships	2	23,846		(10,720)
		229,534	(68,563)	(10,720)
Group relief re LR deficit		(10,720)		10,720
Group relief re trading losses	3	(68,563)	68,563	–
Taxable total profits (TTP)		150,251	NIL	NIL

Corporation tax payable:

	£
Pawn Ltd	Nil
Rook Ltd	Nil
Queen Ltd:	

	£
TTP	150,251
FII (£9,000 × 10/9) (Note 4)	10,000
Profits	160,251

	£
Lower and upper limits (£100,000 and £500,000)	
£150,251 × 21%	31,552.71
Less: Marginal relief	
(500,000 − 160,251) × 150,251/160,251 × 1/400	(796.37)
Payable on or before 1 January 2016	30,756.34

Losses forward:

Pawn Ltd (80,000 − 16,890)	63,110
Rook Ltd	Nil
Queen Ltd	Nil

Notes

1. The PAYE interest is not tax deductible.
2. The interest payable by Pawn Ltd is for a non-trading purpose and is, therefore, deductible as a loan relationship, rather than a trading expense. This deficit can be group relieved to Queen Ltd.
3. The trading loss of Rook Ltd is available via group relief to be offset against the trading income of Queen Ltd.
4. As the dividend was received from the French company after 1 July 2009, it is assumed that it qualifies for one of the exemptions and is not therefore taxable. It must, however, be grossed up by 10/9 and included as FII.

Payment of the Dividend

No tax effect on company when paid.

Chapter 10

Question 10.1

Sale in June 2014

The conditions to qualify for substantial shareholding exemption (SSE) are as follows:

Shareholding requirements

- The holding must have been substantial (i.e. at least 10%). This condition is met as at time the holding was 100%.
- The substantial shareholding must have been held throughout a 12-month period in the two years before disposal. This conditions is also met as the shares have been held since 2002.

Investor/investee conditions

- Must have been a sole trading company or member of a trading group in the qualifying period (generally 12 months before disposal).
- Will be a sole trading company or member of a trading group in the qualifying period immediately after disposal.

Both of these conditions are met as both are trading companies and both will be so immediately after. Therefore SSE is available and the entire gain in June 2014 was exempt, saving corporation tax at the maximum rate of 21%. It should also be noted that the substantial shareholding does not have to be held in a UK resident company, so the German residence of the company is not an issue. There may also be foreign tax payable in Germany on the disposal and any tax thereon would not be available for double taxation relief in the UK as the gain is entirely exempt in the UK.

Proposed sale in May 2015

The 5% shareholding appears not to meet the substantial shareholding test as it is less than the 10% requirement.

However, as long as the less than 10% requirement is met throughout a 12-month period in the two years prior to the proposed disposal, then the disposal will qualify.

Hence the 5% disposal in May 2015 will also qualify for SSE, because in the two-year period prior to this (i.e. from 1 June 2013 to 25 June 2014) the company held 100% and this constitutes holding a substantial shareholding for a 12-month period in the previous 24 months.

If the remaining 5% shares are to be sold at a loss, no capital loss will arise as the loss is also subject to SSE.

We would recommend delaying the transaction until after 25 June 2015, when the substantial shareholding requirement required for SSE will not be meet and a capital loss will crystallise, which can be used by the company against any current period chargeable gains or carried forward to be utilised in the future (carry back is not possible).

Question 10.2

Report to the board of directors
Solar Group
Corporation Tax Position – Accounting Period Ended 31 March 2015

Introduction

(a) The group's corporation tax liability for the year ended 31 March 2015 is £37,018 and is payable to HMRC by 1 January 2016. None of the companies in the group have taxable total profits in 2015 in excess of £300,000 (£1,500,000/5), hence corporation tax was not due on an instalment basis. Calculations of the corporation tax position are set out in Appendix 1.

(b) (i) Set out in Appendix 2 is a calculation of the capital gain on the disposal of Solar's investment in Saturn. The gain after indexation allowance is £335,750. Ordinarily, Solar would have been assessed to tax on this gain at the appropriate rate. Given the number of associated companies in the group, it is likely that the full gain would have been taxed at 21%.

However, under the substantial shareholdings exemption (SSE) legislation, there is an exemption from tax on gains and losses made by companies on the disposal of shares. There are a number of conditions that must be satisfied to qualify for the relief.

The main exemption will apply where a trading company or a member of a trading group makes a disposal of all or part of a substantial shareholding of shares in another company or member of a trading group. For this purpose, substantial means at least 10% of the ordinary shares of the company concerned, together with an entitlement to at least 10% of:

▪ the profits available for distribution to equity holders; and
▪ the assets available to equity holders in a winding up.

Trading company means a company carrying on trading activities whose activities do not include, to a substantial extent, activities other than trading activities. Substantial in this context is not defined, although in common with other tax reliefs, 20% is typically taken as the benchmark.

A further condition is that the company making the disposal must have been a trading company or a member of a trading group throughout the period:

▪ beginning with the start of the latest 12-month period within the preceding two years during which the company met the substantial shareholding test mentioned above; and
▪ ending with date of disposal.

It must also be a trading company or a member of a trading group immediately after the disposal.

Based on the above, Solar would appear to satisfy the conditions so that the gain on the sale of the shares in Saturn will be exempt from corporation tax on the potential capital gain arising of £335,750.

(ii) *Degrouping charge*

I have set out in Appendix 2 my calculations of the gain arising from the transfer of the property from Solar to Saturn, as a result of Saturn leaving the group. When Saturn ceases to be subsidiary of Solar, it will be deemed to have sold the freehold property acquired from Solar at the date it was originally acquired from that company (i.e. March 2007). The deemed sale proceeds will be the market value at that time.

A gain of £126,500 will be deemed to have been made by Saturn in March 2007 under TCGA 1992 section 179 (referred to as a degrouping charge) by virtue of the fact that where a company leaves a group and has, within the six years ending at the time, acquired an asset from another group member, the company leaving is treated as having sold the asset when it was acquired from the other group member at its market value at that time and immediately reacquired it.

Although computed as if the asset had been disposed of in March 2007, the gain is regarded as arising at the start of the accounting period in which Saturn leaves the group and would ordinarily be charged corporation tax at the rate applicable to that accounting period.

However, under the legislation, where a degrouping event takes place on or after 19 July 2011, the degrouping charge arising is treated as deemed proceeds on the disposal of the relevant shares for calculating the gain or loss on the disposal of the shares. A consequence of this is that SSE is also available on the degrouping charge, meaning both the chargeable gain on the share sale and on the £126,500 degrouping charge are fully exempt from corporation tax.

(c) (i) *Proposed property transfer*

The proposed transfer of the property from Solar to Neptune will not give rise to a chargeable gain arising for Solar even though the sale to an independent third party would result in a capital gain of £100,000 by virtue of the fact that Neptune is a wholly owned subsidiary of Solar and assets transferred between both companies are treated as transferred on a no gain, no loss basis under section 171 TCGA 1992 (i.e. no gain will be deemed to have arisen).

Corporation tax on the capital gain will therefore be deferred until such time as the asset is sold outside the group or if Neptune leaves the groups within six years, subject to the rules for degrouping charges which apply after 19 July 2011.

(ii) *Sale of Neptune property*

The disposal of the property currently occupied by Neptune will be a disposal outside the group giving rise to a chargeable gain in Neptune. To mitigate the gain arising, advantage can be taken of TCGA 1992 section 171A. Neptune can jointly elect with Solar, within two years of the disposal, that the property is deemed to be transferred on a no gain, no loss basis to Solar with Solar being deemed to make the disposal. This enables the group to use the capital losses of Solar against the capital gains of Neptune without having to physically transfer ownership of the asset intragroup before making the disposal outside the group.

Alternatively, if advantage of capital loss relief available from say Solar is not taken, the chargeable gain may be rolled over or held over against a qualifying acquisition by Neptune or a qualifying acquisition by another group company. The usual 12 months before and three years after rules relating to rollover relief would apply.

(d) *Acquisition of Mars*

The group should be aware that anti-avoidance legislation is in place to prevent companies buying other companies and taking advantage of existing trading losses. These provisions disallow the carrying forward of trading losses incurred before a substantial change in ownership of the company's shares. The disallowance will apply if there is a change in the ownership of the company and either:

- there is a major change in the nature or conduct of trade carried on by the company within three years; or
- at any time after the change in ownership, the scale of activities of the trade carried on by the company has become small or negligible.

Given that the board of directors intends to make significant changes to the products sold, customers and markets, it is possible that (b) above would apply and the £500,000 losses would not be available to carry forward. These would be effectively wasted. We would recommend that the exact changes proposed are reviewed in more detail, taking into account HMRC guidance in this area before a decision to purchase Mars is made, as the availability of these losses should be factored in to the price paid for the company. We would also stress that even if the acquisition of Mars does not fall foul of this specific anti-avoidance rule, if there is any suggestion that the Mars acquisition is being undertaken to access these losses, then relief will also be denied.

Appendix 1 – Computation of Corporation Tax Liability

Solar Group – Year Ended 31 March 2015

	Solar	Neptune	Venus	Saturn	Mercury
	£	£	£	£	£
Trading profits	67,550	47,087	72,680	82,793	0
Chargeable gains			8,260		
Current year loss offset		(47,087)			
Profits before group relief	67,550	0	80,940	82,793	0
Less:					
Group relief	(2,760)	0	(20,940)	(22,793)	0
Taxable total profits	64,790	0	60,000	60,000	0
CT @ 21%	13,606				
CT @ 20%			12,000	12,000	0
Marginal relief					
(£300,000 – £64,790) × 1/400	(588)				
Corporation tax due	13,018	0	12,000	12,000	0 **37,018**

Total: **37,018**

Notes:

The upper limit and lower limit for corporation tax purposes must be divided by 5, as there are 5 associated companies in the group:

£1,500,000/5 = £300,000 £300,000/5 = £60,000

Group relief has been surrendered in order to bring as many companies as possible into the small companies rate, being profits up to £60,000.

Workings
Working 1: Trading profits – Saturn

	£
Profits before capital allowances	112,559
Capital allowances	(29,766)
	82,793

Working 2: Trading loss – Neptune

	£
Loss b/f	75,000
Current year offset	(47,087)
Loss c/f	27,913

Working 3: Loss memorandum – Mercury

	£
Adjusted loss	46,493
Group relief:	
Solar	(2,760)
Venus	(20,940)
Saturn	(22,793)
Remaining	Nil

Working 4: Capital gain – Venus

The capital gain of Venus (£55,260) will be reduced by capital losses brought forward (£47,000), leaving an amount assessable to corporation tax of £8,260. (If a student had stated that they wished to treat the capital gain in Venus as reallocated to Solar under the rules for chargeable gains relating to groups of companies, this would have been correct also.)

Appendix 2

Capital Gain on Sale of Solar's Shares in Saturn

	£
Proceeds	300,000
Deemed proceeds: degrouping charge	126,500
Cost	(55,000)
Gain before indexation allowance	371,500
Indexation allowance: 55,000 × 65%	(35,750)
	335,750

Capital gain arising on property transferred to Saturn as a result of Saturn leaving the group within six years – degrouping charge:

	£
Deemed proceeds – March 2007	230,000
March 1982 market value	(50,000)
Gain before indexation allowance	180,000
Indexation allowance: £50,000 × 107%	(53,500)
Gain after indexation allowance	126,500

Question 10.3

Assuming PRI successfully migrates its tax residency to Ireland and ceases to be UK tax resident under section 18 CTA 2009, there are a number of tax issues to be aware of.

If a company ceases to be resident in the UK, certain exit charges and restrictions to rollover relief will apply.

First, under section 188 TCGA 1992, migration gives rise to an "exit charge" on certain unrealised capital gains and losses on chargeable assets. Section 188 creates an occasion of charge immediately before the time (the "relevant time") when a dual-resident company is classed as resident outside the UK by reason of a double taxation agreement. Section 188(2) TCGA 1992 deems the company to have disposed of all its assets at their market value immediately before the relevant time and to have reacquired them at that value at the relevant time. A similar charge arises under section 859 CTA 2009 for intangible fixed assets, such as goodwill, acquired or created on or after 1 April 2002. This would apply to the goodwill value of the trade of PRI as its trade did not commence until 1 March 2003.

On the basis of the statement of financial information provided and assuming there is no significant increase in market value between the current market values and 1 September 2015 (the planned migration date), exit charges totalling £1,604,892 (see Appendix 1) would arise subject to UK corporation tax at 21%, resulting in a liability of £337,027. Payment of these exit charges is dealt with separately.

It is also necessary to establish if PRI recently sold any assets on which rollover relief has been provisionally claimed, as rollover relief would be restricted if the new assets are acquired after the company ceases to be UK resident and any gain arising on its immediate deemed disposal would be outside the charge to UK tax, which would likely be the case.

Other tax issues

When a company ceases to be resident in the UK part-way through a year of assessment, an accounting period ends and another one begins with the corporation tax payment and filing date flowing from that. Therefore a corporation tax return and payment will be due for the short accounting period ending 30 November 2015, with tax due for payment in respect of total taxable profits for that period on or before 1 September 2016 (assuming the company is not subject to instalment payments). The filing deadline for that return would be 30 November 2016.

From 1 December 2015 the company becomes treaty non-resident and it is not within the charge to corporation tax (section 5(2) CTA 2009), so no further returns or payments are due.

As the occasion of migration results in the company ceasing to be within the charge to corporation tax in respect of its trade, the company is treated as if the trade is ceasing, so it should be established if that will result in balancing charges or allowances on plant and machinery on which capital allowances have been claimed. A balancing charge will arise if the tax written down value of those assets is less than their current market value of £82,000. This would be included in the calculation of total taxable profits in the final corporation tax return to 30 November 2015.

The provisions of section 164(4) CTA 2009 apply to the valuation of the trading stock at the time the trade is treated as discontinued – the "amount which it would have realised if it had been sold in the open market". This is the net amount realisable by disposal of the stock in bulk under practical business conditions. On the basis that inventories have a current market value of less than the accounting cost, this should not result in an adjustment in the final period when the company is within the charge to UK corporation tax.

Payment of exit charges

Following a European Court of Justice judgment, the UK introduced in the Finance Act 2013 a mechanism to allow companies to defer the time at which they must settle some or all of the tax they are due to pay under current tax rules. Two deferred payment plans for exit taxes are now available in the UK.

The first new option is designed to ensure minimal compliance burden. It involves a calculation of the tax due at the time of migration, with staged payments of the tax attributable to exit charges then made in six equal annual instalments, starting with the first payment due within nine months and one day of the end of the accounting period. This option allows all assets to be taken together, without distinguishing between different classes and without the need for them to be tracked individually after migration. If this option is selected by PRI, six equal instalments of £56,171 plus interest would fall due for payment, with the first due by 1 September 2016 and the remaining five due on 1 September of each year thereafter.

The second new option, called "the realisation method", is more directly related to the economic life of assets. It involves a calculation of the tax due at the time of exit, with the tax attributable to exit charges allocated on an asset-by-asset basis as calculated at Appendix 1. PRI would be obliged to provide HMRC with an annual statement identifying the realisations of assets in that period, and the tax would become payable in respect of those realisations. For intangible assets, in this case goodwill, the useful economic life of each asset would have to be determined at the point of migration. Tax would then be payable in equal annual instalments over the useful life of the asset.

Overall, tax related to the exit charges under either deferred payment plan may be deferred for up to a maximum of 10 years, or in cases of chargeable assets until the disposal of the asset (if sooner).

The amounts deferred under either of the above options will be subject to interest from the normal due date.

So, while the exit charge tax is sizeable, PRI would be able to choose the most suitable plan to defer payment of this tax.

Procedure for notifying migration

The company must also follow the procedure laid down in section 109B TMA 1970 in relation to its migration. A penalty of up to the amount of tax unpaid is chargeable for failure to comply with this section. Four conditions required to be satisfied are as follows:

1. the company must give notice to HMRC of its intention to cease to be UK resident;
2. the company must specify the date of migration;
3. the company must provide a statement of the tax outstanding at the proposed date of migration; and
4. the company must set out a proposal for securing the unpaid tax – at this point PRI would outline which option it is choosing for deferral of the exit charges.

Appendix 1

Calculation of exit charges – PRI Limited

Property – section 188(2) TCGA 1992	£	£
Market value	1,500,000	
Less:		
Original cost	130,000	
Indexation allowance:		
*270.0 – 179.9 × 130,000	65,108	
179.9		
Exit charge		1,304,892
Goodwill – section 859(1) CTA 2009	£	
Market value	300,000	
Less:		
Original cost	Nil	
Deemed profit on intangible		300,000
Total exit charge		£1,604,892

Plant and machinery is treated as having a useful life of less than 50 years and classed as "wasting assets" with those that are also chattels (i.e. moveable tangible property) usually exempt assets for CGT purposes. Where capital allowances have been claimed in relation to such wasting chattels (in this case, the plant and machinery), those assets are no longer exempt and the CGT rules for non-wasting chattels apply. However, one of the CGT rules for non-wasting chattels is that any gain is exempt where the original cost and the market value of the asset are less than or equal to £6,000.

It should therefore be noted that no exit charge capital gain will arise on the market value of plant and machinery on which capital allowances have been claimed as there is no single item therein with an original cost or current market value in excess of £6,000.

Chapter 11

Question 11.1

Liquidation of Kay and Sons Ltd

The company's shareholders have decided to voluntarily liquidate the company in light of the imminent cessation of its business. This will be a members' voluntary liquidation as the company is solvent.

As an aside, a licensed insolvency practitioner will need to be appointed as liquidator to hold what's left of the company's assets, oversee the discharge of the company's liabilities and distribute any surplus to the shareholders.

Prior to 1 March 2012 it was possible to wind up a company and use the strike-off procedure in the Companies Order under Extra-Statutory Concession (ESC) C16. However, this ESC has now been legislated and is only available where the total distributions to be made on the liquidation are £25,000 or less, which is clearly not the case here. The more expensive formal procedure will therefore need to be followed, given the size of the potential distribution.

The end of an accounting period will be triggered by the appointment of the liquidator. As the liquidation is due to take place on 1 August 2014, the accounting period beginning 1 April 2014 is shortened to 31 July 2014 and another accounting period begins on 1 August 2014, which will run until 31 March 2015.

Therefore a corporation tax return and payment will be due for the short accounting period ending 31 July 2014 with tax due for payment in respect of total taxable profits for that period on or before 1 April 2015 (assuming the company is not subject to instalment payments). The filing deadline for that return would be 31 July 2015. The normal filing and payment dates will apply to the accounting period ending 31 March 2015.

A corporation tax charge will arise if there is a gain on the disposal of any of the assets remaining in the company's ownership. A balancing charge is also likely to apply in respect of any remaining plant and machinery, as 100% allowances will have been claimed in respect of more recent additions. Any current trading losses should be available to set against any gains or balancing allowances.

The distributions made to the shareholders will be taxed as a capital gain under section 122 TCGA 1992, as section 1030 CTA 2010 specifically excludes distributions made in respect of share capital on a winding-up from being taxed as income.

The rate of CGT will depend on the amount received by each shareholder, and will be a maximum of 28%, with the potential for entrepreneurs' relief (ER) available for shares held in the company that qualify as a holding in a personal trading company (i.e. ownership of more than 5% of the shares and having worked full time for the company for at least 12 months prior to the date of the distribution). ER will be available on the capital distribution received, provided that the distribution is made within three years of the cessation of the business and the company is a trading company.

For the purposes of ER, a company is a trading company provided that it does not have substantial non-trading activities. Substantial in this case is more than 20%. The high cash balance should not prevent trading company status, as it likely to have resulted from relatively recent sales of property and is intended for distribution to the shareholders rather than investment. If there is any doubt as to the trading status of the company, then an opinion on the matter can be sought from HMRC using the Non-Statutory Business Clearance service.

ER, if available, affords qualifying disposals with a 10% rate of CGT on gains up to the lifetime limit (currently £10 million).

Chapter 12

Question 12.1

Salary versus Dividend
Scenario 1 – Company perspective

Payment of a gross bonus of £100,000

	£
Bonus	100,000
Add employer's NIC @ 13.8%	13,800
	113,800
Less corporation tax saved @ 21.25%	24,183
Cash cost to the company	£89,617

Payment of a gross dividend of £100,000
The payment of a dividend by a company is from after-tax profits. Therefore there is no further tax cost or saving on the payment of dividend and the cash cost to the company is £90,000 (£100,000 × 90%) as the gross dividend of £100,000 includes a 10% notional tax credit.

Scenario 2 – Tax position of Annette

Receipt of a gross bonus of £100,000

		£
Bonus		100,000
Less income tax:	£30,000* × 40%	12,000
	£70,000 × 45%	31,500
Employee's NICs @ 2%		2,000
Net cash received by Annette		£54,500

Receipt of a gross dividend of £100,000

			£
Gross dividend			100,000
Income tax	£30,000* × 32.5%	9,750	
	£70,000 × 37.5%	26,250	
Less tax credit		(10,000)	26,000
Net cash received by Annette**			£64,000

* Gross remuneration £120,000, therefore £30,000 left of higher rate band.
** Net cash is the £90,000 less the income tax and NIC (*Note:* it is not the £100,000).

Overall
Dividend

	£
Cost to the company	90,000
Tax cost to the company	–
Net receipt by Annette	(64,000)
Net cost	26,000

Bonus

Cost to the company	100,000
Tax cost to the company	13,800
Tax saved on the bonus	(24,183)
Net receipt by Annette	(54,500)
Net cost	35,117

Payment of a dividend is more tax efficient by £9,117.

Question 12.2

Mr and Mrs Andrews
Andrews Transport Limited
Any Road
Any Town
15 March 2015

Dear Mr and Mrs Andrews,

Remuneration Strategy

Further to our meeting of last week, please find attached my analysis of the current remuneration structure of Andrews Transport Limited ('ATL') and my proposed changes to it under the following headings:

- Salary
- Dividends
- Pension planning
- Recommendations

When planning to benefit from tax-free payments in the future, it is important to bear in mind that that tax law can change and impact the rules and benefits in these areas.

When you have considered the opportunities outlined in the attached, please contact me so that we can decide how you will proceed with implementing any changes.

Changes to the remuneration structure of ATL – improving tax efficiency

1. *Salary Payments*
    - At present you, Mr Andrews, are the sole member of your family to be paid a salary by ATL, despite the fact that Mrs Andrews and the Andrews children also work in the business.
    - At present you receive a salary of £100,000 per annum from ATL. As Mrs Andrews does not receive a salary from the company, you can only avail of one personal allowance and one basic rate band of £31,865. I would recommend considering making salary payments to Mrs Andrews and possibly reducing your own salary. Making salary payments to Mrs Andrews will allow you to avail of another personal allowance and another basic rate band of up to £31,865.
    - I also recommend making salary payments to your children to reward them for their part-time work in the business. Payments up to the personal allowance of £10,000 would represent tax-efficient remuneration for your children. But you must be aware of national

minimum wage legislation and that details of the salary should be reported to HMRC under Real Time Information. The national insurance implications should also be addressed.

▨ ATL could receive a corporation tax deduction for the gross salary payments plus employer's NIC to both Mrs Andrews and your children. Given the level of pre-tax profits, the corporation tax deduction is likely to be at 20%.

2 *Dividends*

▨ As shareholders in ATL, both you and Mrs Andrews are entitled to receive dividend payments from the company. Assuming that both of you are receiving the maximum salary payments possible from ATL, you will be liable to income tax at 25% on the net dividend received from ATL (or 30.56% if your taxable income was greater than £150,000).

▨ Unlike with salary extraction, there is no NIC on dividend payments.

▨ ATL will not receive a corporation tax deduction for the dividends paid to you.

▨ Dividends tend to be more tax efficient than salary/bonus, but there are other non-tax considerations to be addressed.

3 *Pension Planning*

▨ I would also recommend increasing the pension contributions to your pension fund. This could be done by you or ATL. The funding by you personally could be up to the level of your salary. You can contribute up to £40,000 per year to your pension scheme (known as your 'annual allowance') and receive tax relief on the contribution.

▨ It is also possible to use any unused annual allowance from the past three financial years. This is likely to be relevant in your case as only low pensions contributions have been made to date through your company pension. It is possible to contribute more than the allowance but no tax relief will be given on the contributions.

▨ Alternatively, ATL could make the contribution. If this is done, then this limit does not apply. The limit on the contributions by the company is the funding required to pay your pension, subject to an overall fund limit of approximately £1.25 million.

▨ As your pension is underfunded, there should not be an issue of a limit on the contributions that ATL can make. Your pension advisor could advise regarding this pension issue. ATL should get a corporation tax deduction for the contributions it makes to your occupational pension fund (subject to the spreading provisions). Also, contributions are only deductible if paid.

▨ In addition, the pension scheme is exempt from income tax and capital gains tax in respect of assets held in the fund.

▨ On retirement you can take a tax-free lump sum from the pension fund equal to 25% of the pension fund. Withdrawals from the pension scheme are taxed as emoluments and are subject to tax.

▨ An associated benefit of the pension contributions is that they extract cash out of the company to you/your pension fund. This should prove to be tax efficient for you from a capital gains tax perspective if you wish to sell the business in the future, as the company's available cash will have been extracted by you at a minimum tax cost and the value for CGT purposes on a sale will reflect the value of the business and assets only and therefore could qualify in full for entrepreneurs' relief.

5 *Recommendations*

▨ There are opportunities for you to save tax by rewarding yourself and your family adequately for the work that you do for the company. ATL should pay your two children for their work. This will lead to a saving for you as you will not need to fund them because of

their earnings from ATL, i.e. instead of you funding them from income taxed at 40% they will fund themselves from income not taxed if kept within their personal allowances.
▦ Mrs Andrews should be paid for the work she does for ATL. This will allow her to use the full basic rate band and possibly benefit from termination payment relief at a later time.
▦ Consideration needs to be given to whether dividends should be paid.
▦ Consideration should be given to increasing your salary to maximise any pension contributions. If a large pension contribution is envisaged, it would be more tax efficient for ATL to make the payment rather than you personally.

Chapter 13

Question 13.1

1. Maurice – CGT Computation 2014/15

	£	£
Sale proceeds		80,000
Incidental costs of disposal		(750)
Net proceeds		79,250
Deduct:		
Base cost	20,000	
Costs of acquisition	600	
		(20,600)
Chargeable gain		58,650
Less: annual exemption		(11,000)
Taxable gain		47,650
CGT liability:		
£31,865 − £30,400 = £1,465 @ 18%		263.70
£47,650 − £1,465 = £46,185 @ 28%		12,931.80
Total		13,195.50

2. Vincent – CGT Computation 2014/15

	£	£
Sale proceeds		9,300
Deduct: Allowable cost		
Market value at 31 March 1982	1,200	
		(1,200)
Chargeable gain		8,100
Less: Annual exemption		(8,100)

Taxable gain   Nil

£2,900 of annual exemption is wasted.

Question 13.2

1. James – CGT Computation 2014/15

	£	£
Sale proceeds		650,000
Deduct: Allowable costs:		
Market value at 31 March 1982	230,000	
Enhancement expenditure − July 1993	10,000	
		(240,000)
Chargeable gain		410,000
Less: Annual exemption		(11,000)
Taxable gain		399,000
CGT @ 28%		111,720

Note: the gain is taxable at 28% as the level of James's taxable income for 2014/15 exceeded the basic rate band threshold.

2. Declan – CGT Computation 2014/15

	£	£
Sale proceeds		400,000
Deduct: Allowable costs:		
MV 31 March 1982	55,000	
Expenditure August 1984	20,000	
Expenditure February 2003	39,250	(114,250)
Chargeable gain		285,750
Deduct: Annual exemption		(11,000)
Taxable gain		274,750
CGT @ 18% of £5,000 (i.e. £31,865 − £26,865)		900
CGT @ 28% of £269,750 (i.e. £274,750 − £5,000)		75,530
Total CGT payable on 31 January 2016		76,430

Question 13.3

Capital Gains Tax Computation 2014/15

	£
Sale proceeds	80,000
Less: selling costs	(3,500)
	76,500

Less: cost

$$\frac{80,000}{80,000 + 145,000} \times £18,000 \qquad (6,400)$$

Chargeable gain	70,100
Less: annual exempt amount	(11,000)
Taxable gain	59,100
Taxable as follows:	£
£(31,865 − 25,000) = £6,865 × 18%	1,236
£(59,100 − 6,865) = £52,235 × 28%	14,626
CGT liability	**15,862**

The above liability falls due for payment on 31 January 2016. The base cost of the remaining land is £11,600 for any future disposal.

Chapter 14

Question 14.1

(a) Janet is not resident in 2014/15 as she meets an automatic overseas test, in that she was resident in one or more of the previous three tax years and visits the UK for fewer than 16 days in the current tax year.

(b) Paul is resident in 2014/15 as he does not meet an automatic overseas test but does meet an automatic UK test in that he is present in the UK for at least 183 days in the tax year.

(c) Victor is not resident in 2014/15 as he meets an automatic overseas test, in that he works full time overseas and visits the UK for fewer than 91 days, with the number of days in the tax year on which he works for more than three hours in the UK being less than 31.

(d) Christine is resident in 2014/15 as she does not meet an automatic overseas test but does meet an automatic UK test, in that she has a home in the UK for more than 90 consecutive days (of which at least 30 days fall in the tax year), more than 30 days are spent there in the tax year and she has no home overseas.

(e) Terry is not resident in 2014/15 as he meets an automatic overseas test, in that he was non-resident in all of the previous three tax years and visits the UK for fewer than 46 days in the current tax year.

(f) Margaret is resident in 2014/15 as she does not meet an automatic overseas test but does meet an automatic UK test.

This is because:

- she carries out full-time work in the UK for a period of 365 days, with no significant break (i.e. at least 31 days) and all or part of that 365-day period falls within the tax year;
- more than 75% of the total number of days in the 365-day period when more than three hours per day are worked in the UK; and
- at least one day in the tax year is a day on which she works more than three hours in the UK.

Margaret may be entitled to split-year basis in her year of arrival to the UK (2014/15) and the year of departure (2015/16).

(g) As Ned does not meet any of the automatic overseas tests or any of the automatic UK tests, residence will depend upon the number of UK ties that the he has and the number of days spent in the UK.

Ned is resident in the UK in the tax year 2014/15 by meeting the sufficient ties test in that:

- he spent between 121 and 182 days in the UK; and
- he has a sufficient UK tie (90-day tie), having spent more than 90 days in the UK in one or both of the previous two tax years.

As a leaver, Ned only required one tie to be resident in 2014/15.

Question 14.2

Jessica states that she left the UK in June 2013 and intends to return by December 2017.

As Jessica had always lived in the UK before June 2013, she would have been resident in the UK for four out of the seven tax years prior to the tax year of departure. This means that, unless she remains outside of the UK for a period of more than five complete years, she will be treated as if she had remained resident in the UK for CGT purposes under section 10A TCGA 1992.

The period between June 2013 and December 2017 includes only four complete years (June 2013–June 2017).

If Jessica returns when she intends to later this year, she will be charged to UK CGT on the gain made on the disposal of the painting she inherited from her aunt in 2010. She will be treated as if the gain arose in the 2017/18 tax year and the CGT will be payable by 31 January 2019. The CGT liability could be as high as £64,400 ((£750,000 − £520,000) × 28%). Jessica will be responsible for advising HMRC of the gain by either contacting the self-assessment helpline or completing and submitting a form SA1 and submitting her 2017/18 tax return by 31 January 2019.

These rules do not apply to assets acquired whilst overseas, so the gain on the disposal of the Australian flat will not be caught under section 10A TCGA 1992. However, if Jessica were to become tax resident in the UK before she disposes of the flat, the gain will fall within the UK CGT net though it is likely on the facts given that in such a scenario the disposal would qualify for principal private residence relief under section 222 TCGA 1992. Jessica could avoid this and a CGT liability on the painting sold during her time in Australia by simply delaying her return to the UK until after June 2018, at which point she will have been non-resident for more than five complete years.

Question 14.3

Capital gains tax position under the arising basis

	£
Foreign chargeable gain	220,000
Less: annual exempt amount	(11,000)
Chargeable gain	209,000
CGT at 28%	58,520

Under the arising basis of taxation, an individual who is UK resident is taxed on the arising basis on their worldwide income, hence Sophia would be taxable on the foreign chargeable gains in full in addition to her employment income.

Capital gains tax position under the remittance basis

	£
Remitted foreign chargeable gain	25,000
CGT at 28%	7,000
Remittance basis charge	50,000
Total CGT	57,000
Additional income tax on employment income	4,000
Overall tax bill under remittance basis	61,000

As Sophia is not UK domiciled, she can elect to be taxed on the remittance basis. However, as she is a long-term UK resident (resident in more than 12 out of the last 14 tax years), she is required to pay £50,000 as a remittance basis charge. Under the remittance basis, Sophia loses entitlement to both the capital gains tax annual exempt amount and the £10,000 personal allowance for 2014/15 (resulting in additional income tax of £4,000 (i.e. £10,000 × 40%)). Therefore it would be more beneficial for Sophia to be taxed on the arising basis as the tax payable would be £2,480 lower.

Chapter 15

Question 15.1

Shauna Quinn – CGT 2014/15

	Painting	Vase	Shop	Land	Total
	£	£	£	£	£
Chargeable gains	47,000	0	125,900	55,000	227,900
Capital losses current year					(8,000)
Capital losses c/fwd					(208,900)
Net chargeable gains					11,000
Annual exemption					(11,000)
Chargeable gains					Nil

	£
Capital losses b/fwd	210,000
Used against 2014/15 gains	208,900
Capital losses c/fwd	1,100

Workings

1. Painting

	£
Proceeds	50,000
Less: costs of sale	(500)
Net proceeds of sale	49,500
Less: cost	(2,500)
Chargeable gain	47,000

2. Antique vase

	£
Proceeds:	4,000
Deem gross proceeds to be £6,000	6,000
Less: costs	(14,000)
Loss	(8,000)

3. Freehold shop

The transfer from Darren to Shauna is a no gain/no loss transfer. The base cost for Shauna is therefore £55,000.

The value of the unit at the date of the transfer is irrelevant.

	£
Proceeds	185,000
Less: costs of sale: Legal fees	(2,250)
Estate agents fee	(1,850)
Net proceeds of sale	180,900
Less: cost	(55,000)
Gain	125,900

4. Land

	£
Proceeds	80,000
Less: costs	

$$£40,000 \times \frac{80,000}{80,000 + 48,000} \qquad (25,000)$$

	£
Gain	55,000

The small disposal rules do not apply.

5. Car

Exempt from capital gains tax.

6. Capital losses

The current year capital losses must be used in their entirety against any available current year gains and in priority to any capital losses carried forward. However, the capital losses carried forward can be tailored in how they are used so as not to waste any of Shauna's annual exempt amount.

Question 15.2

MEMO
From: An Accountant
To: John Smith
Date: 3 July 2014
Subject: Outline of UK capital gains tax system

As discussed in our recent meeting, I have outlined below the basic principles of the UK capital gains tax system. Please do not hesitate to contact me if you have any queries in relation to this memo.

(a) Capital gains tax is payable in the UK at a flat rate of 18% on chargeable gains in the available basic rate band (£31,865 in 2014/15) with 28% charged on gains in excess of the basic rate band. A rate of 10% is available on any gains qualifying for entrepreneurs' relief, e.g. sale of shares in a personal trading company up to the lifetime limit per individual of £10 million. As you have income in excess of £100,000, any chargeable gains would be taxed at 28% subject to the availability of entrepreneurs' relief or other reliefs that might apply.

(b) Any capital gains tax due for the year ended 5 April 2015 will be due for payment by 31 January 2016.

(c) The capital gains should be declared to HMRC by filing in the relevant sections in your self-assessment tax return for the 2014/15 tax year.

(d) The first £11,000 of chargeable gains arising in the 2014/15 tax year will be exempt from tax.

(e) For sales of assets by individuals prior to 6 April 2008, the UK gave an inflationary increase to your capital gains base cost (called 'indexation allowance') for any assets that were acquired prior to April 1998. The indexation was calculated based on the increase in the RPI from the date of acquisition to 6 April 1998 even if the asset was sold after April 1998. However, from the 2008/09 tax year, no indexation is available. Note that companies still receive indexation on capital assets they sell from the month of acquisition to the month of sale.

(f) The following types of expenditure qualify as deductible for capital gains purposes:
   - Consideration given wholly and exclusively for acquisition of the asset.
   - Incidental costs of acquisition and incidental costs of disposal. These are limited to stamp duty and professional fees directly related to the acquisition and/or sale.
   - Expenditure incurred on enhancing the value of the asset that is reflected in the state and nature of the asset at the date of sale and expenditure in preserving or defending title to the asset.

(g) Unused capital losses are carried forward to set against capital gains arising in future periods. They cannot be carried back. However, as the capital losses will be used in periods after the period in which they arose, they can be partially set against gains arising to bring them down to the level of the annual exemption so that this is not wasted (rather than being used to reduce the gain to below the annual exemption or £Nil).

(h) If the asset had been sold to your brother, this would be a sale to a connected person. Therefore the capital loss would be 'ring-fenced' and could only be used against a capital gain arising on a future sale of a capital asset to your brother. It could therefore not be used against general gains on sale of capital assets.

(i) The capital gains base cost of the rental property will be the probate value of the property. This is likely to be the market value of the property at the date of your grandmother's death.

(j) As you are 'connected' with your grandmother under the capital gains tax legislation, then the gift of the property to you would be deemed to occur at the market value of the property at the date of gift – which would then be your capital gains base cost. Gift relief under section 165 TCGA 1992 would not be possible as the gift of rental property is not a business asset. The gift before death would also have IHT consequences. At the time of the gift, it will be classed as a potentially exempt transfer. However, if your grandmother died the next day (which is within seven years), the gift would fall within her death estate potentially liable to IHT at 40% after any available annual exemptions. Section 260 TCGA 1992 gift relief, which is available on non-business assets, would not be available here as the gift was not immediately chargeable to IHT in your grandmother's lifetime.

Chapter 16

Question 16.1

The house will have been James's principal private residence (PPR) as it was the only house he owned when he purchased it and he lived in it as a residence on acquisition.

Therefore the periods of qualifying ownership for PPR exemption are as follows:

- First three years (actual occupation).
- Last 18 months (always treated as a period of ownership).
- Years 4, 5 and 6.

These years qualify because there was actual occupation both before and after the period of absence, and the legislation contains a deemed period of occupation to cover three years of absence for any purpose.

The three years of deemed occupation are available even though the house was let in the period of absence. Thus, 7.5 years of ownership count as occupation and 2.5 years do not. The gain subject to tax is therefore £800,000 × 2.5/10 = £200,000.

However, as the property was let for residential purposes, letting relief is available to further reduce the chargeable gain that arises.

The letting relief is the **lower** of:

- gain arising in the letting period – this is £400,000;
- gain exempt under the PPR provisions – this is £600,000; or
- £40,000.

Thus, an additional £40,000 of the gain is exempt. The tax due is then calculated as follows:

	£
Gain after PPR relief	200,000
Less: lettings relief	(40,000)
	160,000
Less: annual exemption	(11,000)
Chargeable gain	149,000
Capital gains tax at 28%	29,800

Question 16.2

Mr Jack Bates
Your Place
Your Town
Spain

24 June 2014

Dear Jack,

Further to our recent conversation, I have set out below responses to your queries regarding capital gains tax in relation to your UK property.

Principal private residence relief

The general rule is that a gain on the disposal of an individual's only or main residence is exempt from capital gains tax. Grounds of up to half a hectare (approx. 1.24 acres), or larger areas that are appropriate to the size of the house, also qualify for the relief.

Full exemption applies where the owner has occupied the house throughout his entire period of ownership. Where occupation of the house has been only for part of the period of ownership, the exempt part of the gain is the proportion given by the following formula:

$$\frac{\text{Period of ownership post-31/03/1982}}{\text{Total period of ownership post-31/03/1982}} \times \text{Chargeable gain}$$

Where there is a delay of up to a year (extendable to a maximum of 2 years) in taking up residence of a property (e.g. complicated sale, house built, redecorations, etc.) then the period of non-residence will count as a period of residence. Providing a property has been an individual's only or main residence at some time during his total ownership (whether before or after 31 March 1982), the last 18 months automatically count as a period of residence (this was 36 months prior to 6 April 2014).

Certain other absences also count as residence, if preceded and followed (not necessarily before and after) by a period of actual residence and provided that relief is not being claimed for another main residence during the absence. These are:

- Up to three years for any reason.
- Any absence throughout which the individual is employed abroad. Up to four years during which the individual is prevented from living in the house because of work distances or because his employer requires him to live elsewhere.

There is further relief for owner-occupiers who, at any time during their period of ownership, have let all or part of the property as residential accommodation. This is known as "lettings relief". Lettings relief is restricted to the lower of:

- the gain accruing during the letting period;
- the part of the total gain that is exempt under the PPR provisions (including deemed periods of occupation); or
- £40,000.

CGT consequences of potential sale

I attach at Appendix 1 the capital gains tax calculation associated with the proposed sale of your Belfast property. You will note from same that the potential capital gain arising on disposal is £221,045, which would be taxed at 28% as you are an additional rate taxpayer.

Should you have any further queries in connection with the above, please do not hesitate to contact me.

Yours sincerely,
ABC & Co
Chartered Accountants

Appendix 1 – Sale of Apartment

	£
Sale Proceeds – July 2014	1,300,000
Cost (09/82)	(65,000)
	1,235,000
Less:	
Exempt element of gain:	
223/286 × £1,235,000	(962,955)
Lettings relief:	(40,000)
Lower of £40,000	
Exempt gain of £962,955; and	
Letting gain:	
63/286 × £1,235,000 = £272,045	
Chargeable gain	232,045
Annual exemption	(11,000)
	221,045
CGT thereon @ 28%	61,893

Workings

Total duration of ownership:

01/09/1990 to 01/07/2014 – 286 months being as follows:

	Months	
01/09/1990–01/01/1998	88	
01/01/1998–30/04/2006	100	Letting
30/04/2006–31/01/2012	69	
31/01/2012–01/07/2014	29	Letting
	286	

Exempt proportion:

Owner occupied	88 months	88 months
Deemed owner occupied	48 months (max.)	48 months (max.)
Owner occupied	69 months	45 months
Last 18 months deemed	18 months	36 months
Total exempt portion	223 months	

Chapter 17

Question 17.1

	£
Sales proceeds re: 2,500 shares	30,000
Cost: 2,500/6,450 × 21,225	(8,227)
Taxable gain	21,773
CGT @ 28%	£6,096.44

Due for payment on 31 January 2016

Note:

As the disposal cannot be matched with any acquisition on the same day or the following 30 days, it must be matched with the section 104 holding, which is as follows:

Date

		No. of shares acquired	Cost £
5/10/2001	Purchase	1,500	8,000
10/4/2004	Purchase	2,800	10,000
18/3/2006	Rights issue, 1 for 2 held at £1.50 per share	2,150	3,225
Section 104 holding		6,450	21,225

The average allowable cost per share is therefore £3.29.

Chapter 18

Question 18.1

Meets Condition (1)	£
Gain	900,000
CGT payable @ 10%	90,000

Question 18.2

ER not available – Condition (1) is not met, as she did not own business for at least one year prior to the disposal.

Question 18.3

Meets Condition (1)	£
Gain	10,300,000
CGT:	
£10,000,000 @ 10%	1,000,000
£300,000 @ 28%	84,000
Total CGT	1,084,000

Note: gain exceeds lifetime limit of £10 million.

Question 18.4

ER not available – Condition (1) is not met as it is not a qualifying business, i.e. not a trade, profession or vocation. A letting of unfurnished property is not a furnished holiday let; therefore, it is a property letting under rental provisions and is not a trade.

Question 18.5

Meets Condition (2)	£
Net qualifying gain (£360,000 − £90,000)	270,000
CGT @ 10%	27,000

Gain (on subsequent disposal) 2015/16	£
Condition (2) is met	72,000
CGT @ 10%	7,200

Question 18.6

ER not available as Condition (3) is not met. Must have at least a 5% interest.

Question 18.7

	£
Meets Condition (1)	
Gain	630,000
CGT @ 10% (2014/2015)	63,000
Gain on second disposal (2015/16)	10,000,000
CGT at 10% on £9,370,000 (i.e. £10m − £630,000 = £9,370,000)	937,000
CGT at 28% on £630,000 (i.e. excess over lifetime allowance)	176,400
Total CGT 2015/16	1,113,400

Question 18.8

No chargeable gains arise on cessation as there is no disposal at that time. The actual disposal will qualify for ER as Patricia meets the criteria of Condition (2) above. If Patricia sold the property after 30 April 2017 instead, then no ER would be available.

Question 18.9

	£
Meets Condition (1)	
Gain	190,000
CGT @ 10%	19,000

Question 18.10

Report to James Devlin – Tax Implications of Recent Transactions
April 2015

Introduction
This report outlines the tax consequences of the disposal of both your shares in Devlin Communications Limited and the Dungannon property. Both transactions constitute chargeable gains; therefore we have also considered reliefs available and outlined our recommendation that capital gains tax entrepreneurs' relief (ER) is claimed as this is available on both transactions (although only partially available on the Dungannon property disposal). ER reduces the rate of capital gains tax from the maximum rate of 28% to 10% and applies on a 'lifetime cap' of £10 million for gains arising after 6 April 2011. Your full lifetime limit of £10 million is available as these are the only assets you have ever owned.

Details of the timing of tax payments and of available elections are also included with detailed calculations outlined at Appendix 1.

Devlin Communications Limited share disposal

To qualify for ER on a disposal of shares in a trading company or holding company of a trading group, the company must be your 'personal company', which means that you must be an officer or employee and must hold a 'material interest' of at least 5% of the ordinary share capital and voting rights. These conditions must be fulfilled for a period of 12 months prior to the disposal.

You appear to meet all of these conditions as the company is a trading company, you were a director at the time of the disposal, you held 40% of the shares and you did so for a period of over 12 months prior to disposal. Therefore entrepreneurs' relief is available on this transaction.

Dungannon property disposal

ER is also available for the disposal of an asset owned personally by an individual if it can be 'associated' with a relevant 'material disposal'. Three conditions must be satisfied:

1. The individual makes a 'material disposal' of either the whole or part of their interest in the assets of a partnership or the shares in a company. Your disposal of your entire shareholding in Devlin Communications Limited fulfils this condition.
2. The associated disposal is made as part of the withdrawal of the individual from participation in the partnership or the company. This condition is also clearly fulfilled as the Dungannon property disposal is tied into the share disposal.
3. The assets are in use in the business for one year ending with the earlier date of material disposal of (in this case) the shares in Devlin Communications Limited. As the property was used and rented by Devlin Communications Limited since 2006, this condition is also met.

Therefore ER is available, however the amount of ER is restricted because the shop was not used throughout the entire period of ownership by Devlin Communications Limited and it is further restricted because a rent was payable by Devlin Communications Limited – see Notes 2 and 3 in Appendix 1 for further explanation.

Conclusion

As noted above, we recommend that ER is claimed. This represents a saving of £174,245 (i.e. £1,200,000 − £11,000 @28% less £158,675). You should note that ER is not automatic and must be claimed by the first anniversary of the 31 January following the tax year in which the gain arose. As both transactions happened in the 2014/15 tax year, the claims for ER on each must both be made by 31 January 2017.

The capital gains tax that arises on the gains, which totals £158,675, must be paid on or before 31 January following the end of the relevant tax year. Therefore the liability must be paid by 31 January 2016.

Appendix 1 Capital gains tax position

	Shares £	Shop £
Proceeds	851,000	475,000
Less: cost	(1,000)	(125,000)
Gains before relief	850,000	350,000
Less: gains on shop not eligible for relief		
£350,000 × 3/12 (Note 2)		(87,500)
		262,500
Less: restriction for rent charged		
£262,500 × 70% × 7/9 (Note 3)		(142,917)
Gains eligible for entrepreneurs' relief	850,000	119,583

Total eligible gains (£850,000 + £119,583)	£969,583	
Total gains not eligible for ER	£230,417	
	£1,200,000	
Less: Annual exemption (Note 1)	(£11,000)	
Chargeable gains	£1,189,000	

Capital gains tax liability:	£
£969,583 @ 10%	£96,958
£220,417 @ 28%	£61,717
Total CGT liability	£158,675

Notes:

1. The annual exemption should be set against the gain subject to the highest tax (i.e. the gain not qualifying for ER (28%), rather than those qualifying for gains (i.e. 10%). This reduces the non-qualifying gains to £220,417.
2. The shop was only used in the business for nine out of the 12 years of Sean's ownership. Therefore only 9/12ths of the gain on this associated disposal will qualify for entrepreneurs' relief and 3/12ths will not.
3. The shop was used in business from 1 April 2006 to 31 March 2015 (nine years). The period falling after 6 April 2008 is seven years.

James received rent on the shop which represented 70% of the market rent (£1,575/£2,250). Therefore the gain eligible for entrepreneurs' relief is further restricted but only for the period after 6 April 2008 (i.e. seven years out of the nine).

Chapter 19

Question 19.1

	£
Proceeds	43,000
Less: Cost	(5,000)
Gain	38,000

The gain is then reduced to amount not reinvested i.e. £18,000 (being £43,000 – £25,000).

Capital gains tax is payable thereon as follows:

	£
£6,865 @ 18%*	1,235.70
Remainder (£11,135) @ 28%	3,117.80
	4,353.50

*Available basic rate band is £31,865 – £25,000 = £6,865. Hence £6,865 of the gain is taxable at 18% and the remainder at 28%.

Question 19.2

This is Sarah's personal company as she owns at least 5% of the company and its voting rights. The assets are broken down between chargeable business assets and chargeable assets as follows:

	£	£	£
	MV 2015	**CBA**	**CA**
Goodwill	410,000	410,000	410,000
Land and buildings	470,000	470,000	470,000
Plant and machinery	2,500	Exempt	Exempt
MV	4,000	Exempt	Exempt
Debtors	40,000	n/a	n/a
Stock	3,000	n/a	n/a
Cash	500	n/a	n/a
Rental property	120,000	n/a	120,000
	1,050,000	880,000	1,000,000

(a)	Proceeds – deemed		£
	Proceeds		105,000
	Less: cost		(50,000)
	Gain		55,000
	Less: gift relief $55,000 \times \dfrac{880,000}{1,000,000}$		(48,400)
	Taxable gain		6,600
	Annual exemption		(11,000)
			NIL

(b)	Base cost for Emily under (a):	
		£
	Market value	105,000
	Less gift relief	(48,400)
	Base cost	56,600

(c)		£
	Indexed gain	55,000
	Annual exemption	(11,000)
	Taxable gain	44,000

(d)	Base cost for Emily under (c):	£
	Base cost = Market value	105,000

Question 19.3

Aine Taylor
Belfast

26 November 2014

Dear Aine,
I refer to our recent meeting in relation to the proposed factory disposal. I have outlined the information requested below:

(a) Tax due
UK capital gains tax will be payable on the sale of the factory. The calculation below indicates that, in the absence of suitable reliefs, capital gains tax of £276,920 will be payable.

As you are trading as a sole trader, this tax will be payable by you personally. As the disposal will be made in the 2014/15 tax year, the capital gains tax will be payable on or before 31 January 2016. As you are an additional rate taxpayer, the rate of capital gains tax is 28% before any reliefs. This is calculated as follows

	£
Proceeds	1,500,000
Less: base cost	(500,000)
Taxable gain	1,000,000
Less: annual exemption	(11,000)
Taxable gain	989,000
Tax @ 28%	276,920

(b) Rollover relief

Rollover relief is available when a sole trader such as yourself sells a capital asset which is in their trade and uses the sales proceeds to acquire one of a number of specified assets that is immediately brought into use in the trade.

Qualifying assets include:

- Land and buildings.
- Goodwill.
- Fixed plant and machinery.
- Ships, aircraft, hovercraft, satellites, space stations, spacecraft, milk quota, potato quota, fish quota and ewe, suckler cow premiums and payment entitlements under the new agricultural subsidy Basic Payment Scheme.

However, the asset acquired does not have to be the same as the asset sold.

Rollover relief is only available if the new asset is acquired in the period twelve months before and three years after the date the factory is sold. If you are unsure when the new investment will be made, as long as it is within the three years from disposal (i.e. by 8 November 2017) a provisional claim for relief can be made. In addition, it would be recommended that you review expenditure in the year prior to disposal (i.e. from 9 November 2013 to 8 November 2014) to check if any qualifying spend was incurred in that period.

However, in order for full rollover relief to be available, the entire proceeds of sale of the first asset must be reinvested in the second asset.

If all of the proceeds on the sale of the factory (i.e. £1,500,000) are not fully reinvested, a gain equal to the lower of:

- the full gain (i.e. £1,000,000); or
- the cash retained

is left chargeable. If the amount of cash retained exceeds £1,000,000, then no rollover relief may be claimed. So for every £1 of cash that is not reinvested (up to £1,000,000 not reinvested), £1 of the gain is subject to capital gains tax. Therefore, rollover relief will only be available in respect of every pound reinvested over £500,000.

The gain rolled over reduces the capital gains base cost of the new asset by the amount of that gain.

Rollover relief must be claimed in writing to HMRC within four years after the **later** of:

▦   the end of the tax year in which *disposal of the old asset* took place (i.e. by 5 April 2019); or

▦   the end of the tax year in which *acquisition of the new asset* took place.

In your case, if reinvestment did not occur until 8 November 2017, the date for the claim for relief would be 5 April 2022. The earliest date a claim would be due will always be 5 April 2019 even if you had reinvested in sufficient qualifying assets in the period 9 November 2013–8 November 2014.

You should note that hold-over relief is another form of deferral relief that may be available should you decide instead to lease property instead of purchasing a freehold investment.

(c) Enterprise Investment Scheme relief

On the basis that Shoe Manufacturer Ltd is a qualifying company, it may be possible to claim Enterprise Investment Scheme (EIS) deferral relief if you subscribe for shares in this company.

Relief given under EIS deferral is the lower of:

▦   the gain itself (i.e. £1,000,000);

▦   the amount specified in the claim (compared to rollover relief which cannot be tailored); or

▦   the amount subscribed for new shares in the EIS company.

This is a significant difference from rollover relief as only £1,000,000 would need to be subscribed for shares in the company for the capital gains tax on the gain to be fully deferred. Under rollover relief, the entire £1,500,000 would need to be reinvested to fully rollover the gain.

However, whereas rollover relief reduces the base cost of the new asset, under EIS relief the capital gain is merely deferred and will crystallize when certain specified events occur (normally sale of the shares). Though it can be said that rollover relief does significantly reduce the base cost of the new asset when disposed of in future, unless it is again replaced with a further qualifying asset.

Again, the relief will only be available if the shares are subscribed for within the period 12 months before to three years after the date the factory is sold.

EIS deferral relief must be claimed in writing to HMRC within five years from the tax filing deadline for the tax year in which the shares were issued. So if you reinvested £1,000,000 in Shoe Manufacturers Ltd shares in 2014/15, the claim should be made on or before 31 January 2021.

There are also a number of other valuable reliefs available under the EIS, including income tax relief at 30% on the initial investment (assuming you will not hold 30% or more of the shares) and capital gains tax relief on their eventual disposal if they are held for a minimum three-year period.

I hope this is helpful. However, if you have any queries please give me a call.

Yours sincerely,
An Accountant

Chapter 20

Question 20.1

Mr Andrew Jameson
Andrewstones Limited

11 December 2014

Dear Andrew,

As requested, we have set out below the tax consequences of the proposed purchase by the company of your shares in Andrewstones Ltd.

(a) Conditions for capital gains treatment

If the following conditions are met, the share buy-back of an unquoted trading company (which Andrewstones Ltd is) will be treated as a capital transaction taxable as a capital gain on you. We have also assessed whether, in the case of the proposed transaction, each of the conditions below is met:

- *Wholly or mainly for the benefit of the trade and not in the course of a scheme whose main purpose is the avoidance of tax.*
  In Statement of Practice 2/82, HMRC accepts the circumstances in which the trade benefit test will be met. The company's sole or main purpose in making the payment must be to benefit a trade carried on by it or by its 75% subsidiary. If the purpose is to ensure that an unwilling shareholder who wishes to end his association with the company does not sell his shares to someone who might not be acceptable to the other shareholders, the purchase will normally be regarded as benefiting the company's trade. Included within the examples of unwilling share-holders are a controlling shareholder who is retiring as a director and wishes to make way for new management. Therefore the trade benefit test should be met in this case. In addition, there is no suggestion that the transaction is being undertaken for a tax avoidance motive.
- *Vendor must be UK resident when the shares are bought back.*
  Andrew has always been UK resident and there is no suggestion that this will change in any respect, hence this condition will be met.
- *Vendor must have owned the shares for the preceding five years (three years if acquired on death). If the shares were acquired from a spouse or civil partner, then the spouse or civil partner's ownership period will also count as your ownership period for the purposes of this test.*
  Andrew has held the shares since 1991, clearly satisfying the five-year ownership test.
- *Must make a substantial reduction in shareholding: after-sale vendor and associate's interest must be reduced to 75% or less of interest before disposal.*
  Andrew is disposing of 100% of his shareholding and thus clearly meets this condition. We do not count his son John's 25% shareholding as the shareholding of an associate in this case because John is not a minor.
- *After the transaction the vendor must not be connected with the company (or any company in the same 51% group). Connected means one can control more than 30% of the ordinary share capital, issued share capital and loan capital or voting rights in the company or is entitled to 30% of the assets of the company if it were to be wound up.*
  Andrew will no longer hold any shares in the company, hence this condition will be met.

OR

▓ *If the buyback facilitates the payment of an IHT charge within two years of the death of the individual whose death gave rise to the liability crystallizing – N/A in this case*

On the basis of the above, it would appear that each of the necessary conditions are met in order to obtain capital treatment. However, please be advised that it is possible to obtain HMRC advance clearance that capital treatment will apply to the transaction. We would recommend that this clearance procedure is availed of to provide more certainty given the significant tax saving to be achieved (£253,900 capital gains tax vs. £779,167 income tax distribution).

(b) Anticipated CGT liability

If the above tests are met (which is likely to be the case), we anticipate that you will have a capital gains tax liability of £253,900 (see Appendix 1) as entrepreneurs' relief is available on the chargeable gain, reducing the capital gains tax liability from 28% to 10%. This assumes you have your full lifetime limit for entrepreneurs' relief available.

(c) Consequences if capital treatment is not obtained

If capital treatment is not obtained, any payment the company makes in respect of its shares will be treated as an income distribution (i.e. a dividend), apart from the amount that represents repayment of the nominal value of the shares.

We understand that you originally subscribed £75,000 for 75,000 £1 shares in 1991. As such, if the company paid you £2,625,000 in exchange for these shares and capital gains tax treatment was not obtained, then you would be treated as in receipt of a cash dividend of £2,550,000. The gross dividend would be £2,833,333 (£2,550,000 × 10/9) and as you are an additional rate taxpayer (because your income is over £150,000), tax of £1,062,500 (dividend additional rate of 37.5%) would be payable against which a tax credit on the dividend of £283,333 (10% of the gross dividend) would be available, giving a net tax charge on the purchase of your shares of £779,167 (which is effectively 30.56% of the net dividend). No capital gain/allowable loss arises on the £75,000 that is treated as the repayment of the nominal value of the shares.

(d) Stamp duty reserve tax

Please also be aware that the company (Andrewstones Limited) will be subject to stamp duty reserve tax on the share buy-back in the amount of £13,125, being 0.5% of the £2,625,000 proceeds that the company will pay for the shares. There is a 30-day time limit after execution (when the share transfer documents are dated and signed by all parties) for getting the document stamped and paying the required stamp duty. If the share transfer document is not presented to the Stamp Office until after 30 days from the date the transaction is executed, then a late filing penalty and interest may be charged.

I hope the above is helpful, however if you have any questions, please do not hesitate to contact us.

Yours sincerely,

Appendix 1

	£
Proceeds: 75,000 × £35	2,625,000
Less: original cost	(75,000)
	2,550,000
Less: annual exemption	(11,000)
Chargeable gain	2,539,000
CGT @ 10%	253,900

Entrepreneurs' relief is available to reduce the rate of capital gains tax on the gain from 28% to 10% because Andrew has disposed of a 75% shareholding in his personal trading company. The company is a trading company and Andrew has held a shareholding of more than 5% for a 12-month period as he has held a 75% shareholding since 1991. Andrew also meets the director/officer condition, thereby enabling a 10% rate of capital gains tax. We are not aware of Andrew having used his lifetime limit for entrepreneurs' relief and assume the full lifetime limit of £10 million is available.

Question 20.2

The Directors and Mrs Sarah Donaldson
Maddon Engineering Ltd

11 March 2015

Gentlemen and Mrs Donaldson,

Company buy-back of shares

First, may I once again extend my condolences on the recent death of Aaron.

I refer to our recent discussions in relation to the forthcoming share buy-back by Maddon Engineering Limited ("Maddon"). You also requested information explaining the tax treatment, together with an explanation (with associated calculations) of how Sarah will be taxed and whether the capital treatment is available.

Tax legislation specifies that if the consideration payable by Maddon for the shares exceeds the amount of capital originally subscribed for them, the excess will constitute an income distribution unless the capital treatment applies. In this case the consideration for the shares clearly exceeds the original consideration, as Maddon will be paying £1,500,000 to Sarah for the shares (10,000 shares × £150 per share).

From Sarah's perspective, the buy-back is a taxable disposal. Essentially there are two possible tax treatments i.e. taxable as a capital gain or taxable as an income distribution. Calculations for each treatment are outlined in Appendix 1 and as you can see the capital treatment is more favourable as the rate of tax is less at 28% compared to an effective rate of 30.56% under the income treatment.

The remainder of this letter therefore assesses whether the capital treatment is available as Sarah has indicated the transaction will not proceed unless this is available.

Share buy-back – capital treatment

The capital treatment only applies where:

- *The repurchase is by an unquoted trading company whose trade does not consist of dealing in shares, securities, land or futures.*

  Maddon is a trading company, therefore this condition is met.

- *The repurchase is wholly or mainly for the benefit of the trade.*

  Sarah does not wish to retain the shares she will inherit from Aaron later this month – HMRC is likely to accept this scenario as meeting the wholly or mainly for the benefit of the trade test.

- *The shares must be bought back from a UK resident vendor who has held the shares for at least five years (three years if acquired on a death).*

  On 4 April 2015 Sarah will not have held the shares for three years; however Aaron's ownership period can also be taken into account. As he acquired the shares in the 1990s, this test is clearly met. Sarah is also UK resident; therefore the residence test is also met.

- *The vendor must, as a result of the buy-back, reduce his or her interest in the company by at least 25%.*

  Sarah is disposing of the entire shareholding, hence this condition is met.

- *The vendor must not be connected with the company following the buy-back. The vendor will be treated as connected with the company if they either possess, or are entitled to possess, more than 30% of the issued ordinary share capital, loan capital, or voting power, or are entitled to receive more than 30 % of the assets on a winding-up of the company.*

  Sarah will no longer be connected with the company as she will hold no shares after the transaction is completed, therefore this condition is met.

- *The share buy-back is not undertaken solely for tax avoidance reasons.*

  There does not appear to be any tax avoidance motive and hence this condition appears to be fulfilled.

Based on all of the above, the capital treatment will be available for the transaction and will provide a tax saving for Sarah of £41,157. More certainty can be obtained by applying to HMRC in advance for clearance.

Stamp Duty

Please also be aware that the company, Maddon Engineering Limited, will be subject to stamp duty on the share buy-back in the amount of £7,500, being 0.5% of the £1,500,000 proceeds that the company will pay for the shares.

If you have any further questions, do not hesitate to contact me.

Yours sincerely,

Appendix I

(a) Calculation of capital gains tax/income tax liability re: share buy-back

Income treatment

	£
Amount received on share buy-back (10,000 × £150)	1,500,000
Less: original subscription price	(10,000)
Net dividend received	1,490,000
Gross dividend (£1,490,000 × 100/90)	1,655,556
Income tax @ 37.5%*	620,833
Tax credit (10% × £1,655,556)	(165,556)
Income tax due at effective rate of 30.56%	**455,277**

*Sarah is an additional rate taxpayer so the dividend additional rate applies
Under the income treatment, Sarah will also have a capital disposal as follows:

Sales proceeds (original subscription price)	10,000
Less: actual cost	(10,000)
Capital gain/loss	**0**

Capital treatment

Sale proceeds (10,000 × £150)	1,500,000
Less: cost	(10,000)
Chargeable gain	1,490,000
Less: annual exemption (2014/15)	(11,000)
Taxable gain	1,479,000
CGT payable @ 28%	**£414,120**

Sarah is not an employee or director, therefore entrepreneurs' relief is not available to reduce the gain arising.

(b) Briefing note

To: Any Partner
From: Any Accountant
Date: 25 March 2015
Subject: Shares in Maddon Engineering Limited ("Maddon")

Further to my recent conversations with Sarah, this briefing note addresses two matters:

1. The availability of business property relief for the Maddon shares.

2.   The IHT and ethical implications re: the chargeable lifetime transfer.

Each of those is dealt with in turn below.

1.   The availability of business property relief for the Maddon shares
Business Property relief will be available at the rate of 100% on the 10,000 shared held by Aaron at the date of his death. This is because the shares qualify as shares in an unquoted trading company. There is no minimum holding requirement, so the fact that Aaron only held 1/3 of the shares has no impact. The shares have also been held since the 1990s, hence the two-year holding period requirement is also met. BPR is also fully available as there are no excepted assets on Maddon's statement of financial position.

However, if BPR was not available it should be noted that no inheritance tax (IHT) liability would arise as the shares are being transferred to Sarah on Aaron's death and are thus fully exempt from IHT under the spousal exemption.

The value of the shares to be included in Aaron's estate is therefore calculated as follows:

10,000 shares × £150 per share	£1,500,000
Less 100% business property relief	(£1,500,000)
Value in death estate	£NIL

2.   The IHT and ethical implications re: the chargeable lifetime transfer
The transfer of cash to the discretionary trust comes within the relevant property regime and IHT should have been paid thereon in lifetime as follows:

Lifetime IHT

December 2011		£
Gift to discretionary trust		500,000
Annual exemption – 2010/11		(3,000)
Annual exemption – 2009/10		(3,000)
Chargeable lifetime transfer		494,000
Inheritance tax threshold – 2010/11	325,000	
Less cumulative chargeable transfers in the previous seven years	0	
Available inheritance tax threshold	325,000	
Less nil rate band		(325,000)
Chargeable lifetime transfer		169,000
Lifetime IHT thereon @ 20%		33,800

On lifetime transfers, the primary liability for payment lies with the donor (unless the donee agrees to pay tax). For chargeable lifetime transfers, the due date is the later of:

▪   six months from the end of the month in which the transfer is made; or
▪   30 April following the end of the financial year in which the transfer is made.

As the gift was made in December 2011, the liability was due for payment on or before 30 June 2012. Interest and penalties will arise for failure to pay this liability.

The gift is required to be included in Aaron's death estate as it was made in the previous seven years. IHT arises as follows:

Death estate

December 2011		£
Gift to discretionary trust		500,000
Annual exemption – 2010/11		(3,000)
Annual exemption – 2009/10		(3,000)
		494,000
Inheritance tax threshold – 2014/15	325,000	
Less cumulative chargeable transfers in the previous seven years	Nil	
Less available inheritance tax threshold		(325,000)
		169,000
Inheritance tax:		
£169,000 @ 40%		67,600
Taper relief @ 20%		(13,520)
Lifetime tax paid		(33,800)
Additional IHT payable on death		20,280

Please note that Sarah has suggested that if the transfer to the trust fails to be included in Aaron's estate, she would like us to turn a blind eye to this as she believes HMRC have no way of finding out about this. On the basis of the foregoing, the transfer to the trust is required to be included. As you know, it would be unethical to omit this from the inheritance tax return and under the Code of Ethics of Chartered Accountants Ireland we cannot do as Sarah wishes.

Could I suggest that when we next meet we agree how best to approach this with Sarah. I would also suggest that we take the opportunity to discuss with Sarah the importance of ensuring that the inheritance tax return is complete and the potential penalties that could arise for failure to include all relevant items.

Chapter 21

Question 21.1

(a)

Transfer of value made by Mr Grey for IHT:

Value of shares before transfer (78,000 × £35)	£2,730,000
Value of shares after transfer (48,000 × £14)	£(672,000)
Value transferred	£2,058,000

Anne has received the shares by way of gift from her father. Anne is treated as a connected person under section 286 TCGA 1992, hence Anne's base cost of the shares in Grey Ltd is deemed to be their open market value unless a joint election for gift relief is made. On the basis of receiving a 30% shareholding which is valued at £14 per share, Anne has a base cost for capital gains tax of £420,000 (30,000 shares × £14).

Question 21.2

In cases where assets (other than shares) are owned jointly by husband and wife, and one spouse makes a transfer of value for inheritance tax purposes, the value transferred is calculated as below.

	£
Value before transfer:	
800,000 × [375,000/(375,000 + 110,000)] (Note 1)	618,557
Value after transfer:	
500,000 × [250,000/(250,000 + 110,000)] (Note 2)	(347,222)
Transfer of value	271,335

Note 1:
6 chairs are worth £800,000, Stephanie has 4 of these.
4 chairs are worth £375,000.
Martin's 2 chairs are worth £110,000.

Note 2:
5 chairs are worth £500,000. Stephanie has 3 of these.
3 chairs are worth £250,000.
Martin's 2 chairs are worth £110,000.

Question 21.3

(a) Gift of shares in family company to daughter
    Yes, this is a transfer of value because it is a gift. The transaction would also have capital gains tax implications as a transaction with a connected person.
(b) Sale of a painting to a local art dealer
    No, this would not be a transfer of value because it is a genuine arm's length transaction between the parties and there is no loss to the original donor as cash has replaced the asset.
(c) Waiver of dividend in family company
    No, this would not be a transfer of value as long as the right to the dividend is waived within 12 months before the right to the dividend accrues. The waiver must also be by way of legally enforceable deed.
(d) Payment of daughter's school fees
    No, this would not be a transfer of value. While the donor's estate would be reduced, there is no associated gratuitous intent.
(e) Purchase of Lamborghini from a local car dealership
    No, this would not be a transfer of value because it is a genuine arm's length transaction between the parties and there is no loss to the original donor as a car has replaced the money paid for it.
(f) Gift of an investment property to a family trust
    Yes, this is a transfer of value because it is a gift. The transaction would also have capital gains tax implications.

Question 21.4

(a) Zelda's domicile of origin is outside the UK. As she has not been resident in the UK for at least 17 out of the last 20 years (she has been UK resident for 15 years), she remains non-UK domiciled and is only subject to inheritance tax on a transfer of her UK assets.

(b) Willem has acquired a UK domicile of choice and is therefore subject to inheritance tax on transfer of both his UK and overseas assets.

(c) Cerys is no longer UK domiciled but she remains UK deemed domicile for three years after changing her domicile status in November 2013 and is therefore subject to inheritance tax on transfer of both her UK and overseas assets. It may be advisable to delay transferring her foreign assets into the UK resident trust until after November 2016, at which point she will be not be deemed UK domiciled. However, at that point Cerys would still be subject to IHT on the transfer of any UK assets.

Question 21.5

Currently Penny's domicile is a domicile of origin in the United Kingdom, as an individual acquires their mother's domicile at birth where their parents are unmarried. This means that should Penny die before she leaves the UK, she will be UK domiciled for IHT purposes at that time and subject to inheritance tax on all her worldwide assets, including the London property and the Italian property inherited from her mother. This would also apply to any gifts in lifetime. This is the most robust form of domicile and can only be displaced by acquiring a domicile of choice.

Penny plans to emigrate to Australia before the end of 2015; she plans to cut off all remaining ties with the UK. This is suggestive that Penny intends to acquire a domicile of choice in Australia by being both physically present there **and** sufficiently evidencing the intention of staying there permanently. It should be noted that there will be a heavy burden of proof on Penny to demonstrate to HMRC that she has displaced her domicile of origin in the UK with a domicile of choice in Australia.

This is because if Penny is not UK domiciled she will only be subject to UK IHT on her UK assets (including the London property if she still owns it at the time) with relief available for any inheritance tax she might pay on her UK assets in Australia. However, the deemed domicile rules are also relevant. These mean that any individual previously UK domiciled will be considered to be UK domiciled for UK IHT purposes (only) for three years after they cease to be UK domiciled. So if Penny permanently leaves the UK for her new domicile of choice in Australia in December 2015, she will remain UK deemed domicile for IHT until December 2018. Once again, all of her worldwide assets will be caught.

In addition, where a non-UK domiciled individual has been resident in the UK for 17 out of the previous 20 years of assessment, ending with the year of assessment in which the relevant event falls, deemed domicile will again apply. At the point that Penny becomes non-UK domiciled in December 2018, she will only have been non-UK resident for three complete tax years (2018/19, 2017/18 and 2016/17 as in 2015/16 she will have been UK resident until the date of her departure), meaning she will have been UK resident for 17 out of the previous 20 years of assessment. Penny remains deemed domicile under this rule until 5 April 2019. Four complete tax years of non-residence are therefore required to shake off deemed domicile. Thereafter, Penny will be non-UK domiciled for IHT purposes and only subject to UK IHT on any UK situs property with credit available for any IHT she may also pay on those assets in Australia.

Chapter 22

Question 22.1

At the time of the transfer by Sean in July 2014, the value transferred of £1,500,000 is exempt to the extent of £325,000 only as Gita is non-UK domiciled and a PET to the extent of £1,175,000. Sean dies less than seven years later in June 2017, meaning the failed PET is chargeable and, after deducting the nil rate band, £850,000 is subject to tax. No taper relief is available because Sean died less than three years after the original gift.

The £200,000 transfer by Gita in January 2016 was a transfer of excluded property under IHTA84/S6(1) by a non-UK domiciled individual holding non-UK property. Following Sean's death, Gita has the choice of electing to be treated as domiciled in the UK. If she does so, the gift from Sean in 2014 will become fully exempt as a transfer where both spouses are domiciled in the UK. This would result in an IHT saving of £340,000 (£850,000 × 40%).

However, Gita will then be treated as domiciled in the UK from 2014 for all IHT purposes. This means that the £200,000 transfer to the trustees would no longer be one of excluded property and will be subject to UK IHT. As a transfer to a trust, it will be immediately chargeable to tax as a chargeable lifetime transfer. However, it will be fully covered by the nil rate band.

It seems that an election would be worthwhile given the tax saving of £340,000, however Gita will need to consider all the consequences of making an election in the context of her of her entire asset portfolio.

Question 22.2

▨ The land valued at £80,000 gifted to her daughter Ana is reduced to £69,000 by applying the marriage exemption of £5,000 for a marriage gift to a child and annual exemptions of £3,000 for each of 2013/14 and 2014/15.

▨ The gifts to her grandchildren are likely to be fully exempt as 'normal expenditure out of income', as they are habitual, paid out of surplus income and presumably Annette is able to maintain her usual standard of living.

▨ The first £325,000 of the gift from Annette to Stefan is exempt as it is from a UK domiciled to a non-UK domiciled spouse. Prior to 6 April 2013, the limit was £55,000. Stefan may wish to consider electing to be deemed domicile as £55,000 constitutes a transfer of value by his wife.

Chapter 23

Question 23.1

Lifetime IHT arises as follows:

	£
Cash gift	400,000
Less: annual exemption:	
2010/11	(3,000)
2009/10	(3,000)
Net gift	394,000
Less: 2010/11 NRB	(325,000)
Chargeable transfer	69,000

Primary responsibility for any lifetime IHT rests with the donor unless Frederick specifically requests as a term of the gift that the donee bears the IHT. Thus IHT due in lifetime is 20/80 × £69,000 = £17,250.

Should Frederick die on 10 April 2014, additional IHT falls due on the gift on death as follows:

	£
Net gift including lifetime tax	411,250
Less: 2014/15 NRB	(325,000)
	86,250
Less:	
Taper relief (3–4 years) 20%	(17,250)
	69,000
Less:	
Lifetime IHT paid	(17,250)
Additional IHT on death	51,750

Question 23.2

Portia di Rossi – Inheritance tax calculations 2014/15

Lifetime Gifts

Portia has made a number of lifetime gifts which need to be assessed from an IHT perspective to establish tax payable in lifetime and potential additional IHT payable thereon on death.

None of the gifts qualify as a PET as Portia died less than seven years after making the earliest transfer of value.

The following CLTs arise during Portia's lifetime:

2008/09 Tax year	£	£
Gifts to children in 2008/09	18,000	
Less: annual exemption 2008/09	(3,000)	
b/f annual exemption 2007/08	(3,000)	
		12,000*
2009/10 Tax year		
Gift to USA charity	25,000	
Wedding gift to godson	6,000	
	31,000	
Less:		
Annual exemption 2009/2010	(3,000)	
Marriage exemption	(1,000)	
		27,000*
2013/14 Tax year		
Discretionary trust	380,000	
Less:		
Annual exemption 2013/14	(3,000)	
Annual exemption 2012/13	(3,000)	
		374,000
Total chargeable		413,000

* No tax in lifetime as it was then a PET nor on death as both are covered by the IHT NRB.

Tax payable on death by trustees of discretionary trust

	£	
Value liable to tax		374,000
NRB at death	325,000	
Utilised by PETs now chargeable on death	(39,000)	
		(286,000)
Liable on death		88,000
IHT thereon @ 40% on death		35,200
Less: IHT of 20% paid on CLT of £49,000 (CLT £374,000 less NRB £325,000)		(9,800)
Additional IHT on death		25,400

IHT treatment of assets at date of death

Calculation of taxable estate on death

	Notes		£
Armagh house	2		645,000
House contents	2		48,500
Villa in Portugal	3		225,000
Belfast Ceramics Plc shares – 18,000 × £1.45	4		26,100
British Meats Plc shares – 3,500 × £13.60	4		47,600
Belfast bank accounts			69,000
Guernsey bank account	3		228,000
Italiana Wine SA shares	5	180,000	
Less: Business property relief	5	(180,000)	
Nil			0
Taxable estate			1,289,200

IHT payable by Portia's executors on her estate at death:

As Portia's £325,000 NRB has been exhausted by lifetime transfers, the whole of the taxable estate is chargeable to IHT at 40%, being £515,680.

Notes

1. Lifetime Gifts
   The annual Christmas gifts to Portia's grandchildren are covered by the £250 small gifts exemption and are therefore exempt from IHT.
      As only gifts to EU charities are exempt from IHT, the gift to the US charity is not exempt.
      The first £1,000 of the gift to her godson is exempt as a gift in consideration of marriage, with the remainder being a transfer of value.

2. House in Armagh

The property was sold for less than its probate value. Under post-mortem relief, where an interest in land is sold within four years of the date of death, a claim may be made that the sale price is treated as the date of death value for IHT purposes. The sale value has been included in the estate tax calculation on the basis that such a claim would be made. The value of the contents of Portia's Armagh house also falls into her estate.

3. Overseas assets

As Portia died domiciled in the UK, her worldwide assets are liable to UK IHT. Therefore, both the Portuguese villa and the Guernsey bank account are part of her estate on death.

4. Quoted shares

Post-mortem relief also allows, where quoted shares are sold within 12 months of the date of death for less than their probate value, a claim to be made to substitute the gross sale price for the probate value.

However, the change in value of all investments sold within 12 months of death must be taken into account.

The Belfast Ceramics Plc shares were sold at a loss, whereas the British Meats Plc share sale produced a gain.

Overall, as a claim would be beneficial, the actual sale proceeds after death have been included in the calculation, on the basis that a claim would be made.

5. Company assets

Business Property Relief (BPR) is not limited to UK situated business property.

Since Portia would appear to have held shares in an unquoted trading company, there is no reason to believe that BPR would not be available in respect of these shares.

Chapter 24

Question 24.1

(a) Relevant business property means:
   (i) A sole trader's business, or a partnership share, including professions and vocations.
   (ii) Unquoted securities of a company which, together with any unquoted shares of the company (including related property in both instances), give the transferor control immediately before the transfer.
   (iii) Any unquoted shares in a company.
   (iv) Quoted shares and/or securities of a company that, together with any related property, give the transferor control immediately before the transfer.
   (v) Land, buildings, plant or machinery which immediately before the transfer were used wholly or mainly for the purposes of a business carried on by a company of which the transferor then had control, or by a partnership of which he was then a partner.
   (vi) Any land, buildings, machinery or plant that, immediately before the transfer, were used wholly or mainly for the purposes of a business carried on by the transferor and were settled property in which he was then beneficially entitled to an interest in possession.
   Shares on the Alternative Investment Market (AIM) are treated as unquoted.
(b) A business, or an interest in a business, or shares in or securities of a company, are not relevant business property if the business, or as the case may be, the business of the company, consists wholly or mainly of:

(i) Dealing in securities, stocks or shares (except for market makers and discount houses).

(ii) Dealing in land or buildings.

(iii) Making or holding investments.

(c) The relief applies to transfers of value in lifetime or on death or to the 10 yearly charge on discretionary trusts, the value attributable to relevant business property being reduced by 100% in respect of (a) (i) to (iii) above and 50% in respect of (a) (iv) to (vi).

Question 24.2

(a) Agricultural property relief is available on the transfer of agricultural property. This includes agricultural land or pasture; woodland and any building used in the intensive rearing of livestock or fish if the occupation of the woodland or building is ancillary to that of the agricultural land or pasture; and also such cottages, farm buildings and farmhouses occupied with the agricultural land as are of a character appropriate to the property.

The provisions for agricultural property relief are very similar to the rules for business property relief, in that the agricultural value is reduced by 100%. Agricultural property relief is given at the rate of 50% where the land is let to a farmer and the lease was signed before 1 September 1995 and there is still more than two years left to run on the lease. If any of these conditions are not met, then 100% relief is due. Where a farmer runs a farming business, business property relief may be available to cover any market value not otherwise covered by agricultural property relief. Therefore agricultural property relief should be applied first.

(b) Agricultural property relief is available on the transfer of shares or debentures in a farming company, provided that the holding gave the transferor control of the company immediately before the transfer and the agricultural property forms part of the company's assets. Relief is given only on that part of the value of the holding that reflects the agricultural value of the underlying property. The rate of relief is 100%.

Business property relief is available on the non-agricultural value of a holding where the relevant conditions are satisfied at 100% on holdings in unquoted farming companies and at 50% on quoted controlling holdings.

Question 24.3

Transfer to Discretionary Trust

Tax due on gift in June 2011

	£
Gift	500,000
Less: two annual exemptions (2011/12 and 2010/11)	(6,000)
Less: nil rate band for 2011/12	(325,000)
Taxable	169,000
Taxable @ 25% (as grandmother paid the tax)	42,250
Total value transferred as a result of gift	536,250

Additional tax now due on death

	£
Initial transfer of value	536,250

Less: nil rate band for 2014/15	(325,000)
Chargeable on death	211,250
Inheritance tax due @ 40%	84,500
Less: taper relief (20% as 3–4 years between gift and death)	(16,900)
Tax due	67,600
Less: lifetime tax paid	(42,250)
Tax now due	25,350
Payable by trustees of estate	

Gift of family home is now a failed PET and is chargeable to IHT

	£
Value of gift	600,000
Less two annual exemptions of £3,000 (2013/14 and 2012/13)	(6,000)
Value now chargeable (no nil rate band remains)	594,000
Inheritance tax due @ 40%	237,600
Payable by Chris personally	

Death Estate

	£	£
Rental properties (Note 1)		525,000
Cash – UK bank account		250,000
Cash – IoM bank account		40,000
Art	250,000	
Less: associated debt (Note 2)	(50,000)	
		200,000
Holiday home in Iceland	78,000	
Less allowable probate costs (max. 5% so restricted)	(3,900)	
		74,100
Total		1,089,100
Less debts of estate:		(15,000)
Less: funeral costs – headstone		(2,000)
Less: funeral costs – clothes		(550)
Death estate		1,071,550
Inheritance tax due @ 40%		428,620

Nil rate band all used by lifetime gifts.

Costs incurred by executors in administering the estate are not allowable.

Note 1:

As the buildings have been sold by the executors within three years of death and the sales price is lower than market value at the date of death by more than 5% of that value and £1,000, the sales price can be used in the death estate.

Note 2:

The loan secured against the art collection is deductible in full and is not restricted because it meets all of the following conditions:

- the loan was not used to acquire, maintain or enhance excluded property;
- the loan was not used to acquire, maintain or enhance assets that qualify for business, agricultural or woodlands relief; and
- on death, the liability will be repaid out of the estate.

Question 24.4

MEMO
TO: Any Partner
FROM: Any Accountant
Date: 30 April 2015
Subject: Fionn O'Shea estate

This briefing note deals with the following matters:

(a) Calculating the lifetime inheritance tax (IHT) payable for lifetime gifts.
(b) Calculating the inheritance tax due on Fionn's death estate, making any appropriate claims or reliefs available to reduce the liability arising.

Each of these matters is considered in turn below.

(a) Lifetime IHT on gifts

10 March 2009 – gift to Shay

	£	£
Gift to Shay		9,000
Marriage exemption		(5,000)
Annual exemption – 2008/09		(3,000)
Annual exemption – 2007/08		(1,000)
		NIL

No inheritance tax due.

28 December 2009 – gift to a discretionary trust

		£
Gift to discretionary trust		300,000
Annual exemption – 2009/10		(3,000)
Annual exemption – 2008/09 (already used)		0
Chargeable lifetime transfer		297,000
Inheritance tax threshold – 2009/10	325,000	

Less cumulative chargeable transfers in the previous seven years	0	
Available inheritance tax threshold £300,000	325,000	
Less: nil rate band		(297,000)
		NIL

No inheritance tax due.

25 November 2010 – gift to a discretionary trust

		£
Gift to discretionary trust		175,000
Annual exemption – 2010/11		(3,000)
Annual exemption – 2009/10 (already used)		0
Chargeable lifetime transfer		172,000
Inheritance tax threshold – 2010/11	325,000	
Less: cumulative chargeable transfers in the previous seven years	(297,000)	
Less: available inheritance tax threshold		(28,000)
Amount liable to inheritance tax		144,000

£144,000 @ 20%		28,800

(b) Death Estate

10 March 2009 – gift to Peter

Exempt transfer due to marriage exemption and annual exemptions.
No inheritance tax due.

28 December 2009 – gift to a discretionary trust

		£
Chargeable lifetime transfer		297,000
Inheritance tax threshold – 2014/15	325,000	
Less: cumulative chargeable transfers in the previous seven years	NIL	
Less: available nil rate band		(297,000)
		NIL

No inheritance tax due.

25 November 2010 – gift to a discretionary trust

		£
Gift to discretionary trust – fall in value relief applied*		75,000
Annual exemption – 2010/11		(3,000)
Annual exemption – 2009/10		0

Revised chargeable lifetime transfer		72,000
Inheritance tax threshold – 2014/15	325,000	
Less: cumulative chargeable transfers in the previous seven years	(297,000)	
Less: available inheritance tax threshold		(28,000)
Amount liable to inheritance tax		44,000
£44,000 @ 40%		17,600
Less: taper relief 40% (4–5 years)		(7,040)
Less: lifetime tax paid		(24,400)
Additional IHT payable on death		NIL

* When death tax is payable on a gift because the transferor has died, but the value of the gift has fallen between the date the gift was originally made and the date of death, then a claim may be made to have death tax charged on the reduced value of the gift.

31 March 2015 – death estate		£
Main residence		225,000
Cash and investments		85,000
Chattels		15,000
Value of interest in possession trust		276,000
Gross value		601,000
Inheritance tax threshold – 2014/15	325,000	
Less: cumulative chargeable transfers in the previous seven years		
Chargeable lifetime transfer – 28/12/2009	(297,000)	
Chargeable lifetime transfer – 25/11/2010	(172,000)*	
Available inheritance tax threshold		NIL
Amount liable to inheritance tax		601,000
Less: claim to use wife's NRB		(325,000)
		276,000
Inheritance tax payable £276,000 @ 40%		110,400

* Where a lifetime gift has fallen in value, relief is only available against IHT payable in respect of the gift itself. The reduced value does not get cumulated or carried forward to the death estate. The original transfer value is still included in the death estate calculations.

Question 24.5

IHT due on Andrew's death estate:

	£
Death estate	575,000
Less: remaining NRB*	(175,000)
Taxable estate	400,000

IHT @ 40%	160,000
NRB*	
Lifetime gift	156,000
Annual exemption 2010/11	(3,000)
Annual exemption 2009/10	(3,000)
	150,000
NRB	325,000
Utilised	(150,000)
Remaining NRB	175,000

James's death estate	£
Value of death estate	1,500,000
Less:	
NRB	(325,000)
Chargeable estate	1,175,000
IHT payable @ 40%	470,000
Less: quick succession relief	
$\dfrac{415,000^*}{415,000 + 160,000} \times £160,000 \times 40\%$	(46,191)
IHT due	423,809

* Estate of £575,000 − IHT £160,000 = £415,000.

Chapter 25

Question 25.1

Capital Gains Tax

As Shay is Sean's son, he is treated as a connected party under section 286 TCGA 1992, hence market value is imposed on any transactions between them that are gifts or at undervalue.

(a) The gift of his residence is a deemed disposal at market value for capital gains tax purposes. However, as Sean has lived in the property all his life, the entire gain will be exempt by virtue of principle private residence relief.
(b) The gift of cash is not a chargeable asset for capital gains tax purposes, hence no chargeable gain arises.

Inheritance Tax

(a) The gift of his house will be treated as a gift with reservation of benefit, and as such is treated as follows:

(i) as a PET at the time of the gift (using the valuation at the time of the gift); and

(ii) as part of Sean's death estate (using the valuation at the time of death) because it is assumed Sean will die within seven years of making the gift.

This results in a potential double charge. HMRC will select the treatment giving rise to the higher total tax payable and will require two computations as denoted above.

(b) This gift would be subject to the pre-owned asset rules.

The gift of cash to Shay by Sean is a PET and is likely to fall into Sean's death estate given he is unlikely to survive for seven years. However, under the pre-owned asset rules Sean will suffer an annual income tax charge. As the painting is a chattel, the income tax is calculated by way of a notional interest charge on the value of the painting multiplied by the official rate of interest, which would give an annual charge of £150,000 $\times$ 3.25% = £4,875.

Question 25.2

Both are liable for pre-owned asset tax (POAT) charges because:

▨ Diarmuid now occupies the flat and Aisling uses the chattel in her own home; and

▨ they both provided the consideration to buy the assets.

In respect of the flat, POAT is charged on the annual value less the amount contributed by Diarmuid (£15,000 − £4,000 = £11,000).

Regarding the home cinema system, POAT arises on the value of the chattel multiplied by the official rate of interest (i.e. £15,000 $\times$ 3.25% = £488). But as this is less than £5,000, no charge arises.

Question 25.3

(a) A pre-owned asset income tax (POAT) charge will arise as Sean has provided the funds for the acquisition of a chattel of which he has possession without that asset being included in his IHT estate.

The income brought into charge will be the value of the chattel as at the date that the POAT first arises multiplied by the official rate of interest, being 3.25% $\times$ £190,000 = £6,175.

The resulting tax charge on Sean in 2014/15 will therefore be £6,175 @ 45% = £2,779.

(b) Sean could elect instead to mitigate the POAT charge by agreeing to treat the gift as falling within the gift with reservation rules instead. As a result of that election, a proportion of the print's value would be included in Sean's estate for as long as it hangs in his house. The proportion that would be included in his estate would be calculated as follows:

£150,000 (consideration provided)
£190,000 (value at first date of "occupation" in his home)

Any election to do so must made by 31 January 2016. This election is irrevocable. If Sean returned the painting to Steven, then the above proportion would fall out of his estate, but only after seven years had elapsed.

Chapter 26

Question 26.1

(a) The due date for payment of the lifetime IHT is the later of:
   - six months from the end of the month in which the transfer takes place (i.e. 31 May 2011); or
   - 30 April following the financial year 2010/11 (i.e. 30 April 2011).

   Hence the due date was 31 May 2011. The IHT100 is due for filing within 12 months from the end of the month in which the gift occurs, hence the filing date was 30 November 2011.
(b) The due date for additional IHT payable on the lifetime gift as a result of Fionn's death on 31 March 2015 is six months from the end of the month in which death occurs (i.e. 30 September 2015).
(c) Payment of IHT on the death estate is due on the earlier of:
   - six months from the end of month in which the transfer takes place, assuming this occurs on 31 March 2015 (i.e. 30 September 2015); or
   - the date of delivery of the IHT400 return (i.e. 29 July 2015).

In this case IHT on the death estate is due on 29 July 2015. The due date for filing the IHT400 for any CLTs, failed PETS and details of the death estate is within 12 months from the end of the month of death (i.e. 31 March 2016).

Question 26.2

Calculation of IHT on failed PET to Eileen – 14 June 2010

No spouse exemption is available despite the subsequent marriage.

The value is the loss to the donor which will be more than half of the total value of £900,000.

Peter's 50% retained is worth less than 50% of the whole. Using a 15% discount the value is £382,500

	£	
Value of PET (loss to estate)	517,500	
Less: annual exemptions 2010/11 and 2009/10	(6,000)	
Net chargeable transfer £511,500		
Available nil rate band (Note 1)	(105,000)	
Taxable amount	406,500	
		£
Tax @ 40%		162,600
Less: taper relief at 40% (gift more than 4 but less than 5 years before)		(65,040)
Tax payable		97,560

Note 1:

The chargeable transfer in 2005 (less £6,000 for two annual exemptions) used £220,000 of the nil rate band, so the nil rate band for calculating IHT on the failed PET reduced from £325,000 to £105,000.

Tax on estate at death – 1 January 2015

	£
Bank accounts, investments, etc. net	240,000
Shotguns, etc.	48,000
Smyth Farm	1,900,000
Windy Farm	950,000
Smyth Farm Ltd shares	425,000
Total	3,563,000
Less: agricultural and business relief (Note 2)	(1,175,000)
Total value of estate net of reliefs	2,388,000
Less: nil rate band (nil due to all used by PET in 2010)	Nil
Net taxable value	2,388,000
Inheritance tax @ 40%	£955,200

Note 1:

The half-share of Primrose Farmhouse passing to Eileen, as the surviving beneficial joint tenant, is exempt by virtue of the spouse exemption. Thus it is ignored.

Note 2: Business property and agricultural property relief

Business property relief (BPR)

Total value of Smyth Farm Ltd shares (seemingly a trading company, so 100% BPR available) is £425,000.

Agricultural property relief (APR)

Windy Farm: no APR available for Windy Farm as Thomas has never occupied it for farming, so seven years of ownership would have been needed for APR to apply.

Smyth Farm:

1. No APR available for stables as they are not occupied for agriculture.
2. APR is only available on £600,000 (agricultural value) of £750,00 (market value) of the farmhouse.
3. As the tenancy is prior to 1995, APR only available on 50% of £150,000 (£1900,000 less £300,000 for stables and £100,000 of farmhouse value): £750,000.

Total value of reliefs £1,175,000.

Chapter 27

Question 27.1

There are several tax consequences of the proposed transfer of the warehouse from the company at undervalue.

Corporation tax
The transfer of the plot of land from the company to Stewart is a disposal of a capital asset; any gains arising on the disposal are liable to corporation tax for the company. Stewart is connected to

the company under section 286 TCGA 1992 as he controls the company through his ownership of the majority of the company's share capital. As a result, section 18 TCGA 1992 imposes market value on any capital transaction between Stewart and the company. The market value imposed by section 18 forms the base cost for any future disposal by Stewart of the warehouse.

The corporation tax payable by the company will be as follows:

	£
Deemed proceeds – market value	625,000
Less: Original base cost	(100,000)
Indexation allowance:	
$\dfrac{255.7 - 171.1^*}{171.1} \times 100,000$	(49,445)
Chargeable gain	475,555
Corporation tax thereon @ 21%	£99,866

*Actual indexation factor for April 2014 used.

Close company implications

Furthermore, there are both IHT and CGT implications if the transaction is proceeded with as a transfer at undervalue. The company is a close company under section 439 CTA 2010 as it is controlled by five or fewer participators as Stewart holds 100% of the shares.

CGT

The provisions of section 125 TCGA 1992 mean that a transfer at undervalue by a close company can result in the reduction in the base cost of company's shares by the amount by which the asset is undervalued, thereby reducing the base cost Stewart can use in the calculation of CGT arising on a future disposal of the company.

However, section 125(4) TCGA 1992 provides an exception from this legislation in several cases, including where the transferee is a participator, or an associate of a participator, in the company and an amount equal to the undervalue amount is treated as a distribution or a capital distribution; or in cases where the transferee is an employee of the company and an amount equal to the undervalue amount is treated as the employee's employment income.

In these circumstances, it is likely that the transfer at undervalue would be treated as an income distribution under section 385(1) ITTOIA 2005, unless Stewart is an employee. This works by treating the amount by which the asset is undervalued as a dividend liable to income tax. Therefore, if Stewart only pays £350,000 to the company for the land plot, he will be treated as receiving a dividend of £275,000. A distribution of this size would be subject to income tax at an effective rate of 30.56%, resulting in an income tax liability of £84,040.

IHT

There are also potential IHT implications to consider. Sections 94–102 IHTA 1984 contain anti-avoidance rules applying to transfers of value (e.g. sales at undervalue) by close companies. The transfer of value is apportioned between the close company's participators for IHT purposes. In Stewart's case, the entire transfer of value of £275,000 would be apportioned to Stewart for IHT purposes as he holds 100% of the shares.

Assuming Stewart made no other transfers of value in the same tax year, or in the previous seven years, the entire amount would be covered by his nil rate band (£325,000) and annual exemption (£3,000 plus a potential £3,000 from the previous tax year if it remains unused). Though there would be no IHT payable in lifetime, this chargeable lifetime transfer could affect the level of IHT on Stewart's death estate if he died within seven years.

Chapter 30

Question 30.1

Private and Confidential
Mr Symon Cawell,
Grove House,
2 Maybury,
Belfast

1 March 2015

Dear Symon,

First, may I start by thanking you for your time at our recent meeting.

You asked me to consider the stamp duty implications of your various transactions during the 2014/15 tax year and these are now outlined.

Stamp Duty on transactions

Rental of property
Stamp duty land tax (SDLT) is chargeable on the premium at a rate of 4% as the premium falls in the 4% band for property over £500,000. The SDLT on the premium is 4% of £575,000, which equates to £23,000. However, SDLT is also chargeable on 1% of the net present value of the rent exceeding £150,000. The SDLT on the rent is, therefore, 1% of £35,000 which comes to £350. Therefore, the total SDLT payable amounts to £23,350.

Purchase of house by son
SDLT is payable at the rate of 1% i.e. £2,250. A relief for first-time buyers of residential property up to £250,000 was withdrawn from 25 March 2012.

Sale of Government securities
No stamp duty arises on this purchase as the purchase of Government securities and loan stock is an exempt transaction.

Shares received in satisfaction of debt
You received shares worth £175,000 in lieu of repayment of the loan originally provided. Consideration subject to stamp duty is any money or money's worth provided by the purchaser. Therefore, the loan provided constitutes consideration and is thus chargeable to stamp duty as being consideration for the purchase of shares at a rate of 0.5% which comes to £875.

Gift of shares to daughter
No stamp duty arises on this as it is a gift for no consideration.

Should you require anything further, do not hesitate to contact me.

Yours sincerely,

An Accountant

Question 30.2

For the purpose of claiming group relief for SDLT on the transfer of the two warehouses by Armour Ltd, Armour's ownership of Destiny Ltd was 82% at the time of the transaction and thus no SDLT was payable on the sale of the warehouse to Destiny Ltd for £750,000. However, within a three-year period, and by 1 January 2015, Destiny is no longer a member of the group as Armour's ownership has fallen to 74%. As this is below the 75% ownership threshold, group relief will be withdrawn. SDLT of £30,000 is now payable (£750,000 × 4%).

Gaston Ltd did not qualify for group relief for SDLT purposes at the time it acquired the warehouse from Armour Ltd as its ownership by Armour Limited is less than 75%. However, as the chargeable consideration of £120,000 is below the non-residential threshold of £150,000, no SDLT is payable.

Question 30.3

If it is sold for £200,000 after the mortgage is paid off, the consideration is £200,000. The relevant rate of tax is 1%, so £2,000 of stamp duty land tax (SDLT) will be due. If it is sold for £200,000 with the son taking over the mortgage, the consideration is £250,000 (as assumption of a debt is viewed as consideration). The relevant rate of tax is still 1% (as the 1% band is up to and including £250,000), so £2,500 of SDLT will be due.

The sale for £350,000 means consideration is £350,000. The relevant rate of tax is then 3%, so £10,500 of SDLT will be due. The mortgage is not taken on by his son and so has no impact on the SDLT due.

Question 30.4

Assets subject to stamp duty land tax (SDLT), typically land and property, can be transferred between 75% group companies without any stamp duty liability, provided the transfer is not part of arrangements for the transferee company to leave the group or consideration for the transfer is not being provided directly or indirectly by a third party.

In this situation, no stamp duty liability will arise. However, relief from stamp duty will be withdrawn if Neptune was to leave the group within three years of the execution of the instrument of transfer while still holding an interest in the freehold property. Relief would also be withdrawn if Solar's ownership of Neptune fell below 75%.

Question 30.5

Apple, Banana, and Date form a group for SDLT group relief purposes, as Banana and Date meet the 75% subsidiary test. The sale to Date Ltd was eligible for SDLT relief and one condition for that relief is that Date Ltd must remain within the SDLT group for three years after buying the warehouse.

Grape Ltd was never in the same SDLT Group as Apple Ltd, but no SDLT was due as the consideration is less than £150,000.

Chapter 31

Question 31.1

(a) The chargeable consideration is £150,000; it is irrelevant that a £30,000 deposit was paid first followed by the balance of £120,000. This is subject to stamp duty land tax (SDLT) at 1% as it falls within the 1% band for residential property. Therefore SDLT of £1,500 is due.

(b) A SDLT return is required if the chargeable consideration is more £40,000.

(c) The SDLT return is due 30 days after completion (i.e. 30 November 2014).

Question 31.2

Stamp duty land tax (SDLT) will be payable by the purchaser of the Dungannon Property in the amount of £14,250, being 3% of the £475,000 proceeds. There is a 30-day time limit after execution for getting the document stamped and paying the required stamp duty. Therefore, as the transaction occurred on 31 March 2015, the SDLT and associated return must be presented to the Stamp Office by 30 April 2015, otherwise a penalty and interest may be charged. The SDLT is a liability of the purchaser and not the vendor of the property.

Question 31.3

Apple

As the amount being paid for the shares is below the "nil duty rate" of £1,000, no stamp duty reserve tax is payable.

Peaches

As the amount being paid for the shares is above the "nil duty rate" of £1,000, the rate of stamp duty payable on the purchase of the shares is 0.5%.

So the stamp duty payable is 0.5% of £6,725 = £33.62

However, stamp duty, which is levied on paper-based transactions, is rounded up to the nearest £5, so the actual amount payable is £35.

Blackberry

There is no duty payable on foreign shares, so the stamp duty here is nil.

There is a 30-day time limit after execution (when the share transfer documents are dated and signed) for getting the document stamped and paying the required stamp duty.

Therefore, assuming the transaction proceeds on 30 April 2014, the share transfer document must be presented to the Stamp Office by 30 May 2014 with the correct duty payment of £35 to avoid a penalty and interest being charged.

Question 31.4

(a) A transfer of UK unlisted shares worth £90,000 on divorce from husband to wife is exempt from stamp duty.

(b) A sale of shares in a UK listed company for £524,000 to a registered UK charity is exempt from stamp duty (subject to being adjudicated).

(c) A sale of shares in a UK unlisted company for £150,000 between unconnected individuals is stampable at 0.5% × £150,000 = £750.

(d) A sale of UK shares worth £895 between unconnected parties does not attract a stamp duty liability because the consideration is less than £1,000.

(e) A sale of shares in a UK unlisted company for £60,000 in cash and an agreement to waive £20,000 of debt owed by seller to purchaser attracts stamp duty at 0.5% on £80,000, being £400, as the debt waiver counts towards consideration.

THANKS FOR JOINING US

We hope that you are finding your course of study with Chartered Accountants Ireland a rewarding experience. We know you've got the will to succeed and are willing to put in the extra effort. You may well know like-minded people in your network who are interested in a career in finance or accountancy and are currently assessing their study options. As a current student, your endorsement matters greatly in helping them decide on a career in Chartered Accountancy.

How can you help?

○ If you have an opportunity to explain to a friend or colleague why you chose Chartered Accountancy as your professional qualification, please do so.

○ Anyone interested in the profession can visit **www.charteredaccountants.ie/prospective-students** where they'll find lots of information and advice on starting out.

○ Like us on **Facebook**, follow us on **Twitter**.

○ Email us at **studentqueries@charteredaccountants.ie**

We can all help in promoting Chartered Accountancy to the next generation and in doing so, strengthen our qualification and community. We really appreciate your support.